GOLD IN
THE WATER

GOLD IN
THE WATER

The True Story of Ordinary Men and Their
Extraordinary Dream of Olympic Glory

P. H. MULLEN

Thomas Dunne Books
St. Martin's Press ❧ New York

THOMAS DUNNE BOOKS.
An imprint of St. Martin's Press.

www.stmartins.com

All photos, except where noted, are courtesy of Greer Photography.

Library of Congress Cataloging-in-Publication Data

Mullen, P. H.
    Gold in the water : the true story of ordinary men and their extraordinary dream of Olympic glory / P. H. Mullen.—1st ed.
        p.   cm.
    ISBN 0-312-26595-6
    1. Swimmers—United States—Biography.   2. Swimming—Training—United States.
    3.   Olympic Games (27th : 2000 : Sydney, N.S.W.)   I. Title.

GV837.9 .M85   2001
797.2'1'092273—dc21
[B]   2001031955

10   9   8   7   6   5   4   3

FOR KAREN

I am honored to be in her story.

CONTENTS

OLYMPIC ODE I

We may sing of no contest greater than Olympia,
Just as water is the most precious of all the elements,
Just as gold is the most valuable of all goods,
And just as the sun shines brighter than any other star,
So shines Olympia, putting all other games into the shade.
                              —Pindar, c. 500 B.C.

INTRODUCTION: SINK OR SWIM

Four laps to go. Four laps to define a place in the world. Four laps to justify an existence.

Moments before the race begins, eight Olympic finalists prepare themselves behind the starting blocks. He stands among them. He stands in front of the world and he empties his body of everything except power. Power and the singular, nonnegotiable passion to touch the wall first.

This is the swimming finals of the 2000 Olympic Games in Sydney, Australia. The air temperature inside the largest natatorium ever built is a constant seventy-nine degrees Fahrenheit. The 18,000 spectators have grown quiet except for various shouts of final encouragement. Frightened birds career through the rafters. The structure is enormous, a marvel of millennium technology and artistry containing the fastest water in the world. Hundreds of feet separate the liquid from the roof's steel beams and nothing exists between them except passion, hope, and the chance to fulfill a dream.

The eight swimmers behind the starting blocks have each swum more than one million laps to get here. Nearly all Olympic swimmers—and the tens of thousands who chased the Olympic dream but fell short—train more than a decade to live a moment like this. Their arms have logged nearly enough miles to swim from Sydney's nearby harbor to Los Angeles—and back again.

Swimming has a grooved, recognizable order to the start of every race. This is an orderly sport, one full of boundaries and enforced structure. First, the eight finalists will be introduced one by one. And so it happens. When his name is called, he waves to the crowd and then steps out of his sweatsuit and gets down to the business of racing. In swimming, as in many sports, there exists a powerful force that compels athletes to withdraw from the outside world before the battle commences. They zero in, not on their competitors, but on their battlefield. And so these Olympic finalists preparing for the most important race of their lives stare only at the still pool water, which is bubbled upward with the slightest shimmering convexity. Could the water itself be rising to meet its racers? It seems so. When you are a swimmer standing behind a starting block, what you see is the black line on the pool's bottom that runs down the middle of your lane. Through the water, it appears jagged, like a lightning bolt, which is exactly how you feel. This line becomes a focus point. Here at the Olympics, the water explodes with the reflected light from tens of thousand of camera flashes.

The finalists adjust and readjust their goggles; they swing their arms in fast circles and jump explosively upward. They adjust their goggles again, taking care to press the hard plastic into their eye sockets to create a watertight seal. Standing among them, he exhales mightily until his head faintly spins and all the carbon dioxide has cleared his lungs. The others do the same. Their movements have become specific and ritualized over the years. In the big picture, isn't that what all of sport is? Ritual, specificity, and hungry want? And in turn, isn't that what defines the human experience? We watch sports because within their careful choreography and their constant pursuit of perfection there will forever exist endless variation, chance, struggle, and the slightest imperfection. It is in these variables that we find the drama, and the drama is why we watch.

He shakes his hands as if throwing off water. He jiggles his long, hammocked triceps. These unconscious moves are intended to loosen the muscles although all they really do is release nervous energy. Several other swimmers heave their shoulders and then slowly roll them backward as if shrugging off overcoats. He scowls at the pool. In this, the 2000 Olympic finals, there is only one goal on everyone's mind: to move through the cool, blue water one-hundredth of a second faster than anyone else in the world.

Swimmers, step up to the blocks.

On the starting blocks, the athletes needlessly press and repress their goggles yet again. The craving for simple reassurances. The swimmers set their feet. Their starter is a man with a tan and creased face, and he announces the event in a voice that is authoritarian and slightly tinny.

The sound of it echoes through the natatorium and the spectators fall silent. Now the voice turns quiet to speak directly to the competitors. There's a rounded softness to the words, a sense of grandfatherly intimacy. The swimmers hear what's said through the small, waterproof speakers embedded beneath every block. The voice says:

Judges and timers, ready.

There is a suspended silence that lasts about two seconds. Just enough time to laser-focus on the race. Or just enough time to falter and become undone.

. . .

By now we know the 2000 Summer Olympic Games were the most successful in history. We know the Olympic swimming competition will probably go down as one of the greatest swim meets of all time. Fourteen world records and fifteen U.S. national records were set. It was a wonderful story. But this book is not about that story, at least not at first. The Olympic Games serve as this book's final exclamation point, its rousing inflection at the end of a two-year journey. In the twenty-four months that precede every Olympics, legions of swimmers all over the world stop their lives to train for the opportunity to represent their country in the Olympiad. Their passionate quest is the greatest singular goal in individual sports. It is a hard and solitary journey. But it is also noble. It is noble because one of the most important things to do in life is at least once chase a dream with every ounce of power and conviction we can muster. That dream-chasing is what this book is about. It's also about the dreaming itself, about the quest for immortality, and the failures and triumphs that occur along the way. These mostly anonymous athletes spend their whole lives backseating friends, social life, academics, and normal adolescence for the chance to chase this dream. They must first reach the national level and then the international level. They wait their entire lives for the chance to pursue greatness and then they embark upon it. This book is a record of one group's journey.

At the storied Santa Clara Swim Club in northern California, a corps of two dozen American swimmers, one of the largest elite groups in the country, made a run at Olympus and immortality. Long ago, the Santa Clara Swim Club had been the center of the swimming universe. But by the time these individuals began training there in the late 1990s, it was a tired institution trying to reclaim any measure of its fabled past. That, too, must be part of this story, for while America is the land of opportunity, it is also the land of reinvention and improbable resurrection. Some of the Santa Clara group gave up nothing more than a summer to train. But others gave up everything—school, home, work, and love—to swim inexorably and unwaveringly toward their common goal.

These athletes grew up eating out of a bowl of common experience. Their lives were cramped in a rhythmic cycle of swim-eat-sleep. Their adolescences were wet and chlorinated, and commitment was a part of childhood. By age ten, most were shaving downy body hair to gain extra speed and realizing the reward for a year of hard work was improvement measured in tenths of a second. By age fourteen, most were in the water by 5:30 A.M. to swim several miles before school. They returned every afternoon after classes to swim several more. From ages fourteen to twenty-two, for three to four hours a day, forty-eight to fifty weeks per year, they stared at a black-tiled line on the pool bottom. What they shared was a bone-deep knowledge that life involved sacrifice and that its rewards, while worthwhile, were often few and far between. To be a contented swimmer, one must first learn that happiness cannot depend on the outcome of a race.

If you are a sports fan, you believe that all sports build character and strengthen human will through tests, setbacks, and triumphs. You believe that all sports reinforce the notion that we improve ourselves through work and dedication. That is true, but there is something intrinsically unique about swimming. It is an incredibly personal pursuit and its athletes reflect that. They exist in an isolated, sensory-deprived world, where communications consist of barked commands, and external stimuli are limited to the rush of water in the ears and a fogged view of a pace clock. As a result, swimmers possess a keen level of self-awareness, even balance. They are not in it for the fame or the money, because there is little of either. It's unlikely they are in it for team camaraderie, because it is difficult to conceive of a more individualistic sport, except perhaps extreme sports like ultra-marathon running or rock climbing.

To be a swimmer is to be willing to exist within the paradox that you may win a race but still fail because a time is not fast enough. Or you may finish dead last and feel victorious because a best time is achieved. Those are odd lessons to accept in youth. They are odd because they require a willingness to accept that victory, its meaning and significance, is nuanced and multi-layered—just as life is. And regardless of a how a race ends for a swimmer, neither the clock can be beat nor the swim can be completely perfect. That makes the sport one of the most humbling on the planet. Ultimately, satisfaction must come from within. This may be the most important lesson sports can teach a person about life.

The parallel between swimming and life is intentional, for in both individuals must ultimately be wholly accountable for their own success or failure. Much of today's world fails to remind of us of that. But never was the ethos of personal responsibility more in force than at the barebones, no-frills Santa Clara Swim Club. The moment you stepped through the center's slatted gate, honor and pride became not just buzzwords but badges of merit. I liked that immensely. So did the swimmers. They found it funky, gritty, and honest. At Santa Clara, the swimmers lived body and soul in a universe that offered no favors. Nowhere in evidence were the trappings of today's modern elite athlete. There were no spoiled attitudes, no excesses, no expectations of financial reward. The athletes in the water subjected themselves to one of the most difficult and intense training regimens in existence. Their commitment was attacked, their values questioned, their security challenged. Weaknesses were exposed and viciously torn down. Because swimming is so rote, most of today's programs inject endless variation into daily workouts to keep their athletes fresh and enthusiastic. It seems a logical expression of a millennium culture that offers endless forms of stimulation. But at Santa Clara, the opposite values held true. There, the athletes swam virtually the identical workout twice per day, six days per week. It was a dreadfully monotonous routine—unheard of anywhere else in the swimming world—that forced daily comparisons to previous efforts and created an environment of unremitting hardship. There were joys so great they could not be articulated, disappointments so profound tears did no justice. Some quit; some succeeded. It was sink or swim.

I was a lifelong competitive swimmer, first in Indiana with the Michiana Marlins and later at Dartmouth College. After college, I became a professional marathon swimmer and for several years competed internationally in rivers, lakes, and oceans. I won national team championships, cashed small checks from foreign banks, and even finished the world's longest swim race, Argentina's fabled 89-kilometer (55-mile)

Hernandarias-Parana swim. The longer the race, the better I became, not because I was fast (I wasn't) but because I could endure. Several years ago, I successfully swam the English Channel and wrote about the experience in *Sports Illustrated*. That little article indirectly led to this book.

I was training recreationally at the Santa Clara Swim Club when the team's head coach, an intimidating man named Dick Jochums, told me I should be writing about his swimmers' Olympic journey. Jochums doesn't talk to you as much as he informs you. I knew him only by reputation. He was said to be ferocious, a man with an explosive temper and a monstrous ego. There is an unwritten rule in journalism that says you never write about someone who asks for it and I declined his invitation. But I wanted to see how the elite trained, so it soon happened that I watched a closed practice. Two swimmers were performing a breaststroke set. These were no ordinary athletes. One was ranked No. 1 in the world in the 200-meter breaststroke; the other was No. 2. Except for this fact, the set was unremarkable until the end. That was when the younger athlete pulled ahead of his older teammate and convincingly won. At the wall, the younger one tried to hide his pleasure while the older one's face twisted into a mask of private anger. What happened next was the reason this book exists. The kid turned to the veteran and asked for advice on how to swim even faster. For the next several minutes, they worked together on their techniques, openly sharing tips that would presumably make one victorious over the other. I wasn't sure what this meant, but I knew there was a story.

The book follows those two athletes and several others for the two years leading to the 2000 Olympic Games. It travels with them around the country to competitions; it goes into their homes and into their heads. Hundreds of interviews were conducted, and the result is a character-driven story that tries to capture the grace of the Olympic pursuit. This book is not meant to be the definitive and final word on the sport of swimming. It does not, for example, address in detail the use of illegal performance enhancers. Nor does it delve into the sport's rich history or compare various programs. Most notably, it does not try to follow the sport's biggest stars. I could have done that, and I'm very glad I didn't. *Gold in the Water* is about one team and its common dream. None of us knew where the story would go or how it would end.

When this project began, I didn't particularly like Dick Jochums and he didn't particularly like me. It made for nice balance. Two years later, I personally believe this complicated man, an unknown beyond U.S. swimming circles, is one of the great American motivators of the twentieth century. I am forever indebted to the unlimited access he provided. I'm equally grateful to the other subjects and acknowledgments appear at the book's end. However, one person must be thanked here. Santa Clara Assistant Coach John Bitter does not appear very often in these pages. That is because of editing constraints. He spent countless hours educating me about the sport and the Santa Clara swimmers. Just as much of Santa Clara's rebuilding success is due to Coach Bitter's work, *Gold in the Water* is a much better book because of his support.

I became friends with the people who appear in these pages, and while that is a dangerous thing for a journalist, it was impossible to avoid. For the price of breakfast at nearby Noah's Bagel, they let me into their lives. These are likable, well-rounded people, the kind you want as sons, daughters, and neighbors. Each had engaged in the process of becoming a champion and had dared to pursue greatness. Their journey still gives me chills every time I think about it. Don't let anyone ever say sports don't matter. Sports matter more than almost anything else.

. . .

It is the Olympic finals and the natatorium has fallen silent as everyone leans forward in hushed anticipation. Nearly one billion television viewers worldwide can see his rib cage rise and fall. But no one can feel the power coursing through his body. He doesn't think. He has no past or future; everything he has ever dreamed, everything he has ever done, thought, or hoped for, is synthesized in the crystalline air of the moment. The fans are ready to scream themselves hoarse.

Swimmers, take your mark.

He brings his hands down between his feet and grips the edge of the starting block. He leans forward ever so slightly. His soul aches for the race to start. The world will never again be this simple.

PART I

NEVER PANIC

January 1998 to May 1999

PROLOGUE

O h my God, is this really happening?!"

It was halfway through the 200-meter breaststroke finals at the 1998 World Championships and the rookie Tom Wilkens was silently gliding four feet beneath the water's wind-rumpled surface. He had just made the second turn of his four-lap race. Above him, 15,000 spectators were on their feet and roaring encouragement. More than 1,000 television, radio, and print reporters were on hand and millions were watching on live television. Every one of them could see what Wilkens and the seven other finalists could not—the actual race as it unfolded.

Breaststroke is swimming at its most precise and measured, and one of the stroke's inviolable rules is that swimmers don't turn their heads during the race. It remains rigid and the eyes stare directly down at the water. A quick glance at the competition can throw the whole body out of alignment and require two strokes to correct. That kind of error is more than enough to lose a race. Above all else, breaststroke is a science of exactitude.

Coming off the wall at the 100-meter mark on this hot, windswept evening in Perth, Australia, Wilkens didn't know if he was in first place or last. All he knew was that his lungs were beginning to ache. It was a familiar enough sensation, that brief period when fatigue existed but had not yet overwhelmed the muscles. In the middle of Wilkens' underwater pull, with his arms at his sides and his legs beginning to curl upward into a kick, the swimmer had one fleeting instant to peek at his competition without disrupting his streamline.

Wilkens' glance down the width of the pool shattered his concentration. For a split second he couldn't believe his eyes and had to do a double take, which probably cost him a tenth of a second. But it didn't matter. A bucket of adrenaline was dumping into his gut and flooding his arms and legs. He wanted to laugh and shout in joyful surprise. Is there any greater joy than feeling unbridled power course through the body at the exact instant it is needed most? But the young swimmer immediately felt a second wave run through him like a cold chaser. It was fear.

"Don't blow it," he thought. "Control yourself, dummy. Legs feel good; arms feel good. You're fine. You're in charge. You make the other swimmers hurt. You can do this. Go now!"

He burst through the surface with a tremendous forward surge and began his first stroke with a ferocious outsweep of the arms.

What did Wilkens see? Rather, what he *didn't* see was the competition at this 1998 World Championship, the most significant swim meet between the 1996 and 2000 Olympics. Five of the seven other finalists were so far behind they were completely out of view. In the middle of the pool, just two swimmers—their heads tucked tightly into their chests so they looked like torpedoes—glided evenly with him. Wilkens caught sight of the American flag on the white bathing cap of one of them and knew it was his teammate, friend, and older mentor, Kurt Grote. He couldn't distinguish the other swimmer but knew he was fast. Wilkens began stroking for all he was worth. The twenty-two-year-old, sweet-tempered senior from Stanford University was competing in his first truly major international meet and had merely hoped to swim well enough to prove that qualifying for the United States national team was no fluke. Now he suddenly found himself vying for the title of world champion.

"No way!" he shouted to himself as he felt his power growing greater with each stroke. "I'm even with the best swimmers in the world—and I haven't even turned it on yet!"

. . .

The 6'2", 180-lb. Wilkens didn't have a race plan when the gun went off and he dove into the water. Or if he had a plan, it was simple: Swim like hell and see what happens. His coaches would have killed him if they knew that, for race management was the most critical aspect of his ongoing development. Control was crucial to success, yet the men who understood that, who knew the calculated give-and-take it required, were wise with age and standing on the pool deck as coaches. It is so hard to teach the lessons of control to the young. That was especially true for a person like Tom Wilkens, who had built a career winning races not because he managed them well but because he fought harder than his competitors. He was a warrior, but a reckless one.

Yet on land, Wilkens was anything but a warrior. A person meeting him for the first time would be struck most by the happy earnestness of this New Jersey shore native with kind eyes and a receding hairline. If anything, he was the little-brother type. He was garrulous and genuine and liked to make friends with strangers. He laughed often and after his workouts ended it wasn't unusual to see him playing in the water like a kid. But in races—at least his best ones—he transformed into a different person, one full of underdog vigor and an incredible determination to succeed.

That determination was the first thing that set him apart during a competition. It was crucial for him because he had always been a water thrasher, a technically challenged swimmer with no particular natural talent who relied on strength and mental toughness to muscle out victories. In fact, it was a safe bet that Tom Wilkens was among the least naturally gifted swimmers emerging on the U.S. national scene in the latter half of the 1990s. His presence at the World Championships was testament to his drive and will to win.

The second thing that distinguished him was his profound love of racing itself. Swimming is a sport that downplays direct competition in favor of the more sterile pursuit of man versus clock. In this environment, Wilkens was a refreshing antidote. Competing always filled him with a surging gladiatorial joy. *Forget about swimming your fastest time,* he seemed ready to whisper to opponents. *Forget about the clock, the crowd, or your race plan. It's just me against you.*

It was an attitude that had delivered startling results. Four years prior to this 1998 World Championships, Wilkens had arrived at Stanford as a wide-eyed freshman with the dream to walk on to the greatest men's swim dynasty of the modern era. That was the fall of 1993, and the only thing he had going for him was his competitive spirit. From the first day, he hit the water with such vehemence that soon the coaches warned him to pace himself in order to survive the season. Instead he swam harder, constantly scanning the other lanes to find the blurry shape of a teammate to race. Even to the untrained eye, it had been abundantly clear that the boy swam on passion instead of talent. Natural swimmers have a "feel" for the water, which means they work intuitively with the medium instead of against it. They form a relationship with the water and instinctively adjust every part of their bodies—hips, elbows, shoulders, head—to reduce drag and move forward more efficiently. The changes are minute and often indiscernible: a subtly altered hand pitch, a few extra degrees of hip rotation, an invisible tempo change to the kicking. It takes years of refinement and practice, but on a cellular level, a natural swimmer seems to know how to manage this, just as a natural musician can adapt to a new instrument.

Swimming technique gurus posit that fewer than three percent of competitive swimmers are truly "natural swimmers." Typically, those are the athletes at the top of the sport. The rest are like Wilkens, swimmers whose races often become contradictions within themselves because the harder they fight the water, the more they lose their streamline, increase their resistance, and slow down. One of the many paradoxes of the sport is that harder swimming does not usually lead to faster times.

Upon arriving at Stanford, Wilkens realized his only hope of being a national-level athlete was to dismantle his stroke and rebuild it from the ground up with proper technique. Because most swimmers entering college realistically have only four years remaining in their careers, few would have been willing to engage in the multiyear reconstruction process Wilkens required. But because he was not a star, because he had no scholarship to risk, he had nothing to lose. And so he became a disciple of biomechanics. Three years later, he was winning NCAA championships, capturing national titles, and in the hunt for a world championship. He had always dreamed of the Olympics in an offhand way because he was a swimmer and that is what swimmers do. But by 1998, thoughts of the 2000 Sydney Games, which had once seemed so utterly unattainable, sent shivers down his body.

There was something distinctly and robustly American about this young swimmer and his journey, about his improbable presence at the World Championships, and about his blue-collar work ethic. He did not even possess the benefit of a swimmer's body, did not enjoy the same abnormally broad back, the huge hands or willowy physique of his competitors. Standing on the blocks, Wilkens seemed to offer a simple message that any dream is possible with enough drive and sacrifice.

But while he had become an NCAA and U.S. national champion, standing on deck with the world's best in Australia left him feeling young and incredibly naive. That, too, had elements of a symbolic American spirit because it was steeped in idealism and wonder. Every time Wilkens donned his Team USA sweats, he felt simultaneously giddy and unworthy. By twisting before his hotel mirror, he could see the letters "U-S-A" stitched on his back. Every time, it made him burst into a wide grin. Then he'd lean close to the glass, stare himself down, and say, "Remember, you deserve to be here as much as anyone else."

What does a rookie do in a pressure situation except look to an older, wiser role model for comfort? Wilkens had turned to Kurt Grote, who now—in the middle of the World Championship final—was swimming three lanes away. Several years older than Wilkens, Grote was a weathered veteran and a former Stanford star. When Grote was an undergraduate, he had shown Wilkens around campus during the younger swimmer's recruiting trip. Subsequently, Grote received a thank-you note from Wilkens that read like a fan letter. As teammates, they had become fast friends.

Anyone looking for a role model would be lucky to find Grote. He was a collegiate All-American breaststroker with a 3.5 GPA who competed in three events at the 1996 Atlanta Olympics. Like Wilkens, Grote had been a Stanford walk-on who improbably made the varsity team and by senior year was a team captain. Like Wilkens, Grote privately battled severe asthma. Like Wilkens, Grote came from a stable family that encouraged its children without being overbearing. From the day Wilkens arrived in California, Grote had helped him improve his breaststroke, converting the younger swimmer's outdated, flat-stroke style to the faster and more efficient wave-action style. The flat-stroke style, which had virtually disappeared from competitive swimming a decade earlier, involves sheer pulling and kicking against the water. The newer wave-action is a rolling motion that emphasizes the torque and power gained by dipping and raising the body like a porpoise.

But in Australia, Wilkens had discovered the veteran was not particularly disposed to being helpful. After all, they were competing in the same 200-meter breaststroke race. Even if Wilkens didn't yet fully understand what that meant, Grote surely did. The older swimmer, a quiet and intense San Diego native with a body Michelangelo might have sculpted, had spent years grooming himself to be America's next great breaststroker. He was only twenty-four years old—only two years older than Wilkens—but he always seemed much older, just as Wilkens always seemed younger. Grote had graduated from Stanford in 1995 and now was in the middle of his second year at Stanford Medical School. In the pool, he had put in the work, suffered setbacks, and patiently waited his turn for glory. He had arrived at this World Championship meet ranked No. 1 in the world in both the 100-meter and 200-meter breaststroke events. Nothing against Wilkens, but Grote wasn't about to let the hot upstart steal a crown that was rightfully his.

As they now sprinted down the windswept pool on the third length of their four-lap championship race, it was impossible to tell who was ahead. Wilkens' strokes were monstrous lunges that pushed wave after wave in front of him; Grote stayed stiletto-precise as he cut through the water. Overhead, the sun had set and the air had turned a dusky yellow that was the color of a fading bruise. It was a portentous sky, one that promised unusual things. Wilkens knew he and Grote were battling for the lead. He also knew Grote closed his eyes during his turns and therefore would have no idea that they were running neck-and-neck. That offered the rookie a distinct advantage. A person can spend a lifetime asking his body to do incredible things, and every so often the body actually complies. Even as the race advanced, Wilkens could feel his arms growing stronger. He quickened his pace.

These two swimmers, the rookie and the veteran, had been on identical trajectories for some time. Both made monstrous time drops as soon as they entered the Stanford program; both evolved into team captains and Academic All-Americans; both were destined to win multiple NCAA titles. Grote set a Stanford school record when he won the 200-yard breaststroke at the 1995 NCAA championships. Three years later, Wilkens would win the same event and tie Grote's time to the hundredth of a second.

They were following the same path, but using different means. Wilkens was a workhorse who had to swim beyond his capabilities to reach the international level. Grote was a beautifully natural swimmer who began the sport at the ancient age of fifteen years (six years later than Wilkens) and who had put himself on the national level the first time he ever swam a breaststroke time trial. One swimmer had learned to defy his own limitations; the other had been able to unlock his potential.

Now in the gloaming of the western Australian sky, the time had come for their parallel careers to collide. It was ironic but also appropriate that these two friends could train side by side every day, but had to travel to the opposite side of the world for a showdown that was about to change and interlock for all time the twin courses of their careers.

Neither man was well prepared for this inevitable moment. They liked each other too much. Any relationship is resistant to change, but that is especially true when the bond is between a mentor and his protégé.

Just before departing for Australia, Wilkens and Grote had moved their twice-daily training sessions from Stanford to the storied Santa Clara Swim Club, located fifteen miles south of Stanford's campus. Santa Clara once had been the global center of swimming, but those days were so long gone that no current swimmer had any memory of them. Both swimmers (as well as many of their college teammates) trained at Stanford during the school year and came to Santa Clara for the summer season. But the 1998 World Championships were being held in January, which meant Grote and Wilkens' last days of stateside training had occurred during Stanford's Christmas break. Rather than swim in an empty college pool, they headed south. At Santa Clara, Head Coach Dick Jochums told Wilkens his stroke was unbalanced and immediately started making adjustments that flatly contradicted the instructions Wilkens had received only days earlier from his Stanford coach, Skip Kenney. Wilkens listened attentively to both men; after all, Kenney was the head coach of the 1996 Olympic team and one of the best team coaches in swimming history, while Jochums was regarded as one of the premier developers of individual Olympic talent. Wilkens, always eager to please, had tried to incorporate both sets of ideas. That had made his stroke even worse. He was so green with inexperience, he seemed ready to grow leaves.

During his last workout at Santa Clara, Wilkens had been pulled aside by Jochums (pronounced Joe-comes). The coach was an imposing bully of a man charged with the daunting task of restoring the Santa Clara Swim Club to its former glory. He liked to buttonhole swimmers and proclaim the country was going to hell because "goddamn corporate America" rewarded mediocrity. He could make athletes tremble in fear, reexamine their souls, and swim far beyond their natural talent. He was a throwback to an earlier time, a time when men coached with iron fists, spoke what they thought, drank hard, and believed sport was a form of war. This was American swimming's bête noire, a demon genius with both a terrible temper and a storming passion for excellence. His record of success ranked among the sport's best, but what he was known for was the stain of being the first collegiate swim coach ever fired for cheating. Most people found him frightening and unapproachable. His swimmers adored him.

"Tom, you know what your biggest problem is?" Jochums had asked Wilkens.

"I bet you're going to tell me."

"You listen too much," Jochums had said. "That, and you take advice from any chump who gives it. Stop listening to others and start thinking for yourself. Do that, and at the World Championships you're going to give Grote the race of his life."

Wilkens had nodded eagerly, missing the irony. Although it wasn't yet apparent, Dick Jochums was soon going to become the most influential person, outside of family, to ever enter Wilkens' life.

That short conversation between swimmer and coach had elbowed its way into Wilkens' head in the final minutes before his championship race began. " 'Give Grote the race of his life.' " Wilkens had smiled to himself. "That's a good one, because maybe Kurt can win this thing."

It had been a ridiculous thing for the coach to say. Or had it?

• • •

Kurt Grote had an ideal race. In it, he's swimming the 200-meter breaststroke in perfect form, he feels great, and the water is utterly still. He's in the lead and by himself. Grote's idealized race was always the Olympic finals. He swims in a self-contained, whited-out world with no noise and no people. The stadium might as well be empty. The opponents are always generic, for Grote never personalized races the way Wilkens did. Indeed, at this World Championships, Wilkens was right when he guessed that Grote would not glance at the competition. In his dream race, Grote executes everything perfectly and when he touches the wall he has won the Olympics in world-record time. His vision ends with him standing alone on the Olympic podium. He leans forward as the official ceremoniously places the gold around his neck.

If that was the dream, were the 1998 World Championships his nightmare? Grote wondered that repeatedly. While externally sanguine and confident, he was having technique issues with his breaststroke, too. And as a more polished swimmer than Wilkens, he needed absolute precision to swim fast. But what was really dragging him down was life away from the pool. Grote had just emerged from a grueling semester of medical school that required seventy hours per week. As a professional athlete with multiple endorsements (Wilkens, as a collegiate swimmer, was still an amateur), Grote was one of the most successfully marketed male swimmers of his era. That kind of exposure involved business obligations which couldn't be postponed. He had also married his college sweetheart just months before the World Championships and was still navigating through a labyrinth of unpacked boxes in their new apartment. How many balls could a man juggle at once? If that man was Kurt Grote, as many as he wanted. But the fatigue of school plus world-class training would eventually take its toll on anyone.

Grote had put himself into this position. In addition to an intense seriousness—personified by piercing blue eyes that rarely broke eye contact—he was defined by his ambition, a person famous among friends for setting outrageous goals and then methodically achieving them one by one. Some people are driven to succeed by an unnameable force. When Grote arrived at Stanford in the fall of 1990 as a walk-on who had been swimming for only four years, he had said he would win an NCAA title. That had been amusing at the time, but it became prophetic after he won three NCAA individual titles and one relay crown. When he had announced he would go to medical school, he was accepted at Stanford, one of the country's toughest programs. After he went on one date with a pretty a cappella singer he had met at a dormitory concert, he informed his father he would marry her. Four years later, he and Amy

Hunn exchanged vows in Stanford's chapel. Grote took for granted that he always accomplished what he set out to do.

He exemplified the best of the modern American ideal of a Renaissance man. In sixteenth-century Florence, the Renaissance ideal meant an individual was cultured and full of intellectual and scientific curiosity. It meant refined artistic sensibilities and a healthy appreciation for sport. Five hundred years later, the United States had sharpened that image to suit the country's sprawling ambitions and goal-oriented mind-set. Our modern Renaissance man has dropped art and culture. Intellectualism is imperative, but it must twine with tangible, real-world economic applications. Athletics, meanwhile, have been pushed to the fore. Grote was a stunning scholar and an athlete (not necessarily in that order), but it wasn't enough. He was a perfectionist who had to be the absolute best at both. When a person cradles the soft head of a newborn, is it possible to divine whether the child will grow into a perfectionist, one who sets great expectations and lives by higher standards than the rest of us? And if that kind of existence could be intuited just as the infant is starting life, is the trait something to encourage or discourage? It is great to be a perfectionist. But it is often a hard way to live.

In typical Grote fashion, in the months prior to the 1998 World Championships, he had set a goal to be ranked No. 1 in his gastrointestinal physiology course. His intention was to become a teaching assistant the following year. Already, he had finished No. 1 in his class of ninety students during the previous spring's cardiovascular physiology class. As both his school finals and the World Championships had approached, he had known his grades were at the top of his class. But while his grades were outstanding, his breaststroke splits were not. In fact, they had been slipping, and he could feel himself losing strength in the water. At a U.S. Open meet a few months earlier, he'd performed dismally. It was a shock. The careful Renaissance balance he'd so well fostered between sport and school began to tip dangerously, and he was forced to make a choice. It was a small moment in time, but an important one for understanding his priorities. Grote had backed off the teaching idea, painfully letting his grades slip so he could refocus on lowering his times in the pool. Shortly before leaving for Australia, he had finished his physiology course ranked somewhere in the class's top third, and the teaching job had gone to someone else. Now he was in Australia to see whether the decision had been a smart one. Trade-offs were not something to which Grote was accustomed.

From the moment he arrived in Perth, he had been far more stressed than Wilkens could have imagined. In his heart, Grote was a worrier, and he knew his times were slow. Few would understand this, because he came to Australia at the height of his career.

Two years earlier, Grote had made the 1996 Olympic team in both the 100- and 200-meter breaststrokes. He had been favored to win at least one individual medal, but he hadn't, and ever since that disappointment he had been on a passion-filled mission to become the undisputed king of the stroke. Per usual, he met with incredible success: four national championships in two years, plus a double victory at the 1997 Pan Pacific Championships. He came to the World Championships in January 1998 not only ranked No. 1 in the world in both breaststroke events, but able to lay claim to being the best all-around breaststroker of the previous twelve years. That was how long it had been since someone had owned the No. 1 spot in both distances. In many ways, Grote represented the future of American swimming.

But in Australia he knew—by the way his kick lacked its usual snap and by the slowness of his arms—that he was not the same swimmer he had been just months earlier. His training regime had plummeted from its normal thirty-five hours per week to less than ten hours. The med school grind made no exceptions for athletes. As the meet began, he stopped talking about swimming, which others assumed was a display of confidence and cool control. It was anything but.

In the opening event of the World Championships, he was upset in the finals of the 100-meter breaststroke and finished third after having been touted to win. He was dismayed. Just months earlier he had swum a time that would have won the race.

"That went exactly how I planned it and I am really happy because it was my first medal at a World Championships," he told dozens of reporters in the pressroom after the race. He managed a strained smile. "I just want to go and celebrate."

Alone, the perfectionist in him was on fire. "I could have won; what did I do wrong?" he had said to himself. "Did I go out too slow? Did I finish my kick? Did I spin? Could I have turned faster? Was I stretching enough? Did I want it bad enough?" He couldn't talk to people and the next morning could barely eat. Grote was prone to mood swings, but this was like falling off the edge of the earth. There are no rules for how a person should experience hurt, no calibration to distinguish a great pain from a small one. This was a small pain, but Grote's suffering was inordinate. He could sense the muted criticisms, even if he couldn't hear them. They would have begun the moment he lost the race: *Here's a solid enough performer, but when it counts, he chokes. Look at the Olympics. Look at this World Championships.* He was beginning to believe the words were all true.

. . .

In retrospect, Wilkens' sneak peek at the competition midway through the 200-meter breaststroke probably made all the difference. When he realized he was vying for the world championship with less than 100 meters to go, the adrenaline rushed like hot liquid into his arms and legs. He pulled his arms wide to catch more water and began thrusting farther forward on each recovery. He could feel himself planing high in the water as his hips rose and fell during the kick cycle. Suddenly he was "outside smoke," the term for a swimmer in the slower outside lane who tries to steal the race from the favorites in lanes four and five.

He increased his tempo until he seemed to fly through the water. As he completed the third lap, he felt a miraculous second wind and knew, knew in his bones, that he had never felt this strong at the end of a race. The crowd was on its feet and the noise was deafening, for Australians seem to love swimming more than their rugby, soccer, and cricket combined. Coming toward the finish, he saw the yellow touch-pads and the huge Arena advertisement flanking his starting block. The timers and judges, dressed in matching Wimbledon whites, stood in unison and approached the pool's edge. Wilkens saw the fluttering flags five meters from the wall and he was under them, he had one more stroke and then he was touching, hard, and a wash of water spilled into the pool gutter.

"What if I won," he thought. "What if . . ."

In the stands, Team USA was going nuts. His American teammates were dancing in the aisles, chanting, "U-S-A! U-S-A!" and ecstatically hugging each other. All over the stadium, American flags were waving wildly. He turned and looked at the scoreboard.

He had finished seventh.

Shock superseded anger. Anger would come later, in the warm-down pool when he pounded the water with his fist.

"How can it be?" he thought incredulously. "I worked the second half so much harder than the first."

He squinted to make out the scoreboard's legend. He found first place and followed it to the winner's name. Then he understood his teammates' joy and he was already in lane two, then lane three, and moving to the center of the pool. Over in lane five, the dour and worried Kurt Grote, his blue-mirrored goggles on his forehead, had been transformed into an ecstatic little boy with a smile that stretched from ear to ear. He had won by two one-hundredths of a second (2:13.40), a margin of victory too close to see. Grote whooped gleefully, pumped his fist in the air, and turned to his celebrating American teammates with his index finger raised in the air. *No. 1.*

Wilkens forgot his own race and was overcome with happiness for his teammate. He spontaneously grabbed the top of Grote's head and shook it back and forth as if he were wrestling a family dog. They burst into laughter.

Wilkens happily waved to his parents in the stands and headed to the warm-down pool. All he could think was, "Kurt's world champion! Kurt's world champion!" It wasn't until he swam in the quiet water of the warm-down pool that he reviewed his own race.

"What happened?" he asked. "The race started and then it was over. I feel like I've come out of a dream and don't know where I am."

Only later did he realize that he was a full two seconds behind the winners. He was more puzzled than anything else. His best time would have won the event, but all eight finalists swam slowly because of windy conditions. Although he thought his second 100 meters was exceptional, it clearly wasn't—as the No. 7 next to his name on the scoreboard made clear to everyone.

What about his fast swimming? It was really spinning through the water. There are trick mirrors at every turn in life, devilishly turning perceived reality into its exact opposite. Wilkens had moved his hands too quickly and they had failed to fully catch and pull. In his excitement, he had also begun his arm pull without waiting for his legs to finish kicking from the previous stroke. That eliminated the advantage of a brief but crucial full glide between each stroke. When he swam with technique, he had been third in the world and feeling strong. When he traded that technique for power, he fell apart and thrashed like he was back on the New Jersey shore racing in the YMCA pool of his youth.

Grote briefly joined him in the warm-down pool and then exited. He had to dry off and accept congratulations, shake hands, sign autographs, answer questions, meet the press, find his dad, and call his wife. He needed to start planning. The long-overdue coronation had finally arrived. In just over two minutes, Grote had become the hands-down favorite to win Olympic gold in Sydney in 2000. There was a sense of entitlement and rightness to it.

"I deserve this," Grote was thinking to himself as he dried off. "I am the best in the world and this affirms it."

Meanwhile, as Wilkens continued gliding through the warm-down pool, a new idea suddenly occurred to him. "I did pretty well tonight," he allowed. "I swam stupid and my time was slow. But for three laps I stayed with those guys."

It was just a fleeting thought. But later that night, and in the days that followed, the idea crawled under his skin and insinuated itself on his psyche. He began to undergo a fundamental mental shift.

"It was a bad swim and one of the more forgettable races of my career," he mused in the days that followed. "It felt like a warm-up swim. Even so, even though it wasn't my best effort, for three laps out of four I stayed with the best in the world. *I stayed with Grote.* What would have happened if I had swum a good race?"

It would be several more days, in the fog of a fifteen-hour transpacific airline flight, before the next logical thought occurred to him. This came hard and fast and made him sit up.

"I'm not only as good as the best swimmers in the world; I am one of the best in the world," he thought. "Not only can I stay with Kurt, but I can possibly beat him."

There was only one logical last step to his thought process, and when it came moments later, it was as if the plane's bottom had fallen away. Wilkens' heart was suddenly trying to beat its way out of his chest. He felt jolts of electricity run down his legs. He looked at his sleeping friend in the seat next to him. The Olympics were only thirty-one months away.

CHAPTER ONE

More than a year had passed since those defining moments at the 1998 World Championships. Tom Wilkens swam back and forth in the otherwise empty pool at the Santa Clara Swim Club. It was a gray morning in spring 1999, the kind of listless dawn that dulls enthusiasms. The rain had come earlier and left the deck slick and cold. Somehow, colorless days like this always seem an appropriate backdrop to hard work and the formation of dreams. Each of Wilkens' strokes resounded crisply against the ugly concrete landscape around him. There was an unadorned blandness to the Santa Clara facility, and it created a sense that here only the basics mattered. So, too, was there a seriousness in the air. The entire ethos of sport and the pursuit of excellence seemed to have been distilled down to the image of a single figure beating out laps in a massive pool.

Wilkens had grown in the past year; his muscles were better defined and his armstrokes had more power. But more important, he had gained confidence. Although he was still an underdog, he now knew he could compete on the elite level. That kind of internal awareness reveals itself in the way an athlete moves, talks, and even stands still. As Wilkens stroked slowly and methodically through a 3,600-yard pulling set, his hands rhythmically flashed bright yellow. That was because he wore wide yellow hand paddles. Clasped between his thighs to prevent his legs from kicking was a foam pull buoy. He also wore a thick inner tube around his ankles for resistance. Pulling was a cornerstone of Santa Clara's training and doing 2,000 yards wearing a tube was akin to running several miles with a medicine ball.

"I am so bored doing this," Wilkens said irritably when he stopped briefly at the wall. He pushed off again before the coach, Jochums, could respond.

"Write it on your tombstone, asshole," Jochums said to no one in particular.

Wilkens was physically broken down and frustrated. He was lonely, too. For the previous two months he had been training alone, showing up at 7 A.M. just as the high school swimmers finished their workouts before school. He hated the solitary grind, hated the windswept emptiness of the vacant pool and the unrelenting intensity of the man who was now his full-time coach.

Santa Clara Swim Club (SCSC) had more than one hundred and fifty swimmers between the ages of six and eighteen, but Wilkens wasn't a part of their practices. It wouldn't be until summer that the lanes around him would fill with the annual influx of more than thirty college-aged swimmers. These swimmers came every summer, taking part in the sport's traditional westward migration to the best clubs in California, Arizona, and Texas. That is what Division I college swimmers do if they aren't required to stay on campus to train or take classes. Most can't conceive of working a summer job until after graduation. In Santa Clara's case, many would hail from nearby Stanford University. The majority would leave in September, but several had already committed to staying full-time afterward. Together they were going make a run at the Olympic Games, which were now only eighteen months away.

Included in the group joining Wilkens would be some of the fastest, most dominating swimmers the country had ever produced. Also included would be slower athletes with no realistic hope of making a U.S. Olympic team. The faster ones had NCAA titles, endorsements, supplementary income from swimming's national governing body, and a genuine shot at the Olympics. The slower ones should have been formatting their résumés and preparing for the rest of their lives. But all were gripped by the same Olympic fever and a desperate optimism that their breakthrough swims were only a race away.

As Wilkens awaited his peers on a gray and soulless morning in early 1999, he had good reason to be suffering. Not only was he physically exhausted, but the mental drudgery of Jochums' workouts was taking its toll. Since 1975, the coach had not changed his practices in structure or substance. Not through several cataclysmic training revolutions, not in the face of libraries of scientific research. In the late 1970s, when American swimming believed success was based on mileage and demanded its swimmers churn out as much as 25,000 meters per day (15.6 miles), Jochums had ignored the movement. Ten years later, the pendulum had swung in the other direction and swimmers practiced as little as 5,000 meters (3.1 miles) per day. Jochums had ignored that, too.

Joining his program was like stepping into a time machine and going back three decades, to a time when all swimmers had crew cuts and military push-ups were the primary form of dryland exercise. At Santa Clara, the daily workout was the most basic and simple in all of swimming: First came a ten-minute warmup, followed by a 1,000-meter kicking set done hard to exhaust the legs for the remainder of practice. Then came the main set, usually between 1,800 and 2,400 meters of fast swimming that descended to all-out, race-pace efforts. Immediately following was a 400-meter "lungbuster" pull, where the swimmer breathed less each lap while simultaneously trying to recover from the previous set. Next was a hard pulling set, followed by a second 400-meter lungbuster. The workout usually ended with an aerobic warmdown and totaled about 7,500 meters (4.7 miles).

It was the unforgiving daily intensity of the main set and the pulling set that made the system different. There are so many myriad combinations of strokes, distances, and intervals in swimming that a coach can easily go an entire season without repeating a main set, and many take pride in doing so. But for twenty-five years, Jochums had employed less than two dozen total. An individual swimmer might be exposed to as few as a half dozen main sets during a year.

Some swim programs engage in as many as forty unique sets during a single workout. Santa Clara repeated its same six-set routine twice a day, five or six days per week, for a weekly total of some forty-five miles. This was not much mileage in comparison to other top programs. But if sport were religion, the coach's training, with its rote, unchanging formula, was a spare Catholic mass, one found in a cloistered, high-walled environment and stubbornly conducted in Latin. And indeed, there was a righteous zeal permeating the Santa Clara clubhouse, a sense that the group existed in an earlier time and was pitted against the modern world beyond its gates.

Something incredible had happened to Tom Wilkens after the 1998

World Championships. Already one of the best swimmers in the United States, he had not lost a 200-meter breaststroke race again. In fact, he had barely lost at all. After returning stateside, he promptly stormed through his senior year undefeated in dual meets. At the NCAA championships, he captained Stanford to its sixth national title and won all three of his individual races, the 200-yard individual medley (usually called I.M., it combines all four strokes: butterfly, backstroke, breaststroke, and freestyle), the 400-yard I.M., and the 200-yard breaststroke. He continued winning through the subsequent summer, capturing the high-point award at the 1998 U.S. nationals and qualifying in three events for the upcoming Pan Pacific Championships, the final international tune-up before the Olympics.

Something else had happened during that amazing string of victories. At the 1998 nationals, Wilkens had defeated Grote in the 200-meter breaststroke. Not by much, and at the time it didn't seem like a big deal. Grote had been swamped by medical-school work and was at a low point while Wilkens was on a roll. But still. One day Grote had realized with a mixture of surprise and odd pleasure that his younger friend had become not just another competitor but his primary rival. The two of them had ended the 1998 season with Wilkens ranked No. 1 in the world in the 200-meter breaststroke and Grote No. 2. Grote was also ranked No. 2 in the 100-meter breaststroke, a remarkable achievement considering that he could barely train because of his school work. In fact, the reason Wilkens was training alone was because Grote's current schedule only allowed him time to train on his own during lunch. Meanwhile, Wilkens' world rankings told the tale of his improvement: He had jumped from No. 10 to No. 1 in the 200-meter breaststroke, from No. 33 to No. 7 in the 200-meter I.M., and from No. 10 to No. 6 in the hard-to-crack 400-meter I.M.

Now it was April 1999, and Wilkens, improving on an almost daily basis, was entering realms of training performance that made Jochums shake his head in amazement. The swimmer had Olympic fever; it had pushed into the whorls of his brain until the image of the five interlocking rings and the distinct Olympic anthem had seared his consciousness. Word had been getting around the swimming world that the Stanford graduate could sustain levels of peak training longer than nearly any other elite swimmer. It wasn't just what he did on a particular day; it was what he did on a daily basis. And it wasn't just breaststroke. Jochums was pushing him hard toward the 400-meter I.M., the sport's decathlon, and Wilkens was responding with practice times in all four strokes that would have made him competitive with any swimmer on the planet in any discipline or distance except sprint freestyle.

But the fatigue was setting in. Swim training is oddly cyclical. An athlete will experience multiple weeks of steady improvement and then inexplicably hit a wall that can last for weeks or even months. It is a frustrating and trying sport, and Wilkens was about to enter an unwanted period of slowdown. The previous afternoon, Santa Clara's youth workout had ended and about fifty squealing kids raced across the deck to the locker rooms' warm showers. An astonishing number were Asian, perhaps signaling the future of what has traditionally been an all-white, country-club sport. Among the pack was Wilkens, 2½ feet taller than everyone else and flushed bright red from a hard final set. He ran like a swimmer, awkward, his chest puffed out and his shoulders thrown too far back. In the shower area, fifteen over-amped ten-year-olds screamed, spit water at each other, and fought for shower space. A white-bearded grandfather, his eyed bugged with impatience, stood in the doorway shouting for his grandson, Steven, to hurry up. In the middle of the chaos but also outside it was Wilkens, hands clasped on top of the showerhead, his head lolling in exhaustion as water streamed over it. He was so tired he could barely stand. A kid whose head was frothy with shampoo lathered his hands and smacked them together. White suds coated Wilkens from head to toe and he didn't notice. Someone else threw an empty bottle of conditioner that bounced off his foot and he didn't move. The cacophony was incredible. The grandfather continued to yell for Steven. Had Wilkens fallen asleep on his feet? His eyes were closed and his slumping body slowly relaxed until he suddenly snapped upright with a start.

That was yesterday. Today, he finished his pulling set and removed his equipment without speaking. He left his goggles on, which Jochums knew was a sign things weren't going well. The coach gave him an "easy" warm-down set, 6 × 100 yards on a rest interval of 1:15. That meant he had one minute and fifteen seconds to swim 100 yards and he would repeat it six times. All of swim training—as well as the training for track and other sports—is based on this type of "interval training." For the set, Jochums wanted him to swim the first twenty-five yards backstroke and the remaining seventy-five yards breaststroke. Wilkens nodded. For the average college swimmer, the set would have been nearly impossible to make.

"You ever have anyone go 3:45?" Wilkens mumbled.

A smile twitched on the coach's lips and quickly disappeared. Wilkens was asking about a time in the 400-yard I.M. that would win NCAA championships, and when converted into Olympic swimming (meters) could come close to winning the Olympics. The question was an indication that Jochums' relentless insistence that the 400-meter I.M. was Wilkens' best race was beginning to pay off. Though Wilkens was a remarkable 400 I.M. swimmer (he twice won NCAAs in the event), his No. 1 ranking in the breaststroke logically suggested he should place all his focus there. That was even truer considering his training environment enabled him to track his primary competitor, Grote, every day.

"I've never had anyone that fast in the 400 I.M., but I will," Jochums now said to Wilkens. "I've never seen breaststroke sets like the ones you're giving me. I've seen freestyle sets like yours only a few times, and they always led to the Olympics. You're the whole package. You're not a breaststroker. You're not a 200 I.M. swimmer or any other bullshit thing. You're a 400 I.M. swimmer and you're going to be the best the world has ever seen. You'll be a lot faster than 3:45."

Wilkens was impossible to read through his smoked goggles as he listened to his coach. He began swimming.

You're a 400 I.M. swimmer. Those are words on which dreams are built. In swimming, the 400-meter I.M. stands alone. It is the aquatic decathlon, a punishing eight-lap medley of all four strokes (butterfly, backstroke, breaststroke, and freestyle) that is at once the most difficult event in swimming and the most intellectual. It requires not only phenomenal fitness but cunning, strategy, and execution. Parry and strike, check and checkmate. That is the dance of the 400-meter I.M. Leads may change a half dozen times as swimmers attempt to neutralize their opponents' strengths and exploit their weaknesses. The first two legs, butterfly and backstroke, depend on arm strength and technique. The third stage, the breaststroke, abruptly switches the race's emphasis to the legs.

It's a major transition point and a key moment for offensive strikes. The final freestyle segment is an all-out brawl won on guts and training base, not on strength or technique. The 400-meter I.M. is so keenly different from all the other events that even accomplished swimmers avoid racing it out of fear they won't finish. Coaches use it as a form of punishment in practice.

The 400-meter I.M. is the closest thing swimming has to heavyweight boxing, and its champion is the King of Swimming. During much of the 1990s, that title had belonged to the pale and scowling Tom Dolan, the most dominating male swimmer in the United States and the 400-meter I.M.'s world record-holder. At 6'6" and 180 lbs., the two-time American Swimmer of the Year was thin as a reed and as angled as a paper clip. He was unbeatable in the two medley races, virtually unbeatable in any freestyle event over 200 meters, and one of the best backstrokers in American history. He owned most of the Top 10 all-time fastest times in both the 200-meter I.M. and 400-meter I.M. In the five years since setting the world record in the 400-meter I.M., no one had come within two seconds of his time. Dolan knew it, too.

With tattoos showing above his suit line, a glinting earring, and an I-will-destroy-you countenance, the University of Michigan graduate was the bad boy of squeaky-clean American swimming. He had anger juicing through his veins, although it was hard to figure out why. Dolan had grown up comfortable in an affluent suburb of Washington, D.C., and swam for the renowned Curl-Burke Swim Club. His father was a prominent courtroom lawyer who twice unsuccessfully ran for Attorney General of Virginia, the traditional stepping-stone to the governorship. His mother taught at a local Catholic university. Yet the swimmer acted as if life had done him a grave injustice. Opponents were pursued and cut down as enemies. He refused to make friends with competitors—even those who were teammates. Behind the blocks before races, his eyes turned flat and ruthless. Never a glimpse of mercy, never a flicker of doubt. He was unstoppable, perhaps the greatest competitor in the sport. Athletes racing him seemed braced for punishment. If there was one race in all of swimming to avoid because its top spot was locked up, it was the men's 400-meter I.M.

Yet it was the 400-meter I.M., with its mystical allure and invincible champion, that Wilkens thought about when he closed his eyes. Wilkens had only one dream race, and it was in the 400-meter I.M. He's racing at some major competition, but not necessarily the Olympics, and is swimming out of his mind. On the butterfly leg, his kick is phenomenal. On backstroke, his weakest link, he stays even with the leaders. They move to breaststroke and for all practical intents the race is over because no I.M. swimmer in the world can stay with him. Wilkens gains a two body-length lead, and coming home doing freestyle, he increases it another several feet. He nearly blasts a hole through the wall when he touches and the crowd roars because he has set a world record. But he doesn't care. He turns to his right. Tom Dolan comes into the wall several seconds later. In this fantasy, the unbeatable King of Swimming turns to Wilkens and gasps, "That was the best race of my life and you killed me."

Every time Jochums talked about the 400-meter I.M., every time he insisted Wilkens could be the greatest ever in it, the swimmer ached to believe him. He was currently No. 2 behind Dolan in the United States, but by more than six seconds. That gap was so great Dolan might not even have known Wilkens existed.

This is how Olympic dreams are built. Wilkens needed such feedback, needed to trust that he had made the right decision when he put his post-collegiate career in Jochums' hands. The coach grinned as he watched the swimmer move across the pool. Jochums was living a dream of his own. He woke up each morning anxious to get to the pool. It had been years since an athlete had made him feel this way. As Wilkens continued with his warmdown, Jochums folded his arms and stood over the vast pool like a prison guard.

· · ·

When you thought of a swimmer's body, with its chiseled abdominals, broad pectorals, heavy triceps, and platter-sized hands, you did not think of Tom Wilkens. Shirtless, he looked like a guy who lifted weights with friends and ran an occasional campus loop. Put a *Wall Street Journal* under his arm, stick him on a morning commute train, and with his open face, thinning hair, and ready smile, he could have been a General Mills product manager.

If Kurt Grote represented the modern Renaissance man, then Wilkens embodied what we think of as the American Dream, the quaint notion that nothing is impossible with enough persistence. He was an All-American Everyman, smiling and "yes, ma'aming" and working his way toward a single, lifelong goal. Apple pie served hot on the countertop of the American middle class. Wilkens, with his soft eyes and humble demeanor, was the Cal Ripken of the swimming world. While his teammate Grote strove to maintain a balance, Wilkens was ready to give up everything in life for swimming. Tom Wilkens was, literally, from Middletown, USA. His personality was not a contrived archetype, but a salient reality, one that friends and coaches teased him about. Freshman year, his Stanford teammates looked him over and nicknamed him Captain America.

Born in 1975, Wilkens was raised in the New Jersey shore community of Middletown and spent summers at the Middletown Swim and Tennis Club. There, his adoring older sisters, Lynn and Christine, taught him to swim by making him paddle after Matchbox cars they held above the water. Their parents, Peter and Laney, were high school sweethearts from Brooklyn who had met when their respective single-sex Catholic schools held a coed dance. When Peter walked Laney home that first night, they were chaperoned by Laney's mother, an older sister, and the family dog. This was sock-hop romance in the 1950s of neighborhood Brooklyn. Out of this innocence came Wilkens' family, and it was hard to imagine a more cozy, idyllic life. Peter served in Vietnam and then returned home to become an insurance broker. The two sisters, five and three years older, fawned over their little brother. The family didn't have a lot of money, but it was never missed.

Wilkens attended Catholic grade school and became first an altar boy and, later, an Eucharistic minister. Catholicism was integral to family life, and on a very deep and personal level Wilkens saw his swimming as a kind of homage to God, as a reflection of the spirit. His favorite movie scene was from 1981's *Chariots of Fire,* when the missionary runner Eric Liddell tells his sister that he feels God's pleasure when he runs fast. Wilkens could recite the scene's dialogue and knew exactly what Liddell meant. Exactly.

Laney volunteered so frequently at her children's school that eventually the priests offered her a full-time job as the parish sacristan and put her in charge of managing their day-to-day welfare. Wilkens couldn't remember ever coming home from school to an empty house without seeing an explanatory note and the time of his mom's return. He dated one girl in high school, earned exceptional grades at the Christian Brothers Academy, never touched alcohol, and was an average swimmer who couldn't stay away from the water except when his recurring asthma left him gasping for breath. It was an uncomplicated suburban life, complete with mowed lawns, bedtime prayers, and family meals.

From a distance, it seems too saccharine, too easy and complete. It seems modern athletes must have documented hardship. We look for their broken childhoods, their loveless years, and the towering obstacles they overcame. It's as if today's athlete, to command attention and respect, must have first suffered. Wilkens, with neither baggage nor hang-ups, was out of place in the world of modern sports. "That was just how our family lived," the swimmer said. "We were close to each other and any problem that seemed big really wasn't. I grew up thinking this was how everyone lived."

He started swimming in earnest when he was nine years old. In the United States, as many as one million kids participate in summertime swim leagues, which are the starting point for nearly every serious competitor. Approximately 200,000 become wintertime "age-group swimmers," a term used because swimmers race according to age (8 and Under, 9–10, 11–12, 13–14, 15–16, 17–18, and Senior). For someone choosing to swim in the winter, there are generally two paths: Join the YMCA or join a team affiliated with U.S.A. Swimming Incorporated, the amateur sport's national governing body (until 1998 it was called United States Swimming, or U.S.S.). U.S.A. Swimming is the dominant system. Out of these clubs come the majority of Division I collegiate swimmers, as well as nearly all of the U.S. Olympians. The YMCA system is largely looked down upon, sometimes unfairly, as a minor league operation for less serious swimmers. But YMCA swimming, which Wilkens joined because a better-than-average team was close to home, often has a key advantage over U.S.A. Swimming: It races all the time, often in weekly meets that are small enough to personalize the competition. In those meets, beating the swimmer in the next lane was more prized than delivering a fast time.

In contrast, U.S.A. Swimming structures its seasons around two or three big invitationals and a championship meet. These are largely three-day weekend events with hundreds of competitors, crowded decks, and overworked coaches. After training weeks and months for one of these meets, a swimmer's only priority is to deliver fast times. It's a shame, for on an elemental level it sterilizes the competitive instinct. So big and anonymous are these meets that it becomes foolhardy to focus before a race on beating a competitor, because chances of being in the water at the same time are slim unless both swimmers make the finals. Most U.S.A. Swimming athletes don't get their first taste of head-to-head, winner-take-all racing until high school dual meets. Some aren't exposed until college. All other things being equal, Wilkens had a distinct advantage over them because he had been sharpening his racing skills his whole life.

Wilkens' Red Bank YMCA focused equally on all four of the competitive strokes, which is typical because teams want their young swimmers to be proficient in all disciplines before they gravitate to a specialty. But specializing had never made sense for Wilkens because he consistently improved in all strokes. The summer before his senior year in high school, in 1993, he competed in the junior national championships, which at the time were the premier meet in the country for swimmers younger than eighteen. The previous summer he had competed in the meet but finished so far back in the field he never knew his final place. This time he won the 200-meter I.M. and was runner-up in the 400-meter I.M. It was a breakthrough moment, exactly what an average swimmer like him desperately needed to garner the attention of the Division I college recruiters. Afterward, he cried with gratitude in his car and thought, "It will never get better than this."

But it did. Because he was a good but still not great swimmer, when it came time to pick a college he let academics drive the process. He was an outstanding student, which is relatively common in swimming (often the men's and women's university swim teams boast the top GPAs in a college's athletic department), and was accepted by both Harvard and Princeton. Had he attended either he could have stayed near his close-knit family and been a star athlete. But he was also accepted at Stanford, a school he applied to because every swimmer in the United States dreams of attending it. Stanford is to swimming what Notre Dame is to football. And nowhere else did top academics and top athletics walk in such lockstep.

Wilkens had no right to think he could compete at Stanford. But he chose it because he wanted to know if he could be great, and as a freshman walk-on he improbably made the NCAA championship finals in both the 200-yard I.M. and 400-yard I.M. Already, he was engaged in the multiyear process of breaking down and rebuilding his stroke. Sophomore year at the NCAA championships, Wilkens was a finalist in all three of his events, the medleys and the breaststroke. That was 1996, and two weeks later he traveled to the Olympic Trials, where he surprisingly placed fifth in both individual medleys. That summer, with America's best swimmers like Grote away at the Atlanta Olympics and many others newly retired, Wilkens won three events at senior nationals and was runner-up in a fourth. That earned him the national high-point award. Even though he had been improving consistently, there had been no flash, no defining moment in his emergence as a national-caliber swimmer. Almost no one saw it happening, which is unusual in this sport because athletes can be easily tracked through their time improvements. The next year as a Stanford junior, he won the 400-yard I.M. at the 1997 NCAA championships, took third in the 200-yard breaststroke, and fifth in the 200-yard I.M. Suddenly there was no denying that he had become one of the best swimmers in the United States.

That had been two years earlier. During this time, Wilkens' quiet development was overshadowed by the sparkling emergence of his teammate, Grote, as the sport's most visible male star. At the 1997 summer nationals, all eyes were on Grote when he easily won the 100-meter and 200-meter breaststroke titles in some of history's fastest times. But anyone watching closely would have seen Wilkens sneaking up to capture second in the latter event. The finishes put the two teammates on the 1998 World Championship team, which then traveled to Perth several months later. It was there that Grote had been crowned world champion and Wilkens finished seventh.

• • •

Wilkens continued with his warmdown back at Santa Clara on this gloomy spring morning. While he swam, Jochums gazed at his watch and mused. In four hours, Kurt Grote the Med Student would begin his last medical exam of the year. Grote would finish by 2:30 P.M. and would finally become Kurt Grote the Swimmer. Jochums couldn't wait. Like the younger swimmer, during the past year Grote had formally decided to entrust the Santa Clara Swim Club with his Olympic dream. It was a boon to the team because Grote was one of the biggest names in American swimming. His presence practically guaranteed other top athletes would soon follow.

The year since the 1998 World Championships had not been charitable to the champion. For months now, he had been so busy as a second-year medical student that he never knew when he could break free to train. And when he could swim, his mind was always fogged with medical jargon. More than once he was so lost in thought that he ran headfirst into a wall. In the last year, Grote's Renaissance symphony of balancing two lives had caught up with him in a big way. He was weaker than he had been in years, his aerobic conditioning had deteriorated, and on the rare occasions when he was able to train with Wilkens, the younger swimmer consistently beat him. The only saving grace was that when practice ended, Wilkens went home to nap, while Grote attended lectures, worked more than sixty hours per week, and spent late nights underlining information in 10-lb. textbooks. If, Grote reasoned, he could remain relatively competitive under such strain, what did that mean for the future, when he took a year-long leave of absence from Stanford to devote his entire life to preparing for the 2000 Sydney Olympics?

Grote would find out the answer sooner than expected because he had decided to begin his leave four months earlier than expected. It was an abrupt departure from the original plan, in which he would stay in school until mid-summer.

"You can't train for the Olympics, go to medical school, study for the boards, and be married," he reasoned. "You'd come up short in not one, but in all. I need these extra months to build this summer's base, and the base is what I will need for next summer to win at Trials."

Jochums had a more succinct explanation: "You're quitting med school because Wilkens is kicking your ass," he told his swimmer.

It was true. Even though Wilkens was still seen as the upstart protégé and Grote was the established master, the power had shifted. The son had nearly become his father's equal. Although it was left strangely unspoken, both men knew the shift had taken place. The coming months promised to be exciting. There was no way Grote was going to stay second-best.

Grote had been born in 1973 in San Diego, and twenty-six years later the premature crow's-feet creeping around his eyes were a dead giveaway that he had grown up under a hot sun. He owned a beautiful body of hard, sculpted muscle, sunken, intense eyes and blond hair bleached almost translucent by the sun. His body fat was at less than six percent and he was a monster in the weight room. His seriousness occasionally made him appear standoffish, but he had an implausible boyish streak, and when happy his face lit a whole room. As primarily an upper-body swimmer with tremendous quickness, he swam his breaststroke high in the water, hunched and precise. When everything clicked together, he looked remarkably like a master jeweler bent over a precious stone.

Grote didn't start swimming until he was fifteen years old. Until then, swimming was a thing he only did to retrieve his surfboard after riding a wave. Soccer was his game and he was an average but hard-working player. But he suffered from severe childhood asthma which several times had become life-threatening and made him a frequent flyer at the local emergency room. His doctor prescribed a water sport because there were no grasses or pollens in a pool. Grote essentially had no other options.

Swimming begins grooming athletes at age eight and has the gifted ones training six miles per day by age thirteen. Some swimmers *retire* at age fifteen. When Grote arrived for the first day of high school practice, he wore baggy beach trunks and was the slowest on the team. But by the end of that first year, he was the fastest. It was as if his body could express its vigor for the first time. The asthma was still there—he would probably take medication his whole life—but had abated significantly. By junior year in 1990, he qualified for junior nationals in the 50-meter freestyle. The day after his season ended, he dove into the empty pool and for fun swam his first-ever 100-yard breaststroke. The time was fast enough to qualify for junior nationals, at the time the country's premier meet for age-group swimming. That got him thinking in a big way. A year later, he was the 1991 junior national champion in the event.

In the college recruiting tear sheets, Grote had a huge question mark next to his name. No one could remember someone starting as late as he did. Not only that, but his training was limited to a minor team and he had nearly zero experience swimming in big meets. His singular achievement was winning junior nationals. While a compelling story to Division I schools, he could also be a fluke. Time-based sports like swimming and track are extremely easy to recruit because a coach only has to review a time. As a result, great personal stories like Grote's are secondary to putting up consistently fast numbers. Grote had not fully proved himself and it wasn't clear whether he could withstand the rigors of a college program. Yet what if his unhoned talent was just beginning to emerge? If so, what did that mean for the next four years?

It was the kind of gamble the gunslinging college coaches of American swimming loved, but not enough to open their wallets. At Stanford, he was welcome to walk on and because Grote grew up believing the only way to live life was to pursue perfection, the only team he wanted was the almighty Cardinal, which was about to surpass John Wooden's legendary UCLA basketball program to become the longest consecutive PAC-10 champions in any sport, all of them under Skip Kenney (nineteen straight titles by 2000). At the time, Stanford already had nearly 600 All-American honors, over two dozen NCAA individual and relay titles, and the best Olympic swimmers of the day, from Pablo Morales to Summer Sanders. Since the 1981–1982 season, the Cardinal had never finished lower than fourth at the NCAA championships. So Grote headed to Palo Alto instead of to his second choice, Berkeley, which cost twenty-five percent of Stanford and had a team nearly as good. His parents were not wealthy—his father was an engineer and Grote grew up middle-class—but they agreed to pay for half of college if he assumed the remainder.

Freshman year he could barely handle the workouts, and when he wasn't around, teammates joked that if someone needed a recovery day, he should hop in the serious freshman's lane. But he persisted and ended the year not only qualifying for NCAAs, but taking sixth in the 100-yard breaststroke and fourth in the 200-yard breaststroke. Grote continued to improve, and as a junior in 1994 won the 200-yard breaststroke at NCAAs. Senior year the former walk-on was elected captain and captured both NCAA breaststroke events while leading Stanford to the 1995 NCAA runner-up finish. When he graduated in 1995, having never received more than a ten percent scholarship, he wasn't thinking seriously about the Olympics. Friends and coaches couldn't believe he had applied to med school, been accepted by Stanford, and planned to begin courses in the fall. They talked him into swimming seriously for the summer.

Just give us eight weeks of hard work to measure where you are, they said.

By summer's end, he could only measure the competition if he turned around. At the U.S. nationals, which were especially important because they were in the lead-up year to the 1996 Olympics, Grote, after having never finished better than fifth at the meet, won the 100-meter event and was runner-up in the 200-meter race. Using email (a novelty back then), he sent a deferral request to med school, and Stanford, which adored its scholar-athletes, granted the deferment immediately.

At the 1996 Olympic Trials the following year, he qualified for the Games in both the 100-meter and 200-meter breaststroke. That made him one of America's few double Olympians in Atlanta. What he remembered most about the experience was the sheer enormity of it all. Cafeterias seating thousands of the world's greatest athletes. A pool complex twice the size of an airplane hangar. The pressure heaped on his shoulders and incessant talk about winning medals.

His 100-meter breaststroke on the first day of the 1996 Olympics was a best time (1:01.6) and placed him sixth. He was delighted because it signaled tremendous things for his better event, the 200-meter breaststroke on day five. It would be a fight, but the gold medal was his for the taking. In prelims, he swam relaxed and nearly achieved a best time. But in finals he self-destructed. He had done the math after the 100-meter event and projected that his 200-meter time would be fast enough to win. But the pressure and expectations overran his race plan and he went out too hard in finals. By halfway, the race was essentially over. He finished eighth and had no one to blame except himself.

"I put my whole life into training. If I swam a smart race, maybe I would have said, 'That's it, time for the rest of my life to begin,' " he said afterward. "But I wanted to win so badly that it overwhelmed everything else. I was so ready for an amazing race."

Even more frustrating, when it came time to swim the 4 × 100-meter medley relay, he was relegated to swimming on the "B" team. That meant he competed in the prelims and then sat in the stands wearing street clothes for finals when his teammates won the gold and set a world record. He received his gold medal because the Olympics awards them to all relay members, but he felt like he didn't deserve it. Back home he hid it in an unseen place. It was a peculiar thing in his life, a memento that simultaneously embodied his most prized possession and a deep source of embarrassment. He had been dry when it was won. He had also failed in his own primary event. Like so many other American relay swimmers, he called his award "my gold medal with an asterisk." This is a strange phenomenon in American swimming: Many relay winners who fail to meet their individual goals possess a sense of failure and letdown.

Perfectionists are cursed with moodiness that can swing from great peaks to dark depths. It was positively frightening how ruthless Kurt Grote was with himself when he failed to meet a goal. After the Olympics, he slipped into a deep hole of self-pity and anger. It felt like acid ran through his veins. Then one day at a public event an adult man shyly asked if he could wear the medal Grote was displaying. The stranger reverently put the hardware around his neck, felt its unusual weight, and burst into tears.

This episode was destined to happen, for in a world teeming with symbols, cross-symbols, cultural signposts, and endless layerings of meaning, an Olympic gold medal is one of the last objects that transcend the cultural noise, and remains precious and inherently good. There is a reason there is more widespread moral outrage over Olympic athletes cheating with drugs than over political corruption or inner-city poverty. The simple idea of sports, of beating another in a test of fair play, is hallowed and protected. Despite being buried beneath money and ego and many associated problems, the concept of winning or losing a contest remains somehow pure and simple. If you ever hold an Olympic medal, you feel how quickly it draws heat from your hand until the alloy is warm. The medal draws from you, just as you draw from it. And when you carefully hand it back to the owner, you can be fairly certain he or she is one of the best athletes to walk the planet.

The incident with the crying stranger stunned and humbled Grote. The swimmer needed that encounter, because from then on his medal assumed a new significance. There was more pride, and Grote felt like a caretaker. Caretaker of something, although he wasn't sure what. Maybe just the Olympic ideal. Maybe the concept of greatness. And so began his furious, passionate attack on the sport. Grote had something to prove. Within twelve months after the Atlanta Games, he became the undisputed king of the breaststroke. He convincingly won the 1997 Pan Pacific championships in both events, and in the 100-meter breaststroke delivered a time that for three years would hold up as the fastest in the world. Months later came the 1998 World Championships and his victory in the 200-meter breaststroke.

Immediately after those World Championships, he had returned to California feeling fundamentally different. His moment of greatness had arrived and the stigma of his unfulfilled dreams at the 1996 Olympics had finally washed away. Now he was a world champion, and the race had obliterated all lingering doubts: Could he race tired? Could he handle the pressure? Could he bounce back from a bad race and swim with his heart and not his head? Yes. Everything was going according to plan.

In the weeks and months that followed his victory, while Wilkens stormed through his senior year undefeated, Grote had resumed his studies. Externally he was the same: conscientious, serious, confident. He liked letting results speak for themselves and loved the anonymity of medical school, where his classmates were only peripherally aware that he was an athlete. The separation of his two worlds was somehow essential and offered a duality few elite athletes could imagine. Even his wife knew very little about swimming and they both preferred it that way.

But during the droning lectures on the vascular system or pharmaceutical derivatives, Grote held a thrilling secret: "I can walk into a crowded room and know I am the best one at what I do. I can walk into a bigger room and it's the same. You can take a map down from the wall and point to any place and know that you are faster than anyone there. No one takes a win away from you ever. 'Kurt Grote, world champion.' I don't care about the publicity. No one ever has to know except me."

Meanwhile, after the 1996 Olympics, his sculpted body and tale of being a late bloomer had made him a hot commodity in the marketplace. Like thousands of others, by 1999 he was dreaming of the Olympics day and night. But unlike most of them, Grote was a man who calculated, and he had already considered the financial windfall that was in store for the 2000 Olympic heroes. If he could make the Olympic team and then win one or more gold medals in Sydney, the sky might be the limit. Marketed the right way, a single gold medal would be worth $500,000 in the first year alone. An athlete with a good story was practically guaranteed a spot on the lecture circuit for at least four years, until the next wave of Olympians arrived. Grote was in the sport for all the right reasons, but he was also a professional who understood the financial possibilities. The money at stake represented his parents' retirement, a comfortable life during residency, and a chance for his wife, Amy, to pursue her career as a choir director without worrying about the paycheck.

He was a hard and reserved man. And maybe he was a little prideful, too. When a unique opportunity to tell his story presented itself to him one morning during breakfast at Flames Coffeehouse in Santa Clara, he coolly blew on his coffee, weighed his options, and asked only three questions: "What does this mean for me?" "What kind of time commitment are we talking about?" "What will be the result?"

Nike, which couldn't have designed a better spokesperson for its new swimwear line, successfully courted him and agreed to pay for medical school, which covered approximately $200,000. Winnings and other earnings gave him enough money to buy a town house in San Diego. Deals with Revo sunglasses and Zura sports equipment provided disposable income. Typically, the first, the most lucrative, and often the *only* significant endorsement deal a professional swimmer gains is an apparel deal. Usually it is through Speedo, which has the biggest share of the swimwear market. After that, a professional is often hard pressed to find other opportunities. Even Speedo doesn't bother promoting its swimmers to the mainstream public. Less than five miles from the Santa Clara pool the company had a retail outlet, and although on its walls hung fourteen posters of people wearing its apparel, only one pictured an actual swimmer, and she was retired (Summer Sanders, who had made the 1992 Olympics).

Meanwhile, swim magazines began using Grote in photos more frequently than any other 1996 Olympian except Jenny Thompson. He spoke to audiences of 500 or more, sometimes for several thousand dollars, and swiftly became adept at analyzing business opportunities. His story could be told numerous ways to numerous groups: the accidental swimmer, the asthma battler, the modern Renaissance man, the moonlighting med student, the driving perfectionist, the devoted husband. All the while, Grote's grades at Stanford were excellent. By 1998 Kurt Grote had become *the* face of men's American swimming.

But now it was a year later, April 1999, and it seemed Grote's protégé, young Tom Wilkens, wanted to race. Very well, bring it on. Grote could think of no better motivator for the coming year. Even as he sat in a classroom and performed a last-minute review for his final exam, Grote's thoughts settled briefly on his friend. The kid might have the edge now, but Grote would soon catch up. This was his last day at medical school, and he was already thinking ahead, thinking of the pool water's crisp splash, the burn of the lungs, and the clang of the weight room. Grote could barely contain his excitement as he said goodbye to his professors. Swimming was about to become a full-time job for the first time in his life. Just $500,000 for a single medal? Why stop there? Although Grote was not the kind to talk about it, there was no question in anyone's mind that he was in line for three Olympic gold medals in Sydney.

In a matter of hours, the world's two best 200-meter breaststrokers would begin training side by side from now until the Olympics, eighteen months away. Not only that, but thirty other national-level athletes were about to join them. The chase for the 2000 Olympics was starting in earnest, and back at the pool, an electric feeling was in the air. Jochums had called a team meeting in two weeks to officially launch the process and was already mentally scripting his speech.

"It's beginning," Jochums said as he continued watching Wilkens glide down the pool. "In a few weeks this place is going to be overflowing with guys thinking they've got what it take to be Olympians. A few got a shot, though most don't have a prayer. But I'll tell you what. Starting tomorrow, we have two gold medal winners in this pool, Wilkens and Grote. I'm saying it right now and it's nonnegotiable. It will happen if they do everything I say. There's people out there who may be faster than these two, but they won't be come Sydney because they don't have what it takes. These kids do. I've never been more sure of anything."

Jochums squinted at the formless sky. During the previous twenty minutes, dark clouds from the nearby Pacific Ocean had come in from the west, following the rain clouds from earlier in the morning. This new air mass had rolled down the Santa Cruz Mountains and was now gathering above the club. In minutes, a light rain began dimpling the pool's surface. Jochums often retreated from deck during warmdown. But not today. Even though by now Wilkens had finished his set and was just swimming lazy laps for fun, the coach stayed planted at the pool's edge.

Grote and Wilkens. How many coaches get a chance like this? Two champions and one Olympic gold medal. But that was just the simple version of the story. There were other races to consider, other chances at Olympic gold medals. The possibilities seemed endless. Jochums was impervious as the rainwater gathered on his shoulders and began running down his sleeves. He watched Wilkens continue swimming. Fifteen miles north, Grote was bidding his classmates farewell and clearing his student locker. Others were independently readying themselves to join Santa Clara in the most important journey of their lives. The race to Sydney was about to begin.

CHAPTER TWO

Two weeks later, fifteen male swimmers from Stanford University entered Santa Clara Swim Club's meeting room. They came in groups of twos and threes. Jochums peered intently into the room. "I'm going to scare the hell out of them," he said.

He seemed larger than normal, more coiled and packed for action. A man's body telegraphs his thoughts. The message is transmitted in the calculation of narrowed eyes. It's seen in the way he will slope against a wall while seeming to be simultaneously edgy and in control. Jochums was possessed by a kind of deadly Eastwood patience, a smooth-muscled readiness of someone waiting with the full assurance he will get his way.

"It's time to stare straight into the greatest challenge of your lives," he muttered as he watched the crowd. "Are you going to talk about being great, or are you going do what it takes to become great?"

Outside it was a cold and drizzling Saturday, a harbinger that the spring of 1999 was going to be the coldest in northern California in 100 years. The men were gathered to hear Jochums' Olympic dream speech, his official launch of the campaign to the 2000 Olympics. They were as wired as he was.

Most of these straw-haired athletes were enjoying the only multiweek break from swimming they had all year. This is a sport with no real off season and many of its athletes move almost directly from collegiate racing that lasts from September until March to club swimming, which runs from mid-April to August. Several milling in Santa Clara's heatless meeting room were fuzzy with hangovers. Others were fretting over upcoming exams. In a remarkable and unconscious display of esprit de corps, every swimmer wore some piece of Stanford swimming jockwear, either a monogrammed jacket, a parka, sweatpants, or a T-shirt. Santa Clara in general was a male, testosterone-dominated world and many female swimmers had trouble feeling comfortable there. But today there were no females present because the Stanford women's team had its own summertime club organization while the men's team did not.

For weeks, the 6'2", 230-lb. Jochums had been plotting this meeting. This, his chance to convince some of the country's top stars to train with Santa Clara for the 2000 Olympics, was a critical juncture for him. If his message didn't stick, many of these swimmers would return to home-town teams or stay north at Stanford. He needed these men, more than they knew. Once upon a time, Jochums had been the brightest-burning coach in U.S.A. Swimming. That was a lifetime ago, back in the halcyon days of the 1970s when he was named American Swim Coach of the Year before age thirty-five, back before reckless acts and arrogance de-stroyed everything he had built and knocked him out of the sport for years. He was fifty-eight years old now, graying and closer to the grave than the crib. The 2000 Olympics and these young individuals might be his final shot at redemption.

How does one tell the difference between a major life event and a minor one? Jochums didn't know. Perhaps life is nothing more than a series of small moments strung together like Christmas lights through the spanning years. What Jochums did know was that neither his family nor friends had wanted him to return to coaching. When he had assumed control of Santa Clara four years earlier, people predicted he'd be gone within six months. His wife refused for a year to sell their home in south-ern California partly out of fear he would be fired. But he had shown them. And now he was preparing to commit the next eighteen months of his life to the 2000 Olympics.

The swimmers seating themselves in front of him had dreamed of the Olympics thousands of times before—in bed at night growing up, in their hometown pools during workouts, in the car driving home from meets. If you are a swimmer, the Olympics will fill your imagination until there is no room for anything else. This is not a possibility, but a fact. You do not dream of fast times, a perfect stroke, or a collegiate scholarship. You dream of the ultimate goal, just as your swimming friends do. Young swimmers automatically come to see life in four-year partitions, as blocks of time between summer Olympiads.

For nearly all, the fantasies ultimately die natural and gradual deaths, to be replaced by more realistic ambitions and loves. But the men who were now vigorously rubbing their arms and stamping their legs to get warm in the cold room represented perhaps the single most talented collection of male swimmers in the United States. They had emerged from high school as the nation's top recruits. Nearly all were collegiate All-Americans many times over. Over the entire room hung the specter of the Olympic rings. But even on this day, the Olympics were not something to talk about, at least not seriously. It is easier to reproduce the ceiling of the Sistine Chapel on the head of a pin than it is to make a U.S. Olympic team as a swimmer. That's what made this meeting all the more significant. They were about to begin a journey that would almost certainly end in heartbreak. But it also represented a chance to become part of history.

Olympic swimming had debuted at the first modern Olympic Games in Athens in 1896. Organized by Baron Pierre de Coubertin, a French educator and philosopher who never personally competed in sports, the Athens Olympics were a weeklong celebration of the character forged by athletics. There were four swimming events, and they took place the morning of March 30, 1896, in the icy, choppy waters of the Mediterranean. Not until 1912 in Stockholm would Olympic swimmers actually compete in a pool.

The first event was the 100-meter crawl, so named because swimmers appeared to "crawl" over the water; eventually the stroke would be called freestyle. The race was won by an eighteen-year-old Hungarian named Alfred Hajos, who beat twelve others in a sprint from an offshore boat to a red flag close to shore. The seas were bad and the water was so cold it could be considered life-threatening. Hajos's time was 1:22.20 and he afterward said, "My will to live completely overcame my desire to win." This was not a frivolous sentiment by swimming's first-ever Olympic medalist: He had learned to swim only a few years earlier after his father had drowned in the Danube. There is something else interesting about Hajos: His real name was Arnold Guttman, but he raced under a more Hungarian-sounding pseudonym because of anti-Semitism. That means, in an ironic tidbit of history, that while modern competitive swimming traditionally has been an elitist endeavor—for decades country clubs were private Protestant enclaves for the wealthy, while public pools were open only to whites—not only is the sport's most famous Olympic champion Jewish (Mark Spitz, winner of seven golds in Munich in 1972, all in world-record times), but its first Olympic winner was, as well.

After the 100-meter crawl, the next event at the 1896 Games was the 100-meter swim for "professional navy men," followed by a 500-meter crawl race. The 500 crawl was particularly disappointing because twenty-six of the twenty-nine competitors refused to get into the cold, turbulent water. The final competition, a 1,200-meter swim, was also won by Hajos. By noontime, the meet ended and everyone broke for lunch. A single American swam that day. Gardner Williams finished fifth in the 100-meter crawl and promptly disappeared into history. It wouldn't be until 1904 in St. Louis that the United States captured its first Olympic swimming medal.

But despite the late start, the United States quickly grew to dominate the sport like it has no other. The first great American swimmer was Charles Daniels, who inadvertently created the sprinter's six-beat kick while trying to stay afloat as he learned the front crawl, and then used it to win four Olympic gold medals between 1904 and 1908. He passed the mantle to Duke Kahanamoku of Hawaii, who won three Olympic golds and two silvers and who, for an amazing two decades (from 1911 to 1932), was ranked as one of the world's best swimmers. The Duke was first defeated at the 1924 Paris Olympics by Johnny Weissmuller, perhaps the greatest of them all. During his career, Weissmuller won five golds, set sixty-seven world records, and didn't lose a freestyle race in ten years. After retiring, he became Tarzan, a broad-chested sex symbol who represented the perfect male athlete. Meanwhile, in 1926, New York's nineteen-year-old Gertrude Ederle, an Olympic champion, was the first woman to cross the English Channel and in so doing destroyed the previous record by an hour. And so it went. One year the Olympics were dominated by the Japanese, who had studied Weissmuller's stroke on then-novel video. Another time the Australians dominated thanks to revolutionary training techniques. Olympics are "won" and "lost" not by a point system but by simple medal count. The country with the most gold wins. In the rare instances when the United States did not collect the most gold, it was second. And always it roared back to life at the next Olympiad.

In the last thirty years especially, not even the modern supremacy of basketball's Team USA Dream Team compares to what Americans have done in the water. Through the 1996 Olympic Games, the United States had won 387 Olympic swimming medals—more than most countries had won in all Olympic sports combined, and more than triple what second-place Australia earned in the pool. In addition to Spitz's eleven medals in 1968 and 1972, Matt Biondi also won eleven between 1984 and 1992. Shirley Babashoff took home eight in 1972 and 1976. But it wasn't just the individual stars, it was the depth of every American Olympic team that made it so strong. By the 1976 Montreal Olympics, the U.S. Olympic swim juggernaut had become so powerful that the Olympic Committee imposed a kind of affirmative-action policy on the sport by reducing the number of swimmers a country could enter in an event from three to two. That was specifically to prevent the United States from sweeping the gold, silver, and bronze medals, something that had become habit. It seemed other countries had begun questioning why they bothered fielding teams. It was a good decision, for it increased global excitement about the sport, but it did little to slow the U.S. dominance. Once every quadrennium, American swimming shrugs off its tarps of obscurity and whips the world. It is an expected thing, a regularly scheduled reassurance that all is well in the republic.

Yet as every U.S. swimmer knows all too well, there are no Olympic Games without first triumphing in what is often the fastest swim meet in the world, the U.S. Olympic Trials. American swimming is so strong and deep that it requires more energy and resolve, and very often more speed, to qualify for the U.S. Olympic team than it does to win an Olympic gold. Nearly every U.S. Olympian jokes that the pressure of the Games is nothing compared to the lurching drama of Trials. Every man on the premises of the Santa Clara Swim Club had accepted that paradigm years earlier. It was inconceivable for any of them to think of the Trials and the Games as two unique events. They are wedded together, inseparable, and they require one long, sustained moment of greatness.

Nations can select their two Olympians per event in any manner they choose, provided the athletes meet the Games' very fast "A" qualifying standard. If a country does not have two swimmers that fast, it can still

43

send one representative per event, provided he or she meets a slower "B" time. Some nations tap their Olympians years in advance so they can train without distraction; others simply say whoever first achieves the "B" qualification in an event is automatically guaranteed an Olympic spot. The United States takes a more streamlined approach: one meet, one race. Touch first or second at the Trials and get a plane ticket. It's a given that the Olympic "A" standard will be met (the 4 × 100-meter and 4 × 200-meter relays each take six swimmers, which means the first-through sixth-place finishers in the 100-meter and 200-meter freestyle make the team).

The U.S. Trials have an almost sinister and despairing air because the talent is so great that nearly every finalist would be close to making the finals of the actual Olympics—if only allowed the chance. As a result, the meet is like a bleak Russian morality tale designed to illustrate life's inescapable harshness. This is particularly true for the third-place finishers. Which is worse, pursuing a single dream for a decade and then missing it by a margin too close to see or missing it by a green mile? Nearly all third-place finishers at U.S. Trials would be legitimate contenders for an Olympic medal, often the gold. But of course they never have an opportunity to prove it. Through the years, literally hundreds of American swimmers have watched the Games on television when they could have easily been racing. In American swimming, when people talk about the sport's greatest pain, its most searing agony, they don't talk about a fourth-place finish in the Olympics. They talk about taking third at Trials.

Every man in the room knew the eight-day Trials would start on August 9, 2000, in Indianapolis. A month later, the victors would be in Sydney marching in the Olympics' Opening Ceremonies. The U.S. Olympic Trials is the one U.S. meet where no team score is kept. Team banners are prohibited from being displayed in the pool facility, as are sponsors' logos and related paraphernalia, per Rule 61 of the Olympic Charter, which tries to minimize—and this is said with a straight face—the intrusion of professionalism into the Olympic moment. To swim at Trials, it costs $7.50 per event. Faxed entries would be accepted until the very last minute, August 6, 2000, at 11 P.M. At the meet's conclusion, the 2000 U.S. Olympic swim team would number a maximum of twenty-six men and twenty-six women.

Back at Santa Clara, a swimmer told a dirty joke and everyone cracked up. Would he be an Olympian? Would any of them? They were so young and hopeful. But while the goal of everyone in the room was the same, only four Santa Clara swimmers would have true shots. In addition to Grote and Wilkens, there was the enigmatic and Hollywood-handsome Dod Wales. Silent as a shadow, He had glided into the room unnoticed. Instead of striking up conversation, he selected a seat and settled in. Wales had the secure ease of a loner, that quiet confidence of someone who knew exactly what he was doing. He had already decided he was going to be as selfish as possible from now until the Olympics. Chisel-jawed and statuesque, he sat with a straight back and carefully smoothed the front of his jacket. Here was a meticulous, careful man, and as he surveyed the scene, he seemed impenetrably cool, even critical. This was not a person who revealed himself. Nor was it one who made mistakes. Dod Wales, easily the most stubborn and controlled person in the room, was also on many days the best. Just weeks earlier he had shattered a thirteen-year-old American record in the 100-yard butterfly mark and captured the event's NCAA title.

Wales was an analytic, and he saw swimming the way a classical engineer would: as an emotionless set of systems, theorems, rules, and processes. He didn't study mathematics (he was a history major), but his mind was directed by a kind of narrow, Euclidean determination. His Olympic journey had begun light-years before his teammates', perhaps before any other active swimmer in the United States. His father was not only the former president of U.S.A. Swimming Incorporated, but a bronze medallist in the 1968 Mexico City Olympics. The son was following his old man's footsteps; both were among the best butterflyers who had ever walked the Earth.

The fourth swimmer with a real shot at the Olympics was a 6'7", condor-like swimmer named Tate Blahnik, one of the most naturally gifted backstrokers the world had produced. Yet he was miserable in swimming. Blahnik cursed his talent, but his gift was too great to forsake. The backstroker regularly avoided the pool, sabotaged his body with soda and candy, and dreamed of the day no one would ever ask him to race again. Only weeks earlier at the 1999 NCAA championships, Blahnik had won his second consecutive title in the 200-yard backstroke. Since then he had been AWOL. Some of his teammates assumed he had finally quit. There were fifteen eager and expectant faces in the room, but Blahnik's wasn't one of them. He was the only one who had failed to show.

There were others who might come close to Olympic glory. An NCAA champion butterflyer named Matthew Pierce had a shot if he could recover from shoulder surgery in time. NCAA champion freestyler Julie Varozza, who would join the team later, could be a dark horse. In the room were at least six additional athletes who could be within inches of making the Olympic team.

But it was Santa Clara's big four who stood out: Grote and Wilkens, the cool, collected Wales, plus the unhappy Blahnik. They were the thunderbolts and lightning of the 2000 Olympic effort. Each had been an NCAA champion. Each knew what it was like to dominate his event and to grasp the golden chalice of Olympus. In Greek mythology, that chalice was carried by Ganymede, a human so beautiful and athletic he was allowed, briefly, to live among the gods. So it was for these four: Mortal though they were, their talents had brought them to the mountaintop of greatness.

If you were to stand in the club's meeting room on that rainy day in April 1999, you would have seen a cluster of redwood-sized athletes milling about and utterly indistinguishable from one another. But already there were hints as to who they were. Grote and Wilkens were already recognizable. Wales' silent presence became the calm center amid the bustle. Backstroker Blahnik's absence spoke volumes. As a unit, the fifteen athletes wore the same clothes, ate the same meals, and laughed at the same jokes. But their individuality was soon going to emerge. Jochums specialized in building individual champions and in Santa Clara's waters the swimmers would separate and take form as unique beings, each with different stories and lives, each with the same burning goal.

The room was still settling when Jochums stepped forward. The swimmers looked up expectantly. Then the coach did a funny thing. He abruptly swiveled and left the room. He wasn't ready. Even the smallest of life's moments should be paced correctly. Once he opened his mouth, there would be no turning back. You don't ever ask to be a part of people's dreams and then later change your mind. But did he really want this? He ached for this chance at redemption, yes, but did he really want it? He knew how rich the coming months were going to be. But he also knew how much they were going to hurt.

. . .

Coach Richard Marion Jochums had many wishes, but this one was special: "I hope to God my children aren't like me—like a hard-ass, like it's my way or no way—because it's a difficult life and I've been through things I wouldn't wish upon my worst enemy."

Indeed. Jochums, a thick mountain of a man, was difficult, argumentative and explosive. He bubbled with ego and was forever righteous. But he was also outrageously witty, intelligent, and impassioned. This was the Teddy Roosevelt of swimming, a charismatic, hell-bent, larger-than-life character who charged, pushed, and shoe-horned his way through his days. He was terrible and he was awesome. "You get me, warts and all, the good, the bad, and the ugly," Jochums liked to say. To some men, life is about character. And so it was with Jochums. He did not care for personality, professional success, or civic values, just blunt, craggy character. He told many little lies to get through the day, but turned remarkably and dangerously honest when it mattered. In the same workout he might explode with a tirade of obscenities at an unmotivated swim from his best swimmer, and be brought close to tears at a gut-filled effort from his worst. He judged a person the old-fashioned way, by a handshake. He fought your enemies if you were an ally and indiscriminately disparaged anyone outside his circle of trust. Like many great coaches, he was forever defensive and paranoid, could hold a grudge for years, and was among the most immovable men on the planet.

That the winds of life had deposited him on a pool deck among soft, sandaled coaches in Hawaiian T-shirts proved nature's wicked sense of humor. He was meant to bestride a muddy gridiron, where he could throw clipboards, swear at Vince Lombardi, and charge at Mike Ditka. Jochums was meant to be surrounded by helmets and groans of pain, war cries and dirtied blood. Instead, he coached kids who worried about sunburns. None of them had ever seen anything like him.

People downplay emotions; they try to separate them from the daily congress of their lives. Jochums knew that, and so he expertly used emotion, particularly anger, to force home his messages and win his arguments. There was an element of genius in this. His volatile outbursts were legendary in the otherwise gentle and decorous world of swimming. There were tales of him punching walls, chasing swimmers, and climbing fences to fight coaches. He once threatened to beat up a roomful of swimming's most important people when they didn't elect him to a national team. At a Santa Clara meet, Jochums was temporarily managing the parking lot when a driver refused to pay the nominal entrance fee. The fifty-eight-year-old coach left his station, stalked down the car, scuffled with the youthful offender, and before a crowd of age-group swimmers and their horrified parents, flattened the driver on his back. For weeks afterward, Jochums blew on his knuckles and bragged about it. The parking admission had been $3.

At Santa Clara, he spoke a language most swimmers had never heard before. The younger swimmers were children of privilege and wealth, the sons and daughters of Silicon Valley's vast riches and comforts. They carried cell phones and were picked up in expensive imported cars. Jochums talked to them about the need to separate themselves from their lives and discover internal heroism. He showed them a world where success had nothing to do with money and external trappings. Most swim coaches preached that success was based on speed and purity of feel; all Jochums wanted to discuss was courage, the process of the struggle, and the eventual defeat of fear. Times, splits, rankings, and finishes were just outcomes.

Born in 1941, he grew up blue-collar and tough in Berkeley, California. Berkeley of the 1940s and 1950s was a middle-class town for working families and men who earned their paychecks bending metal in the nearby shipyards. His father was the production supervisor at a linoleum and paint plant, and the neighborhood teemed with servicemen who had returned from World War II. Jochums was twelve years old when he decided to be a coach, and his mother frequently caught him staying up past bedtime to draw elementary football and basketball plays. The first book he remembered reading was about great football coaches and he was enthralled with the story of D. X. Bible, a legendary coach from the early 1900s to 1940s at Texas A & M, Nebraska, and Texas. Bible inspired such high expectations in his players that after one bad game, his team supposedly climbed into the stands and walked out of the stadium rather than face him in the locker room.

"The common theme of great coaching is that the great coaches are all developers of men and their spirit," Jochums remembered years later. "I didn't know what that meant but I knew it was me."

In the neighborhood, he was one of the few whites who would play street sports with blacks. But he was mouthy and often came home welted and bruised from fighting. His overprotective mother decided to put him in a noncontact sport and for a while Jochums was a figure skater. When that failed, she brought him to a pool because swimming was the one sport where he couldn't shoot off his mouth. At the time, a revolution was beginning in northern California that would affect every swimmer for generations. It had started fifty miles south of Berkeley, where a small team named the Santa Clara Swim Club was laying the foundation that would make it the most powerful swimming force in the world. Less than two years after Jochums started swimming, he was ranked No. 1 in the country in the 100-yard butterfly for his 13–14 age group.

He never did so well again, but it didn't matter, because he was intent on becoming a coach. He attended the University of Washington on a swimming scholarship, captained the team his senior year, and was a conference champion. He then remained for three years as the assistant coach while earning a master's degree in physical education. Swimming in California, he had learned that "technique was everything." But in Washington, the coach preached that "quality was everything." Rather than seeing the incompatibilities, Jochums blended the concepts, and they became the twin pillars of his unique and stark coaching philosophy. This is a sport that globally spends tens of millions of dollars per year enhancing optimum training techniques, advancing the understanding of physiology, and improving conditioning. Yet through his whole career, Jochums remained unwaveringly committed to precise technique and daily race-speed quality. In the 1990s, his swimmers considered him a throwback; twenty years earlier his swimmers had been saying the same thing.

Armed with his master's degree, he returned home to Berkeley for a second graduate degree, this one an educational doctorate in physical education. It was the late 1960s and the university was ground zero for the psychedelic freedoms of drugs and free love, anti–Vietnam War protests, and equal rights. The crew-cutted Jochums marched through it with his eyes straight ahead, teeth gritted, and chest thrust forward defiantly. He was a husband (he had met his wife, Mara, in college) and young father, and the anti-war movement disgusted him. First he worked as a

Cal assistant and then as head coach of Cal State–Hayward, a small state university. He also started a youth team in nearby Concord. It is typical even today for many swim coaches to hold several jobs to make ends meet. During this period, he began consciously adjusting the swimmer–coach relationship so that while he remained an authoritative figure, he forged equal, adult partnerships with his athletes. It was a style wrapped in discipline but also possessing an unusual amount of freedom and personal responsibility. More than anything else, this was what had drawn older post-collegiate swimmers like Grote and Wilkens to his club.

In 1971, the proverbial magic phone call came. In southern California, a famous coach named Don Gambril was immediately leaving Long Beach State to coach Harvard. If Jochums would take over Gambril's job and buy his house, the program would pay him nearly $1,000 per month. If Jochums took the job but *didn't* let Gambril unload the house, the pay would be only $400. Without consulting his wife, Jochums accepted the job and bought the property site unseen. He was not a rich man by any stretch of the imagination. He and Mara had just closed escrow on a new home in northern California without yet selling their first one, and it had been so stressful that Mara, pregnant with their second child, had gone into early labor. When Jochums informed her they now had *three* homes and to pack for southern California, she packed her bags all right, but for her parents' home in Washington State, where she stayed until she cooled down. It was neither the first nor the last major blowup in their more than thirty years of marriage. Dominating men like Dick Jochums often pair themselves to deferring, meek women. That couldn't have been further from the truth in this case. Mara Jochums was elegant, acutely intelligent, and as iron-willed as her husband.

The next spring, in 1972, the ex–Long Beach coach, Gambril, returned to train elite swimmers for the Munich Olympic Games. The coach was possessed by Olympic fever, and Jochums was bumped to assistant. Gambril's stars took over the pool and most of Jochums' young swimmers quit the team in frustration. Jochums was livid but attentive: He saw how Gambril's demands for knowing his swimmers' times created a daily expectation of excellence, just as the football coach, Bible, had done in Texas's dusty stadiums forty years earlier. Jochums decided he would make similar demands on his athletes. But by the time Gambril's Olympic group left for Munich, Jochums' age-group team had been reduced to just seven young kids. He looked around and wondered how to start over. One of the swimmers was a scrawny thirteen-year-old named Tim Shaw.

Shaw was the youngest of four children. Both parents were teachers and his father led hymns in the local church. Shaw was a rail of a boy, all knobby bone, ears, and glasses, and he didn't have much natural talent. But he had guts and willpower and over the next several years Jochums single-handedly built him into the best swimmer of his day. By 1975, Shaw was a shy teenager who owned world records in the 200-, 400-, 800-, and 1,500-meter freestyle, at the time the only man except Mark Spitz to ever hold that many records simultaneously. (A quarter century later, another teenage star would become as dominant as Shaw and own world records in the same four events. The boy's name would be Ian Thorpe.) Shaw graced the cover of *Sports Illustrated*, won the Sullivan Award for the nation's best amateur athlete, captured three world championships, and was twice named *Swimming World Magazine*'s Swimmer of the Year. In eighteen months, he set and rebroke nine world records and was touted as the next Spitz. He was actually stronger than Spitz had been at the same age, and looked to be an equal of John Naber (winner of four gold medals at the 1976 Montreal Olympics). The year prior to the Olympics, Shaw was the most recognized amateur athlete in the Unites States and the one most assured victory in the 1976 Montreal Games.

And then Jochums destroyed him. Not all at once, but over the course of a year. Jochums wanted it so bad: the gold, the glory, the universal acknowledgment that he, Dick Jochums, had built the world's greatest swimmer. Jochums loved Shaw like a son; in fact, he thought more about him than about his own children during this time. But he drove Shaw to inhuman depths of training and when Shaw began to break under the physical strain, the coach was blind to the deteriorating situation.

Passionately convinced he could do no wrong, certain anyone urging reason was a saboteur, Jochums, his veins bulging and spittle flying, screamed daily obscenities at Shaw. The coach accused the swimmer of the worst things, of being a quitter and being unmotivated. Shaw, by then a freshman at Long Beach State and utterly trusting, never knew to question or complain. He had become anemic, his eyes sunken and hollow, his weight down from 192 lbs. to 170 lbs. When Jochums finally let up, it was too late. Tim Shaw could have possibly won four gold medals in Montreal; instead he barely qualified for one event, the 400-meter freestyle, in which, through pure grit, he took an Olympic silver. He never set another record or won a major international race again.

"Everything I know about coaching I learned on Tim Shaw's body," Jochums said more than two decades later. "All my theories, all my mistakes. I will love Tim Shaw until the day I die more than any swimmer I will ever coach, and you know what? I ruined him as a swimmer. The one who will always mean more than anyone else. First I made him; then I broke him."

Jochums sent seventeen swimmers to the Olympic Trials in 1976 and seven made the team. But the only one he thought about twenty-four years later was Shaw. He saw Shaw's ghost on Santa Clara's gray solitary mornings when Tom Wilkens swam at levels Jochums had never expected to witness again. He saw Shaw when Wilkens looked at him with those same trusting eyes. Both swimmers were willing to do anything that was asked of them. Jochums still shivered at the memory of his own unchecked hubris. But really, what had changed in a quarter of a century?

What happened to Tim Shaw in 1976 was a bleak, footnoted tragedy that no one thought about anymore but the coach. More than twenty years later, Shaw had a great family and had returned to his old high school, Long Beach Wilson, where he worked as a Special Ed teacher for mildly disadvantaged kids. His students were the kids society had written off, but some made it to community colleges, and in a very real way he could say he changed the course of their lives. He also coached water polo (he had made the Olympic water polo team in 1984 and earned a silver medal), and although he didn't reflect on his swimming days very often, he lived his life according to his old coach's principles. When he did think about his career, what Shaw remembered were not the frustrations but the lessons Jochums imparted and their impact on his life. Shaw couldn't talk about his old coach without bringing up, again and again, the lifelong positive effect "Jochums' philosophy" had had on him.

Jochums moved to the University of Arizona in 1978 and for the next decade delivered a number of top twelve NCAA finishes, even though his true strength was always building individuals, not teams. In 1984, he developed the great American male distance swimmer George DiCarlo, who won Olympic gold in the 400-meter freestyle and silver in the 1,500-

meter freestyle. DiCarlo's American record in the 1,500 (15:01.51) would remain on the books for an unprecedented sixteen years. But both Jochums' hellfire and his enemies caught him in the Tucson desert.

Despite his own belief in discipline, Jochums looked at rules more as guidelines, things to which one adhered unless a higher personal purpose overrode them. The history books are filled with such men. Of course, so are cell blocks. In 1988, Jochums' training group for the Seoul Olympics fared poorly and just one person qualified for the team. On the pool deck, his relationships with his team members deteriorated. First came an anonymous letter accusing him of stealing funds from his club program. Then came more accusations of misappropriating money and providing illegal loans to his swimmers. A firestorm was building and the university's administration, led by Athletic Director Cedric Dempsey (who soon thereafter would be tapped as executive director of the NCAA), was already weary of its uncontrollable, renegade swim coach.

In November 1988, Jochums rested his team for the National Dual Meet Championship at the University of Alabama. Despite the heady title, this kind of early-season meet has little or no bearing on a season. It's a sizing-up exercise, a chance to evaluate various strengths and to swim fast before entering an intense training period during Christmas break. Right before Arizona arrived at the meet, Jochums learned one of his best swimmers had lost his eligibility because of poor grades. Jochums swam him anyway. It was an easy decision even though it was illegal. He wanted to see what kind of shape the boy was in. On the first day, the athlete competed under his own name, but on the second day, in blatant violation of every rule of competition, the swimmer raced under an assumed identity. A former team member went to the athletic department with the information. Jochums had hardly been a model citizen and this proved the final straw. In fact, he acknowledged providing a personal loan to a swimmer who, he said, was starving and needed food money. Two weeks later, the athletic director, Dempsey, handed Jochums a typed resignation letter and told him to sign it. In an invitational like the National Dual Meet Championship, the top teams score hundreds of points. Jochums' ineligible swimmer had earned a single point for his team.

"I knew I was breaking a rule," Jochums defiantly told the *Tucson Citizen*. "My intention was not to cheat, to gain an advantage. It was to know where the hell I was . . . His point didn't make any difference in the meet. There are no trick plays in swimming. But it was not morally wrong because it wasn't going to make any difference. If we had won the meet because of him, I'd have forfeited."

To the *Arizona Daily Star* he was equally unrepentant: "People talk about Dick Jochums and they'll say he may do a lot of things and he may be nuts. But Dick Jochums does not steal. Dick Jochums does not pay people under the table. And Dick Jochums does not cheat."

He was a forty-seven-year-old disgraced man with four children to feed. Friends disappeared and enemies celebrated. He was ostracized from coaching, the only job he had ever known. Having to escape town, he moved his family to southern California, where for six years he was a pariah working as a construction manager for his brother-in-law and selling insurance. Until then, he didn't know what hell was. As the years advanced and his bitterness hardened into something permanent but manageable, he started coaching part-time, just to remind himself what it felt like to feel his heart beating again. When he learned the struggling Santa Clara Swim Club needed a new head coach, he applied against his wife's advice. Three coaches were seriously considered and he landed the job only after the first two turned down their offers. This was in 1995, and Jochums was given a clear mandate: Return the once-glorious club to immediate respectability.

Jochums secured the job because no other top coach in the country had been interested in it. Yet once upon a time, the very mention of its singsong name, Santa Clara Swim Club (SCSC), had quickened the pulse of every swimmer in the world. Tucked between a public library and a softball field in the center of what later became Silicon Valley, the club had been founded at a local high school in 1951 by a man named George Haines, a young World War II veteran who had grown up swimming in an Indiana rock quarry. Three years after inception, SCSC had its first national champion. That was the beginning, and by the mid-1960s, when the American Dream was fast evolving into an image of palm trees, the Beach Boys, convertibles, and California sun, the Santa Clara Swim Club became the first and greatest American swimming Mecca. The club employed what was then a still novel approach of combining fast interval training with regimented and ordered workouts. Only a few years earlier, swimming had been a sport of low volume and low intensity. Interval training—that is, using a pace clock to swim a series of sets—is today the foundation of the sport.

Soon the country's best swimmers moved to the sleepy town of Santa Clara, and SCSC was winning one national championship after the other. It sent top athletes to the Olympics in 1960 and 1964 and won a bushel of medals. In 1964, Don Schollander became the first swimmer to win four gold medals in an Olympics. The same year, Donna DeVarona was the darling of the Tokyo Games with her two victories in the individual medleys, which she parlayed into a job as the first female sportscaster in the United States. But those Games were just warm-up acts for the 1968 Mexico City Olympics. For all intents, the U.S. team might as well have worn Santa Clara's blue and yellow colors instead of red, white, and blue.

That was the year an SCSC swimmer named Claudia Kolb broke DeVarona's 400-meter I.M. world record in practice by *nine* seconds. It was also the year the men's squad was so powerful that at a California invitational, Haines fielded five separate teams in the 4 × 200 freestyle relay and, to no one's surprise, they finished first through fifth. By the time the Mexico City Olympics were over, athletes from the orchard community of Santa Clara had accounted for twenty-three of the thirty-three gold medals U.S. swimming won, making it far and away the most powerful swim force in the world.

By then, Haines had built the Shangri-la that Jochums would later inherit, the nine-lane, 50-meter, $700,000 Santa Clara International Swim Center, and the city had been anointed "the swim capital of the world," according to the *San Jose Mercury News*. When converted to a 25-yard short-course pool (accomplished by stringing the lane lines widthwise instead of lengthwise), the facility had twenty-three lanes, enough to run two meets simultaneously. The year the foundation was dug, the 60-mile peninsula area between San Jose and San Francisco was an agricultural zone known as the Valley of the Heart's Delight. Miles of orchards surrounded the complex. Prunes, apricots, and cherries. Pink and white blossoms carpeted the earth every spring. Del Monte, the fruit cannery, was a major employer. But changes were already underway. The fields were being replaced by monolithic, windowless buildings where thousands of engineers were toiling day and night to beat the Soviet Union into space. Less than two miles from the swim center, a new company with no business plan was breaking ground on a plant. It was going to call itself Intel Corporation.

When the city-owned pool was finished in 1967, it was inaugurated with the first annual Santa Clara International meet, an invitational so immediately important that it garnered nearly twenty articles in the *San Jose Mercury News*. And that was before the racing began. Haines hand-picked the world's 200 best swimmers to compete, and the meet became *the* society event of the swimming world. Foreign athletes from every corner of the globe scrambled to attend. It was the height of the Cold War, and swimming was a major battleground where East-versus-West ideologies played out. Santa Clara became a major venue for determining athletic supremacy. The "Cadillac of swimming pools" boasted wider than normal lanes, the world's "best gutters" for minimizing turbulence, and a 1,000-person seating capacity that expanded to 5,600 with bleachers. Tickets for the first international meet sold out at eleven Bay Area outlets, and before a stroke was taken that first year, the event already overshadowed U.S. nationals in importance. It would continue to do so for years to come. By 1999, 22 world records had been set in Santa Clara's waters, as well as 333 American records and 57 foreign national records. Through the years, the club captured 48 national team titles and developed 49 Olympians, including Spitz, Schollander, DeVarona, Pablo Morales, Chris Von Saltza, Claudia Kolb, Steve Clark, Brent Berk, Greg Buckingham, Mitch Ivey, Karen Moe, Jenny Bartz, Brian Job, Joe Bottom, John Hencken, Tom Jager, Troy Dalbey, and hundreds of others. Its Olympic haul included 33 gold medals, 12 silvers, and 9 bronzes. Haines, who would be named Swim Coach of the Century by *Swimming World Magazine,* served on an unprecedented seven Olympic staffs and coached his swimmers to more than 150 world records. This was a history neither Wilkens, Grote, nor any other present-day swimmer knew anything about.

By the mid-1980s, the Santa Clara Swim Club had lost its magic luster. Haines, the club's guiding force, had departed in 1974 for collegiate coaching. Other programs around the country gained prominence. The team slid into a period of fallow years. Coaches came and went, usually on bad terms, and the talent steadily drained away. The situation had reached its nadir at the 1996 Olympic Trials when only a single SCSC swimmer qualified for finals. Jochums had stepped in just months earlier with his mandate to win again and a four-year window in which to do it.

Sadly, as Jochums prepared in April 1999 to launch his 2000 Olympic campaign, the club had virtually no reminders of its glorious history. The one permanent acknowledgment was a Hall of Fame wall with black-and-white photos. But the display was in a public reception area that was inaccessible during team workouts and many age-group swimmers had never been in there. Because of a missing letter that had never been replaced, visitors entering the area were informed this was the "Hall O Fame."

The club had several photos of past Santa Clara Olympians, including ones of Olympic heroes DeVarona and Morales, collecting dust in the lifeguards' room under a box of unused gauze pads. More photos were in a small cupola office, but it was opened only several times per year. In the team room, dominated by a hideous blue carpet, there were virtually no trophies from the glory days on display. Most been lost, stolen, or given away years before Jochums had arrived. Trophies from the 1990s sat on dusty shelves with insect exoskeletons littering their bases (the shelves would be cleaned in early 2000, dramatically improving their appearance). History doesn't endure very well at pools in general because the damp environment causes trophies to rust and photos to curl, and at Santa Clara in particular. Dozens of the biggest names in swimming had suffered, endured, and triumphed in these waters, yet there was barely a trace of them.

What had endured for Jochums to inherit was the original monument to excellence, the sparkling 50-meter pool with its deeper-than-normal depth and its odd ninth lane, which was put in to expand the pool's width to 25 yards (the competitive distance for winter swimming). As the 1960s had turned into the 1970s and the pool continued to host its famed invitation once a year it became the aquatic equivalent of the Roman Coliseum, where warriors and ideologues arrived to fight. As American swimming gained more parity, the *Mercury News* had gradually shifted its news stories from celebrating SCSC's dominance to focusing on East-versus-West dramas, so even though the world records eventually stopped falling, the racing always had a heightened importance. But by now the Cold War was long over and the meet had existed for years primarily as a moneymaker for the club, earning as much as

$50,000 annually. Somewhere through the years, the qualifying standards had been lowered to attract hundreds of additional entrants and therefore boost revenue. Soon after, top teams had stopped putting the meet on their calendars. Jochums' predecessor had managed the considerable feat of getting the meet televised by ABC, but even that failed to fully restore its luster. When Jochums arrived, one of the first things he did was raise the meet's qualifying standards, revenue be damned.

During his first four years at the club, the coach had maintained a low profile. He was careful and tentative, and in truth he was quieter now, less of an absolutist and less likely to explode. Almost immediately, he had begun reversing the club's fortunes, and for three straight years—1996, 1997, and 1998—Santa Clara had won the men's national championship title. In 1997, it had captured the overall team championship by a single point. Jochums was engineering swimming's biggest turnaround story, thanks in no small part to the summer influx of Stanford stars. Things were undoubtedly going well.

But national championships only take a person so far. The real test of a coach, and his club, is to put someone on the Olympic team. At the end of the day, that is the differentiator. Jochums had done it before, but that had been years earlier. He constantly wondered if he had what it took to do it again. He believed he did, but every time his mind went down that path, he also had to think about the destruction of Tim Shaw. One thought could not exist without the other. This was his self-imposed punishment and he was going to carry it to the grave.

That first summer when he had moved into the head coach's office, which was no bigger than a walk-in closet, he refused to decorate it with personal effects. Several seasons passed before his assistant coach, exasperated, would finally do it himself while Jochums was away. The assistant knew Jochums' soul and on the walls he put two posters. One held a Vince Lombardi speech about the true meaning of winning. The other was a twenty-five-year-old black-and-white photo of Shaw. These were Jochums' twin reference points, his constant reminders of how precarious the distinction is between success and failure.

. . .

Dick Jochums took less than two minutes to collect his thoughts and then he stepped back into the room. He was a dramatic motivator, one of the sport's best, and for a long, extended moment he let the silence billow. Several younger athletes who had never swum for him shifted uncomfortably. The older ones slouched and waited.

"I don't need you to stand up and sing the national anthem today," Jochums began in his gravelly voice. "You know why we're here. We're here to begin an eighteen-month process that starts today. Not tomorrow. Today. We're here to make a commitment."

As if on cue, church bells at nearby St. Jude's Catholic Church began ringing. It was 12:20 in the afternoon. The swimmers smiled at one another. Was this Jochums' way of emphasizing the sanctity of the journey?

These men were the best and brightest the country had to offer. As athletes at Stanford, where academic excellence was demanding, they epitomized the ideal concept of the scholar-athlete. They were children of the millennium, the people best equipped to succeed in the new epoch. But they were also all Watergate babies who had been born at the height of American cynicism. Their first years were informed by a U.S. President's downfall, fallout from the Vietnam War, and the Iranian hostage crisis. They had grown up without much by way of heroes and noble acts. They also belonged to the first American generation in decades not to experience the blossoming of courage that occurs during a shared crisis. Their great-grandparents' generation had the Great Depression; their grandparents had World War II. Their own parents had Vietnam. Each was a vastly different situation, but they all required mettle and inner resolve. In comparison, these men had had it easy. They weren't weaker or less prepared for life, but they were certainly less tested. And this, at a core level, bothered them. They recognized their own lives as privileged and relatively frictionless. After all, most enjoyed scholarships to one of the world's premier learning institutions. They wore shorts to class and walked among palm trees. There was something inauthentic to it all. As a result, they sensed in Jochums some unnameable and ancient force and it drew them. He offered steadfastness and immovability, things that were lacking in their own constantly shifting age. He spoke the language of their grandfathers, a language chipped by hard living. It made those in the room hang on his every word. When he yelled at them, they shook like children. The ones who couldn't stand his crude style— and that included many people—had been weeded out during the previous two summer seasons.

The coach waited until the bells stopped ringing and continued: "The next eighteen months you need to dedicate to yourself. That's first. Then, if you want to take a run for the Olympics, you must go for it. For most of you, this journey will be the most important thing you ever do in your life. I will treat you as adults, and as adults you will be expected to make your own decisions. But before beginning, you, as a whole person, must come first. Your primary priority must be to yourself. Once that is established, you take care of your life in this order: school, social life, and swimming. I strongly recommend you realize as soon as possible that swimming is a lousy lover."

This was a speech Jochums had used for more than twenty years and it was wholly disingenuous. Anyone wanting the Olympics was going to eat, breathe, and sleep them until the Trials came and went. Sitting in this room was no group of wildmen. Those had gone in different life directions long ago. The ones present were ready to commit their lives to pursuing greatness.

"Every workout will be designed to build you, not tear you down," Jochums continued as he paced the room. "Every day, there will be a major set, which we will ask you to swim at one hundred percent race speed. Nowhere else in the country do they demand that kind of daily intensity. I do. But I say it now: We do not guarantee you a spot on the Olympic team."

The mention of "Olympic team" sent a crackle of energy through the room. These young men had waited a lifetime to hear these words. Jochums stopped pacing, and no one moved.

"We do not guarantee you a spot on the Olympic team," Jochums repeated. "However, I personally guarantee you will work harder than anyone else in the world to make that team. If you do as I say, you will be in the best shape of your life. I will take responsibility for your lives in the hours that you give me, but this is a personal journey for you and you alone."

He stepped close to the first row of swimmers, so close into their space that they grew uncomfortable and seemed to lean away without actually moving. He was close enough for them to see the bristle of his unshaven face and smell his breakfast.

"If you come here every single day between now and Olympic Trials, if you make no excuses and if you allow no bad days, you will have done everything possible to make the Olympic team," he said. "That is our goal. If you begin this journey but don't meet those requirements, you're someday going to be my age and you're going to be at a cocktail party. You'll be having a good time until you suddenly hear yourself telling people how good you could have been.

"Very simply, you cannot have any off days. Your body is a machine and tuning the machine is the key. I do not believe in high yardage. I do not believe in new ideas. In workout, we stick to basics. Some of you will call this 'boring,' but that's how it is going to be. In workout, we fix technique at race speed, not in drills. I don't believe in drills. You will not hear us making new corrections at meets, because it will already have been taken care of on the practice deck.

"In 1976, I trained seventeen people for Olympic trials. Seven made the team; ten did not. Of those seven, one is a millionaire. Of the ten who did not make the team, every one considered himself a failure the day Trials ended. Today, nine of them are millionaires. If money is the measure of success, and much of today's society tells us it is, then those nine are true success stories. All ten came to me and said even though they missed their dream, they wouldn't have traded anything in the world for the chance to go for it. I'm therefore asking you to commit yourself as individuals and as a group. I am providing you the mind-set and framework for success; your job is to step forward and accept it."

He explained how the program would be tailored to each individual. For most, this would be their last two years swimming. They would be allowed to be selfish, Jochums told them. He talked several minutes and then paused. He gazed out the window and suddenly he looked much older. There was something he needed to say. He had been struggling to find the words for two weeks. Outside a light rain had begun falling on the pool's bright blue tarps. How do you explain in clear, simple sentences who you are and what you have done with your life?

"Some of you know my history," Jochums said very slowly. "You know I've done wrong in my life and I've made mistakes. Some of you realize how bad I want another Olympic swimmer and another world record. Some of you think you know how bad I want to be an Olympic coach. You can't possibly know. But I need to tell you something. I am old enough to realize I can't hang my own dreams on you, any of you. I've learned the hard way that I can't do that."

He stopped and waited, as he later said, until the difficult memories of Tim Shaw and several others rose from his knuckled brain folds, briefly lingered, and then cleared. It was almost certain the weight of the Olympic dream was going to crush some of these eager young athletes. Add a coach's expectations, and the burden may be too great for anyone.

Jochums switched gears to discuss training. The days at Santa Clara would seem robotic and mind-numbingly dull, he reminded them, worse than any training they had ever encountered. But every day, they would leave the pool knowing whether they were faster than the day before. It was all about personal responsibility and rising to the daily challenge, he said. The men responded to words like this. They wanted hardship and challenge; they needed to face a steep mountain that must be climbed.

"I want you to be the toughest sons of bitches in the world," the coach groused. "I want you hurting. But I want you standing tall."

The swimmers liked the way this sounded. Sports are about the struggle, not the final result. Wilkens nodded appreciatively to a teammate. There was the general shifting of bodies that occurs when a room agrees. The earlier feeling, that of caged energy, dissipated. But Jochums wasn't through. He had their heads, but he thought he could clutch their hearts, too. What bothered the coach most was people's inability to directly confront something they cared deeply about. Jochums could never have been a psychologist—he would have bullied and intimidated all but the strongest patients into straightjackets—but coaching allowed him a unique position to push directly against people's deepest desires. He thrived on the psychological brinkmanship involved in his job, and as it happened, he was masterful at it.

"In this room, there is potential to break the current Aussie freestyle dominance," he said. "There is someone sitting in front of me who could be looking at an Olympic medal in the two-hundred-meter freestyle. I don't know if anyone has ever told him that, but I'm telling him now."

In one simple statement, the personalized Olympic dream was suddenly in the room, crowding everywhere at once. It was as if a car air bag had exploded, and it was glaringly obvious this group, with all its national honors and accolades, had not walked down this path before. For an exhilarating instant, all the shared longing and dreaming seemed to collide in one big mash. In an era when every fast swim creates suspicion about performance-enhancing drugs, when the Olympics themselves have devolved into crass commercial affairs touting Coke and Visa, when the height of American pride is watching multimillion-dollar professional basketball players dominate teams so weak there's no actual contest, somehow, incredibly and almost naively, the original glory of the Games still existed. It was here in this room, glowing bright for the people sitting in Santa Clara's clubhouse on a drizzly Saturday in April 1999.

All eyes fixed on a nervous Stanford sophomore in the front row. Indeed, no one had ever said anything like that to him, although he thought about it all the time. Jochums stood directly over the swimmer, who tried to make eye contact but couldn't get his eyes above the coach's waistline. Jochums kicked the kid's foot and they locked stares for a long, silent moment. Then Jochums turned to two sprinters. He said that in case they weren't aware of it, both had legitimate shots at making the Olympic 4 × 100-meter freestyle relay team, which took the top six finishers in the 100-meter freestyle at Trials (instead of the top two for individual events). Both began fidgeting.

Jochums continued around the room individually assessing each person's potential. He informed one athlete he'd be the surprise of the 2000 Games if he ever pulled his head out of his ass. He told another his fear of failure would haunt him for life unless he faced into it. Meanwhile, the sophomore in the front row was engaged in a fit of nervousness. He crossed his legs once, twice. He folded and unfolded his arms. From several feet away, Kurt Grote watched the swimmer's jumpiness with a veteran's casual amusement. Soon nearly everyone was staring out the window or bouncing nervous legs. Jochums was pleased. Winning them over had been easier than he thought. All would swim for him in the summer of 1999. The college graduates would stay through the winter, and in the summer of 2000 nearly all would return to Santa Clara to train for the Trials. He had the foundation for his team.

When the coach had finished his speech, he again told them it would be the hardest, most emotional year of their lives. He asked them to go home, make a commitment, and bring it back to the pool. The meeting broke up, and everyone began to leave.

"It's real now, isn't it?" Wilkens asked a teammate who had been biting his fingernail during the meeting. The friend nodded vigorously, too vigorously. He resumed his nailbiting. The Olympics did that to people.

The 2000 Games were less than two years away, and there was precious little time. The coming months would be devoted to finding an inch here, an inch there. Finish a race one stroke sooner. Increase a bench press by 40 lbs. Get the kick to generate one additional pound of propulsive force per stroke cycle. Find a way to shave a tenth of a second off every turn. There was so much to do and not a day to waste.

For Wilkens and Grote, the campaign started on Monday. The others would swim at Stanford for several more weeks until school let out for summer. Walking toward the exit, Grote turned and realized the sophomore in the first row was frozen in his seat and staring out the window. It was a poignant image. The swimmer's lips were moving, and three times in succession he wiped his sweating palms against his blue jeans. *The dream.* The swimmer exhaled hard, as if he were moments away from stepping on the Olympic starting block. *The chance for immortality.* Smiling, Grote returned and put a friendly hand on the kid's shoulder. That was part of the moment, too.

"Are you ready?" Grote asked, and the swimmer nearly jumped out of his skin.

CHAPTER THREE

A new urgency materialized at Santa Clara in the weeks that followed the Olympic dream meeting. It bubbled in the pool, percolating from the cracked bottom with its criss-cross pattern of black lines, its glinting, child-thrown pennies, and its floating tangles of public-swimmer hair. The urgency rose from the knowledge that every day now mattered, that every squandered practice could never be regained. A hard-fought set on a Monday night had to be the starting point for Tuesday morning. When a swimmer faltered, he had to step back, shake off his failure, and resume plunging forward. Nationwide, nearly 1,500 of the best U.S. swimmers were preparing for Olympic Trials and the fifty-two slots available for the 2000 Olympic swim team. Perhaps as many as 5,000 more were still trying to qualify for the meet's difficult time standards.

The first collegiate swimmers from the East Coast began filling the lanes. Every morning and afternoon, Jochums stood on deck wearing the same blue warm-up suit and never moved more than twenty feet from the pool's edge. He looked huge. He kept his left hand balled in his pocket and gripped in his right a beautiful analog stopwatch which he glanced at constantly.

Jochums was unable to get Grote off his mind. The club's best swimmer, its surest hope for the Olympics, was considering leaving the team. A month earlier, shortly before the Olympic kickoff meeting, Grote had traveled to Hong Kong for the 1999 Short Course World Championships. He had performed poorly, losing a race he should have won after leading at the halfway mark and being under world-record pace before fading to fifth. The star was partially blaming Santa Clara for the loss and debating his options. This threatened everything Jochums, was trying to build. But the meet in Hong Kong had been swum in short-course meters, a distance American swimmers race so rarely they often have trouble adjusting their stroke to the turns. Grote wasn't sure whether his poor performance reflected his spotty training, poor coaching, or was simply a case of competing in an unfamiliar pool.

U.S. swimming has major schizophrenia about swim distances. There are three legal formats, each with its own records, specialists, and racing strategies. The established international standard is "long-course meters," which refers to an Olympic-sized, 50-meter pool. It is used for every national and international championship of consequence except the NCAA championships, although someday they, too, will probably become a long-course meet. But long-course swimming is not the predominant format in the United States. More than ninety percent of pools in the United States are 25-yard facilities, which means the majority of U.S. swimmers spend most of their careers swimming "short-course yards." It is shocking how variant the two formats are. Short-course swimming is based on strength, on muscling through the water and leveraging the frequent turns. Long course involves a steady build up of speed during each lap, and a better management of stroke turnover, technique, and breathing. You have to be a racer for short course and a strategist for long course. American swimmers have separate sets of personal best times for each distance, and many young swimmers carry conversion charts to translate their times between formats. It's an inaccurate science, but in rough terms a race in a 50-meter pool is approximately fourteen percent slower than its equivalent in a 25-yard pool.

But Grote had raced neither of those distances. There is a third format, "short-course meters," which is raced in a 25-meter pool. In the United States, this is the sport's aardvark, its alien animal in an organized world. Virtually no short-course-meter pools exist stateside and most American swimmers have never competed in one. But short-course-meter swimming is used by the rest of the world during the winter season, and the format has its own World Championships and World Cup Series. Until the late 1990s, the United States had largely ignored these competitions, and as a direct result they carried diminished importance. And as a consequence of the United States' overall disregard for the format, the world records for short-course-meter swimming are significantly slower than their long-course equivalents.

That was precisely why Grote went to Hong Kong, even though he wasn't in top shape. The meet offered a $15,000 purse for breaking a world record and he was within striking distance in both breaststroke events. Had he set two records, the $30,000 payday—paltry by most professional athletic standards—would have shot him into the top five percent of swimming moneymakers for the year. Instead, he hadn't even covered his plane fare.

Since returning from Hong Kong, Grote's times had been slow and his workouts sporadic because he had a final medical school obligation to complete. This was the medical boards, the biggest exam of his life. The test would largely determine where he spent his residency after graduation and required inordinate amounts of studying. Some days, Grote sat at his desk for sixteen hours. What kind of hubris would lead a man to believe he could do that and still swim fast? Yet Grote was so used to perfection he refused to acknowledge how draining his situation was. As a result, his frustration was building. He was being pulled in too many directions at once but was too proud to admit it. The situation made Jochums' stomach ache.

Happy Tom Wilkens was the coach's antacid. For the past month every practice had pivoted on perfect technique. His control was coming. Day by day, what first looked clunky and difficult was becoming more graceful and flowing. These were the final months of any major stroke work. By winter, Wilkens—and everyone else—had to be ready for final fine-tuning to have any shot at Trials.

"You build a Volkswagen, you drive a Volkswagen," Jochums often said. "You build a Porsche, you drive a Porsche."

The precision and efficiency of Wilkens' freestyle had become breathtaking. His hands entered the water and seemed to stay in place as his body pulled over them. He employed little of the crawl's well-known "S-stroke," which for thirty years had formed the foundation of how we thought swimmers moved through water. Instead, Wilkens pulled his arms straight back with elbows high. He breathed to the left side, so his right arm pulled slightly wider than his left in order to balance the body as it rolled back and forth on its hips through each stroke. He had his Porsche all right; the engine was already there, so was the chassis. He was now down to the details.

The S-stroke more accurately resembles a Z-stroke. It refers to the way a swimmer's hand sculls outward, inward, and then outward again as it completes a stroke, and its history shows how a major Olympic sport entering the new millennium can remain at a loss to answer its most fundamental question: *How do people swim fast?* Science can map the human genome in record time, but it can't yet fully figure out how the human body moves through the water. A marvelous book called *Science in the Summer Games* points out that a swimmer needs more than 1,000 watts of power to reach maximum velocity in the water (a pokey 4 miles per hour) when the fastest fish achieve speeds of 70 miles per hour without, figuratively speaking, breaking a sweat. More remarkable, a dolphin uses only one-eighth of the power that physics says is required for its movement. What can the dolphin know that we don't? Why can a human outsprint a horse but not a guppy? There is a need to understand the secrets of this mystery.

The sport of modern swimming is surprisingly young (while the act of swimming is probably nearly as old as the act of running, and the first recorded swim races were in Japan nearly 500 years ago, modern racing was organized just 150 years ago in England). For much of that time, theorists steadfastly believed a swimmer moved forward by pushing directly against the water. The effort created drag forces, just like a riverboat's paddlewheel, and was supported by Newton's Third Law of Motion, "For every action there is an equal and opposite reaction." However, in the 1960s one of the sport's great pioneers, Indiana University's James "Doc" Counsilman, discovered when his best swimmers swam, their hands appeared to remain in place in the water while their bodies moved over them. Counsilman realized the world's most natural swimmers didn't pull straight back in a paddle motion as was long thought; instead, they made several distinct sweeps, or sculls, within a single armstroke. As the hand changed its pitch and angle while moving, it seemed clear that not only did the best swimmers possess an innate "feel" for the stillest water, but they employed more than just Newtonian physics to their stroke. Instead of a paddlewheel, the swimmer's hand was working as a propeller blade.

This gave rise to the conviction that Bernoulli's Principle, not Newtonian law, was primarily responsible for propelling swimmers through the water. Bernoulli's Principle, which explains through lift forces how airplanes and kites rise off the ground and fly, posits that during an armstroke a swimmer constantly adjusts the hand's direction in such a way as to put greater pressure against the palm than the hand's back. This creates propulsive lift. A layman can stick a hand out the window of a moving car to understand this. By adjusting the hand's pitch, the hand will ride up and down on the currents. This is what it does while moving through the water during a stroke. For three decades, nearly every swimmer's development was based on Bernoulli's Principle. The problem is, the theory might not even apply to swimming.

Several studies in the 1990s have questioned the sculling idea, in part because while lift forces have been documented in sculling, no drag forces have ever been conclusively found. There can be no Bernoulli's Principle without drag. At least two studies found that truly natural swimmers, the ones with the best intuitive feel for the water, actually make less of an S-stroke when they are swimming in the water than they do when they are asked to demonstrate the "proper" stroke on land. That means while they accurately perform the traditional stroke when moving their arms through the air, once they enter the water their bodies intuitively restrict and limit the sculling motions. But what these naturals seem to share, though, is tremendous hip rotation. Just as a golfer or batter starts swinging the club or bat with the hips, so, too, do natural swimmers tend to lead each armstroke with a hip rotation that creates substantial torque. And what about the legs? It's estimated the legs contribute only thirty percent to forward movement while using up to sixty percent of the body's oxygen.

One indicator of efficient swimming is the amount of water bubbles and turbulence involved in a stroke. To a layman, this is far easier to understand: More bubbles and turbulence following the hand mean the swimmer is failing to fully "catch" the water. A slipping hand is akin to clawing at pebbles while climbing a steep hill. So much better to grasp solid rock. As Wilkens swam his workout, his left hand created no bubbles—zero—even when it entered the water. On his right hand, only the thumb made the thinnest white bubble trail, and that hung motionless in the water like a necklace. Similar to a ballroom dancer, he was always aware of maintaining a high elbow placement throughout the stroke.

Laminar flows, bound vortices, intracycle velocity fluctuation, flinging mechanisms. The biomechanics of swimming is an exhausting jargon, while the secrets of forward propulsion remain elusive. Scientists are captivated by the mystery and devote their lives to studying it. Meanwhile, in the United States, the sport has so many participants that it takes years for any changes in swimming's science to reach the masses. As a result, while the grassroots continue to overemphasize the principles of sculling, the top programs long ago changed their focus to building more centralized power. By 1999, elite swimmers were attuning themselves to their body "cores," rather than to their hand motions, swimming low in the water instead of higher, burying their heads for better balance (instead of raising the head to reduce drag), and working once again on the drag-based propulsive force found in Newtonian physics.

Wilkens was becoming a glowing example of physics fused with power. He finished an 800 freestyle that required he swim increasingly faster every 100 yards. He had managed to hold his perfect stroke for the entire swim, although it wasn't easy. His body had wanted to thrash and cut loose. He spluttered when he heard his time and complained that he could have swum much faster.

"Speed was not the goal; technique was," the coach said. "Swim like that and by next year no one can touch you."

Wilkens began his next set and Jochums glanced at his stopwatch. "It's coming," the coach said. "All great swimmers had it, this oneness with the water. Timmy Shaw had it and now Tom's learning it. He could already swim at this speed. But never with such effortlessness. He's building his racecar and every day he gives me the chills. This kid has no idea what he's got."

· · ·

But Wilkens did know. And because he knew, in the dark-wooded pews of Stanford's gilded chapel he knelt and prayed for guidance.

Sunday was his one day off from swimming, and Wilkens often drove north to Stanford to attend an afternoon Catholic mass. It was a chance to see friends, students and priests alike, a chance to forget about the narrow world in which he lived between two lane lines. Attending church regularly made him feel connected to something bigger than himself.

His days were boring, but he was frequently executing Jochums' simple sets with such flawless precision and mastery that the moments shimmered with transcendence. He knew he was moving in a sacred space, and believed if he thought about it too much it would be snatched from him. But it felt, honest-to-God, like he could point a flashlight at heaven anytime he wanted and for a split second glimpse some veiled majesty. The feeling of complete joy he had when he swam hard must be similar to what mystics experience as religious ecstasy.

Stanford's chapel is a soaring and beautiful offering to a higher power. A first-time visitor finds himself shrouded in the cool and private darkness of the pews, where the light is so dim it's difficult to read a songbook. Yet the chapel's gilded ceiling bursts with golden illumination, with angels and prophets heralding promises of a radiant afterlife. Darkness and light, heaven and earth. The chapel was designed to humble its worshipers, to make them bend their knees and accept their smallness.

Through him, with him, in him, in the unity of the Holy Spirit, all glory and honor is yours, almighty Father, for ever and ever.

Returning to his seat after communion one Sunday, Wilkens bowed his head, and tried to grab ahold of his whirlwind life. It was a remarkable time for him. But it was also frightening. There was no doubt he was in a sustained breakout moment, the kind of symphony an athlete dreams of. At nearly every meet, he was winning the high-point award for the outstanding male swimmer. Kids suddenly wanted his autograph; recently a *competitor* had asked for it. At first, Wilkens hadn't understood what his fellow swimmer wanted, and when he finally realized it, he had flushed red and laughed awkwardly. In practice, his times continued to defy anything he believed he was capable of. Wilkens rarely thought about Grote right now. But he knew Grote was thinking about him all the time and that made him uneasy. He had always been the hunter, not the hunted. Now that was no longer the case. In the year since the 1998 World Championships, Wilkens had become the second best all-around U.S. male swimmer, after the King of Swimming, Tom Dolan. Away from the pool, sports agents had sought him out and, after interviewing several, Wilkens had chosen the agent who represented Olympic track star Michael Johnson. This fantastic new world seemed surreal and implausible.

Wilkens was giddy, even as he prayed for help. He needed to know how to act, how to be a role model, how to express his gratitude for this chance at greatness. These were ridiculously premature sentiments. The sporting world didn't care one whit about an unknown swimmer named

Tom Wilkens. Nor would it anytime soon. He was just another pale, down-looking face in a dark pew.

Yet he found it somehow essential to be thinking about these things. Pressure manifests itself in different ways. So does responsibility. The Olympic pursuit is the ultimate example of selfish individualism. But Wilkens was not born with a gene that encourages solitary pursuits; nor was he raised in a way that allowed him to be self-centered. Self-centeredness, at least a degree of it, is a requisite for a professional athlete to be great in today's competitive world. But for this young man it seemed to cause a chemical imbalance. People who want to give back to the world often feel this way. *Make the right impression,* Wilkens told himself. *Always remember how lucky you are.* He gave time to every child who asked for an autograph, and recently at meets he had begun swimming his preliminary races much harder than necessary so no one would think he loafed. It was all so genuine and earnest. How many athletes think this way? Jochums wanted to kill him.

The service ended. Still thinking, Wilkens filed out of the chapel. There were no answers, only more questions. He shook hands with friends who had been at the mass; he joked and asked the usual questions a person does to catch up and show interest in someone else's life. The hum of church people on the steps after a service is always low and friendly. Wilkens didn't yet know it, but this problem of his, this difficulty of fitting into the emerging role assigned him, was going to grow much worse over the next year.

But there was something else on his mind, something that was clicking in the back of his head even as he slapped people on the back, talked Stanford sports, and smiled broadly at various stories. It was something momentous that not even spiritual contemplation was helping him handle. The previous week, Wilkens' world had been tipped upside down. For years, Tom Dolan had been Wilkens' primary motivation. Dolan was the quarry, Wilkens the relentless pursuer. Now the two of them were No. 1 and No. 2 in the United States in the medley events. It was a comfortable paradigm for Wilkens, but it had unexpectedly changed a week earlier. Dolan had been training at the U.S. Olympic Center in Colorado Springs when he went on a fast break during a pickup basketball game. The king cut left, cut right, and crumpled to the court floor as pain seared through the torn medial meniscus of his right knee. Days later, he had been wheeled into St. Francis Hospital in Colorado Springs for emergency surgery. The 8 A.M. operation lasted only two hours, but in that time, the entire landscape of the 200-meter I.M. and 400-meter I.M. had seismically shifted. Rumors had Dolan out for the year, and possibly for his career. Without swimming a stroke, Tom Wilkens, by abrupt default, was now the country's No. 1 medley specialist and best all-around male swimmer. Was he ready for this?

As he stepped into Stanford's pretty Spanish-style courtyard, the swimmer gazed at the wide sky above him. Everything in his life was changing so fast. He exhaled deeply and rubbed his hands together. Mass was supposed to calm him, but his heart was beating too fast.

. . .

Two weeks later, Jochums was grave and troubled. Had been for three straight days. The stomachache he blamed on Grote had migrated to his head, making him lose sleep.

"Someone raced them," he said bitterly. "Tom and Kurt went to a Stanford practice over the weekend when I was out of town, and someone put them against each other. It was disaster and it's going to take ten days minimum to repair the damage."

Oddly enough, it was the first time the world's No. 1 and No. 2 breaststrokers had swum against each other in months, ever since Jochums had decreed they must no longer race head-to-head during practice because there was too much at stake between them. Now the coach was genuinely aggrieved. He had spent months masterfully dealing with a delicate competitive undercurrent that ran through Wilkens and Grote's complex relationship. All three of them had handled the subtle reordering at the pool after the protégé beat his mentor for the first time the previous summer. More recently, Jochums had muzzled his growing excitement about Wilkens' progress whenever Grote was on deck, and he treated Grote's ongoing frustrations with patience. Grote, still the better and more exciting swimmer, was so tough on himself that things were either great or terrible, and it had not been a good spring.

In his younger days, Jochums relished pitting two top athletes against each other. For weeks he'd have them go at it until one emerged victorious and hardened. The problem was, to have a winner, there had to be a loser. When Jochums' most well-known Olympic champion, George

DiCarlo, had shown up at Arizona as a freshman, he immediately began racing Doug Towne, Arizona's defending NCAA 500-yard freestyle champion, every lap of every practice. "If you want to be the best, you have to take on the best," DiCarlo remembered thinking.

Coaches like that kind of attitude, but within months Towne's spirit was broken. DiCarlo knew it the day the other swimmer avoided racing him during practice. Towne's unhappiness grew and soon thereafter he left the sport. With the path cleared, DiCarlo went on to twice win Towne's event at the NCAA championships, capture gold and silver Olympic medals in the 1984 Olympics, and turn into a motivational speaker for young swimmers. Nearly twenty years later, DiCarlo was still one of the biggest names in swimming while no one at Arizona seemed to have any idea what had happened to Towne, not even the school's alumni-records office. There is a lesson in that story. Jochums had begun his season with two potential champions and ended with one. As a result, Santa Clara teammates like Wilkens and Grote almost never raced each other in practice once they became direct competitors.

Wilkens and Grote knew they weren't supposed to race. They knew they trained differently—Wilkens like a wild animal, Grote like a meticulous surgeon—and most important, they knew Grote was not in top shape. But who would back down from a challenge? Wilkens in particular had been thirsting for a head-to-head matchup. A part of Grote had been dreading it. After they had squared off, Wilkens returned to the apartment he shared with Santa Clara's top assistant coach, thirty-four-year-old John Bitter. The swimmer was grinning from ear to ear.

"What are you so happy about?" Bitter had asked.

"I dusted him," said Wilkens, breaking into an even wider smile.

"Oh, shit," said Bitter, understanding immediately.

"Not even close."

The damage was done. During the following practice, Grote began driving himself so hard he suffered an asthma attack, something that hadn't happened in months. Jochums made the swimmer get out of the pool, which Grote never would have done himself, and told him not to come back until the next day.

"Did you race Tom last week when I told you not to?" asked Jochums once Grote returned.

Grote, standing in the shallow water, indicated it was no big deal. "Did he dust you?"

Grote managed a grim smile and said, "Yeah, he dusted me."

"Well, did you consider that he had been sick for three days beforehand, and during that time he did nothing except sit on his ass and rest? While you were making two workouts per day and devoting all your mental energy to the biggest exam of your life?"

Jochums jutted his chin toward Grote, daring him to challenge the information. The swimmer hadn't thought of it that way. All Grote knew was that there was too much unwanted information hitting him at once. He was a world champion who couldn't beat his own teammate and that selfsame teammate was now his top competitor, and who knew how this had come about so fast, although in fact it had all started years earlier, because he, Grote, was the one who had taken the kid under his wing and shown him how to swim faster in the first place. That last part made Grote feel good, like he was the person he wanted to be, but the irony ticked him off.

Also, it piqued him that Wilkens could swim breaststroke so fast when he didn't even practice it every day. Grote had swirling in his breast anger, confusion, and, worst of all, a sense of slipping. Here he was, the most mature and accomplished swimmer at Santa Clara, and suddenly he looked like a lost boy. The coach stepped to the pool's edge and spoke quietly so the other swimmers couldn't hear.

"Look, Kurt. I never said you were guaranteed to win gold in the two hundred," Jochums said. "But I will guarantee the two of you will go one-two in Sydney. I will guarantee that you—you, Kurt—become the first man in history to break one minute in the one-hundred-meter breaststroke. You will hold the world record in that event. That is what I am telling you."

Grote attempted a loose smile and faltered. Something significant had just been said and a line had been crossed. Jochums was indirectly telling the swimmer that he could not defend his own world-championship event against Wilkens. Grote looked perplexed, as if he had misheard.

"You don't have to be the fastest in workout," Jochums continued. "In fact, you never will be. Tom is a once-in-a-lifetime workout swimmer. You know that. Are you going to train to become the world's all-time greatest practicer? Last time I checked, they don't give out gold medals at the end of workout. You don't have to beat him here; you don't even have to be close. Be smarter. Be craftier. That's how you'll win."

This was a paradigm Grote was willing to accept. He pushed off the wall and swam the rest of practice a little smoother and a little higher. He even joked between sets. But the strain was apparent. Never before had he been less than perfect. If his times didn't start improving, he could be in bad shape.

Two lanes away, Wilkens was in the middle of a crushing 20 × 100-yard freestyle set. Every fifth repeat he dropped five seconds off his rest interval until he swam each 100 yards on a 1:05 interval and averaged 52 seconds. It was a monstrous set, something fast enough to intimidate most national-level freestyle specialists. Wilkens' face and back were scarlet and his breath came in horrible gusts. But his arms churned like twin blades, seventeen strokes each lap in the 25-yard pool, five more per lap than he used when swimming easy. Strokes shorten as fatigue sets in, and a swimmer has to compensate by taking more of them. Wilkens' intensity was frightening, his stroke flawless. When the set ended after twenty-five minutes, he retched in the gutter so hard the veins on his neck bulged like bridge cables.

Grote watched the scene from a distance, his eyes flinty, his face set hard. How dare Jochums say Grote couldn't beat Wilkens in the Olympic 200-meter breaststroke. The world champion had understood the words all right, and he was going to prove them wrong. But even as he had that thought, in his gut he could feel the first waves of concern. He swallowed hard against them. This was not a sensation he had ever expected to feel, least of all in his own pool. Grote climbed from the water and headed for the locker room without looking back.

Meanwhile, the coach talked calmly at Wilkens even as the swimmer continued to gag: "That was better than good. You were hurting, but you didn't panic; you stayed in your stroke. Remember this, because everything you will ever do in life comes down to one message: Never panic."

PART II

HOW WE DO IT

June 1999 to August 1999

CHAPTER FOUR

By June, the Santa Clara national team workout teemed with forty bronze collegiate bodies gliding across the pool's azure surface. Three weeks earlier, the senior workout was nearly empty; now Santa Clara boasted the most powerful men's team in the nation. It was a good time. Wilkens had someone to race against every lap. Grote, having scored so well on his medical boards he could attend nearly any residency program he wanted, had loosened up and stopped thinking about leaving Santa Clara.

The forty athletes in the sparkling water were so beautiful to watch that people had begun coming to the pool to spectate and Jochums closed practices, literally slamming shut the pool's slatted gate that led to the outside world. The complex had an official entranceway (this was where the "Hall O Fame" wall was located), but it was locked during team practice hours and the SCSC members reached the pool deck by entering through a chain-link gate on the south side of the complex. Whenever that gate closed, it made a stinging sound of metal crashing on metal and a large section of surrounding fence shuddered for several seconds. At the Santa Clara Swim Club, where everything had stripped-down meaning and simple symbolism, the biggest symbol of all was this drab gateway between two worlds. Outside teemed chaos and confusion. Inside was a universe unto itself, one with its own organization, systems, rewards, and codes of behavior. Once through the gate, the angles always seemed sharper and everything gained heightened meaning. It was like seeing the world through a pair of polarizing sunglasses. When a swimmer crossed the threshold and the gate swung shut with its unnerving, jailhouse clang, it was a sound signaling clarity and purpose.

Maybe the symbolism itself was what had been keeping Tate Blahnik away. But this was a rare day indeed because the unhappy athlete, possibly one of the most naturally gifted swimmers in the world, had actually joined a practice. Jochums watched as the 6'7" backstroker delicately practiced his stroke using small children's paddles. They helped him feel the way his hand entered the water. Jochums hated drills. He watched Blahnik's matchstick arms—they were about half the circumference of either Grote's or Wilkens'—rise and fall slowly. The swimmer moved with the deliberate slowness of a geriatric. He was rail thin, with no visible muscle tone. Yet he could out-bench-press most of his teammates. He could hold his breath 4 ½ minutes. Most important, while he specialized in backstroke, he could outswim nearly every swimmer in the world in any stroke, at any distance. The coach was deciding what kind of morning this was going to be. He could get mad at the swimmer's drag-assing or walk away. He walked.

All spring, Blahnik had been telling Jochums he was training at Stanford. Simultaneously he had been telling the Stanford coaches he was at Santa Clara. The ruse might have worked except for the simple fact the two staffs talked several times per week. Blahnik knew they conversed; it had been his way of making a point.

"Get off your pinkies," Jochums said to the swimmer. The coach hadn't been able to stay away after all. "Enter the water riding your first two fingers; that's where the stroke starts. You keep wearing those baby paddles until you feel it."

"It feels terrible," Blahnik said.

"So does watching the Olympics when you could be winning them," Jochums said.

"If you say so," the swimmer replied dully.

He resumed his lethargic swimming. He was twenty-two years old and already his black hair was flecked with gray. His arms were double jointed, and as he swam the length of the pool, they hyper-extended so dramatically at the elbows, they looked like outward-turned parentheses ready to snap. It gave people the heebie-jeebies. Hyper-extension is a secret gift bestowed upon many of the best swimmers. It provides several crucial extra inches of reach and range of motion. Jochums impatiently waited as the swimmer traveled down the pool. When Blahnik reached the far end, he stopped and stared back blankly. Jochums shouted to hurry back. Blahnik languidly began the return trip.

"He's petrified," Jochums muttered. "I can fix the stroke, but it's up to him to fix his own head."

It hadn't always been like this. But the hotter they burn, the more spectacular the flameouts. Blahnik was, and always had been, a creature of compulsive addiction. Whatever he liked, he devoured, and for years swimming was his greatest craving. The sport attracts this kind of personality. It draws those who seek to accumulate laps as well as those who find security in the layerings of numbers. The fact that improvement is always available, even though perfection is not, also draws people. Another country club sport, golf, has the same insistent pull. Blahnik could swim at thirteen months (before he could walk), and by the time he was ten years old it was apparent that he was the kind of swimmer coaches spend their careers dreaming of.

Blahnik had become a certifiable teenage phenomenon about the time his family moved from his Texas birthplace to Suffern, New York. At the magically young age of fifteen, he announced he would qualify for U.S. nationals and then not only qualified, but also made the cut for the 1992 Olympic Trials. The number of fifteen-year-old males who make Olympic Trials may be counted on one hand. Soon he was the second-youngest member of U.S.A. Swimming's national junior team.

"Whatever I decided to do, I just did," Blahnik remembered. "I never gave failure a second thought. I did not even know what failure was."

He performed an inordinate amount of mileage, an average of fifty miles per week, much of it on his back. Studies have indicated one mile of swimming is the physiological equivalent of four miles of running. That suggests Blahnik's fifty weekly miles would be the equivalent of running two hundred miles per week—more than a marathon every day. Even top collegiate swimmers don't train that much. He possessed a lurching, unpolished stroke and absent kick. Yet observers had never seen such natural strength in the water. Fueled by his all-consuming compulsion, he was on a trajectory to greatness.

But that compulsive intensity was a double-edged sword. It so frightened him that in high school he had made a lifelong vow to never touch alcohol. There had been no history of alcoholism in his family, but Blahnik feared the pleasures of a single buzz would lead to permanent addiction. It had been that way with swimming.

Midway through high school, things began to change. He caught mononucleosis and subsequently began exhibiting classic behaviors of depression, lethargy, and oversleeping. Soon he was diagnosed with Seasonal Affective Disorder (aptly acronymed SAD), a light-based disorder that creates patterns of depressive episodes. A person with SAD suffers depression-like symptoms during the winter when the sun appears only a few hours per day. Blahnik may have always had the condition, but hadn't realized it until he left sunny Texas. He had readily accepted the diagnosis—he knew it wasn't normal to sleep sixteen hours at a time—but by then he also knew much of his unhappiness was related to swimming. As often happens with athletic prodigies, he found the sport was turning on him. By this time he was one of most exciting young swimmers in the world. But the faster he grew, the more difficult it was to meet his lofty goals. Swimmers are notorious perfectionists, but Blahnik hovered on the outer edges. As he grew older, his unhappiness with his performances, which continued to be remarkable, became increasingly profound. His compulsion to do better every time he raced had become a curse. The swimmer had always had a fragile psyche—a childhood speech impediment had made him permanently shy, while reading-comprehension problems made him a subpar student—but until then swimming had been his glowing salvation. Yet by the end of high school his flame was burning too hot and his expectations were too great. It was a dangerous way to start college in the autumn of 1995.

Blahnik selected Stanford in part because it is located in one of the country's sunniest regions and his swimming prowess gained him admittance. But he didn't finish freshman year before the twin sledgehammers of anguish and heartache knocked him to his knees in the spring of 1996. They had come suddenly, without warning, and then they simply didn't stop their pounding. The pain was nearly unbearable. Blahnik had known disappointment in his nineteen years of existence. But nothing could prepare him for taking third at the 1996 Olympic Trials.

The two Americans who beat him in the 200-meter backstroke at Trials won the gold and silver at the 1996 Atlanta Games. Had he competed, Blahnik would likely have captured a bronze. Perhaps even better. But he was still remarkably young. He could have used the experience to harden his resolve for the 2000 Trials, when he would be at his peak. Defeat builds character. Adversity fuels excellence. Yet Blahnik became a walking zombie. In nearly every important meet, he finished in the top three. But there was little drive or passion behind the effort. He had been so programmed to make the 1996 Olympic team that the loss was like shrapnel tearing through his heart. There are people who suffer a defeat that then plays in cruel slow-motion in their mind's eye for years afterward. It wasn't like that for Blahnik. It was more like an all-over body hurt. It felt like death. Depression set in and there were times when he couldn't rise from bed to attend class. Days would pass. Eventually, he made another vow, just as he had when he decided to abstain from alcohol: He would never put himself in a position to feel that kind of sustained hurt again.

A decision like that closes a person off from the world. It turns him into a spectator and life moves on without him. The backstroker wanted to quit in 1996. He wanted to quit again in 1998 after a female swimmer deliberately kicked him in the ear during a meet warmup because she was apparently frustrated by overcrowding in her lane. The blow permanently damaged his hearing. But when you are as good as Tate Blahnik, quitting isn't easy. He was a de facto favorite to vie for backstroke gold in 2000 with an up-and-coming star from southern California named Lenny Krayzelburg. Teammates, friends, and family were counting on him. He was a star in the country's best collegiate program. As a practical matter, swimming was paying for his education. A part of Blahnik also felt duty-bound to develop his talent as far as it would go. That was the mark of Blahnik's generation; it knew how to push individual potential to its limit. Blahnik realized he had a chance to be an Olympic champion, and on the deepest level he very much wanted to triumph. It was just that he also knew he couldn't survive another near miss. He was a haunted young man.

Duress always finds a way to express itself. Feeling damned by his talent and terrified of experiencing another devastation, after 1996 Blahnik had begun acting out against the sport. Almost unique among the insular Stanford team, he cultivated friendships away from the pool. He lost himself for days in computer-simulation games the way he once lost himself in swimming. An expert computer programmer, he took refuge in the established and predictable patterns of coding. After all, when a system fails to boot or a runtime error flashes on the monitor, there is always a logical way to fix it, a way to convert a failure into a success. That provided the same sense of order and safety swimming once did.

The swimmer had always possessed a keen edge of individuality, but now he asserted it by painting his fingernails and even donning women's clothing. It was all about shock value, about thumbing his nose at the straight-laced establishment that had made him feel so miserable. He wore shorts during winter, ate candy bars for dinner, and swigged Coke all hours of the day and night. Despite it all, in his junior year in 1998 he won the NCAA championship in the 200-yard backstroke. But that had barely changed things. His girlfriend was also a Stanford swimmer, but they rarely talked about their shared sport.

Then Blahnik began senior year at Stanford. That had been just nine months earlier, in the fall of 1998. The swimmer tentatively allowed himself to begin caring again. The moment he stepped back into the world of the pool, he started posting phenomenal results. It was as if he had been wearing a diver's weight belt before. During one ordinary day at Stanford's practice, he swam a set of 4 × 200-yard backstroke and finished the final repeat on 1:42.8. That was not only under the Stanford pool record by half a second, but it scraped near the American record. And Blahnik had done it from a push, not a dive. A dive can take as much as two seconds off a swim. Coaches and teammates were convinced he would break the American record at the NCAA championships. Blahnik, badly wanting to believe them, opened himself up even more. He was so earnest and sensitive, so genuinely likable that everyone wanted him to succeed.

Then, with the NCAA championships looming, Stanford decided to swim him in two new events, the 500-yard freestyle and the 4 × 200-yard freestyle relay. It was a strategic decision to win points for a team in the hunt for another national championship. But both came before Blahnik's two backstroke events. Mentally, it devastated him. He had trusted the team and come to believe he could redefine the American record in the 200-yard backstroke. He had even gone so far as to tell the Stanford campus newspaper that he was expecting to swim a time (1:38) in the 200-yard backstroke that seemed humanly impossible. Now it was searingly clear to him that he was nothing but a cog to win team points. He never considered how such a decision might reflect the team's confidence in him. He had never raced the 500 freestyle in college, yet the team was so in awe of his talent that it suddenly seemed possible—perhaps even likely—that he could finish as high as third. These new expectations were outrageous, but they built upon themselves until they seemed set in stone. At NCAAs, he was a consolation finalist in the 500 freestyle with a time of 4:21, and the effort absolutely wrecked his body. Then, he was removed from his regular backstroke spot in 4 × 100-yard medley relay to concentrate on his new relay, the 4 × 200-yard freestyle. This was another strategic move, but Blahnik interpreted it as a no-confidence vote. He had been a member of the 4 × 100-yard medley relay for three years and considered it his most vital link to the team. As he watched his replacement swim, he could feel his psyche shattering.

By the time the finals of his 200-yard backstroke were swum, it was obvious Auburn was going to beat Stanford for the team title, which meant Blahnik's sacrifices—which was how he saw them—had been pointless. He raced glumly, feeling the fatigue from his two freestyle events as soon as he started. He successfully defended his NCAA crown, but swam three seconds slower (1:41.42) than his goal time and he missed the American record. As his teammates cheered, he hung on the wall, miserable, unable to face his team or parents. He had exposed himself again, and he had failed again. How many times was he going to do this to himself? The hurt he felt was supernatural and all-consuming. Hanging there in dejected victory, Blahnik had wished with all his heart a black hole would swallow him. If you were a friend of the swimmer, you would have been worried.

That had been just three months earlier. Now the June sun stayed in the sky longer each day and Jochums was treating him with kid gloves. There are many ways to coach an athlete. Browbeating and worked-up anger don't succeed with a person like Blahnik. Nor do cookie-cutter approaches. A scared athlete must be reassured and coaxed. He needs to realize his value as a person is not tied to his performance. That's a difficult lesson to teach, although Jochums, much to his credit, was trying. Even so, Blahnik still wanted out. Yet escape was no easier than before. Now he had two NCAA titles. He was also the world's third-fastest active back-stroker since 1996. About this time, Krayzelburg, a Russian-born American, was beginning to dominate the backstroke events. But Blahnik was the last person to defeat him, when he did so at the 1998 NCAA championships. One doesn't walk away from that very easily.

"I can't begin to explain what it does to me when I fail," Blahnik had started to tell Jochums one morning. The swimmer rarely opened up, so this was significant. He was reaching out. But then he saw a look of irritation flit across the coach's face. "Just forget it," Blahnik had quickly said.

In the months ahead, Jochums was going to grow frustrated with the mousy way Blahnik was training. It was inevitable. The coach would abruptly decide he wasn't going to coddle fear.

"You suicidal or what?" he would challenge the swimmer. Jochums had a way of making questions sound like veiled threats.

If Blahnik was surprised by this, he didn't show it. The backstroker was going to carefully consider the question. He would rotate it through his head, view it at different angles to judge its sincerity, and finally answer with the same deliberate slowness with which he swam. "Yeah, I'd say I'm minimally suicidal."

The words would catch Jochums off guard and he angrily snapped, "And exactly what the hell does 'minimally' mean, Tate?"

Blahnik shrugged, and for surely one of the first times in weeks, Dick Jochums didn't know what to say next. Blahnik would finish the workout, unperturbed by the exchange. He did think occasionally about suicide. On and off, he had for several years. But it was in an academic, what-would-it-be-like way. The feelings usually came in the winter, when the SAD made him so miserable he slept all day, and he saw no need to lie about it.

A week later, Jochums planted him in front of a Stanford psychologist. Blahnik told the doctor he didn't want to swim, and the psychologist suggested he quit. Blahnik replied that's exactly what he was trying to do.

That meeting was a bust, but indirectly it would have a tremendous long-term effect on the swimmer. Jochums, in his own pushy and aggressive way, was the first adult outside of Blahnik's family in a long time to demonstrate he gave a damn. It wouldn't mean much immediately. But eventually it would. The long days of California summer were going to turn into the heavy-curtained, dark days of December, and in the descending blackness, both Jochums and Blahnik would find their separate lives backed into corners. Unexpected problems and rising fears of failure would attack from all sides. No two people on earth were more different than Dick Jochums and Tate Blahnik. Yet in the coming months, they were going to discover how much they needed each other to make sense of their worlds.

That was the future. Right now, in the warm June air there was no inkling of the waves of trouble that lay ahead for both of them. Blahnik finished his workout and promised to return. And so he did. Soon, he began appearing with reluctant regularity. But that reluctance wasn't going to disappear anytime soon. While everyone at the Santa Clara Swim Club was counting the days until Trials, even though they were more than a year away, Blahnik was the only one who counted them like a prisoner waiting to be released.

· · ·

Wilkens was in lane five, where he should be. Grote, a much slower seed, was in lane nine. This was the finals for the 200-meter breaststroke at the 32nd Santa Clara International swim meet. Several other of the world's top breaststrokers were in the remaining seven lanes.

The Santa Clara event was once again among the world's Top 15 fastest annual competitions. This year it also served as the most significant tune-up event before launching into a championship season that promised to be one of the most complicated and nerve-wracking in recent memory. Every pre-Olympic year is filled with international events serving to expose athletes to Olympic-like pressures. But this summer of 1999 was particularly onerous. Instead of one or two season-ending championships, there would be four, all stacked within six weeks of one another.

Grote and Wilkens were heading to the Pan Pacific Championships in Sydney, Australia, with U.S. swimming's national "A" team. Pan Pacs were unquestionably the most important competition until the Olympic Games. Joining them was a third Santa Clara swimmer, the handsome and analytical butterflyer, Dod Wales. Jochums would be there, too. For the first time in nearly fifteen years he had been selected to coach a national team on an international trip. His inclusion meant people were noticing his accomplishments at Santa Clara. All four were now on the short list to make the 2000 Olympic team.

While they prepared for the Pan Pacific Championships, several others were members of the national "B" team competing at the Pan American Games in Winnipeg, Canada. Several more were on the national "C" team that would head to Spain for the World University Games. Blahnik would be on this last team. He might have been on the national "A" team, but the injury to his ear—when the swimmer intentionally kicked him—had occurred at the qualifying meet and had knocked him out of contention.

Meanwhile, Santa Clara had nearly twenty others training specifically for U.S. nationals. What a summer. Each group needed a completely customized schedule. On paper, Santa Clara seemed destined to have its most triumphant season in a decade. But it would be a logistical nightmare for the coaches. Already things were beginning to unravel at the Santa Clara International meet.

As the breaststroke finalists prepared to start, Amy Hunn, Kurt Grote's pretty and down-to-earth wife, sat in the bleachers and nervously twisted her hands. She wasn't swimming, but she might as well have been. She twisted, she fretted, and she twisted some more. Amy had made no effort to conceal the dark circles under her eyes. The months of Grote trying to balance swimming and academics had wiped her out.

"He's so down on himself right now," she said. "No one knows how bad he really feels because it's important to him that his teammates don't see the frustration."

Amy was a choir director about to begin a master's degree program at Stanford in music. Everyone expected her to finish with a 4.0 GPA and, indeed, she would. But though she was smart and sensitive, she would never understand what makes some men want things so badly. The desire is total and all-powerful. It tastes like metal in their mouths. It screams to be satisfied and it bangs in their heads like a crazed incarcerate. The need to do better had so consumed Grote that by now there was no place in his life for pleasure or contentment, only caged intensity. Although he was steadily regaining his form, it wasn't fast enough for him. There always seemed to be a latched roar trying to push out of his throat. Amy could only wait and watch in love.

When the race started, Amy's nervous hands stopped twisting. They were a musician's hands, long and lovely, and Grote's race could be deciphered just by watching them. First they lay serenely in her lap. But soon enough they balled into fists. Then they became clenched so tight that the knuckles glowed white. If only they stopped there. But Amy was already pounding them desperately against her legs. She would continue to do so until they would finally slow to a soft, resigned beat. It is so hard to see a loved one struggle.

Most swim races are eerily silent because the spectators know the swimmers don't hear the cheers. But in breaststroke the swimmers' ears rise above the waterline and the crowds chant, "Go! Go!" in rhythm with a specific swimmer's stroke. As this race unfurled, it seemed half of Santa Clara's 1,000 spectators were rooting for Grote, while the others were for Wilkens. But indeed, the race was not going well for the world champion. At the halfway mark, Japan's national champion owned a huge lead with Wilkens in second. Grote was second to last. At 125 meters, Wilkens abruptly shifted gears. Over the next 25 meters, the buzz of the crowd grew pitched as Wilkens closed an eight-foot deficit and drew even with the Japanese swimmer. Grote fell farther back until he was no longer a factor. Those who had been cheering for him now switched allegiances to Wilkens. The transition happened instantly and effortlessly. It was a crowd behaving like a crowd, following its Darwinian instincts, latching to the strongest and seeking a victory.

At the final turn, Wilkens and the Japanese swimmer touched simultaneously. Grote was more than fifteen feet behind. Racing home, Wilkens' turnover exploded a second time. It was as if someone flipped a switch and put him on fast-forward. An electric shiver ran through the crowd. The Japanese national champion fell back three feet, six feet. Grote? By now he was miles behind and forgotten. Only his wife still cheered for him. Wilkens touched in a meet record (2:15.51). The crowd leapt to its feet, not for the record but for the sheer awesomeness of his last 75 meters. You just don't often see something like that in this sport. Not against a national champion, not against anyone. The Santa Clara team whooped and high-fived, then sat down to talk excitedly. Nearly all the spectators missed Grote gliding into the wall six seconds later, a lifetime in a 200-meter race.

All things considered, it was not a bad swim for Grote. It was two seconds faster than the morning prelims and he had moved from ninth to fifth. But he looked tight and out of shape. There was no snap to his kick and never once did his swimming evoke an image of the master jeweler. This was not how he had envisioned taking on Wilkens in their first big race since his full-time return. There was so much ground he had to make up.

Amy watched her husband's face intently, never glancing at the scoreboard because she couldn't distinguish between a fast and a slow time. She relied on his reaction, and when he smiled weakly at her, she let out a long breath that seemed to originate in her feet. Twenty minutes later, Grote bounced into the space next to her and gave her a big hug. He was smiling. She didn't know what to think.

The first thing he said was, "Did you see how great Tommy swam? Forget about how bad I was; did you *see* that swim? The *last lap*? God, I wish I could have watched it."

Next Grote climbed a few rows to where Jochums sat. He said the same thing to the coach and then disappeared to talk to others. Recently, Grote had been finding it increasingly difficult to articulate his relationship with Wilkens. They were friends, yes. But there had always been a hierarchal element to it, with Grote as mentor and Wilkens as protégé. Grote even occasionally referred to Wilkens as a "son" or "younger brother." It was so much more complicated now. Grote had the titles, the prestige, and the mystique. He could walk into almost any pool in the country and be surrounded by fans. But he was now an underdog, although he certainly couldn't admit it. He still wielded considerable influence over his friend and he knew that he could easily inflict psychological damage on the younger man. It wouldn't be hard. Wilkens was always eager to please and he trusted everything Grote said. Grote could suggest an unnecessary stroke correction. Or he could artificially heap on Wilkens an early dose of the pre-Olympic pressure that was soon going to hit all of them. There were many options, and competitive teammates seek the psychological edge all the time. It's an expected part of professional athletics.

That's why the men who swam at the Santa Clara Swim Club were so different. They were grounded in honor and fair play. Grote would beat Wilkens fair and square, and until they raced the finals of the Olympic Trials, he was going to be his protégé's biggest booster. It wasn't paradoxical at all to him. But for a while after Grote disappeared, both Amy and Jochums, sitting six rows apart, wore the same puzzled expression on their faces.

· · ·

A typical U.S.A. Swimming meet runs from Thursday or Friday through Sunday, with prelims in the morning and finals at night. Swimmers typically race about six events, which seems like a lot of swimming but, in fact, is the only available relief from the total drudgery of sitting through a four-day meet. The days are as predictable as they are monotonous. Swimmers rise early and warm up in a crowded pool for about forty-five minutes. Then they dry off and wait for the first event. They bring books, because this often takes hours. Shortly before the race, they loosen up in the warm-down pool for fifteen minutes. This might be the only time to actually have the space to swim a full stroke because the water is not as crowded. After racing, they swim down for twenty minutes to clear the accumulated lactic acid from the system, and then wait several more hours to repeat it all for the next event. In between, they nap, read, play Hearts, and listen to music. They cheer teammates when convenient, but it's hard to get motivated to yell for someone who can't hear the noise.

Major meets like the Santa Clara International might have thirty prelim heats in men's and women's 200-meter freestyle. At three minutes per heat, that adds up to a long, hot day. As the interminable heats go on, often the loudest noise is the sound of crunching water. It is a dreadfully colorless world, yet U.S.A. Swimming seems unwilling to enliven it with innovative alternatives. What these bland days need are some non-standard races interjected between the monotonous events: Have kicking or pulling races to recognize and encourage some young swimmers who may not win their regular events. Stage an event that mimics velodrome cycling by playing cat-and-mouse games of slow and fast swimming over 100 meters. Host round-robin races that emphasize one-on-one racing and excite the crowd. Something. *Anything.*

But since those options existed neither at the Santa Clara International nor nearly anywhere else, the crowd's only diversionary fun after the 200-meter breaststroke was to debate whether Tom Wilkens could win a second race that day. After dispensing with Grote and the other breaststrokers, he had remained in the warm-down pool because his afternoon wasn't over. Thirty minutes later, he was back on the blocks for the finals of the 200-meter I.M. It never sat particularly well with some Santa Clara parents that Jochums absorbed the Stanford men into his summer program and seemed to focus all his attention on them, but Wilkens' breaststroke finish had opened eyes. There was a buzz of expectation as he readied himself.

Anyone belonging to the Santa Clara community knew the 200-meter I.M. was a two-man race. Anyone would also suspect it was also a private grudge match. Two days earlier, Wilkens had lost his first serious competition in the 400-meter I.M. in almost a year to Sergey Mariniuk, a thirty-year-old Moldovan Olympian. Built like a muscled greyhound at 6' 0" and 170 lbs. with three percent body fat, Mariniuk had been a Santa Clara swimmer for nearly a decade. But he did not train under Jochums because he did not believe in the coach's training principles. Instead, he swam alone. In a program where the coach's authority was ironclad, this was unheard of. But that was just the beginning.

In 1999, Mariniuk was one of only two male swimmers born in the 1960s ranked anywhere in swimming's Top 100 fastest times. He was remarkable for his longevity, having been identified as a potential champion at an early age and raised inside the Soviet sports machine for most of adolescence. As a U.S.S.R. superstar, he had barely missed the 1988 Seoul Olympics, and four years later had made the finals of the Barcelona Olympics in both the 200- and 400-meter I.M. Afterward, he had returned home to his former Soviet-bloc country of Moldova as a national hero. But the collapse of the communist world had wrecked the tiny, landlocked nation of four million. Wedged between Romania and Ukraine, the Maryland-sized country had no natural energy sources and one of the world's lowest life expectancy rates for males, just fifty-nine years. The economy had collapsed, some childhood friends had become mobsters, and his neighbors were starving. Alcoholism was so rampant that people fermented vegetables in bathtubs to make grain alcohol.

Mariniuk was soon using his car as a taxicab to earn food money. The one thing of value he owned was a CD player, and for hours he would stare at the cracked ceiling of his family apartment and wonder what had happened to his life. He was a Moldovan citizen, but identified so much more strongly with Soviet culture that he felt like a man without a country. In fact, he could not even speak Moldova's national language. The Soviet Union had lied to him about everything: the equality and prosperity, the promises of security for athletes and their families. Mariniuk had once been a full believer, but now there was nothing to believe in. In 1993, he came to Santa Clara for its meet and then simply stayed. Beforehand, he had sold his CD player and everything else. He didn't know what California had to offer, but it had to be better than what he had at home.

The Santa Clara Swim Club was dazzled by his gentleness, not to mention his speed, and a stroke so beautiful it made the world's best swimmers stop and look. He was to swimming what Mikhail Baryshnikov was to ballet. They even resembled each other. Families opened their doors as they would for a refugee. One secured a green card; another gave him lodging. He became SCSC's assistant coach as well its star, and within weeks his rudimentary English was conversational.

Mariniuk showed his gratitude by winning national titles for Santa Clara, teaching young kids how to swim, and mentoring teenagers. His new Californian friends had wild-eyed capitalist dreams, ambitions to own large homes and make millions on the Internet. They couldn't find Moldova on a map, were only vaguely aware of world events, and failed to notice when the Russian parliament building was bombed by its own army. He found there was something frightening and wonderful about their endless opportunities and optimism. He drove to the ocean in nearby Santa Cruz every chance he could, pushed a surfboard into the green water, and spent hours rocking with the swells. He looked back at this strange new world and, after a time, discovered he could live in it.

In 1996, he had been the only Santa Clara swimmer competing in the Atlanta Games. Swimming again for Moldova, he had placed eighth in the 400-meter I.M., thirteenth in the 200-meter I.M., and afterward retired. He entered the working world for the first time as an apprentice software engineer (naturally, a Santa Clara connection provided the job). He married a beautiful Santa Clara adult swimmer and together they bought a cozy home bigger than anything he could have imagined back home. When he earned enough money, the first thing he did was bring to the United States both his best friend and his childhood swim coach.

When Jochums had arrived to revive the club, Mariniuk was easily the most respected and universally liked personality at the center. The swimmer seemed to have a halo over his head. People were so rankled by Jochums' brusque manner that for many months there was talk of staging a coup to oust him and make Mariniuk the head coach. Nothing had ever happened, but any other person would have lived in true mortal danger, for Jochums was a king who let no rival survive in his court. That was especially true because Mariniuk had been a member of the original committee charged with finding a new coach, and he had voted against Jochums, which of course Jochums somehow learned. But Mariniuk was protected, not because he had no interest in a coaching career or even any knowledge of the revolt, but because his relationship with the club community was so strong.

Mariniuk had trained under Jochums for the Atlanta Games but had not liked the monolithic structure and its emphases. So in 1998, two years after retiring, he began sporadically training on his own, slipping into an empty lane at Santa Clara for a nonstop hour of slow, efficient stroking that emphasized technique and never left him out of breath. Sometimes he swam with the Santa Clara Masters team, a collection of retired collegiate competitors as well as fitness athletes. Within months, Mariniuk realized he was moving nearly as fast with his strange, erratic training as he had when he swam full-time with Jochums. That made him start thinking about the 2000 Olympics. All told, he was training less than most casual recreational swimmers.

Throughout 1998, Jochums had watched without saying anything. Coaches can read an athlete's body language. Long before anyone else, Jochums knew what the swimmer was up to. In Jochums' world, you were either with him or against him, and long ago Mariniuk had made his position clear. The coach and swimmer had a very positive personal relationship—Jochums wanted Mariniuk to represent SCSC in meets; Mariniuk had invited Jochums to his wedding—but it wasn't going to be based on coach/swimmer interactions.

By the 1999 Santa Clara International, it was known that Mariniuk was planning to swim in the Sydney Olympics (Moldova only required he make the minimal qualifying standard, which he did). As a result, the success of his loose training program was an indirect but very real slap at Jochums. The bright welt was there for anyone to see. Mariniuk was swimming for an hour just four times a week. He no longer even used a pace clock. If this were basketball, he was preparing for game day by shooting two dozen free throws and then going home. Before the Santa Clara meet had begun, Jochums told Wilkens his job was to "put the Russian back into retirement."

But surprise, surprise, in the 400-meter I.M., Mariniuk had spanked Jochums' boy wonder. It was close, but not that close. Wilkens became flustered during the race and was disqualified for an illegal backstroke-to-breaststroke turn. It didn't matter, because Mariniuk beat him by more than two seconds. The SCSC spectators had roared for their favorite swimmer while Jochums watched stone-faced, his teeth clenched so hard they might have cracked.

"You buy Sergey a gift certificate," he had growled at Wilkens when he was calm enough to speak. "You write on the card, 'Thank you for the telephone wake-up call. I was beginning to get full of myself because I've had a few months of good practices. You cut me down to size. P.S., You will never, *ever* beat me again.' "

Now the 200-meter I.M. was a grudge rematch between the fatigued Wilkens and the fresh Mariniuk, who had rested for two days. They stayed together for the first half of the race, but on the breaststroke leg— both men's strong event—Wilkens gained the lead. Wilkens was exhausted and could feel the fatigue from his previous event. But races like this defined why he was becoming successful. Swimming on pure grit, he not only held off Mariniuk's last-lap charge, but widened his lead to nearly a full body length and won by a second.

Afterward Jochums didn't smile or look around. He didn't acknowledge Wilkens, who was happily rolling on a lane line and waving to get his attention. Jochums gazed at the blue water stilling itself in the pool's center and said quietly, "That's how we do it around here."

. . .

There was one more story at this meet. At almost any major swim competition during the second half of the 1990s, the men's events were overshadowed by the women's events. That was because Jenny Thompson, who as of 1999 had won five Olympic gold medals (tying her with speedskater Bonnie Blair for the most by any female athlete in history), was usually there to put on a demonstration in excellence. At the Santa Clara International meet, Thompson swam so beautifully she seemed to float above the water. Five events, five easy victories. But that was not the story. As Thompson effortlessly won one race after another, the story was in the stands. That was where an older woman, one hidden behind sunglasses to help her remain anonymous, leaned forward and watched intently. The woman could not believe Thompson's majesty and power. The hair on her arms stood straight up when she saw the breadth of Thompson's sculpted back.

The woman was thirty-two-year-old Dara Torres, a long-retired three-time Olympian who was putting her lingering fame to use in New York City as a television commentator and model. Torres had flown to California to rid herself of a recurring dream. In it, she stood on a starting block preparing to race. That was all there was, but the image had appeared to her again and again over successive nights until she could think of nothing except swimming. Torres had not swum in seven years. She did not own a training suit. She had a life full of commitments and plans, but she deeply believed in signs, and suddenly she was consumed with ideas of an unprecedented comeback. Conventional wisdom said a female swimmer matures in her mid-teens and is running on fumes by the time she's two years out of college at age twenty-four. No American woman over thirty had ever swum on the national level, and certainly not one who'd been retired most of the decade.

Only days earlier, Torres had telephoned the women's U.S. Olympic and Stanford Coach Richard Quick, an old friend, to ask for advice. He told her before she could think about a comeback, she had to see the best. "Come to California and let me show you Jenny Thompson," he said.

Long after Thompson had won her last race, Torres gazed at the pool winking in the sunlight. Really, what did she think she was doing here? She looked at the ugly Santa Clara clubhouse, blunt and squatty. She studied the cheering spectators and the athletes who were half her age. She could tell some people in the stands had recognized her, perhaps young mothers who'd raced against her in a different lifetime. Santa Clara's pool was so blue and beckoning. She exhaled deeply and stood up. She had to get back to New York City as soon as possible to shut down her life. Sometimes life-changing decisions are made without understanding the hows or whys. Torres was going to make a comeback. It was ridiculous; it was a perverse midlife crisis. But she couldn't think about that now. She had to get home and pack. She had no inkling that many months from now, this aging pool would become an unexpected and last-resort refuge for her. Right now, she was only wondering where she could buy a suit and a pair of goggles. Like hundreds of other American sprint freestylers, Torres was thinking about one of those six available Olympic positions on a relay.

CHAPTER FIVE

Summertime swimming is nothing more than a chipshot between spring and fall seasons. There are a few weeks of hard work and then the season-ending taper begins. And so, just four weeks and two weekend meets after the Santa Clara International meet, the SCSC team began resting for its national and international championship competitions.

A taper is a curious, gorgeous thing. Virtually all sports try to peak at the climax of a season, but few need to be as precise as swimming. Its athletes swear up and down they can tell not only the day their taper peaks but the actual hour. The basic premise is to work hard for a long, intense period and then gradually move into a several-week resting stage to hone speed. Some think of it as a trampoline bounce. The harder they jump into the tramp's center, the deeper they sink and the higher they ultimately soar. Hitting a perfect taper is the El Dorado of swimming, but once a swimmer discovers what works for him or her, it is possible to duplicate the methodology. Some lose their edge if they rest longer than seventy-two hours. Others need three weeks. All the Santa Clara swimmers had done enough laps to know what worked and what didn't.

During a taper, most swimmers' strokes temporarily fall apart. Times get slower before they get faster. It's another one of swimming's confounding paradoxes. Faith is essential but confidence often plummets. So much rides on timing, and there are so many variables that can disrupt the precision. When this period of a season kicks into high gear, most coaches intensify their coach/swimmer interactions because it is a period full of second-guessing and worry. But at Santa Clara that premise was inverted. While Jochums gave his swimmers inordinate amounts of individual attention during a season, once the taper started, in the name of personal responsibility, he steadily reduced his involvement. It had to do with autonomy and shouldering the burden of success and failure.

As far as Jochums was concerned, there was no hand-holding in the real world, so there could be none at his pool when it came time for ultimate tests. It was the philosophy of a hard man, one who resisted the fact that the world did not operate that way anymore. He was often struck by how these strong young men became prisoners to their fears as big meets approached. But by then he had usually stepped into a secondary role and let them work things out for themselves. It was an approach that was bound to someday lead to problems, even as it toughened his men for life.

Now in mid-July, fifteen of the finest swimmers in the United States were playful as puppies in a bathtub. The team had hammered intense practices for weeks and resting felt like a resurrection. A taper is a carnival. Jochums tugged girls' ponytails and gave bear hugs to the men. He insulted them; they insulted him back. The coach shadowboxed on the deck and looked exactly like a middle-aged man shadowboxing.

"No Viagra for this guy," he said as he feinted a right uppercut and performed an awkward Ali shuffle.

Jochums danced and jabbed his way to a group of sprinters and told several they would never make the Olympic team until they renounced their soft liberal sensibilities. All Santa Clara sprinters were considered left-leaning, tree-hugging liberals until they proved themselves to be real men—which meant either they had to volunteer to swim the distance workouts or they had to vote Republican. Next, the coach told an off-color joke that sent his team into gales of laughter. They loved him, especially when he was happy like this.

The other swimmers pushed off the wall still laughing, but Dod Wales hung back. Wales was the marvelous butterflyer trying to follow his famous father's footsteps to the Olympics. He'd joined the team a month earlier, after Stanford graduation, and now stood in the shallow water peering slant-eyed at Jochums. The coach sighed. Wales. Of course. Always measuring, always inscrutable. Wales' Olympic journey was a very internal, private one. If Jochums was the spinning generator sparking with excessive emotion, Wales was the black hole that captured the sentimentality and flattened it into a dense, controllable force. The unrevealing swimmer came complete with his serious attitude and a stubborn streak as wide as the sky. For several summers, the 6'2", 180-lb. athlete and coach had worked together, and over time their relationship had grown increasingly strained. Wales possessed a strong, judgmental sense of right and wrong, and he often found Jochums offensive and bullying. He defended other swimmers when the coaches yelled at them, and in the near future he would upbraid Jochums in public for making a sexist remark. Within earshot of others, he told the coach he had "no class." Jochums would pretend to laugh it off, but he was a man who evened scores. Workouts the following week had been hell.

Wales would join Grote and Wilkens on the national "A" team when it traveled to the Pan Pacific Championships later in the summer. Grote and Wilkens were bigger names, but on many afternoons it was the pro-grammatic Wales, the one who saw swimming as a geometric series of laws and systems, who was looking like Santa Clara's best shot for mak-ing the Olympics. He was a remarkable talent and was drawn to the sport for its order and logical framework, for its statistical sense, and for the way individual laps expanded into sets which became organized prac-tices, which in turn added up to a structure of days, weeks, and months. And one thing that set him apart from his teammates was his well-known desire to be in complete charge of his own career.

Still in a good mood, Jochums decided it was time to set Wales straight about life. He knew Wales didn't much like him or trust him. He knew Wales was leaving the club in September for a new team that offered a more sophisticated and technologically advanced approach to training. But Jochums also knew Wales listened to him, listened much closer than he let on.

"America has failed its mission, Dod," Jochums informed him, launching into a favorite theme. "In your lifetime, it will no longer be the dominant world power because it has become a results-oriented country instead of a process-oriented country. You know that, don't you? They taught you that at your fancy school, right? You know no one wants a gold medal more than me. But dumb as I am, I know that's just a result. You don't have to win to be a champion; you just have to race knowing you've done everything in your power to achieve your dream. That's a process, and that's what matters at the end of the day. There are no quick fixes or easy answers when you are building a 'pro-cess,' although it seems you people grew up with mommies and daddies telling you otherwise. Success comes through effort, drive, and commitment. Corporate America used to know that; now they make you rich just for showing up to work."

"Tell us about the time they invented electricity, Dick," Wales said with a grudging smile. He secretly ate up Jochums' rifts on sacrifice, commitment, and courage. In many ways, the two men were remarkably similar. Perhaps that was the source of the regular tension between them. But there were other reasons as well.

While Jochums used emotion as a motivating tool, Wales consciously drained emotion from his endeavors. Subjective emotion, he believed, was a liability because it could never be fully controlled. Then there was the issue of training. Wales wanted to manage his own development and didn't like Santa Clara's old-fashioned approach, which he called "cookie-cutter." The relationship between swimmer and coach had grown so bad that Wales had to train directly with Jochums' assistant, John Bitter. Exactly why this was necessary became evident minutes later, when Bitter gave the sprint group a brief but fast set designed to evaluate speed. The others nodded and readied themselves, but Wales looked suspicious. Bitter had started to walk away but then returned.

"Dod, this whole week I want to focus you on quality kicking and just three hard sets, including this one," the assistant coach said. "That's it, the whole week. The rest of the time I want you floating and just feeling the water. The goal is to peak you at Pan Pacs. That's still weeks away. This set won't harm you."

Wales looked back, squinting in the sun and silent. It was impossible to tell what he was thinking. He was a Midwesterner and owned that region's natural reticence. Oddly, his careful suspicion made him seem mysterious, even alluring. If this man could make the Olympic team, his face, with its high cheekbones, penetrating hazel eyes, and strong jawline, would undoubtedly be put on a glossy poster. And that poster would be sold through various distribution channels, and it would wind up on the walls of teenage girls swimming in the United States. He was that good-looking.

"Well, how does the plan sound to you?" Bitter finally asked after twenty seconds of silence.

Wales might very well have been running quadratic equations in his head. He actually rubbed his jaw in thought. Many sets were like this.

He lived exactly according to the principles of personal responsibility Jochums dictated. But he did so by openly challenging the rationale for various sets, which drove the coaches crazy. Jochums had two inter- changeable nicknames for him, and they served as accurate barometers for gauging their relationship. In good weeks, Wales was "The Prince." In bad weeks, he was "that goddamn stubborn prima donna."

Wales finally agreed to the set. He pushed off with the others. As expected, he proceeded to blaze through it faster than anyone else.

• • •

Wales had been seven years old when he learned about his Olympic bloodline. It was dinnertime at home in Cincinnati, Ohio. The 1984 Win- ter Olympics had recently begun and Wales asked his parents what they were. His mother told him to turn around. She told him to look closely at the medal hanging on the wall behind him. There it was, an Olympic medal. It hung there like any other wall decoration, and no one had ever made a big deal about it. His mother explained that Wales' father, Ross, had won the bronze medal in the 1968 Mexico City Olympics in the 100-meter butterfly. His chief rival had been a swimmer named Mark Spitz, and in their day they had engaged in some great battles. As his mom beamed and his father tried to change the subject, Wales' kid brain struggled to understand what it meant. He asked his father questions, but Ross just smiled and shrugged. That's how it was in the Wales family. You did not put on airs, and you certainly did not flaunt your accom- plishments. Years later, Wales realized he would not have learned about his father's athletic career until he had asked about it.

Swimming has legendary stories of overbearing swim parents, usually dads. Nearly every club has a father weighing his girls and restricting their diets. There are usually several fathers on every team who carry notebooks that hold the details of their children's daily workouts. There are parents who bring children to hotel pools on weekends to work on their technique. It's not unusual for a coach to get multiple requests from mothers of young swimmers to start their kids on twice-a-day workouts years before they are physically ready. At Santa Clara, one over-zealous parent had briefly bribed an assistant coach with $500 per month to give special attention to his offspring during team practices.

All these noxious people should have taken a cue from Ross Wales.

In many ways he was the dean of modern American swimming, having served as the president of U.S.A. Swimming Inc. in its crucial formative years in the late 1970s. Yet whenever his two sons (Dod's younger brother, Craig, swam for Princeton) asked about swimming, Ross maneuvered off the subject. When they wanted personal anecdotes about his great career, he was strangely vague on the details, lest it create a climate of expectation. It wasn't as if Ross was uninterested, but he wasn't going to pressure his children.

He didn't need to, because a dozen years before Wilkens would become consumed by the Olympic ideal, seven-year-old Dod Wales was already videotaping the 1984 Los Angeles Olympics and memorizing the swimming commentary. Those Olympians were his first heroes, and after the Games ended, they began stopping by his house for dinner and to pay their respects to his father. The impact must have been incredible. Butterfly queen Mary T. Meagher came into his home. So did Tracy Caulkins, the greatest U.S. female swimmer ever. These were his rock stars, and they were sitting at his dining-room table and they were complementing his mother's home cooking, and all they wanted to talk about was swimming in the Olympics. By the next summer, he would shoot baskets in the driveway with neighborhood friends and they would tease him about making the Olympics. He was eight years old.

Dod Wales turned into a twenty-three-time YMCA national champion and was one of the best swimmers ever to emerge from the Midwest. He led his high school, Cincinnati's St. Xavier Preparatory, to the mythical high school national championship, and at Stanford, he instantly demonstrated he was capable of climbing to greater heights. But that's when the legacy of his father began bothering him. Consciously or not, for nearly three collegiate seasons Wales avoided his father's event, the 100 butterfly, even though it had been his best in high school. He wanted to cast his own shadow, not step into his father's. He was an All-American in various events, but he wasn't dominant in anything.

Then during the last dual meet of his junior year, Wales swam the 100-yard butterfly for fun. He did well, so well that he swam it again at the Pac-10 Conference championships. When he finished, he not only had won the conference title, but he had broken the Pac-10 record. Several weeks later, swimming the event for only the second time in a finals situation, he placed third in the NCAA championships. As overjoyed friends and family congratulated him, he tuned them out. He was already plotting the next step.

That was another thing about Wales. He was a student of incredible habit and programming. Through all his considerable success, he avoided feeling good about it. He became a machine. Each victory was a step in a long process that would ultimately lead to the 2000 Olympic Games. His ideal of the perfect athlete was one who confronted himself and defeated his own fears and shortcomings. This philosophy had taken form years earlier, before it even had a name or a clear objective. Essentially, he was competing against himself.

He was certainly not the first athlete to approach sport this way, but Wales' mastery of control intimidated his teammates and helped make him something of a loner. Unlike Grote, Wilkens, and most of the other swimmers, he was always aware of his primary competitors but never felt the need to establish a rivalry with any of them. Senior year at Stanford he was far and away the country's best butterflyer. Weeks before the 1999 NCAA championships he slipped into a fog of focused concentration that didn't clear until he won the 100-yard butterfly (45.89) and broke by four-tenths of a second the existing American record. The former record-holder, Pablo Morales, had gone on to win the Olympic butterfly gold medal in the Barcelona Olympics. In capturing the event, Ross and Dod became the first father-son combination in NCAA swimming history to win the same championship race. Afterward, Wales had opened his ears and let the compliments wash in. Several days later, he had closed them again, because while he secretly craved praise, he feared the complacency it often brought. It was time to start thinking about Sydney.

That sweet victory had been six months earlier. As Wales now streaked down the Santa Clara pool with a very fast butterfly lap, any casual observer could see why he was so good. Low and powerful, he seemed to summon all his force from his hips. He was beautiful to watch, the Santa Clara swimmer who possessed the best balance between technique and strength. But there was a problem. Wales was an incredible collegiate swimmer who excelled in the explosive short-course yard format. No American butterflyer had ever moved as fast for four 25-yard laps. But he was not nearly as good at long-course meters, the format used in the 50-meter Olympic races. That format required a different style of swimming, one with better acceleration and management. Nearly all his Olympic dreams hinged on whether he could successfully convert from one type of swimming to the other.

"You swim with that stroke and you're doing a best time in two weeks," Jochums called out when Wales finished his lap.

"It felt easy; it felt so easy." Wales smiled.

"Remember that feeling after you've wrecked your career," Jochums said.

The unprovoked rudeness came from nowhere. Jochums walked away and Wales looked disgusted. This was why the swimmer was leaving the program. This was why weeks would sometimes pass without the coach and swimmer talking to each other. Wales was going to bid adieu to Santa Clara and its old-fashioned ideas after the Pan Pacific Championships and join the U.S. Resident Team at the United States Olympic Center in Colorado Springs. Jochums thought it was the stupidest thing he had ever heard and he mocked the swimmer relentlessly. Wales hated to be mocked. The U.S. Resident Team was an innovative program that trained a pre-selected group of approximately ten elite swimmers. Each participant had a unique, scientifically exact regime engineered specifically to his or her body. There were frequent biomechanical and physiological tests, and workouts were designed with computer assistance. Hydrodynamics, scientific research, exacting speed work, closely watched cycles of recovery, and hard work—the program offered it all. Algorithms, heart-rate monitors, video cameras, computers, blood samples, training matrices, cutting-edge research.

The U.S. Resident Team's success rate was mixed at best, but it was exactly what Wales' analytical mind sought. There was no starker contrast between two major U.S. swim programs than it and the Santa Clara Swim Club. Colorado Springs, with its shimmering aquatic laboratory and state-of-the-art tools, symbolized twenty-first-century precision and all its marvels of modern training. Santa Clara, in contrast, embodied old-school ethos and the blue-collar approaches. Wales thought he wanted the future, not the past. In the Colorado mountains, he believed, he would find everything he needed to get on the Olympic team.

Wales wanted his last weeks at Santa Clara to be good ones. There was even a niggling doubt in his mind about whether he was making the right decision. And Jochums desperately wanted Wales to stay because the swimmer looked increasingly like Olympic material. But the coach's method of expressing that want—which was certain to only grow worse—made Wales' choice easy. The swimmer completed the rest of his workout in a foul mood and left the pool complex without talking to anyone.

· · ·

Two weeks later, nationals were imminent and the taper had turned serious and subdued. The animation that sparked the first days was replaced by a palpable energy that coursed through the team. The swimmers worked quietly on starts or technique and moved to the far end of the pool if they wanted to talk. Underlying the gestures, words, and thoughts was a growing tension, a sense that outcomes mattered.

In the days since the taper began, Jochums had grown more withdrawn and worried. He wasn't liking what he saw one bit. Some swimmers looked to be peaking too early; others seemed strangely flat. With nine lanes in which to juggle four simultaneous tapers (the University Games, the Pan American Games, the Pan Pacific Championships, and U.S. nationals), he realized too late that he hadn't established a priority of importance. Each one needed a customized taper and the crowded pool had made that too difficult. The University Games swimmers had been to Spain and had come back again, and now they required more hard work before starting a second taper that might or might not succeed. The Pan Am swimmers, who had just departed for their championship, had needed to rest earlier than the others. In the big picture, U.S.A. Swimming's nationals were the least significant meet, but they carried the most importance because they were the focus for nearly twenty athletes. Then there were Wilkens, Grote, and Wales, who were resting with the national group even though their big meet, the Pan Pacific Championships, came three weeks later. Everything was mixed up and the coach still didn't know the names of every new swimmer in his pool. A week before SCSC left for nationals in Minneapolis, Jochums privately announced the season was going to end very badly.

But who the hell was Ed Moses? That was all anyone wanted to know as reports from the first morning swims at the 1999 Pan American Games in Winnipeg reached Santa Clara. Santa Clara had sent three swimmers to the meet, which showcased the U.S. national "B" team. In the meet's prelims, Moses, an unknown nineteen-year-old breaststroker with the Curl-Burke Swim Club from the Washington, D.C., area, had blazed a 1:01.06 in the 100-meter breaststroke. Thanks to the Internet, everyone at Santa Clara knew the time the hour it was posted. It was the fifth-fastest performance in history, a spot previously held by Grote. Suddenly Grote was no longer the quickest 100-meter breaststroker in the world since the 1996 Olympics. This Moses kid was.

Swimmers don't come out of nowhere. They are tracked by a community that follows the paper trail of results and rankings. Progress is linear and predictable within a standard range of probability. Yet in one minute Moses went from being nobody to a leading contender for the gold in Sydney and one of the most exciting sports stories of the year. Later in the Pan Am finals, he would slice another .2 seconds off his time to post a 1:00.99, which was significantly faster than Grote's best (1:01.22). In the weeks that would follow, stories in USA Today, The Washington Post, and elsewhere would start to appear, revealing how the 5'10", 160-lb. Moses was a frustrated golfer and military brat who swam only during the winter and spent summers collecting golf balls on driving ranges. He had taken up swimming seriously just two years earlier to see what he could do, and the Curl-Burke Swim Club—which was also Tom Dolan's club—had made him an overnight sensation. However, right now the Santa Clara swimmers were trying to manage the basics: Where's he from? How old is he? Where does he swim? Did they drug test him?

The questions were ironic, considering Moses, by virtue of having swum well enough to place third at the 1998 U.S. nationals and thereby earn a spot on the Pan Am team, was already among the top breaststrokers in the country. But he entered that meet as just another fast swimmer. Winning the Pan American Games race might have been a footnote if it weren't for his time. That, and the preposterous 1.28 seconds he had dropped from his previous best time to achieve it.

"You know what that Ed Moses confirms?" Tom Wilkens asked his friend, a Stanford junior named Clayton Jones. Wilkens was stretching in the shade, legs straight out and nose pressed low between his knees. "He confirms that anyone thinking they're already on the Olympic team is going to be watching the Games at home. There's no free ride."

"Even a dark horse like me has a shot," quipped Jones. So far, this particular swimmer had been unable to make his Olympic Trial cut. Like many at Santa Clara, he thought Wilkens' success offered conclusive proof that the American dream was possible for anyone willing to work hard enough. The slower swimmers often seemed to peer closely at Wilkens, as if hoping to see a bit of themselves reflected.

Grote appeared from a stretching session. He liked to stretch alone inside the club's meeting room while gazing through the doorway at the empty pool. The cool, dark quiet aligned his mind for practice. In the four weeks since the Santa Clara International meet, his body had undergone a miraculous transformation. It had hardened and grown more muscular; the waist had tapered and the shoulders broadened. Muscles popped, bulged, and slid under the skin. His body fat hovered below five percent. He was a gorgeous specimen, an image an artist might render when sketching the perfect body. Grote carried his swim log, in which he wrote his daily workouts. The diary-like book could be purchased in swim shops nationwide. On the cover was his own face.

"Who's Ed Moses?" Grote joked. At the Santa Clara International meet, Grote had raced Moses in the 100-meter breaststroke. In that race, Wilkens had finished second, Moses third, and Grote fourth. At the time, Grote was immersed in studying and hadn't thought much about it. "I'd have to say my life just got more interesting," the world champion added.

Grote made his way to the pool. He seemed relaxed and in command. Later in the practice he would swim a 50-meter breaststroke in a painfully slow 33.5 seconds and Jochums would consider lying and saying the time was faster than it was. Like everything else, there are good lies and bad lies. Jochums wanted to know how it felt.

"Easy," said Grote. "I was going as smooth and easy as I could. Watch what I'm about to do."

He returned to the other end of the pool and swam another 50-meter breaststroke. This time he would work it. The arm sweep would be a little too rushed, yet on every stroke he came out of the water hunched and lunging forward. For the first time in months he would look like a jeweler bent over his work, just as he did when he swam his best. His time nearly broke 30 seconds, great news for him. Grote's swimming was so grounded in technique that his times had been yo-yoing all season as he tried to find his groove. Finally, he had nailed it perfectly. He beamed. His greatness was fast returning. Who cared about this Moses?

As Grote swam, Wilkens continued stretching, grunting as he forced his head even lower between his knees. Jochums had refused to taper Wilkens with everyone else, opting instead to continue his training regimen until the last days before nationals.

"I'm confident," Wilkens said. He was facedown and speaking more to the concrete deck than anything else. What was he talking about? Moses? Moses was a raw sprinter who didn't even swim Wilkens' event, the 200-meter breaststroke.

"I'm confident," Wilkens repeated mysteriously. "I know what needs to be done and I know I'm going to be able to do it."

He stood up and followed Grote to the pool. Never in a thousand years would he have imagined how prophetic that strange statement was someday going to become.

CHAPTER SIX

The Santa Clara swimmer named Clayton Jones padded barefoot down the hotel room corridor carrying a bucket of ice. He and about ten Santa Clara teammates, including Grote and Wilkens, had just finished watching a movie in their hotel on the campus of the University of Minnesota. In less than a day, the 1999 Phillips 66 National Long Course Swim Championships would begin.

The swimmers' routine during these championship meets never varies. They lounge in hotel rooms across the country watching movies and talking about all things great and small. They take naps; they read. It is very unglamorous. A nap was in Jones' plans when he returned to his hotel room. But he was too keyed up. This was a great and significant meet for the twenty-year-old Stanford junior, the moment when he planned to put several years of frustration behind him and join his teammates as an Olympic Trials qualifier. Jones exemplified the manifest hopes and dreams of the majority of the Santa Clara swimmers. He was a symbol, a representative swimmer from the collection of fifteen Santa Clara team members who were at nationals but who had so far failed to qualify for the 2000 Trials.

In swimming, class distinctions between the haves and have-nots are based on speed. You either have an Olympic Trial cut or you don't. You either have a senior-national cut or you don't. At a place like Santa Clara, it can be unbearable to be a have-not. No matter how strong the friendships are, no matter how vibrant an individual is on land, there is a tinge of failure to being left behind.

"You spend your life preparing for one day at one meet," Jones said as he eased gently onto his bed. "That's years of work coming down to two minutes to prove your worth."

Less than two hundred feet outside the hotel window sat the University of Minnesota's natatorium, a light-infused indoor complex. Like most things in Minnesota, it provided the basics without exerting energy on any frills or accessories. Next to the facility was a small field where two swim shop retailers were busy raising blue plastic tents and unfolding tables. There are so few retail stores catering to swimmers that many in the sport must rely on swim meets as their primary opportunity for buying suits and goggles. A swimmer who rips a suit during winter in some regions of the country may lose several days of training while waiting for a new one to arrive via express mail.

Jones, the personification of the gritty mid-level swimmer, was a 100 and 200 freestyle specialist. That's one of the toughest combinations in swimming because it requires both bursting speed and endurance. Few can claim to be equally good at both. A 100/200 freestyler is also the most desirable swimmer for a collegiate program because he or she can score points in the widest range of events: the individual 100-yard freestyle and 200-yard freestyle, plus three relays (4 × 100-yard medley, 4 × 100-yard freestyle, and 4 × 200-yard freestyle). Additionally, the swimmer can be used in a pinch in the 50-yard or 500-yard freestyle. In contrast, a distance freestyler might only specialize in one event, the mile, while a single-stroke swimmer like Grote can contribute in no more than three events, the stroke's 100-yard and 200-yard races, plus the 4 × 100-yard medley relay.

On land, Jones presented a carefree, impish personality, one full of Florida light and boyish innocence. He had grown up in Coral Springs and wanted so badly to be validated as a serious swimmer by his peers that he hid from them his considerable academic success, which included near-perfect SATs (800 verbal and 780 math). He worked as hard as his teammates—did the identical workouts and left on the identical intervals—but for whatever reason, he did not possess the same speed. The sport is merciless that way.

"I always wanted to be Peter Pan, the boy who never grows up," he said. "I can't fly, but swimming is the next best thing. It's harmony and balance. The water is my sky."

But sometimes Peter Pan crashed to earth, and Jones had an intense, dark underside. He had been one of the nation's hottest swimming prospects out of high school two years earlier and had surprised many by matriculating at Princeton, a regionally great swimming school but no one's idea of a national powerhouse. Jones thought he wanted an all-around collegiate experience. However, he quickly became disenchanted with the team, and after missing his NCAA cut by .02 seconds, he had transferred to Stanford. But sophomore season he had done no better, and now he was faced with the chilling prospect that he did not have what it took to be an Olympic Trial qualifier.

Jones was not an elite-level athlete like Grote, Wilkens, Wales, or Blahnik. Those were the swimmers he and the rest of the SCSC team aspired to be. He was extremely fast, but there are hundreds of fast swimmers in the United States. To learn how he finished in national meets, he often had to dry off, walk outside the pool area, and locate the bulletin board where results were posted. He'd wedge between milling bodies and run his finger down the list until he found his name, usually somewhere in the middle. Now in Minnesota, he rose to shut the room's heavy curtains. Every morning for the next eight days, the maids would open them. And every afternoon, as his own frustrations reflected those of the entire team, he would wearily pull them shut and entomb himself in the darkness.

"I need to see how fast I can go," he said philosophically. "It's become essential to who I am. I need to *know*. Realistically, I know the Olympics can't be my dream anymore, but that doesn't—"

He was interrupted by the sound of loud voices coming from the hallway. The sound halted outside his room and there was a loud rustle of someone rummaging through a swim bag. It was the two swimmers staying across the hall. One spoke in accented English. This was Russian-born backstroker Lenny Krayzelburg, perhaps the most dominant swimmer in the world. Once Jones thought he could be a Krayzelburg, a world-beater. He now smiled at the irony as the swimmers' voices disappeared into their room. But then Peter Pan began flying again. It is impossible not to dream great dreams when greatness itself stands right outside the door.

"You know, I'm still going to call myself a dark horse for the Olympic team," the Santa Clara swimmer sighed happily. "Anything can happen if you believe in it."

. . .

The most animated time of day at any U.S. nationals is 8:30 A.M. when the water, packed with approximately 1,000 swimmers warming up in just eight lanes, is so dense with humanity that nearly every swimmer's hand brushes the feet of the person ahead. That was how it was on the first day of the 1999 summer nationals. Already the outside temperature was cresting seventy-five degrees and the natatorium air was turning thick and noxious with chlorine. Large speakers blared summertime hits from the Goo-Goo Dolls, Barenaked Ladies, and Dave Matthews. The walls were lined with photos of Minnesota's numerous All-Americans, more than seemed conceivable for a hockey state on Canada's border. On the over-crowded deck, coaches holding stopwatches aloft wove through the crowds on deck in pursuit of their sprinting swimmers. Several athletes climbed out of the water to cough and complain about the bad air.

Minnesota's indoor complex is neither beautiful nor particularly fast. The tiling is cheap and spectators must sit on concrete ledges. The pool itself was not designed to set records and as a result it does not offer particularly "fast" water. What makes a pool fast? Engineers began pondering the question in the 1970s, which led to two wildly successful experiments, the pool at the University of Texas and the Indiana University Purdue University at Indianapolis (IUPUI) Natatorium. Despite its clunky name, the IUPUI facility in particular was for two decades known as the world's fastest pool. It lost that unofficial status when Sydney opened the International Aquatic Centre, site of the 2000 Olympics.

A pool is fast when its turbulence is reduced and it can maintain still water from one end to the other. Turbulence, often invisible, drags against a swimmer, causing slowdown, and in extreme cases stroke disruption. Another key to fast swimming is clear visibility for the turns, no small feat considering a pool's overhead lighting loses it luminance underwater and light fixtures embedded in the pool wall can blind a swimmer charging toward them.

Pools built for speed must to be deep enough so a swimmer's turbulence won't ricochet off the bottom and return to the surface. At a depth of nine feet, no surface swimmer can disrupt sand or any other substance poured along on a pool bottom. Equally important are the gutters, which must capture the water without letting it bounce back. In use at Texas is a wet-deck system planed to resemble a beach. Indianapolis boasts gutters that are six feet deep. In contrast, the University of Minnesota pool has small gutters and is shallower.

The fastest pools have moveable and semi-solid bulkheads at either ends that further reduce turbulence by capturing and diffusing the thousands of pounds of water displaced when a line of charging swimmers approaches the wall to turn. In old Olympic videos, swimmers can be seen getting clobbered by tidal waves as they come off the walls. That doesn't happen anymore. Lane lines that were once simple ropes are now made of plate-sized plastic discs that block waves. Even so, during races a lead swimmer creates so much drag that his competitors on either side can often move against the shared lane lines and surf his wake. Also important for fast pools is a circulation system that releases water via many small jet streams, preferably on the bottom, instead of through big, current-creating nozzles in the wall.

As the Minnesota pool began to empty for the first day's events, it was abundantly clear that U.S.A. Swimming's nationals barely register on the media's radar. An NBC television crew was there to accumulate background footage on swimmers who'd be vying for the 2000 Olympic team, but its presence only accentuated the absence of all other media outlets. For the whole meet, the coverage would consist of one Associated Press reporter, who seemed to write several short stories before disappearing, and *Swimming World Magazine* Editor-in-Chief Phil Whitten.

American swimming is clearly accustomed to being ignored. U.S.A. Swimming's press liaison was absent for the first several days because she was in Canada at the Pan American Games and the organization didn't send a replacement. Instead, the press desk was manned by a cute, gum-snapping University of Minnesota undergrad who wore a child's barrette in the center of her bangs. The young woman had an infectious, tinkling laugh that unexpectedly spilled into her sentences when she acknowledged she knew nothing about swimming (laugh); no, she had no relevant meet information (laugh); and sorry, but as far as finding a copy of the day's results, her guess was as good as yours (laugh). To write his daily stories, each evening *Swimming World Magazine*'s Whitten had to borrow a results printout from a meet official and Xerox his own copy. This meet was a very intimate, cozy affair. Even the local paper, the *Minneapolis Star Tribune,* was going to fail to include the scoreboard results on some days. At least the swimmers found a silver lining. Since deck space was so limited, right away several athletes commandeered the pool's unused media-viewing platform (it provided a nice view of the diving well but not the pool), and used it for taking naps throughout the meet.

. . .

"Up! Up! *Up!*" Jochums bellowed as Clayton Jones raced the final 12 meters of his 100-meter freestyle race in prelims. Jones touched and Jochums stopped his watch. Both looked at the massive scoreboard on the natatorium wall. Jones grimaced while Jochums swore quietly and noted the time in his water-spoiled blue notebook. Jochums' notebook held all the swimmers' times and splits. In big meets like this, his handwriting was virtually illegible because he shook so badly with nerves he could barely hold a pen. He always told his swimmers the crowd had been jostling him.

Jones had been slow off the blocks and never showed any zip during his race. His 52.12 seconds was bad and he wouldn't be racing at night, not even in the bonus heat for the seventeenth- through twenty-fourth-place finishers. Nearly three years earlier—as a high school swimmer—he had swum the same race in 51.6 seconds. What had happened between then and now? He climbed out of the water and disappeared into the warm-down pool without talking to anyone. Not that anyone would have had much to say. The entire team was swimming just as flat. The preliminary session wasn't over before Jochums knew his fears about the taper turning sour were going to be realized.

That night in the finals, Grote was embarrassed to find himself swimming the consolation heat of his primary event, the 200-meter breaststroke. He finished thirteenth with a dismal time (2:20.19) that didn't even make the Olympic Trials cut. He at least held his stroke together, something he couldn't do a month earlier at the Santa Clara International. But Jochums was angry because Grote concentrated on precise and technically flawless swimming rather than on racing. Being in the middle of a taper for the upcoming Pan Pacs was no excuse. Jochums wanted to see hunger and boldness in his swimmers, and Grote had given a demonstration on perfect stroke.

Next up, Wilkens raced the 200-meter breaststroke finals. He might have expected to win the event, but it would be tough because he had elected to delay his taper until the Pan Pacific Championships in a month. The race began, and at the 100-meter mark, he was in second. Usually, he used the third lap to shift into a higher gear, but tonight he could feel his legs protesting and decided to wait until the final 50 meters. Racing home, he did indeed rev up, and the race looked like it was over. But then he visibly faltered and stalled. The Santa Clara team stood and whistled impatiently for Wilkens' signature surge move, not realizing it had already been made and that the swimmer was in trouble. He finished second to a hotshot teenager and his time (2:16.80) was significantly slower than his time from the Santa Clara International six weeks earlier. He hadn't lost this race in over two years, since the January 1998 World Championships, and on deck afterward he was fuming. This was the type of athlete who takes for granted that his body will do whatever is commanded. The swimmer could fail, be defeated, or lose heart. But his body could never let him down. That was the rule and fallacy of being young and feeling immortal. Wilkens angrily hurled his goggles into the warm-down pool and Jochums hurried over to him. Most coaches let their swimmers cool off and warm down after a race, but Jochums was possessed with a boxing trainer's mentality. He used the cloudy and disorienting seconds immediately after a race to fill his athletes' ears with psychological messages before their own conclusions had time to set in.

When Jochums returned to the team area, he was inconsolable. This meet was supposed to be a test of how adroit he was at juggling different priorities, tapers and schedules. He had seen nearly a dozen poor swims and now his favorite swimmer had fallen apart as well. The taper had been all wrong. This never would have happened in the old days. Jochums had the sudden realization that he was nothing but a tired, old warhorse pretending he owned an edge in a young man's game. The deck swarmed with bright young coaches, men with flat stomachs, new knowledge, and burning ambitions. They seemed connected by invisible cords to their swimmers in the pool. They were the definers and shapers of the world around them. Jochums used to be their leader. And now? He returned to his team, which sat in glum, dejected silence. When a taper is missed, it is nearly impossible to recover. The coach brooded on dark, malevolent things and gave off such a swirling, frightful heat that when he reclaimed his seat on the bleachers, all the nearby swimmers inched away.

"I swear someone needs to kick me in the ass," Jochums said. The words were brittle and sharp-edged. "I've been out of the sport so long, I don't realize when I know what I'm doing and when I don't. I was either going to nail every taper or I was going to miss them all. I can't put a team at risk like that. Dammit, if I'm going to succeed, I have to know in my gut what's going to happen before it does."

The meet continued to be a disaster. But then a wholly unexpected bright spot came when Tate Blahnik swam the finals of the 200-meter backstroke. Behind the blocks, he methodically cracked his knuckles, but his face was so completely vacant of expression that he looked catatonic. Jochums threw his arms up in defeat. Of all the bad swims, he imagined the unhappy Blahnik would deliver among the worst. Blahnik had competed in the World University Games several weeks earlier. That had been the focus of his summer and this U.S. nationals meet was just an afterthought. As Blahnik readied himself, he steadfastly refused to look to his right, where backstroke king Lenny Krayzelburg swung his arms. Krayzelburg's chest was so broad, a family of four might have picnicked on it. Blahnik, with his long, reed-like body and thin arms, looked like he'd been starving himself. Krayzelburg seemed ready to bench-press a car.

Then they were racing and Krayzelburg immediately took the lead. At the first turn, the announcer cried, "Lenny's ahead of world-record pace!" At 100 meters and again at 150 meters, the announcer yelled the same thing. Krayzelburg's father liked to bang a good-luck tambourine in rhythm to his son's stroke, and now it could be heard within the rising roar. The crowd stood up to watch a one-man race against the clock. But what it failed to notice was that this was also a one-man race for Blahnik. Krayzelburg owned a comfortable lead, yet Blahnik was in second with no one remotely close. Krayzelburg finished, narrowly missing the world record, and Blahnik crashed into the wall after him. It was his fastest swim ever and the time would have qualified him for the 1996 Olympic team. He stared emotionlessly at the scoreboard on the far wall and then climbed out.

Blahnik listened dutifully while an exuberant Jochums congratulated him, then shrugged and made his way to the warm-down pool. The swimmer didn't know it then, but in this relatively slow pool he had just delivered what was going to be the world's third-fastest time for all of 1999, No. 2 in the United States. By the end of the season, he would look like a lock for the 2000 Olympic Games.

• • •

The following morning the bad news continued for Santa Clara in general, and for Clayton Jones in particular. When it ended, all the swimmer wanted to do was go to bed and forget the day. But the day wouldn't let him go. Well past midnight he tossed and turned. He had a habit of clicking his right thumb joint whenever he was thinking hard, and in the dark room it sounded like a Geiger counter at a nuclear test site. "I'm dealing with personal demons," he spoke into the darkness. That morning, he had raced the prelims of the 200-meter freestyle with a desperate desire to prove his worth and had self-destructed like a kid in his first race. What was going wrong? There should be no mystery in swimming: Train hard and move fast. It is a straightforward and logical sport.

Jochums had spent the previous week worrying aloud to his top athletes that the taper was off, but he had failed to deliver the same message to the second-tier swimmers. From a practical standpoint, no coach prepares his athletes for subpar performances. But at Santa Clara there was a hierarchy based on speed, and often the athletes near the bottom received less individual attention than those at the top. When a favorite like Grote was in trouble, Jochums, like a Mafia don, would cup his meaty hand around the swimmer's neck in a gruff and loving way and pull him aside for private words. Those words of consolation were what a swimmer like Jones probably needed most of all, but he didn't have access to that kind of relationship.

For the preliminaries of the 200-meter freestyle, he had been in lane eight. Three lanes away was Chad Carvin, a fourteen-time national champion and former U.S. Swimmer of the Year. Jones' original plan had been to start slow and gradually build into his swim for a strong final lap. But only 30 meters into it, he saw Carvin just inches ahead and boldly thought, "I can stay with him. This is how Tom Wilkens would think and Tom wins races."

The Santa Clara swimmer had challenged Carvin for the race's first 100 meters, swimming it two seconds faster than ever before. But by the third lap, he realized it was a mistake even as he fought to stay on pace. On the pool deck, Jochums wrote down the split and ruefully said, "Great courage, but it's now going to bite you in the ass."

"I'm with him; I'm staying in the lead," Jones thought.

As Carvin pulled away, Jones had moved into triage mode to save his disintegrating stroke. First he had tried rotating his hips because the torquing action helps the armstrokes. Then he had downshifted from a six-beat sprinters' kick to two beats, which distance swimmers use to conserve energy. It was in vain; he limped home with a terrible second 100 meters. He'd expected to make the Top 16; instead he finished thirty-seventh. Carvin had eased up on the last lap and glided into finals; that night he would finish third.

Afterward, Jones had hung on the gutter, hating himself with an intensity that frightened him. The line between success and failure is so thin, yet they seem as if they sit on opposite sides of a yawning chasm. Something Jones' Stanford coach, Skip Kenney, had told him months earlier suddenly burned white-hot into him. The swimmer had just finished a disappointing, season-ending swim and the coach, in the throes of a close meet, had said, "Clayton, you have no guts. That's why you didn't swim faster."

"Maybe he was right," Jones thought now.

The warm-down pool was too crowded, so he followed an underground tunnel that led to the University of Minnesota's original swimming natatorium in the next building. The tunnel was thick with heat and chlorine gas. Suddenly the swimmer couldn't catch his breath and his body, needing oxygen badly, went into distress. He staggered onto the original pool's deck and slumped on a bench. A coach he knew happened to be there.

"Clayton, are you all right?" the coach asked.

Jones couldn't answer because his throat had constricted and he couldn't breathe. Then suddenly his stomach turned inside out and he rushed to a nearby trashcan and vomited. He swooned and grabbed the trashcan's edges. Darkness closed in on his peripheral vision. He was about to faint when his stomach heaved again and he bent into the trashcan to vomit everything in his stomach. It was a moment of sad symbolism, not only for him but for the entire Santa Clara team, which had entered the meet with such high hopes. Purged was not only his breakfast but his goal of qualifying for Olympics Trials. In fact, not one of Santa Clara's many mid-level swimmers in Minnesota would make their Trials' cut this week.

Jones, hovering on the edge of consciousness, was full of heartache. It was a sad, humbling thing to witness. Defeat always is. The camera's eye usually follows the victor, not the vanquished. Jones slid to the bench and put his head in his hands to cry. He waved off the concerned coach.

"Oh God, I know I have guts," he thought. "I gave it everything I had. I should've swum a smarter race. But if this is how you define your manhood, that's the kind of man I want to be. But God, what am I doing wrong?"

Midway through the 1999 U.S. nationals, the Santa Clara team, which had thought it might win the meet, was swimming as flat as the Minnesota landscape. It was obvious the taper had been missed with such sweeping entirety that the responsibility for it rested squarely on the coaching staff's shoulders. The team had begun resting too early and lacked the sharpness necessary to race well. At the same time, the meet had turned into a head-scratcher because no one knew who was the fastest swimmer. Athletes on the U.S. national "B" team who had been swimming at the Pan American Games in Canada arrived in Minneapolis en masse via overnight buses. They were fast, but had already swum their real races. National "C" team members like Blahnik had raced at the World University Games and were swimming erratically. Meanwhile, the fastest people, the members of the pre-Olympic national "A" team, were in the earliest stages of their taper for Pan Pacific Championships in Sydney, and most looked terrible.

When Santa Clara's Pan American swimmers arrived at the meet, the first thing they did was talk about how sluggish they felt. That was the final confirmation Jochums needed to slip into a funk that would last the remainder of the meet. He became a black hole on the pool deck, speaking rarely and then only tersely. At meals he drank seriously and silently while Assistant Coach Bitter, the only man Jochums could stand being around, sipped Diet Cokes and said little. At his worst, Jochums was withering in his analysis of a swim. But when an occasional swimmer exceeded expectations, the coach put him or her on top of the world with praise as if he or she had accomplished something mythic. But that was the exception. Team management was left to Bitter. There were no team meetings, and morale visibly crumbled. Jochums had mentally left nationals and was talking about Pan Pacs every chance he had. If his intuition was right, in Australia Grote, Wilkens, and Wales were going to fall flat on their faces.

. . .

Santa Clara had two swimmers in the finals of the 100-meter breaststroke. One was Wilkens. But the other was not Grote; it was a young, up-and-coming athlete. Grote, who had won the event a year earlier, didn't even qualify for the consolation finals; he was stuck in the bonus heat, where he took nineteenth. Jochums intercepted him afterward and filled his head with the reasons he hadn't swum faster. But he didn't have to; Grote had already convinced himself that bad times at nationals indicated he was on course for the Pan Pacs.

In the event's championship finals, all eyes, as well as the NBC cameras, were on the overnight superstar from the Pan American Games, Ed Moses, who had arrived the day before. What was most striking was his size. With all the buzz and excitement surrounding Moses' Pan Am stunning breakout swim, he had grown to gigantic proportions in people's minds. They were expecting another Steve Lundquist, the magnificent breaststroker from the early 1980s who was the size of a mountain. Yet this newcomer was a compact, baby-faced athlete, barely muscled and very generously listed as 5'10". The second startling aspect about him was his air of supreme confidence. It came off his body like halogen. Hands on hips while standing behind lane four, he surveyed the pool area as if he owned it. Two earrings glinted in his left ear and a crooked, smug smile crept across his face. Two weeks earlier, almost no one had heard of him. Now all 2,000 spectators and swimmers expected a world record.

It was never a race. Moses won his first national title in a meet record (1:01.21), and Santa Clara was slammed. Wilkens finished seventh while his Santa Clara teammate finished eighth and was disqualified for an illegal kick. Watching intently on the sidelines, Grote exhaled deeply. Until tonight, he had won the last three summer national championships in which he had raced. Now he no longer had to think about Wilkens as his only major threat. On this night, Moses had just whipped Grote by over three seconds.

· · ·

Toward the meet's end, Dod Wales raced the 100-meter butterfly and despite being unrested and having no expectations, he delivered a time of 54.48, a lifetime best by half a second. He had been in third until the final 10 meters, when he lost speed and slipped to seventh. It was a great swim, not just because it was an unexpected best time, but because it came during a week when the rest of Santa Clara looked as if it were swimming through pudding. Wales' independence had paid off.

In recent weeks, the swimmer had become increasingly ambivalent about leaving Santa Clara. On the one hand, he and Jochums weren't getting along any better. On the other, he arrived in Minneapolis knowing he was improving substantially in the Santa Clara system and it appeared that his critical conversion from short-course college swimming to long-course Olympic swimming was taking place. Meanwhile, the swimmers on the U.S. Resident Team, where he planned to go, were not performing well. Being analytical, Wales had been reconsidering his departure. He knew a decision either way signaled a turning point in his career.

"You and I don't see eye to eye on a lot of things, but we're working on it," Jochums said to him after the butterfly race. "You go think about how fast you just swam in the middle of a taper. You are just months away from reaching your potential, and we can bring you there. I saw where we could gain almost a second in that swim. One second puts you on the Olympic team. Go think on that for a while."

Wales privately decided to stay at Santa Clara. But he didn't immediately tell Jochums, liking the way the coach's voice sounded close to begging. To be appreciated is a great thing. After several days, Wales told him the news.

"To me, coaching is a partnership, not a one-way street," Wales explained. It was a point he had frequently and futilely made in the past. "I have valid input about my training, but you never want to listen to it. You have to accept that coaching requires two people."

"Yeah, two people: the coach and the one who listens to the coach," said Jochums. But he was smiling. Even in this disastrous meet, Santa Clara's Olympic prospects suddenly looked brighter than ever.

Meanwhile, Wilkens was not accustomed to losing. But like most of Santa Clara, he was having a terrible meet. His final event, the 200-meter I.M., was also his weakest. Unlike the 400-meter I.M., which is a race of strategy and endurance, the 200-meter I.M. is four one-lap sprints of each stroke. Wilkens didn't have the kind of speed and natural talent necessary to set himself apart in this event because the race caters more to sprinters. He was also the only competitor unshaved and unrested. When the race began, he immediately fell far back on the butterfly and backstroke legs, and it seemed like another Santa Clara letdown was in the making. But then came the breaststroke segment.

"Oh, no! It's breaststroke time!" shouted a Santa Clara teammate. "Oh, my! Hide the kids and run to the basement! It's breaststroke time!"

Indeed. Over the next 50 meters, Wilkens closed the 10-foot disadvantage with an awesome rush of power. In swimming, no 10-foot gap is closed during a single lap. It simply does not happen. Yet Wilkens had now done it twice, once at the Santa Clara International in the 200-meter breaststroke and now here in Minneapolis. He turned for the final freestyle lap, owning the lead.

"You people weren't far enough ahead!" the teammate shouted. "Bad planning! It's over!"

Wilkens should have lost the race. He was not rested; he was not shaved. It was his weakest event. His team and his coach had already written off the meet. He himself had had a terrible week, and he was not nearly the strongest freestyler in the water. But Wilkens won his race about 35 meters from the finish. He won it then, because that was the instant when he rejected the scene's scripted outcome. The others had caught him. They were faster and hungrier and they needed the victory more than he did. But if a rolling videotape slowed to a frame-by-frame progression, it would zoom onto the swimmer's face and crop out the outside world. The camera would catch Wilkens' armstrokes crashing over-loud in an otherwise silent universe. Perfect water caplets would spring slow-mo through the air. The swimmer's wild eyes would see the two competitors who have drawn nearly even. That was when he engaged it. He engaged whatever it was that set him apart, that let him swim faster each day of his life when that was obviously impossible to do. If you trace a journey through life, you find hundreds of mini-moments like this, moments that add up to the man. By sheer force of will, Wilkens held off the field and won. When he touched, he didn't look at the scoreboard, only the men he had just conquered. He was angry and pulsating with adrenaline and accomplishment.

"Unshaved! Unshaved!" the Santa Clara team chanted. All week, they'd been looking for something to cheer about. Clayton Jones cheered loudest of all, but it was easy to see the longing and confusion swirling on his face. He and Wilkens could train the same sets in practice, eat the same nutritional foods, and dream the same Olympic dream. But Jones would never equal a swim like that. He could try for years to make it different, but finally, what was left but to accept the reality? And in fact, Jones, the personification and symbol of all the hard-trying swimmers at the Santa Clara Swim Club, would never swim another race for the team after this meet. He would compete for one more season at Stanford and afterward retire without achieving his Trials' cuts. Right now, he felt like he was on an island. If he had only looked around. Then he would have realized how many of Wilkens' teammates were struggling with similar introspections.

Jones' final swim was on Santa Clara's 4 × 200-meter "A" team relay, which had an outside opportunity to win the event. But Santa Clara's first two swimmers swam poorly, and when Jones entered the water for the third leg he was in sixth. By the time he finished, he was in seventh. The relay's anchor swam even worse, and the team failed to finish in the Top 10. Adding insult to injury, it lost to Santa Clara's slower "B" squad, something that should never have happened. It was the final nail in the coffin. For three straight years, the club had dominated summer nationals by winning the men's championship; this year it never stood a chance. The meet's final event was the 4 × 100-meter medley relay, which the club had won for three years. It had the potential to challenge the meet record, but finished sixth with an embarrassing time.

There were several bright spots, including Wilkens' dramatic win, Blahnik's surprising 200-meter backstroke swim, and Wales' decision to stay in California. But overall so much had gone wrong that it was hard to catalog. The Pan Pacific Championships, the last major international meet before the Olympics, were in just three weeks. Jochums shuddered at the thought of a repeat performance. He was puckered with a kind of intestinal aniexty.

When the final relay race ended, the few remaining pockets of fans—mostly parents and finished swimmers—stood, stretched, glanced at their watches, scratched themselves, talked about getting dinner, and began tromping to the exit. Jochums had no bag, only his blue notebook, which he clapped shut. He shoved his pen in his pocket. He told the swimmers where to meet the next morning for the bus that would take them to the airplane that would take them home to their aging pool, where the week's mistakes could be corrected. As the coach walked grimly off the deck, he kept his eyes off the natatorium's huge, state-of-the-art scoreboard. There, still frozen in bright, digitized yellow for all to see and mock, was the final disappointing time of the last Santa Clara relay.

CHAPTER SEVEN

His worst fears about missing the taper at the 1999 Pan Pacific Championships had come true and there was not a goddamn thing he could do about it.

Outside the pool complex was Sydney's sprawling Olympic Park, a near-silent city full of empty athletic arenas and hundreds of workers scurrying like mad to complete their work in time for next year's 2000 Olympic Games. Inside the cavernous International Aquatic Centre, his face set like a bulldog, Dick Jochums avoided people as he walked the pool deck, avoided them even when he stood at their sides. When he did talk, his sentences were blunt and devoid of his usual humor. Mostly he swore at himself for failing to trust his instincts. Six weeks earlier, he had a tugging feeling that his taper plans were wrong. He could have done something about it then. He could have stepped back, made necessary adjustments by cycling in ten days of hard work to reset the taper's timing, and moved forward again. Instead he had convinced himself he was overworrying because he had been out of coaching too long. What a knife-twisting irony that was. He had lacked the confidence to trust his own instincts until it was too late. He *had* been out too long.

This meet, the most important event between the 1998 World Championships and the 2000 Olympics, was supposed to be Jochums' redemption a decade after he had been banished from the sport. It was supposed to be a moment of great triumph, a moment when reborn Caesar rides victorious through Rome's gates after a long and difficult campaign. After thirty years of coaching, Jochums could finally assume his rightful position as one of swimming's greatest coaches and motivators. He might have been there years before, but he'd been too hotheaded and self-righteous. But the Dick Jochums of 1999 had matured and softened. He was not only an assistant on the pre-Olympic team, but he was on the short list to be one of three male assistants on the 2000 Olympic staff.

However, he knew his glaring failure as a coach would be obvious as soon as his swimmers hit the water, and he wished he were anywhere but in Australia, even though on paper the 1999 Pan Pacific Championships promised to be one of the most exciting meets in years. For the first time in a long time, there existed a potential challenge to the United States' aquatic supremacy. Host country Australia had assembled its greatest swim team ever and was spoiling to take down the Americans. Upending the United States is a common goal of every country in every international meet. Other nations bond together, they bridge language barriers and customs, cultural incompatibilities and centuries-old grievances, to collectively root against the United States. Meanwhile, Australia is the most swim-crazy nation in the world. It has a population that is only one-fifteenth that of the United States but boasts nearly the same number of competitive swimmers, 200,000. The best Australian swimmers are royalty, earning millions per year in endorsements. This meet was being televised live nationwide, the pool was definitively the fastest in the world (taking that distinction from the Indianapolis Natatorium), and the stands were full of boisterous and knowledgeable swim fanatics.

It was the type of climate Jochums relished, but it couldn't free him from his funk, which had started three weeks earlier in Minnesota. After U.S. nationals, he had considered forcing his trio of Pan Pac swimmers—Grote, Wilkens, and Wales—into a week of intense work. The goal would have been to start over with fresh tapers. But he had listened to them complain about fatigue and had agreed to begin immediately resting. That capitulation now gnawed at his gut more than anything else because it demonstrated weakness and self-doubt. What kind of general prepares for war by asking his troops whether they want to go into battle?

On the first day, Grote proved the coach's fears were well founded. The swimmer was the defending Pan Pac champion as well as the meet record-holder in the 100-meter breaststroke. Yet his bad year continued in the prelims when he raced looking so tight he might have been wearing a straightjacket. Was it possible to look any flatter, any more broken?

He should have left medical school a year earlier. Too late to think about that now. Grote qualified for afternoon semifinals, but barely. You could start writing his epitaph.

"At least I didn't go all out," Grote ruefully told himself after his race. He was dead worried. In all the hundreds of hours of mental preparation, he had never once considered not making finals. That afternoon for the semis, he swam terrified as a jackrabbit in a crocodile pen, blasting his race as hard as he could on the first lap. *"High elbows,"* he told himself as his stroke began breaking up on the second lap. *"Snap the kick, stretch between each stroke, and lift the hips."* It was a brutally ugly swim from an athlete whose success was based wholly on beautiful technique and confidence, yet somehow it carried him to finals. This was not a victory. He hung on the wall gasping for breath. He was exhausted and scared.

Jochums was surprised to his core by Grote's swim. Never before had the swimmer shown him such heart and desire. Until now, it had always been easy for Grote. For the first time, the coach considered that maybe this year-long adversity was exactly what the swimmer needed going into an Olympic year.

"Two things you got to get into your head," Jochums said to the swimmer after the race. "First, this race is my fault, not yours. You've had a bad year of swimming and that's your fault. And it's life's fault, too, because life gave you the gift of being a top student in a top medical school. That's your problem. But this race is my problem, and you have to understand that. Second, you have to realize we only got one year left. You and me are trapped here in Australia when we both know we should be home training. But the best we can do is begin looking toward next year. Forget about being here. The training for the Olympics must start here, today."

Grote nodded. He, too, would give anything to go home and start preparing for the Olympics. He went back to the hotel to ready himself for the finals the next evening.

Jochums faced more bad news the next morning when Wilkens swam the prelims of the 400-meter I.M. The Pan Pacific Championships were to be their special coming-out party, their moment to make Wilkens the world's preeminent medley swimmer. For six months, this four-minute race had been the single most consuming focus in both their lives. With Tom Dolan, the world record-holder and King of Swimming, back home rehabbing his knee, the stage was set.

126

In the first half of his prelim swim, Wilkens looked strong. But on the breaststroke leg, he punched his overdrive switch, revved up, and then sputtered out. In the stands, Jochums was the only one who saw it and he had to sit down as he felt the wind leave his body. He was going to have two swimmers racing in finals that evening, and he wanted to be anywhere but the pool. Around him, Team USA was oblivious to the truth. Wilkens finished the race as the top seed and his teammates began anticipating the victory they'd see later that day.

. . .

"Stay off the feet," Grote reminded himself every day. He used slow steps to move from his hotel bed to the bathroom. He did his business, then stared at himself in the mirror for a long moment, as if to discern a hidden truth behind the eyes. He returned to bed and was soon napping. During the course of the entire meet, he would only leave his hotel room one time for a destination other than the pool. That would be when his parents insisted on dining outside of the hotel. Before agreeing to it, Grote would eyeball the distance to make certain it was close enough to walk. He wore ultra-lightweight sandals, the ones that years earlier his high school coach had instructed he don for every taper to rest his legs.

Grote used to room with Wilkens, but no longer. There had been simplicity in the arrangement, in the yin-yang of the veteran bunking with the rookie. But that was before Wilkens began to beat him. They would return to the room, where Grote would be unable to hide his glumness and Wilkens would subsequently feel guilty about his victory. "You did what you had to," Grote would tell him, and then they'd both stand there feeling embarrassed and stupid. Wilkens had finally asked to be assigned a new roommate. As a result, Grote now bunked with butterflyer Dod Wales.

This was not a bad thing. Both men were no-nonsense as they awaited their races. They saw themselves as warriors anticipating battle. Wilkens meanwhile happily zipped off to tour Sydney with a video camera and his family. Grote and Wales stayed inside and watched T.V., played cards, read books, and talked about racing. A swimmer's hotel room before competition can become a cage of self-doubt, and the two worked hard on psyching each other up. Although naturally a loner, Wales was the perfect roommate for big meets. His coolness and impenetrability dissolved in one-on-one situations and he had a tremendous capacity to listen. Those who knew him for his stubborn ways and emotionless demeanor were inevitably surprised to discover that when he let down his guard, he teemed with ideas, hopes, and plans.

One thing Wales never did in his hotel room was express doubt or fear, because he had trained himself to dispel negative thoughts and stay centered on his objectives. He was serious in general, but at meets he became almost mystic. Kurt Grote, who bounced from one emotion to another without anyone ever knowing it, needed to stay with a person like this. Because of his poor year, Grote's psyche was in terrible shape. In Australia, it grew even worse, especially after his first two swims. He'd been elected co-captain of Team USA, and so around the team he had to bottle up his feelings and comport himself like a leader. Only in the room with Wales did he drop the charade. He was the mighty Achilles retreating to his tent as the Trojans attacked.

"I'm having a hard time," he admitted to Wales. Grote was not a person who reached out, not ever. He was the one who was supposed to give reassuring advice to others. That was how he fit into the larger world, as a lighthouse, not as a nervous boat in a shifting sea. He began to talk to Wales, first in bits and pieces, and then in a stream of unburdened consciousness. The year had been a complete disaster. Grote was nowhere near as physically fit as he'd been the previous season when he was a full-time student. There was no reason for it, just as there were no answers for his ongoing slump. Swimming is not like baseball; there aren't *supposed* to be slumps. One frustration mounted upon another. The perfectionist within him was about to explode. Grote talked incessantly, not about the meet, but about the future. He had to get back to California and start from scratch. And Wales listened, even though he wished Grote would have left the negativity outside the room.

There is a conventional belief in swimming that says the worse a swimmer performs early in a taper, the better he or she performs when the taper peaks. Using that logic, Grote should have been ready to slingshot himself to a world record. But he really hadn't improved since his nineteenth-place finish at U.S. nationals three weeks earlier. Only by a reserve-burning, all-out effort did he even make the finals of the 100-meter breaststroke. "You can do this," Grote said to himself as he prepared for the finals. But he knew it rang false, and from the very start he had a poor swim. His body rocked up and down instead of forward, his hips failed to stay centered, and his kick lacked snap. The ingredients for success were there, but he couldn't put them together. He touched sixth in a time (1:02.79) that was more than 1.5 seconds slower than his best. Worse, in all three races he was beaten by the meet's No. 2 American breaststroker, a University of Georgia swimmer named Michael Norment. That meant Norment had won the right to swim the breaststroke on the final 4 × 100-meter medley relay. Taking nothing away from Norment, it was a terrible blow for Grote. The captain was not good enough for his own team's relay.

Yet it wasn't the race, but the aftermath of the race that was significant. This was a perfect time for Grote to make excuses or slip into one of his dark, "I failed" moods. That's what he had done at the 1998 World Championships after a poor first race. Or he could dump the blame on Jochums, who was trying to shoulder it. But Grote was not the same person he was in 1998; the year of frustration had matured him. He was tired of making excuses.

"This is a test," Grote said to the coach. "It's easy to roll over, but I'm not letting that happen. I'm going to reverse this. For whatever reason, I can't swim close to my best times. But I can still compete like a champion."

This was a watershed moment for Grote, although he didn't know it. The year had been a loss. He was months off his schedule. His coach was accepting the blame. Nothing came easy anymore. He was sliding and could career off in any number of directions, from finger-pointing to self-pity. Instead, he had applied the brakes.

"The two-hundred-meter breaststroke race is the first step of the next season," he told Wales back in their room. "It's going to set the tone. Then I have to get back and go to work. It's going to be harder than anything I've done before, but I can't wait to start."

Wales listened to him plan out his fall and winter. *Stop talking about the future*, Wales wanted to say. Controlling his own destiny, the butterflyer had felt sharp all week. As a rule, he hated staying with people who raced before him. After their events, they lost focus and that threatened his own concentration. Grote wasn't finished, but he was acting like he was. Wales sighed and wondered how people could allow emotions to get the best of them.

. . .

Jochums had fully expected Grote to hit bottom. When it didn't happen on the first day, the coach waited for the second. Still nothing. Grote had now surprised him twice in one meet.

In the days between Grote's two breaststroke events, world records tumbled right and left. The 1999 Pan Pacs had become the fastest swim meet ever. It was part pool (it offered the best of everything: deep gutters, great depth, perfectly distributed circulation, great lighting) and part thrill to be racing in the 2000 Olympic venue in front of thousands of crazed fans. Apart from Santa Clara's swimmers, the U.S. team was doing remarkably well. But so were the Australians. For the first time in years, the United States had itself a worthy opponent as Australia seemed to counter every victory by the Americans with one of their own. It was a mesmerizing duel, with the Australian men dominating the American men while the American women beat their Aussie counterparts. The tension and excitement grew greater each day. Many swim meets, including this one, are scored by a simple point system (for example, 20 points for first, 16 points for second, 15 for third, and so on) and as the close competition advanced, the entire Australian continent seemed to stop to watch the television coverage. A person could sit in a Perth coffeehouse on the opposite side of the country and for hours listen to people debate the action in Sydney. The meet was the lead story in the daily newspapers with swim photos taking up most of the front page.

Against this backdrop, Grote swam the prelims of the 200-meter breaststroke. He tried so hard, he was certain his time was in the neighborhood of 2:15. When he saw the scoreboard reading 2:19.08, his first thought was that the timing system had malfunctioned. The time wasn't even in the Top 12 in the United States. "Man, I'd go home right now if I were Kurt," mused Wilkens, who watched the race and then in the next heat swam an easy 2:15.7. How many times was Grote going to run face-first into the same invisible wall? If only there were an explanation for this. He knew his swimming had fallen off the cliff, but why? He forgot his pledge to remain positive and began spiraling downward. The disintegration was visible in the moments after the race. It all seemed so hopeless.

That was when Jochums grabbed him by the arm and leaned close.

The coach spoke hard and low and with a quivering intensity. It is likely the most passionate and important moments in Jochums' life occurred in the brief seconds it took to grab a swimmer as he staggered from the pool.

"You are not going to feel good at this meet," Jochums hissed at Grote. "You are going to hurt like hell and you have to let it hurt. This is not a meet where you are beautiful or where you achieve your goals. This is a meet where you decide what kind of swimmer and person you are." He shook the swimmer firmly. "You listen close: How you act here impacts the rest of your life."

Jochums let go and Grote stumbled away. In the semifinals that same afternoon the swimmer laid it all on the line, everything he had from the soles of his feet to the crown of his head. He swam the first 100 meters two seconds faster than he had in prelims. It was a stupid, reckless thing to do. But he wanted to feel the power surge through his body, just for a brief, elusive moment, even though he knew he was going to pay for it dearly on the last lap. Racing home, he completely fell apart, and yes, it hurt like hell, just as Jochums promised it would. But he reached the finals with a stunning 2:15.0, his fastest time of the year. It was still several seconds slower than his best, but no one drops four seconds between a hard morning swim and an evening one. And Grote knew he could go faster. He tried not to think about Wilkens, who had easily cruised into finals and was stalking the deck like a caged animal.

Grote's capacity to believe or disbelieve in himself almost simultaneously had astonishing power. After his swim, he thought, "Maybe I can win this thing tomorrow." It was such a far-fetched notion that he went to bed without dwelling on it. But he woke up the next morning and his first thought was, "I can win if I have the right race."

He decided to take it out faster than he ever had before. He decided also to use a higher stroke rate and intentionally spin his arms through the water. It was a dangerous gamble. Swimming like that requires less sheer strength—which Grote seemed to lack—but it also pushes a swimmer into an anaerobic zone much earlier than normal. When that happens, the muscles begin generating massive quantities of lactic acid. Grote could be caught 50 meters from the finish with no reserves. Depending on how bad it got, he might not even be able to finish the race legally. It was a reckless race plan that would be full of pain.

He raced the first 100 meters exactly as planned, with a stroke rate that was sure to kill him. When he made his second turn, he closed his eyes just as he always did. Then, in the silence of the underwater pull, he glanced down the pool. There was Wilkens. It was an exact inversion of the same moment nearly two years earlier, when Wilkens had looked for Grote during the 1998 World Championships. Would it have the same long-term positive impact? The two Santa Clara swimmers were first and second. Wilkens belonged there, but Grote absolutely did not. No one rebounded like this. For an instant they locked eyes and then they were swimming again.

How you act here . . .

On every stroke, Grote lifted his head into a shockwave of sound greater than anything he had ever heard. Then he dove underwater into a watery silence. He forgot about Wilkens and wouldn't know until much later how his teammate fared. Grote was in lane six, and that was significant because the lane had an underwater camera running along a track on the pool's bottom. Controlled by technicians on deck, the camera was trained on the first-seeded swimmer in lane four. For the first two laps, every time Grote dove underwater he saw the camera slightly behind him. But now on the third 50, he watched it move ahead and knew he was being passed. Turning for the final lap, he tried to get back into that isolated and whited-out world he used when he raced. But it was too late. There was the cursed camera, pulling farther ahead on every stroke.

. . . impacts the rest of your life.

The pain was intense. Holding his stroke together was nearly impossible. But he didn't stop racing. He touched fifth with a time of 2:15.41. Wilkens had finished ahead, but not by much. Grote's swim had been as heroic as it was implausible. He had turned a corner. Afterward, there wasn't much for Jochums to say to him. From that moment on, everything people had come to expect from Grote was going to change. He had learned how to overcome adversity and nothing was going to stop him. The coach, who had anguished so frequently over Grote and his ability to respond to adversity, could have talked at him for hours. But it all boiled down to one sentence.

"I will never be more proud of you than I am right now," he told his swimmer after the race.

For Tom Wilkens, there was a clean, uncomplicated order to life: At the end of the day, the race is always won by the fittest. And in his mind, no swimmer on earth was more fit than him. He could say that with certainty because Tom Dolan was on the sidelines. There were faster swimmers, yes; but none was more fit.

So what was going wrong 250 meters into the fastest 400-meter I.M. in history?

Wilkens had entered the meet as one of the only athletes swimming three events. Even so, he was only predicted to win one, the 200-meter breaststroke, in which he was ranked No. 1. But he had other plans. This was to be his moment to show on an international stage that he had become a 400-meter I.M. specialist. Several days before his breaststroke race against Grote and others, he had swum the finals of the sport's decathlon and for the first four laps was below world-record pace. The water had rushed past his body at a blindingly fast speed, but the swimming felt as easy as turning on a car's ignition. Wilkens had arrived and he knew it. For the chess game that is the 400-meter I.M., his original race plan had called for him to stay as close as possible to the leaders during the butterfly and backstroke legs, and then make his signature charge during breaststroke. Yet at 150 meters, he had found himself unexpectedly owning a body-length lead over a star-studded international field.

"Whoa, I'm moving fast," he had thought as he glanced down his body and saw his two closest competitors at his feet. Both should have been ahead of him at this stage, which meant either both were in trouble or Wilkens was making history. It was a great moment for him.

And then a hairline fracture appeared. An athlete in the heat of competition must be utterly closed from the surrounding world. He must think only of himself and the competition next to him. But as Wilkens pinwheeled his arms through the air and water, he momentarily glanced toward the bright ceiling of the biggest pool complex he had ever seen. He suddenly heard the sound of the Australians screaming for their second-place countryman, Mathew Dunn, to catch up. He felt the water rushing past him and had a deep and lasting impression that this was what heaven would feel like when he died. The hermetic seal around his brain had been broken. In the split-second lull between strokes, he relaxed long enough to think, "I'm going to win this."

That was all it took. Wilkens smoothly rolled from his back to his stomach at the 200-meter wall, flipped, and began his breaststroke. In the 400 I.M., the swimmer wants to emphasize the breaststroke's kick more than the arms' pull. This is a major transition from the butterfly and backstroke segments, which primarily leverage the arms. Swimming a leg-based breaststroke provides the upper body a chance to rest before freestyle. Wilkens began the deep kicking that he knew would seal this race. But at 250 meters, he felt a strange and fatiguing heaviness. As he turned, he saw with a shock that a Canadian swimmer named Curtis Myden had caught him. Myden was not someone to mess with. He'd captured bronze in both the 200-meter and 400-meter I.M.s in the 1996 Games. Hanging right behind him was Dunn, the Australian, who in those same two 1996 Olympic races had finished fourth and fifth. Dunn was also one of the strongest freestylers in the world. Never in his career had Wilkens been caught during the breaststroke leg of a medley.

"What's happening?" the Santa Clara swimmer thought. Panic raced through his cortex. He'd been blindsided. His two competitors, both more experienced, had perfectly played Wilkens' own strength against him by resting during the race's first 200 meters and then attacking during breaststroke. They knew Wilkens wouldn't expect it, and that he wouldn't see them coming because in breaststroke the head is rigid. If this were chess, Wilkens was suddenly in check.

He immediately launched an all-out attack. Wilkens knew the Canadian and Australian both had powerful freestyles, knew that if he couldn't break away now, on the last lap they'd reel him in just like a dumb fish to club alongside the gunwale. The swimmer cursed his momentary lapse of concentration and shifted into overdrive. Then he had a second shock. There *was* no overdrive. *The missed taper.*

Wilkens managed to preserve his lead for the remainder of the breaststroke. He even managed to stay next to the others during the first 50 meters of freestyle. But on the race's last lap, it was over. Myden and Dunn no longer even looked at him as they fought for the gold medal. Wilkens began spinning his arms crazily through the water, missing his catch and losing streamline. His expected breakout moment had become a panicky mess. It was as if all the technique work had never taken place. Dunn touched first (4:16.54), Myden second (4:16.77). Wilkens finished third (4:18.58), more than six seconds slower than the world record, after racing below it for more than half the race. He looked as if he had been dragged behind a truck.

He was disgusted with himself. "I didn't get beat; I lost," he thought acidly. "From now on, the 400 I.M. is my event. Nothing else." As he approached the warm-down pool, he saw Jochums heading gravely toward him. The coach probably wanted to take the blame. Wilkens turned away. He was sick of hearing it.

But in the 200-meter breaststroke, the only event he had a chance to win, problems surfaced again. He was aware of the situation and aware the odds were against him, so he attacked the race early in hopes of building an insurmountable lead. This was the race in which Grote displayed his heroism, but Wilkens, of course, didn't notice it. Wilkens led nearly the whole way, but he swam with concern, not authority. He was symbolic of the American men's team, which was finding itself unable to rise to the Australian challenge. As he stroked, the sharpness he displayed nearly every day in practice was lacking. The race felt nowhere near as good as the first laps of his 400-meter I.M. several days earlier, which meant he had slid even further away from his taper's sweet spot. On the breaststroke race's third lap, he attempted to quicken the pace and nothing happened. He struggled to hang on, but all at once his body tightened into a walnut, and on the final 25 meters he utterly disintegrated. An Australian teenager named Simon Cowley sprang ahead to win easily (2:12.98 to Wilkens' 2:13.97).

Now Wilkens was furious. He had spent a year preparing for this? His body's betrayal? Its refusal to respond on command? He was in the best shape of his life, he'd just swum in the world's fastest pool, and his time was more than 1.5 seconds slower than his best. He needed to find an outlet for his fury; he needed the whole crowd to put its collective finger to his jugular and feel the anger screaming through his veins. Wilkens occasionally playacted after a poor race as if to demonstrate how much he cared, but tonight it was no game. Losing that way on the last lap was unacceptable. NBCOlympics.com would later write an online feature about the art of tapering and use Wilkens' Pan Pacific meet to illustrate what happens when the timing is wrong. Right now, the swimmer climbed from the pool and stalked across the wide empty deck. Wilkens saw in himself what everyone else saw: another American man swimming below expectations at the biggest meet until the Olympics. The meet was now half over and Team USA was facing its first-ever loss in a major international competition.

Wilkens personified the mood of the U.S. team as he looked darkly around the deck, as if wanting to settle a score with his fists. In sport, as in war, there are few things sweeter than beating the United States, and the meet was looking to be Australia's finest swimming hour. Wilkens was sick of it all. Poor swimming, the taste of the ozone-filtered pool water, the crowded warmups, Jochums harping about getting home and fixing things, even the familiar pimpled rash on his legs from repeated shaving. If life were literature, then Wilkens was walking along a familiar enough archetypal journey: Youthful exuberance and inattention grows into an unfair hardship. The hardship leads to serious setbacks. The protagonist questions why he's on the journey in the first place. All that was now needed was a storybook ending involving last-minute redemption.

Wilkens approached his final event, the 200-meter I.M., differently from his first two. He locked into a race plan so detailed it accounted for how many breaths he took while standing on the blocks. He let his anger simmer down to a pitchy tar, coated himself in it, and declared he would win no matter what it took. It didn't matter that each day he felt slower in the water and the 200-meter I.M. was his weakest event.

"No one touches me on this one," he said aloud, staring at himself in his hotel mirror.

He created the whole race in his head, start to finish. After the victory he would shrug his shoulders and make a relieved "It's about time" face to his teammates. Then he would close his eyes and recline backward in the water, as if he were being absolved of a great burden. On his way to the pool, he even rehearsed what he would say to ESPN2 commentator Rowdy Gaines after he won. (No wonder Australia had become a swimming power. While every Pan Pacific race was televised live, including preliminaries, in the United States ESPN2 would condense the eight-day meet into a one-hour synopsis and air it at midnight—after bumping it once—weeks after the final race had been swum.)

Wilkens was in lane three and seeded third. The 200-meter I.M. is a drag race of four laps, and Wilkens dove in with no real chance of winning. An argument could be made that he had slim chance of even medaling. Too much raw speed was necessary. Maybe because he knew that, Wilkens raced the first two laps as hard as he could. On the breaststroke leg, he started in a tight pack with the leaders and swam all-out. Several times he tried to achieve the higher gear, failed, and ultimately swam with a lot of hurt. One by one, the competitors dropped off until there was only one. Wilkens finished his breaststroke lap in 33.5 seconds, easily his fastest ever, and turned in first place. But now he was flush against the pain and three lanes away was Australia's Dunn, the winner of the 400-meter I.M. Dunn was so good in freestyle he had swum it on Australia's relay in the 1996 Olympics. Instantly, Dunn began to catch Wilkens. Dunn by all rights should win. He was the freestyler. He had better legs. He had the crowd. Wilkens could feel his arms spinning out of control. He was entering panic mode again, and it would result in disaster if his stroke fell apart.

"No, No!" Wilkens shouted to himself. "Legs first, arms follow. Keep it in the legs!"

In the stands, Jochums' stomach didn't just drop; it plummeted.

"He's slipping; the left hand is slipping," Jochums whispered. He cursed to himself. How could the swimmer forget his primary lesson? Then the coach glanced at his stopwatch, which he used to measure Wilkens' stroke rate. Could that be right? Jochums quickly checked again. Wilkens was in the final 20 meters, then the final 15.

At a moment like this, the body has already entered severe oxygen debt. The pain is blinding. Hypoxic thought is reduced to basic survival commands. Often, a swimmer in distress loses feeling in the tongue and lips. They seem to fall asleep because the blood is shunting to the vital organs. Wilkens' brain repeated over and over, *Win. Win. Win.* He lunged forward, lungs bursting, and touched.

The vacuum of disappointed silence told him he had won. It had been a remarkable race, so sweet and fiercely contested, so hard won. Wilkens had just learned a whole lot about who he was. The Australian crowd sat down. In the final meters, Wilkens had so punished Dunn that Canada's Myden, runner-up in the 400-meter I.M., had actually slipped by him to steal second. The Americans danced in their section. Amid the team's happy jostle, Jochums checked his numbers. Wilkens' freestyle stroke rate had been nearly twenty percent faster than ever before. At the team meeting the following day, National Team Director Dennis Pursley, the man in charge of U.S.A. Swimming's Olympic movement, would recount to the swimmers how he had seen thousands of swims at international competitions. Then he would look hard at them. "Last night," he would say, "that 200 I.M. by Tom Wilkens was one of the top ten greatest swims I have ever seen."

Until now, Team USA had been in a hard spot. But this single race would inject a magical fire into the team, filling the swimmers with an unnameable, throbbing energy. Maybe it was pride. Maybe it was just a reminder of what greatness required. Weeks later, the executive director of U.S.A. Swimming, Chuck Weiglus, would summarize the meet to the swimming community and would naturally try to speak about the team as a whole. But he couldn't resist mentioning one race: "Tom's gold medal in the 200 I.M. was so gutsy, and some might even say that this performance was a turning point for the U.S. . . ."

That would come later. Right now Wilkens still needed to finish his race. As he had planned beforehand, he shrugged to his teammates and made an "It's about time" face. Then he lay back in the water and floated for several moments. A picture of this appeared the next day on the U.S.A. Swimming website and was seen by nearly 100,000 viewers. In the photo, the swimmer looks as if he's reclining while on a Caribbean cruise. In reality, he was offering a quick prayer of thanks. That, too, had been part of the pre-race plan. There was still one more detail. He pulled himself out of the pool and walked toward ESPN2's Rowdy Gaines, who stood waiting with a microphone. Physically, Wilkens looked the same, but this race and this meet had convinced him of something. He was capable of taking his swimming to another level, and the only level that remained was the Olympic Games. As Wilkens approached the sportscaster, he couldn't stop smiling because, regardless of the interviewer's questions, he already knew exactly what he would say.

. . .

Dod Wales avoided the emotions and the roller-coaster frustrations that plagued Jochums and Grote during the meet. He avoided the archetypal journey taken by Wilkens, with his defeat, frustration, and ultimate redemption. Wales avoided it all by remaining the calm center of the storm. He was there, but he was fenced off and remote. Even though this was his first international meet, he felt as if he had been rehearsing for it most of his life. He charged himself with the task of remembering all that passed before his eyes because he would need to call upon it later. This meet was a stepping-stone, nothing more, in the long march to September 23, 2000. That would be the final day of the 2000 Olympic swimming competition. That was his plan, and Dod Wales stuck to plans.

"If I were anyone except me, I'd be excited to be a part of Pan Pacs and the national team," Wales said. "But there's no resting on laurels. I've got the rest of my life to sit back and enjoy. Right now, I need to push forward."

A month earlier at the 1999 U.S. nationals in Minneapolis, he had departed the meet with mixed feelings about his seventh-place finish in the 100-meter butterfly. The bad news was that his dominance in short-course swimming had not fully translated into the long-course Olympic format. But the good news was his progress. A year earlier, at the 1998 U.S. nationals, he had qualified for the finals of a long-course nationals for only the first time. This year he had done it without resting or shaving.

Wales, as a rookie, was a sponge in Australia. He saw how Jochums and Grote had exhausted themselves by letting their emotions get the better of them. He watched how Wilkens had to lose his first two races in order to get angry enough to win his third. Wales saw how demoralized his Team USA teammates became whenever an American lost a race. How much collective energy dissipates into the universe when a friend falls short of a goal? Wales decided not to invest hope or emotion into their races. That is a cold, calculating thing to decide, but he knew he required all his energy for his own competition. He rationalized that he would give back to his teammates by handing them a performance they could cheer about. In Australia, he came to embody Rudyard Kipling's poem "If." "If you can keep your head when all about you are losing theirs . . ." It was something that would stay with him for the remainder of the Olympic journey.

In his 100-meter butterfly event, he qualified fourth for finals but was a good deal behind the top three. For the race, he had preplanned everything the night before, right down to the clothes he would wear. Planning was his form of meditation. He would feel the nervousness welling inside and struggling to shoot out like a geyser. He would divert and quell it through organization and control. By the time he stood on the blocks for any event, he felt almost serene.

He couldn't beat the top three swimmers; that was something to be realistic about. And so he swam against himself and his own limitations, as he preferred. When the race began, he undulated underwater four, five, six times before breaking to the surface for his first stroke. There is something distinct about butterfly. A supple person can kick it nearly as fast as he or she can swim it. The powerful dolphin kick, that sexy two-legged hip thrust, is the single most powerful force in human swimming. There was a reason Aquaman swam that way when chasing villains. The kick is so strong that many sprint freestylers use it after every turn for extra speed. So do backstrokers. All the power comes from the hips and it drives forward the whole body. To prevent swimmers from kicking underwater throughout a race, the rules require surfacing 15 meters after a dive or turn. During a single butterfly stroke, the swimmer actually kicks twice, once at the onset, when the hands first enter the water, and again when the hands pass the hips as they exit the water.

Wales knew he had neither a great kick nor a great pull. What made him fast was the great symmetry he created between the two. He hung with the leaders as long as possible, and when they began pulling away at 40 meters, he clicked on autopilot and swam his own race. That generally meant his first lap was measured and controlled and his second lap became more ferocious as it went along. He finished fourth in another best time (53.38 seconds). Most important, he was the fastest American finisher. That gave him the butterfly relay spot.

The swim signified he would end the 1999 season as the second-ranked butterflyer in the United States, behind a Texas swimmer who had won U.S. nationals in a faster time. This was the second straight year Wales would finish the season No. 2, but to two different swimmers. He'd take that kind of consistency. There were 26 Olympic swimming events, and no race at the 2000 U.S. Olympic Trials was more up for grabs than the men's 100-meter butterfly. There was no dominant swimmer, but as many as a dozen athletes could finish within inches of each other. And none in that hungry group was as steady as Wales, a swimmer who had been raised never to brag, boast, or make a prediction. Yet as he climbed

Kurt Grote winning another NCAA title: "He was defined by his ambition, a person famous among friends for setting outrageous goals and then methodically achieving them one by one." *Photo courtesy of Glenn Cratty, Allsport*

The master jeweler Kurt Grote and his perfect technique *Photo courtesy of Vincent Laforet, Allsport*

Kurt Grote and wife, Amy Hunn *Photo courtesy of Kurt Grote*

The rookie Tom Wilkens *Photo courtesy of Asbury Park Press, by Bob Bielk*

Left: Tom Wilkens racing breaststroke
Photo courtesy of Todd Warshaw, Allsport

Right: Wilkens moments before the
400-meter I.M. at the Olympic Trials:
"Fear and excitement unlike anything
ever experienced." *Photo courtesy of
Donald Miralle, Allsport*

Butterflyer Dod Wales: "He was beautiful to watch, the swimmer who possessed the best balance between technique and strength."

Dod Wales: "He saw swimming the way a classical engineer would: as an emotionless set of systems, theorems, rules, and processes."

Dod Wales catches his breath after a race at the Santa Clara International meet.

Backstroker star Tate Blahnik

Backstroker Tate Blahnik: "He was rail-thin with no visible muscle tone. Yet . . . he could outswim nearly every swimmer in the world in any stroke, any distance."

Tate Blahnik, wishing he were somewhere else

Sergey Mariniuk, three-time Olympian: "He was to swimming what Mikhail Baryshnikov was to ballet."

Mariniuk racing against Wilkens at the Santa Clara International meet: "What if? What if he were to train with Wilkens? What if the two of them went stroke for stroke each and every day in practice?"

Left: Time warp. Dara Torres and her goggles from an earlier era. *Photo courtesy of Doug Pensinger, Allsport*

Right: Dara Torres, the first U.S. woman to compete in four Olympics and the most decorated athlete (along with track star Marion Jones) of the 2000 Olympic Games: "Every thirty-two-year-old needs a thrill like this." *Photo courtesy of Allsport*

Breaststroke sensation Ed Moses: "[An] air of supreme confidence came off his body like halogen." *Photo courtesy of Al Bello, Allsport*

Tom Dolan, King of Swimming *Photo courtesy of Allsport*

Coach Dick Jochums: "He could make athletes tremble in fear, reexamine their souls, and swim far beyond their natural talent."

The keystone, Coach John Bitter (with Wilkens) *Courtesy of Laney Wilkens*

Lord over all: Dick Jochums and members of the elite team

Bitter and Jochums during a workout

Kurt Grote: "He stayed in the locker room over a half hour, exploring the sediments one finds at rock bottom."

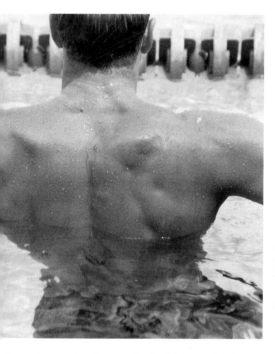

Kurt Grote's back: "He looked like a child's action figure, complete with muscle cabling across his broad shoulders. . . ."

Tom Wilkens fifty days before Olympic Trials: "Halfway to the pool, he felt so tired he lowered himself to the deck's warm concrete and promptly fell asleep."

Left: The start of the 100-meter butterfly finals at Olympic Trials (Wales second from top)

Right: Alone with his thoughts: Dick Jochums at the 2000 Olympic Trials

Left: The Santa Clara Swim Club

Right: The gate leading to the world of the Santa Clara Swim Club

out of the pool after his race, he knew in his heart that he would win the Olympic Trials. He was on a planned trajectory and knew the exact longitude and latitude of his landing.

. . .

Even before Wales' butterfly race, Team USA realized it was in danger of losing its first international meet since the mid-1950s. Australia, with incredible male swimmers like teenage sensation Ian Thorpe and world record-holder Michael Klim, was knocking on the door. Calculating a variety of possible scenarios, U.S. Olympic Coach Mark Schubert, a man with more than sixty national team titles to his credit, determined the meet's outcome would likely be decided on the final event, the men's 4 × 100-meter medley relay. The 1999 Pan Pacific Championships were scored on a point system, with relays capturing the most. Two years earlier at the 1998 World Championships, the Aussies had defeated the United States in this event. The United States had ultimately won the overall competition, but the relay loss signified the first time American men had ever lost the 4 × 100-meter medley. Now at the 1999 Pan Pacific Championships, the Australians were even stronger and the U.S. team might be even weaker. Lose the race and lose the meet. That was the climate when Coach Schubert privately approached Grote. The coach was a straight shooter.

"Stay ready for the relay," Grote later recalled Schubert saying. The coach must have seen the surprise in Grote's face. He added quickly, "Nothing's been decided, but just in case."

Medley relays are particularly easy to organize. You select the fastest American sprinter in each of the four strokes. In Sydney, it was a quantitative, nonpolitical, cut-and-dried fact that Georgia's Michael Norment had beaten Grote three times in the 100-meter breaststroke, in the prelims, semis, and finals. That meant Norment was the breaststroker on the 4 × 100-meter medley relay. But the swimmer had not been at the top of his game for the entire meet, and everyone knew it. In the 100-meter breaststroke finals, he beat Grote, but his time was .85 seconds slower than his best. Afterward, the Santa Clara swimmers and others noticed he didn't seem to bounce back very well. Every time Wilkens turned around, it seemed Norment was in the warm-down pool trying to fix his stroke. That didn't instill confidence in anyone. Meanwhile,

Grote had turned things around after his own dismal performance in the 100-meter breaststroke. His pain-filled race in the 200-meter breaststroke finals had fired up the entire team, and his four-second drop between the event's prelims and finals had resurrected his bravado. He stood taller, prouder. He'd been gritty as sandpaper under adverse circumstances and he knew it. He also had Olympic experience, and that meant he was as battle-tested as they come. Team USA's captain seemed more capable than he had in months.

Before talking to Grote about the relay, the coaching staff had asked Jochums what he thought about making a switch.

"Kurt may be one of the great relay swimmers in the history of the sport," Jochums had said. "He'll go one second faster than he did in his individual race."

One second was the magic number that could earn the Americans a victory.

"So you're saying he should be on the relay," Jochums remembered Schubert saying.

"No, Norment should be on the relay because he earned it," Jochums had said. "You asked my opinion about Kurt. He's my swimmer. I think he should be our breaststroker and I consider that an objective opinion. But it is only an opinion. You make a change and there's going to be a world of trouble. There might be lawsuits. I'm damn glad it's not my decision."

The men looked at each other in silence and let the full significance of this discussion billow around them. There was something unique about Michael Norment. He was the first and only African-American ever to swim on a U.S. national "A" team. The soft-spoken Norment, who quite possibly had the most beautifully sculpted physique in the swimming world, had come from the highly respected Philadelphia Department of Recreation (PDR) program, the country's most successful inner-city, minority-based swim team.

Years earlier, the team had started from scratch with an untrained coach and a few learn-to-swim kids who had trouble completing two unassisted laps. Over the years, it had developed into one of the East Coast's major powerhouses and was almost single-handedly responsible for blowing away the lingering racist notion that African-Americans were poor swimmers. Black athletes on average tend to have less body fat than their white counterparts, and since body fat creates buoyancy, perhaps this physiological difference helped perpetuate the stereotype. But PDR's longtime track record proved success was based on access to pools and coaching, not body composition or skin color. Norment had been one of PDR's first stars prior to attending the University of Georgia, and by the late 1990s he was just about the most successful black male swimmer in the world.

Norment was one of U.S.A. Swimming's Great Black Hopes (notable others included well-known sprinters Sabir Muhammad and Bryon Davis). For years, the sport's national organization had been trying, with increased desperation, to break through the color barrier and dispel its stereotyped lily-white image. There are still hundreds of U.S. country clubs, where grassroots swimming originates, with no black members. At nearly any U.S.A. Swimming meet, there are no more than a half dozen African-American swimmers surrounded by hundreds of white bodies during warmup.

But that could change overnight with one superstar. It had happened in golf, courtesy of Tiger Woods. This wasn't an idle consideration. For years, the number of competitive American male swimmers has been on the decline as young boys left swimming for more glamorous sports. In a very real sense, minority participation symbolizes the future and is a critical issue facing U.S.A. Swimming. Meanwhile, while the media ignores the sport as a whole, it paradoxically follows its few minority swimmers with such intensity that at least one top African-American swimmer, Muhammad, moved to Hawaii, in part to escape the pressures.

But now, at the Pan Pacific Championships, a black man in this white sport had quantitatively earned the right to swim a crucial relay—not once, but three times over—and he was in danger of having a white coaching staff replace him with a slower white swimmer while hundreds of journalists looked on. This was not going to be easy.

. . .

The day before the relay, Schubert asked both Grote and Norment to join him in his hotel room. Grote knew what it meant.

"I want more than anything in life to be on this relay," Grote thought as he approached the room. "But deep down I think [Norment] deserves the spot, not me. I know I can swim faster, but he earned it. That's what I'm going to say if they ask."

They didn't ask. The meeting was short and to the point: Grote on, Norment off. Jochums was right; this was going to create a world of trouble for months afterward, with accusations of racism in the sport. Grote left the room knowing his performance needed to prove the coaches had made the right choice.

U.S.A. Swimming was finally going to find its first African-American Olympian in 2000, when a lightning-fast sprinter named Anthony Ervin would make the team and then tie his Phoenix Swim Club teammate, Gary Hall, Jr., for an Olympic gold medal in the 50-meter freestyle. Ironically enough, after the years of planning and hoping, U.S.A. Swimming would wholly miss this showcase moment. Ervin was a multicultural mix of Jewish, African-American, Native-American, and Caucasian ancestry, and was so light-skinned most journalists were unaware of his heritage. After making the team at Olympic Trials, Ervin would be wholly caught off guard by the barrage of race-related questions because no one had prepared him for the significance of his achievement.

As expected, the 1999 Pan Pacific Championships came down to the final relay, winner take all. Eight teams raced, but all eyes were fixed on the pool's center, where Australia and the United States slugged it out. All of Australia stopped to hold its breath and watch the live national telecast. It was like the final two minutes of the Superbowl with the score tied, the screaming crowd on its feet, and the announcer yelling above the din. Grote was shaking so hard he thought he would lose his balance and fall off the starting blocks. For him, this was ten times more intense than the 1996 Olympics had been. The medley relay's order is always backstroke, breaststroke, butterfly, then freestyle. Lenny Krayzelburg was in the water and swimming. Of the four Americans, only Krayzelburg was certifiably faster than his Australian counterpart. Indeed, he had already set three backstroke world records at the meet. Krayzelburg's job was to create a lead that would be unassailable. Then his teammates would fight to preserve it as the Aussies drew closer and closer.

As Krayzelburg torpedoed toward the wall, he owned a body-length lead. Grote stood on the blocks, waiting for him. The noise reverberated against Grote's skin as it would a drum. He had never felt anything like it. In the next lane was Australia's breaststroker, the teenaged Cowley, who had defeated Wilkens in the final meters of the 200-meter breaststroke. Cowley had also captured the 100-meter breaststroke, and in those two races his fastest times had beaten Grote by 2.4 seconds and 1.2 seconds respectively. In the 100-meter event, that equated to two meters. Krayzelburg's lead was about 1.5 meters.

Grote had to be perfect. "You will not beat me," he thought, breaking his rule of never thinking about the competition. "You will *not* beat me."

Krayzelburg lunged for the wall, the top half of his body disappearing underwater as he stretched backward for maximum reach. He touched in history's second-fastest time just as Grote, his arms swinging, launched. The electronic sensors embedded in the starting block would later show that Grote's feet left the block exactly .03 seconds after Krayzelburg hit the wall, as perfect as it gets. Krayzelburg heaved himself into an empty chair behind the timers to catch his breath.

Grote's race was a blur. The waves of delirious sound pounded his head every time he surfaced to breathe. How was it possible to be more nervous than at the Olympics? He took it out faster than he should have, but at 50 meters he still owned the same lead Krayzelburg had given him. Coming home, he could feel his arms and legs tightening up.

"Long!" he urged himself. "Keep it long. Long! Pull!"

Grote knew Wales was crouched on the blocks, his arms rigidly stretched toward the pool to properly gauge and time Grote's approach. How many years had it been since one Santa Clara swimmer touched the wall and another Santa Clara swimmer dove in during a major international competition? Ten years? Fifteen? There were millions of people watching and not one cared. But if there was one defining moment to signal the triumphant return of the fabled Santa Clara Club, this would be it: Kurt Grote lunging to the wall as Dod Wales flung his body forward with all his might.

Grote touched in 1:01.6, which was 1.2 seconds faster than his individual race. He had done it. His Australian counterpart turned in the same time, which meant the Americans still owned Krayzelburg's body-length lead.

Wales sprinted down the pool harder than he ever had in his life. There was no holding back, none of his usual deliberate caution. He was going to burn all reserves and then try to finish legally. Next to him was an

Australian named Geoff Huegill, the world's No. 2 100-meter butterflyer. In the individual event, he had whipped Wales by .87 seconds.

"Harder, Harder!" Wales shouted in his head. For the first time, he pulled every stroke as hard as he could, not knowing if it would mean disaster in the final homestretch. In the next lane, Huegill was having one of the best swims of his life. But few noticed. That was because Wales was having *the* best. Even as pain flooded his body and he began to shorten up, he held it together. The Australian finished with an astonishing 51.8 seconds, but he did not take over the lead. That was because Wales produced a time of 52.4 seconds, 1.1 seconds faster than his time in finals. The Americans were swimming out of their minds.

On the pool deck, Jochums' thumping heart was nearly breaking his rib cage. Even so, when he saw Wales touch, he sucked in his breath and for an instant the world stopped in place. Jochums had known Grote would exceed expectations, but hadn't known what to expect from Wales. It was one of those rare moments a coach feels only once or twice a year, an instant when everything he thinks he knows about a person is turned on its head. This swim would permanently change the dynamic of their relationship.

"That was it, Dod; that is the race that makes you," Jochums thought. "The boy died, but he did it. He overswam the first twenty-five meters worse than a high schooler. Your country is battling to be number one in the world and it comes down to you and it's your first international meet. How do you respond? Jesus, you respond like Dod Wales."

A year earlier, at the 1998 World Championships, the United States had lost this race for the first time ever. It had lost when Australian Michael Klim, who would later be named World Swimmer of the Year, raced the butterfly leg against American Neil Walker. Bald and bad, Klim had won that duel by nearly three seconds. Now it was 1999 on the Aussie's home turf. Klim was faster than ever, and he was ready to bury the Americans again, this time as Australia's freestyle anchor. Racing him was none other than Walker, who for more than a year had been dreaming of revenge. Earlier in the week, Klim had won the 100-meter freestyle title. Walker had finished second by .2 seconds. Now Wales finished and Walker flew off the block. An instant later Klim tore after him like a shark.

It was the final 100 meters of what had become history's greatest international swim meet. Seven world records had fallen, the most in many years. But more important, true parity had emerged, not only between Australia and the United States, but on all levels. Finally Australia was ready to step into the gap left a decade earlier by the collapse of the Soviet Union. Now one final lap would determine the best team going into the Olympics. The Australian crowd was frenzied with joy. Surely the great Klim would catch the American.

Only he didn't. He couldn't. Klim's first 50 meters would have won nearly every 50-meter race ever held in that distance. He flipped simultaneously with Walker, but somehow the American didn't panic. He protected his small lead down the homestretch and touched first by less than .2 seconds, 3:36.37 to 3:36.54.

Team USA had won. It didn't matter that Klim had actually jumped early by .06 seconds and was disqualified. All that mattered was that Team USA had won.

In the stands, Wilkens felt elation as pure as anything he knew. He wildly hugged his teammates, screamed at the ceiling, and hugged some more. Despite his frustrations, he would leave the meet as the only American to win one medal of each color, gold, silver, and bronze. On the pool deck, the four relay swimmers raised their tired arms in victory. There is almost nothing as singularly beautiful and momentarily complete as winning, and there never will be.

Jochums was being buffeted and knocked around by the ecstatic American swimmers. When the U.S. team had touched first, the coach's body had flooded from head to toe. Flooded with what? Pride? Joy? Relief? He desperately wanted to get back to Santa Clara and prove he could train the world's best swimmers. But it had been so long since he had experienced a moment like this. So many hardships. So much lost, so much regained.

Never. Never in his most optimistic dreams did he believe he could experience this feeling again, this shimmering vibrancy that comes with winning something hard-fought. Around him, young hotshot kids—just children, many not old enough to drink, none old enough to understand how a life could self-destruct or how dreams can eventually yellow and curl—were dancing and high-fiving and squeezing each other's perfect, adrenaline-filled bodies. They were having the time of their lives, not knowing this was a moment they would carry with them always, that they would hold onto the glow from this day until they were old and cloudy-eyed, until they lay on white hospital sheets that smelled faintly of a pool.

Thousands of small American flags fluttered everywhere. They had appeared from nowhere and seemed to gallop and cavort in the happy buck and swoon of the frenzied American spectators. The rest of the natatorium was a shell of disgruntled quiet. But then came the applause. It picked up, growing louder and louder until the natatorium thundered. The fans were sophisticated and knew they had just witnessed the best swim meet ever held. Jochums closed his water-stained blue notebook, the one he had carried to every meet in 1999. Who would read it anyway, besides the few he let come through Santa Clara's slatted gate? Of those, who could ever understand the story written between the lines?

"Two," he thought as he watched the bedlam. "There were four swimmers on the relay, and two were mine."

He had to stop himself right there. He wasn't going to let these people see him cry.

PART III

DARKNESS

September 1999 to April 2000

CHAPTER EIGHT

The pressure increased when practices resumed in mid-September at Santa Clara. Before, there had been an overwhelming sense of being on a mission. Now there was an additional awareness that a clock was ticking. With the summertime swimmers back at school, the pool was again a wide-open prairie with only the elite churning through the waters.

Jochums had returned from Australia knowing exactly how he would adjust the training. An Olympic gold medal in the 400-meter I.M. would come home to Santa Clara or he'd die fighting for it. The day after he returned to California, he began to transfer additional coaching responsibility to his assistant, John Bitter. Jochums would continue to do so from now until the Olympic Trials until Bitter was overseeing most of the team. That way, the head coach could focus better on Wilkens, every lap, every practice.

Wilkens had ended the 1999 season ranked No. 1 in the world in the 200-meter I.M., No. 3 in the 400-meter I.M., and No. 9 in the 200-meter breaststroke. When he stepped through Santa Clara's worn gate and re-entered its insular world, he carried with him a list of his own changes. While the coach wanted more backstroke and more strength through pulling, the swimmer believed he needed more sprint and speed work. They argued lightly about it, testing each other's flex points. Both now wanted the 400-meter I.M. so badly they were willing to forsake the other two events. But they were also daring and rogue enough to think they could make the Olympics in all three. Soon that would be the one thing they could agree on. Neither man realized it as September's golden days warmed the pool's surface, but they were about to enter into a dramatic and confrontational test of wills that would last all winter.

The first time Grote showed up for practice, he flung open the metal gate, cried hello, and bounded happily onto the deck. His Pan Pac relay performance had been nothing short of astounding and it had changed everything. Pushed up against a wall, he had responded like a champion. Finally he had the confirmation that his former level of greatness was returning. The 200-meter breaststroke had proved his heart; the relay had reassured him his speed was still there. Those two mental victories were exactly what he needed to initiate the most intense training period of his life. No more medical school, no more doubt. His muscles crackled impatiently to be put to use. On the flight home, all he could think about was training, and he became so excited, he couldn't sit still. Before, every day had mattered; now every hour did. He had fallen behind his original schedule, but realistically the Olympic push had just begun. He was the only swimmer at Santa Clara who had been through the grind and knew what the coming months would require. There was time to succeed, but no time for any more setbacks. Grote's plan was to supplement his swimming by biking 1,000 miles in September through the rolling foothills of the Santa Cruz mountains west of Stanford University. That would build a foundation of leg strength to last through the rainy winter. He had last biked seriously prior to the 1996 Olympic Trials and was convinced the work had put him on the Olympic team.

Grote also made a decision to ditch Santa Clara's fast-paced dryland program. Three days per week, the swimmers performed a grueling hour of nonstop exercises with medicine balls and light weights. Grote had never fully embraced the program because he preferred power lifting; now he figured the only way he was going to beat Tom Wilkens and the rest of the world was to take command of his own destiny. Immediately when he returned from Sydney—while Wilkens and Wales gave themselves mini-vacations—Grote had thrown himself into a daily three-hour weight-lifting regime at the Decathlon Club, a posh spa in Santa Clara. In exchange for a free membership, he lent his name to the club and occasionally taught celebrity lessons. It catered to nearby high-tech businesses like Yahoo! and Intel, and when Grote began showing up every day for several hours, the other members assumed he was another twentysomething, retired Silicon Valley millionaire.

The world champion had recast himself as the underdog and was feeding off the righteous energy it provided. This was proving easier than he thought, because he had slipped from being ranked No. 2 in both his events to No. 30 in the 100-meter breaststroke and No. 18 in the 200-meter breaststroke. Never in his career, even when he first came on the national scene more than six years earlier, had he been ranked as low as No. 30. He was clandestine about the biking and specifically did not want Wilkens to know of it. The knowledge that he was gaining an edge propelled him up the steep inclines his first days on the bike. *Stay in the saddle,* he told himself. To stand while climbing a hill was a form of defeat. Up on bucolic Skyline Boulevard above Silicon Valley, he sailed through jagged squares of sunlight that filtered through the redwood forests. He rolled in and out of inexplicable cold pockets, listened to the rhythm of his chain, and felt the familiar raw burn in his legs. He had no idea, none whatsoever, that down in the valley Wilkens was simultaneously riding a stationary bike and trying to keep it secret from him.

Meanwhile, Wales had experienced his own transformation Down Under. When he resumed practicing in September, the butterflyer was a changed man. He was still inscrutable and remained outside the collective circle. He was still consciously trying to be selfish. But he now believed with certitude that he could make the Olympic team and join his father on the mountaintop of Olympus.

Wales did not draw conclusions quickly, but once he did, they were set in stone. He had ended the 1999 season ranked No. 2 in the United States and No. 12 in the world. At the Pan Pacs, the three racers who beat him in the 100-meter butterfly finals were fast but not invincible. Wales had studied them deliberately, taking in their supple arms and muscle-bound legs, watching the way they interacted and how they handled the prerace pressures. Even before his own race, he had kept an eye on their movements. He was a student of the sport searching for some physical attribute that gave them an edge. Finding none, he concluded their advantage must be mental. That was something he could compete with, and he had all winter to lay the groundwork. As always, it was a race against himself.

Finally, there was the backstroker Blahnik, who had not raced at the Pan Pacific Championships. He had another semester of schoolwork before graduating with a degree in computer science, so he alternated training between Stanford and Santa Clara. Or so he said. Thanks to his wholly unexpected runner-up finish to Lenny Krayzelburg at U.S. nationals, Blahnik had ended the year globally ranked No. 3 in the 200-meter backstroke. That was a burden he could live without. Everywhere he walked, he could hear the whir of high-tech Silicon Valley beckoning like a siren's song. So while Jochums and the others were in Australia, Blahnik had begun checking out part-time jobs. Any opportunity might offer a backdoor escape from swiming.

The peace he envisioned looked like an office cubicle. It was one of dozens of cubicles that would be mazed together in a long, rectangular room. There would be attached conference rooms, fully stocked refrigerators, and wild-haired coders strung out on caffeine and cowboy dreaming. A person could lose his identity in a place like that. He could slip on a jacket of anonymity, put down his head, and go unnoticed. The cubicle partitions would be gray, or maybe a more stylish beige. There would be a 19" color monitor at the desk and a symphony of tapping keyboards in the air. The room would smell of new computers, freshly laid rugs, and gourmet coffee. The conversations would tumble from all directions, and they would come in the form of coded languages that people from different continents, with different ways of life, used to communicate. Common meanings would be discovered in the strings and patterns of C++ code. Together they would unravel the complex and tangled intricacies of JavaScript, Perl, XML, and HTML.

This was what Blahnik wanted. And no one, no matter how hard he or she might try, could have convinced the swimmer that nearly every worker in every imagined cubicle would have jumped at the chance to have Blahnik's Olympic opportunity. Or maybe he did realize that. If he did, the knowledge was probably one more burden.

Outside the slatted gate of the Santa Clara Swim Club in the fall of 1999, the Silicon Valley that sang to Blahnik buzzed, hummed, and mouse-clicked twenty-four hours a day. The white men in the pool had just become an ethnic minority in California, the first time Caucasians had lost their majority status in any state in the Union. All-night restaurants near the swim center were doing brisk business at 1 A.M. as crack-eyed programmers showed up for omelets that were either dinner or breakfast; they weren't sure which. E-commerce, the Internet, Pentium II, B2B, portals, ISPs, P2P—it was a good time to be gainfully employed. The NASDAQ stock market, which was fueled by Santa Clara County, was hitting record highs every week. Venture capital money flowed faster than SCSC's pool water. Save Blahnik, this was a world the swimmers and coaches rejected every day when they entered the pool.

And so the race to the Olympics resumed. In the movie version, the all-seeing camera would pan around the world to reveal the thousands of athletes engaged in the exact same quest. The camera would come to a halt in a University of Virginia dormitory in Charlottesville, Virginia. There, the new breaststroke phenomenon, sophomore Ed Moses, was standing back to admire the signs he had just posted on his dorm room walls. They offered the Olympic credo, "Citius, Altius, Fortius," Latin for "Swifter, Higher, Stronger." The famous phrase originated with the modern Olympic Games' patriarch, Parisian Baron Pierre de Coubertin. De Coubertin had learned it from a Parisian priest friend, who had discovered the motto while teaching at a French school. The words, apparently of unknown origin, were carved in stone above the school's entrance. Now Ed Moses, the world's new No. 1 breaststroke swimmer, was making them his own. For every mile Grote logged on the bike, Moses was hopping one-footed up a flight of stairs after the rest of his Cavalier swim team had quit for the day.

Then the all-seeing camera would show the Santa Clara swimmers adjusting to the groove of their fall training routine. It would be an idyllic image. Yet the mood would shift and the camera would skitter back across the continent to a windowless, airless pool in Washington, D.C. At first the water would seem empty. But then a dark, ominous form would appear. It would move fast, but the viewer could tell it was a body that had been injured. One could also see that whatever the injury was, it had been pushed aside and ignored. Silently the swimmer churned lap after unremitting lap, real fury parting the waves. The camera would finally show the swimmer getting out, having swum the equivalent of three practices in one session. He would limp, but the knee would not be mentioned by him or his Curl-Burke coach. They had talked about it once and they had agreed to never talk about it again. The swimmer would be back again the next day for more. He alternated between Curl-Burke and his old college team in Ann Arbor, Michigan, but soon he would decide to remain in D.C. permanently, where he had started out so many years before. Tom Wilkens' main medley rival, Tom Dolan, was becoming stronger by the hour.

Everything went smoothly for about forty-eight hours. Then Jochums was waylaid by the most trivial and offensive type of problem: a financial one. But to understand the problem, it is first necessary to understand the man.

Like most great coaches, Dick Jochums detested anything remotely bureaucratic. He hated spreadsheets and financial planning, hated the calculator buttons that were always too small for his meaty fingers and the organizational strategy meetings that lasted forever and went no-where. He found the very act of sitting behind a desk awful. He needed to move and feel the wind in his face. His place was the pool deck.

His single-minded focus on building champions explained why Santa Clara's stunning revival had never been showcased by the local media, for Jochums had no patience for public relations. It explained why each year SCSC scrambled to cover its bills while existing in the world's fastest-growing and most affluent region. It explained why the club had no capital-giving campaign, why no congratulatory banner had hung from the team clubhouse after SCSC won the 1997 national champion-ship by a single point. It explained why few people knew 150 world records had been set in the Santa Clara pool, many by the club's nearly 50 Olympians. To Jochums, everything beyond the froth and passion found in the pool was white noise. He was particularly scornful of money. He thought its accumulation bred complacency and a misguided sense of entitlement. He ridiculed the way it consumed so many lives.

This ethos pervaded Santa Clara. It pervaded to the point where life seemed divided between only two possible choices: Accumulate wealth or lead a meaningful existence. One or the other. To Jochums—and therefore to the club—money represented a means to an end, nothing more. Often when the not-for-profit club was cash-starved, the impatient coach had paid the bills using a personal credit card. It made the problem disappear and let him get back to coaching. Jochums was not a rich man; in fact, he made less than some twenty-two-year-old software engineers directly out of college. But over the previous four years, he had cumu-latively floated the team approximately $60,000 (all of which was re-imbursed). Similarly, when a cash-strapped post-graduate swimmer was too poor to pay for travel, Jochums made a handshake deal to exchange airfare and hotel costs for the swimmer's commitment to teach swim lessons. Meanwhile, dollars were so hard to come by that the team was often unable to address basic shortcomings. The assistant coaches worked in a drafty office that had no centralized heating. The ugly blue carpet in the team room was so old and threadbare Mark Spitz might have stretched on it thirty years earlier. Jochums had an individual to oversee the finances, but they met only several times per month and that was just for a perfunctory review.

The tenuous and loose hand-to-mouth lifestyle had worked for four years. But shortly before Jochums had departed for the Pan Pacific Championships, troubling irregularities appeared in the accounting books. Then, at the first close inspection, the club's fragile financial state unraveled. Tens of thousands of dollars were unaccounted for. It was discovered that taxes which everyone thought had been paid had not been. Looking closer, it seemed nearly twenty swimmers had never been billed for travel and lodging at the 1997 U.S. nationals. That alone represented nearly $30,000 in uncollected outlays. Membership billing (dues were $85 per month) was months behind schedule. The club's adult swim program, which delivered as much as $40,000 in direct annual revenue, was discovered to have no billing infrastructure whatsoever except a much-abused honor-code payment system that had been in place for a dozen years. Anyone could see this program alone was losing thousands of dollars annually in uncollected dues.

"What the hell is going on here?" Jochums roared. Like thousands of struggling not-for-profits, Santa Clara Swim Club had no significant cash reserves or endowment. For such a group, any financial hiccup is a full-blown problem. But this was more than a hiccup; it represented a major crisis.

The club had working for it several office assistants, including one responsible for finances, as well as several assistant coaches and a small army of volunteer parents. Many could have had access to records, receipts, and loose cash. Nearly every dollar passed through several hands before reaching the bank. Rule No. 1 for any nonprofit organization is that one person handles the lockbox while another handles the lockbox's key and records. That wasn't always the case here. SCSC's finances were kept on a simple Quicken computer program that was not password-protected. This was a public pool, but the office was left open even when no team representative was present. Over the decades, the team had had a horrible history with money that included misappropriated funds, accusations of embezzlement, and rumors of outright thievery. When Jochums had arrived in 1995, the club was in hock to the U.S. government for thousands of dollars because of delinquent tax problems. Those inherited problems, he had been assured in a financial report in mid-1998, had been cleared. Or had they?

Jochums was a crafty man who knew how to spin a story to protect himself, but in this case he seemed very truly blindsided. When the first problems had surfaced before the Minneapolis and Sydney competitions, they seemed containable. But by the time the coach returned to California in mid-September, they had grown three heads and were breathing fire. Money was missing. Lots of it. Suddenly, he heard echoes of the long-forgotten and unproven stealing allegations leveled against him at the University of Arizona. He was at a complete loss. In his view, the financial reports he had regularly received indicated the house was in order. Also at a complete loss was the club's volunteer board of directors, which was not expected to perform due diligence and had no reason to question the financial information Jochums had passed along during the previous years. The board had repeatedly requested an external audit, but Jochums rejected the idea on the grounds it cost too much money. What pencil pusher could tell him anything about building champions and running his club? Now he thought that was one of the dumbest decisions he had ever made.

In October Jochums fired the person responsible for managing the club's finances. Subsequently, the individual hit him with a flurry of allegations. Jochums was accused of secretly diverting club funds into a personal insurance policy (he was; only it wasn't a secret, it was part of his original contract) and buying personal items on the team credit card (disgusted, he produced the necessary receipts). The fired worker also charged intimidation, harassment, and other serious personal accusations against both Jochums and the assistant Bitter. Poisoned words flew back and forth. But who was right and who was wrong? It was impossible to tell. In the long run, the angry cross-accusations were never going to be conclusively proved or disproved by either side.

All this was happening behind closed doors with the board. The coach was furious, furious at himself for his lack of oversight and furious at being maligned. He couldn't stop asking what any of this had to do with building the Olympic dream. He produced the paperwork necessary to refute most of the accusations. But some of the personal attacks were grenades guaranteed to send shrapnel far and wide, regardless of their veracity. Most important, Jochums remembered all too well from his last, horrible days at Arizona how quickly lives can be destroyed, how enemies will attack the moment they sense a weakness. And because of Arizona, where no stealing accusation was ever substantiated, much less processed and proved, he forever had a shadow over his head.

Since he no longer had a person overseeing the club's finances, Jochums began opening finance-related mail for the first time. In the first week, he grimly tore open an IRS envelope. As he read its contents, the room seemed to tip. He felt like he had been punched. The letter said the club owed $97,000 in back taxes.

That was when the truth settled on him. The club had nowhere near that much money in the bank. It didn't even own its own pool, which was rented from the city for a nominal charge. The Santa Clara Swim Club was on the edge of financial ruin. How had this happened? Only an instant ago Santa Clara was delivering to Team USA the winning relay at the Pan Pacific Championships. In the coming weeks, Jochums was going to write the SCSC community two emergency letters asking for donations. Then this proud man would go with hat in hand to the city of Santa Clara and ask for an emergency loan to bail him out. Yes, he would have to say, he was in complete charge of his organization and the people who worked there. But no, he couldn't explain what had happened to the money because he simply didn't know.

The possible bankruptcy of the birthplace of modern American swimming would become big news, and the scandal would twice find its way to the front page of the *San Jose Mercury News*' local section. Television crews would huddle outside the pool's slatted gate as their reporters excitedly covered the great club's imminent demise. How did those crews intuitively know not to cross the threshold into the swimmers' hallowed world? When the dust finally settled, the total amount owed the government in unpaid taxes and penalties would be $122,752.23. The amount of additional money lost because of sloppy oversight and management was surely in the tens of thousands of dollars. There were dozens of ungodly wealthy people associated with the club, including many new-wealth millionaires. But during the turmoil, Jochums would collect a single donation of $3,000, and it would come from a board member.

When he had conviction, Jochums was a hell-crazed Hannibal charging unprotected into battle. But here he needed to be more tentative and cautious than ever before. He would tear down the walls of the Santa Clara clubhouse to find who, if anyone, had been stealing from him. But this was an Olympic year and that changed everything. Nothing was more important than preserving the training continuity, not even determining right or wrong.

Days passed. The situation flared up, then seemed to settle itself. Although weeks of focus were lost, everything appeared to be on track. Yet that was an illusion. These early troubles were just a warmup for the real act, a smattering of rainfall before the Category 5 hurricane. Standing on deck as the first cool winter winds began arriving from the west, the coach couldn't possibly fathom that the worst was still to come. Nor would he have been able to believe that money, a thing which has absolutely nothing to do with glory or greatness, would very nearly rip the Olympic dream right out of his hands.

CHAPTER NINE

It didn't seem like much, just some soreness in the left knee about 30 miles into his first bicycle ride in early September. "That's strange," Kurt Grote thought. "What muscle is *that?*" He tried to pull up a mental image of the knee from his medical textbooks. Nothing. It was an odd kind of hurt, but since it wasn't too bad, Grote continued riding for another 50 miles. He remembered to ice it as soon as he returned home.

That had been nearly two months earlier, and Kurt Grote had not kicked breaststroke since. In fact, he had barely swum at all.

It was late October and his world was in flames around him. He was distraught, helpless, and overcome with the pathos of bad luck. He still couldn't understand what had happened. One day he went on a long bike ride and felt a pinpointed pain above his left knee. It was so small it hid under a freckle and it should have gone away in a day. He had biked several more times to stay on course for his 1,000-mile month. But a week later the pain had become persistent, and he visited Stanford's top sports medicine doctors. It wasn't a muscle, they had told him. It was the tendon that connected the left quad to the femur and he'd frayed it.

That type of injury doesn't happen often, and it was almost certainly caused by Grote's enthusiasm. He had attempted to do too much too soon. The swimmer had nodded to the doctor, all the while calmly thinking, *Just tell me how long.* It was only when the physician explained the two options were to either undergo immediate arthroscopic surgery and endure a three-month recovery, or to wait indefinitely for the natural healing process, that the swimmer had felt the office floor fall away.

Jochums had adamantly argued for surgery. It would alleviate the problem and the recovery period was a known quantity. There was simply no other choice with the Olympic Trials ten months away. But Grote instead elected for aggressive physical therapy, which looked like it would take several weeks. He couldn't believe what a senseless, non-traumatic injury this was. The better the athlete, the more impossible it is to accept that a perfect body can fail.

Grote went to one of the world's best physical therapy centers. Also there was the 1996 Olympic decathlon champion, Dan O'Brien, working through a similar injury. Pro athletes came and went. If any place could help the swimmer, this one could. Grote watched silently as the therapist tested his knee. The swimmer had a knot of dread in his gut. The therapist stepped back and said brightly, as if it were good news, "If things go well, we'll have this taken care of in four months."

Grote left the building unable to see straight. It had been an easy bike ride, for God's sake. He had immediately begun intense rehabilitation work. But soon the days had become weeks and the injury was worse than ever. First, it had been impossible to kick breast; next he couldn't push off the wall. Then swimming freestyle had become so difficult, it was necessary to tether himself to an elastic cord and swim in place. The athlete was virtually crippled. A cortisone shot had done nothing to help.

There is an unwritten code in sports that says celebration is public, suffering private. It is a code of warriors and champions, people who don't make excuses. And so Grote refused to talk to his teammates about the injury. For their part, they saw his struggles and steered clear. Bad luck has a way of jumping from one person to another, and no one wanted to risk getting too close. Besides, what could they say? Grote was a proud man and found it unbearably hard to acknowledge weakness. From their cautious distance, his teammates had no way of knowing that after six weeks of struggling with no improvement, his mind had become more frayed than his tendon. It was now mid-October and this was a grave situation. He had lost weeks of critical training. No one realized he was driving 120 miles round-trip to San Francisco three times per week for three hours of physical therapy. Or that everywhere he went he carried an ice bag. It was almost maniacal. A second cortisone shot had failed. There were days when he would give anything for a cast and crutches, just some stupid props to prove his pain was real.

There was one teammate to whom Grote might have turned. But that teammate was the one person to whom Grote could show no vulnerability—Wilkens. There was just too much at stake. Wilkens felt it, too. They talked nearly every day and never once mentioned the knee. Meanwhile, the coaches acted like typical coaches. In sports, suffering is seen as a good thing, as enabling a sharper and more accentuated life. That is, as long as it doesn't interfere with workout. Jochums offered encouragement, but privately wondered whether the injury would be so bad if there were no Ed Moses suddenly burning up the pool.

While Grote anguished, the others forged ahead with their dreams. Wilkens continued to look strong. Wales, collected and deliberate, followed his own path and seemed to grow more confident daily. Blahnik was showing up consistently. Time marched on. Mid-October faded into early November. The sun lost its heat, and Grote, who knew every hour counted if he wanted to achieve his Olympic dream, could still barely flex his leg. He took another cortisone shot, his third in eight weeks, which was extremely unhealthy. Suddenly Grote looked at the calendar and realized it was too late to reconsider surgery. The swimmer who had been so professional and untouchable was now at wit's end. The situation had grown so bad so quickly that five separate times he and his wife, Amy, sat at their small pine dining table and discussed retirement.

It was inevitable Grote would have a heart-to-heart talk with Assistant Coach John Bitter, because both were scraping bottom. Bitter had been in a sour, seriously depressed mood for weeks, partly because of a recent breakup with his girlfriend, but mostly it was due to the acrimony and finger-pointing surrounding the financial scandal. When he had signed on as an underpaid assistant four years earlier, it had been with the verbal understanding that Jochums would retire after the 2000 Olympics and Bitter would be in line to take over the club. The possibility of someday running the famed Santa Clara Swim Club was what had made the assistant's long, thankless hours palatable. But now Jochums was feeling so young and sprightly thanks to his success with Wilkens that he had recently pushed his retirement out to 2004. Like his swimmers, Jochums saw time in four-year blocks organized around the Olympic Games. The decision effectively squashed any ambitions Bitter had about taking over the reins anytime soon. He was a great coach, but he was thinking it was time to get out of the business altogether. For two months, Jochums had worked diligently to help Grote believe he could still achieve his Olympic dream. Then Bitter blew it away with a single sentence. They were standing on the empty deck, surrounded by nothing but gray, wind-swept concrete. Bitter simply told Grote the truth.

"Kurt, quit today so you go out a champion," Bitter said. "You have a full life ahead of you as a doctor. You have a wife who loves you. Your future is brighter than anyone else's at the pool. Walk away now and you'll be remembered as the one who won the Pan Pac relay for the U.S., not as the defending world champion who failed to make the [2000] Olympic team."

Grote looked like a pallbearer. All the robust confidence and excitement he had possessed the day he returned from Australia was long gone. The situation had to be even more dire than he feared if his own coach was telling him to quit. The swimmers trusted Bitter tremendously. If Jochums was all about emotion, then the assistant was about reason. Grote said he needed to think. Jochums later exploded when Bitter told him about the conversation. But it had a remarkable effect on the swimmer.

"He's right; I have an exit," Grote thought that evening. He was home on his couch with an ice bag draped over his knee. Grote's grandfather had been an amateur painter and the swimmer had his artwork hanging on the wall. The cat on his lap was named Carmen, after the opera. Amy's piano was against the wall with sheet music strewn all over it. This was the home of a Renaissance man. Grote suddenly had a memory of swimming for Stanford. The team was often given the choice of swimming an easy interval or a hard one. Of course everyone always took the harder one. That's what athletes did. Grote began to see his current situation the same way. "Do I want the easy or hard path?" he mused. "That's easy: It has to be the hard one. I can't be a quitter; I need to know how this turns out."

Beginning the next day, his attitude changed for the better. He began investing his whole life into getting ready for the day his knee healed. He could once again gingerly push off the wall, so he put away the tethered cord, immobilized his legs with pulling gear, and began pulling his entire workout breaststroke. Breaststroke requires so much strength to be technically correct that most specialists, including Grote, would normally swim it for only about twenty-five percent of their workout. Soon his upper body rippled with new muscle. His back muscles became so huge they seemed to unfold like wings. He added a fourth hour to his near-daily weight-lifting sessions. It was a Rocky-like revitalization. Even though his arms were exhausted by overuse, he soon increased his bench press fifty percent to 285 lbs. At the end of every four-hour workout, he did 100 pull-ups.

But even so, breaststroke is primarily a kicker's event and Grote knew it. That knowledge sent fear running through his bloodstream and made him swim so hard with his arms that he could barely turn his steering wheel on the way home from practice. It was now early November 1999, and with Trials only nine months away, he was a desperate athlete. *If I get my legs back . . .* he would think, never really finishing the sentence. He hadn't cried, not even once. Grote didn't cry because he never cried. But even as his arms grew stronger by the day, he knew his legs were growing weaker. One evening, he and Amy made a very difficult decision. If by February 1, 2000, there was no noticeable improvement, he was going to follow up Bitter's recommendation to be a champion. He was going to quit.

. . .

Autumn, not spring, is swimming's preseason. It is a time to build an aerobic base, develop a routine, and set goals for the year. The few meets held between August and January are dress rehearsals to real racing, which begins in January. However, the routine differed this year. Because of the Trials, the hard fall training would steamroll through the winter and continue until U.S. nationals in early spring. Even then, the break would be short. Hard work would immediately resume and continue until July. For most of Santa Clara's group, the ten months that lay ahead represented the longest period of straight training they had ever experienced.

Jochums and Wilkens had begun their fighting soon after practice resumed. The coach might have been living his days for the swimmer, but he spent many of them trying to break his athlete's willfulness. There was no apparent reason for this except to make the swimmer tougher than he already was. The ancient Greeks had a word, *agon*, that referred to the struggle or conflict inherent in athletics and all of life. Jochums profoundly believed that excellence emerged from *agon,* and by mid-November he was regularly hurtling near-impossible sets at Wilkens, sets so incredible that *Swimming World Magazine*'s Editor-in-Chief Phil Whitten later said he would have published them if he had known. Wilkens took each challenge and angrily shoved it back at Jochums with astonishing results.

On deck, they sounded like they were speaking a foreign language: "You leave on the top doing four by eight hundred [yards] pull with a tube on eight-thirty," Jochums barked at Wilkens. "You descend to seven-forty by number three. You put number four below seven-forty by even splitting, and then go right into a four-hundred lungbuster."

"How 'bout if I . . ." Wilkens started.

"I believe the set begins in ten seconds, and for your sake I hope you're ready," Jochums interrupted.

Even if a layman listening couldn't figure out the jargon, he'd understand its significance. He'd understand when he saw Wilkens' veteran teammates finish their own sets and then watch in a kind of weird holy awe as he swam. Some cheered, and Wilkens smiled between gulps of air before pushing off again.

Jochums, who had thought he'd seen it all months earlier, would be jolted into a zone of disbelief by a performance. It happened several times per week. As he now watched this set, the decades slid together and he started talking about the Tim Shaw, his untouchable teenage star from the mid-1970s. Then Wilkens finished swimming and Jochums' easy smile disappeared as he berated the swimmer for some small flaw no one else saw.

"I think I need to concentrate . . ." Wilkens began to say.

"I think you need to stop talking and begin your lungbuster," Jochums said.

Wilkens' eyes narrowed, but he nodded. If he so much as looked sideways at his coach, Jochums would cut him off. Wilkens seethed. No other Santa Clara swimmer suffered twenty percent of what he did.

It was a mid-November Transylvania morning. The very sky was cold and the air soulless. Wet leaves littered the ground, and outside the gate bare trees raked the sky. On deck, the mood suggested impending calamity. Wilkens had arrived for practice petulant and exhausted. The pressure of Olympic Trials was already breathing circles on his windowpanes. He still was fretting about how to act as a role model. He was haunted by his physical breakdown in Australia. But of all those swirling concerns, he was most worried about his deteriorating relationship with Jochums. Wilkens had never known an antagonistic relationship. He couldn't understand that this was part of the process, that he was being tested and hardened for what lay ahead.

At the pool's edge, Jochums looked ready to swing at anything that crossed his path. He was set on edge by both the ongoing financial troubles and Kurt Grote's knee problem. There were heavy circles under his eyes and he had gained weight around the middle. It was inevitable that all his pent-up frustrations would eventually explode, and today was going to be the day. It so happened that Grote, Wales, Blahnik, and nearly everyone else had the morning off. There would be only four swimmers in the pool's twenty-three short-course lanes to see it.

Not surprisingly, it was a Daphnis sister who started it. The club had two teenage Greek-Americans sisters, Aphrodite and Artemis, who were training for the Greek Olympic team. Their relationship with Jochums was incredibly strained. Neither girl responded to the coach's aggressive style and they showed little enthusiasm for training at Santa Clara. They were phenomenal talents and had already enjoyed great national-level success, but Jochums and Bitter believed they only worked hard enough to get by. In this pool, there was no greater sin. The sisters had borne the brunt of many tirades, some of which were wholly unfair.

On this morning, Aphrodite, the pretty older sister, thought her pulling set was 4 × 200-yard freestyle, even though Jochums had clearly called for 4 × 400 yards. She swam 200 yards and stopped. Her sister briefly stopped swimming to correct her, but a few minutes later Aphrodite made the same mistake again.

Jochums was close to getting very mad when Wilkens glided into the wall. The swimmer was having a terrible workout, and without warning—completely independent of anything going on with the girls or with Jochums—he cracked. The instant the guard is let down, the Olympic pressure can grip the heart. Wilkens had just completed a fast 3:52 for 400 yards while wearing a tube, but wasn't happy with it. Also, the tube's metal air nipple had been gouging deep into his ankle during the whole swim. He yanked off the tube, flung it toward the clubhouse, and swore so loudly it could be heard by anyone walking a dog within 200 yards of the club. Then he adjusted his goggles, looked at the pace clock, and prepared to restart his set.

Jochums snapped. He'd been spoiling for a real fight for weeks, no more of the sissy sniping he and Wilkens had been engaged in since September. The coach spewed a long, epithet-filled barrage of personal insults at Wilkens, attacking his heart and attitude. It was so laced with fury that any nearby dog-walker—already brought up short by Wilkens' primal shout—would have hurried away.

The coach leaned over the water and thundered: "You stupid pea-head! You have no idea how hard that set was yesterday! You have no idea how hard you worked! That's why you're tired and slow. You have no idea what that set meant! Goddammit, get ahold of yourself! Learn how to be a man!"

It was Jochums' style, even in the midst of raging anger, to beat his swimmers down with praise—as if they were too pigheaded and stupid to figure out on their own how talented they were. The coach continued yelling, and Wilkens, staring so furiously at the pace clock he might have burned a hole through it, began talking loudly to himself in order to block out Jochums' voice. If he weren't wearing paddles, he probably would have stuck his fingers in his ears, too. It was the most delightful and juvenile response imaginable. Wilkens defiantly pushed off to start his next repeat.

The previous afternoon, the swimmer had performed four sets of 4 × 200-yard freestyle. The first set was on a 2:15 rest interval, and the interval subsequently proceeded to drop five seconds per set until the final four swims were on 2:00. That is very fast, and Wilkens had averaged 1:52 for all sixteen of them. The 1.8-mile set had been so impressive that afterward Jochums called Stanford to tell the coaches.

Jochums often played up his anger for dramatic effect, but not today. Today, he was truly incensed. As Wilkens swam away, the coach, with a huge windup, savagely kicked Wilkens' heavy swim bag into his lane, where it floated. Aphrodite, still blithely swimming the wrong set in the next lane, could not have picked a worse time to glide into the wall.

"Get that goddamn thing out of his lane!" Jochums yelled at her. Although he swore often, it was almost always reserved for college-age swimmers. Wilkens was already swimming back toward them. With each stroke, the swimmer was angrily smashing his paddles into the water. Poor Aphrodite didn't even know what was going on.

"I said, get that thing out of his way now!" Jochums roared.

Awkward and unable to maneuver her body because the pulling equipment had immobilized her legs, she struggled to navigate into Wilkens' lane. When she got there, she couldn't grab his bag because her paddles were still on.

"What the hell is *wrong* with you?!" Jochums thundered.

He picked up her green Gatorade water bottle and threw it as far as he could. It landed thirty yards away atop the blue tarps that covered the baby pool. Since she couldn't remove the swim bag in time, Wilkens smashed headfirst into it. He ignored it and flipturned as hard as he could, making Jochums jump back to avoid being soaked. For the next several minutes the coach worked at collecting himself. Jochums sent Aphrodite on a five-minute pulling set and watched her closely. Then, before she could take off her pulling gear, he made her to do a final sprint 100.

"Give me fifty-nine seconds on this," he said tersely. "I want one hundred percent, nothing less."

She pushed off and swam away with what was very obviously a half-hearted stroke.

"Hundred percent, my ass," he muttered.

During this time, Bitter was inside the clubhouse talking to the coach of a Top 10 swim school about Aphrodite, who was a high school senior. In swimming, a collegiate coach calls more for a reference check than anything else. An athlete's ability is already out in the open, distilled down to a set of ordered digits that correspond to a time, which corresponds to worth, which is translated into scholarship money to attend a particular university. In American swimming, everyone knows each other, and since there are relatively few programs that consistently develop Division I swimmers, most top college coaches also know a swimmer's training background without having to ask. Whenever a recruiter called Santa Clara about the two sisters, it became an interesting dance. Both were blue-chip national recruits and a number of inquiring coaches would call about the older sister, casually segue to the younger one, and ask how they could convince both to attend the same school.

Aphrodite touched the wall after four laps with a 1:00.3. She wasn't breathing very hard.

"I asked for one hundred yards hard and you gave me hard the last ten yards," Jochums said irritably. "You swim a two-hundred lungbuster and think about why you did that. I know you don't think very often, but you think about that."

She cleared her goggles. Like Wilkens, she refused to take her eyes off the big white pace clock to look at the coach. After the 200 yards, she began to take off her pulling gear.

"No, you give me another one hundred and you hit fifty-nine [seconds]," Jochums said tersely.

He almost never made such a request, just as he almost never gave a surprise set. At Santa Clara, when people failed during practice, they had to live with it until the next go-around. Jochums didn't want them growing accustomed to second chances. They sure didn't have any in competition— or in life. The girl curled her lip and still refused to look at him.

Jochums stepped closer. The earlier indignation and storming fury had drained. In its place was the tone of a guy at the end of a bad morning looking for a little consensus. He quietly said, "Kid, that last one wasn't one hundred percent, and you and I both know it. For Christ's sake, don't do it for me. This matters. What you do right now on this stupid morning when there's no one else here is important to who you are. I know you don't understand why it matters, but I hope someday you will. Do it for yourself. You may be the strongest girl I've ever seen. Do this for yourself."

This was Dick Jochums at his best. The swimming world always heard the explosions, but never the quiet urgings. As Aphrodite began swimming down the pool stronger than before, Wilkens, his own anger still boiling, scorched into the wall. After his outburst, he had retrieved his pulling tube and settled into 10 × 100-yard freestyle pulling on the 1:10 interval. He initially averaged 58 seconds, and in the 12-second window between send-offs Jochums told him to grow up and start acting like a champion. As before, Wilkens looked only at the big pace clock and continued to talk aloud to block out the voice.

Aphrodite touched in 59.3 seconds. Jochums smiled broadly as he read off her time. She refused to acknowledge him as she gathered her equipment and headed to the showers.

By now Wilkens' average had dropped to a low 55 seconds and his back was scarlet. Every time he exhaled, spittle blew out his mouth.

"Set your hands into the wall; don't spin," Jochums said. It was time to get back to business. Wilkens left the wall and Jochums sighed. He was no longer angry. And he was back in 1975.

"When Timmy Shaw was beaten down, he'd say to me, 'That was the best I could do today and I'm proud of it,' " said Jochums as he watched Wilkens flipturn. "There wasn't a damn thing to say to that because he was right. Wilkens doesn't think that way. He's so thickheaded that if it's not an all-time best time, he's pissed. He doesn't consider what he did yesterday or how tired he is. Every day has to be better than the last."

On the last several repeats, Wilkens dropped his time down to 54 seconds. It was uncanny how he regularly channeled his anger into fast swimming. Jochums now had sixteen seconds to talk at him.

"Tom, when you lose your temper, you lose control. Lose control, you lose your edge. Losing your temper doesn't show me you care. I already know you care. Get your stomach right."

By the time the set and the required subsequent 400-yard lungbuster were over, Bitter was back on deck. Wilkens sulked in the water. If anger were oil, the water around him would have been sheeny and rainbowed.

"Feeling a little PMS, Tommy?" Bitter said sweetly. In this male-dominated world, weakness was often associated with being a woman. It happened almost daily. But it never went very far because as a motivating tool, it was a dead end. Nearly every male swimmer spends his formative years, roughly ages eight to twelve, being regularly beaten by girls who have developed earlier and who are therefore substantially stronger and faster. As a result, there may be no other sport where male athletes respect their female counterparts as much.

"What are you talking about, PMS?" Wilkens said irritably.

Bitter gently mocked him until Wilkens smiled. They both knew that they were going to spend the entire evening talking about why Jochums was so hard on Wilkens and what the swimmer could do about it.

"Tom, go swim down and get in touch with your feminine side," Jochums told him. "And don't ever lose control. Get your stomach right."

"I don't even know what that means, 'Get your stomach right,'" Wilkens said. He floated on his back, raised his hands above the waterline, and pretended they were two puppets talking angrily to each other. Then he porpoised away, dipping beneath the surface and pushing off the pool bottom all the way to the other end. He liked the water so much he played in it after practice.

"I used to think mornings like this were the best part of the job," Jochums said as he watched Wilkens. "I loved making them shake. Now I hate it. I'm too old for this. I only do it because I have to."

The anger was gone. But only for today. Jochums put his hands on his hips and turned around to inspect the morning. Outside the pool's gate, the sun had turned the eastern sky a luminous orange. The air was crisp and refreshing. It looked like it was going to be another great day.

CHAPTER TEN

There had been one daily reporter covering the U.S. nationals in Minneapolis. Yet on deck at the fun but meaningless 1999 FINA World Cup Series meet at the University of Maryland outside of Washington, D.C., there were more than thirty journalists from major news sources. Location was indeed everything. But it was also late November and that meant the Olympic Trials were now less than nine months away. That's about the time the media typically begins to notice Olympic sports like swimming. The first stories would be introductions of sorts: Public, meet Swimmer; Swimmer, tell Public what makes you unique. By the time the Olympics rolled around, the average fan would know who to root for and why.

FINA stands for Federation Internationale de Natation Amateur (International Amateur Swimming Federation), and it is the world governing body of aquatic sports. The Switzerland-based organization is in charge of the details that make swimming work: the rules, world rankings, world-record ratifications, drug-abuse detection, arbitration dealings, and so on. Its oversight stretches globally, from Olympic swimming in Sydney to youth waterpolo in Singapore to marathon swimming in Egypt. U.S.A. Swimming Inc., the national governing body that oversees American swimming, is based at the U.S. Olympic Center in Colorado Springs and is a FINA affiliate.

FINA's World Cup Series is a four-continent tour for the world's best swimmers. All competitions on this annual circuit are conducted in the very foreign (at least for U.S. swimmers) short-course 25-meter format. It wasn't until 1991 that FINA began to re-ratify short-course-meter world records. Back in swimming's early days, world records could be officially set in any course. But beginning in 1959, they were limited to Olympic-sized, long-course-meter pools. So from 1959 to 1991, a record-setting swim in a short-course, 25-meter pool was simply classified as a "world best." Only the United States recognizes records in the 25-yard pools, and those are "national records" ("American records" if set by an American).

That means FINA has two separate sets of world records, one for long-course meters and one for short-course meters. It also has two separate World Championships, one for each format. On paper, the two competitions—held in different years—are ostensibly equal. But in reality the Short Course World Championships are so unimportant the United States didn't want to send a formal team to the last one. This is confusing, but it pales in comparison to the inherent schizophrenia of the U.S. national championship picture. Every year, U.S.A. Swimming holds *two* national championships within months of each other, in spring and summer. In the old days, one meet was in yards, the other in long-course meters. That meant in 1966, for example, Dod Wales' father, Ross, could win the 100-*yard* butterfly national title in April, and four months later, in August, Mark Spitz could capture the 100-*meter* butterfly crown.

That was bad enough. But beginning in the 1990s, U.S.A. Swimming switched the spring nationals to meters when it belatedly dawned on everyone that the world wasn't going to embrace yard swimming anytime soon. The move, though largely symbolic, was probably one of the strongest messages U.S.A. Swimming has ever sent that Olympic swimming is its ultimate priority. But at the same time, the switch compounded the fogginess around the national championships. For one thing, the spring meet is significantly diminished in importance, because it falls so close to the NCAA championships that many top collegiate athletes skip it. But far more bizarre, every year U.S.A. Swimming awards two national titles per event.

And the sport wonders why the casual fan gets confused.

But there was no ambiguity at the FINA meet in Maryland. The best thing about the series was that it popularized the art of racing. A meet like this one draws swimmers from all over the world. They come because the series awards purses to the top finishers ($4,000 to win, $2,000 for second, $1,000 for third; an NBA basketball player may make that much during a time-out, but to a swimmer this represents serious prize money), with year-end bonuses to the racers who accumulate the most points and incentive payouts for world records. When combined with the fact that most elite American swimmers care less about time-based success in this format than in long-course or yards swimming, the result is a meet that provides pure drag racing. Professional premeet hype brings in sellout crowds and small venues amp up the enthusiasm.

The series also allowed the American swimming community to perpetuate a cute scam on the media and the casual fan. Since American swimmers compete in short-course meters so rarely, at any serious meet world and national records tend to fall like dominoes. Nothing piques media and general-public interest like a slew of fallen world records in the months before the Olympics. Even the NCAA had jumped into the public-relations game. In honor of the Sydney Olympics, it was going to hold the 2000 NCAA championships in short-course meters.

At the University of Maryland, the atmosphere was informal and relaxed. Santa Clara's half dozen unrested swimmers lounged in the shallow warm-up pool and spent more time catching up with old friends than loosening their muscles before their races. Stars sat on the warm deck and traded jokes. Reporters from NBC, the *New York Times,* the *Washington Post, Sports Illustrated,* and other media outlets comfortably wandered the deck until they bumped into someone like Jenny Thompson, Lenny Krayzelburg, or Tom Dolan. They would tap the swimmer on the shoulder and retreat to a private corner. This is called accumulating "background information" and building "a rapport." The reporters listened to stories and learned about childhoods and talked about the Olympic dream. If you cover sports long enough, it all begins to sound the same. But they, the reporters, diligently took notes in their skinny notepads.

Yet you could tell the journalists' minds were mostly elsewhere. Often their eyes wandered off their subjects and furtively scanned the deck. There was a fresh story here in Maryland, but no one could find him. The journalists had come to see all the top swimmers. But in truth, there was only one person any of them wanted to write about.

. . .

The roar of 1,000 spectators began as soon as the finalists stepped behind the blocks for the 50-meter breaststroke. It grew steadily louder as each athlete's name was called. If applause could climb a staircase, this was what it would sound like. When the announcer reached lane four, the top seed's lane, the yelling and clapping reached a fevered pitch. In the second row of the sold-out stands, Sissy Moses unfurled her huge sign for her son that read: "Part the Water, Moses."

Ed Moses, still stiff from driving for six hours from Charlottesville, Virginia, ignored it all. He stepped on the blocks, diminutive and feisty as always. The starter quieted the crowd. A smirk lingered on Moses' face. The race started. This was one of the world's strongest breaststroke fields, and within three seconds it was apparent that Moses possessed a vigorous, spring-like quickness that no one else could match. It was his secret to success, that quickness. Pound-for-pound, this was the strongest, fleetest man in swimming.

He was challenged by no one and when he won he raised his finger to show he was No. 1. Moses' mother, an elementary school teacher, danced in the aisle and pumped her hands above her head to push up the roof. The hometown crowd roared, and Moses offered a curt bow. In a way, it was a blessing Grote's damaged knee had forced him to scratch the meet and stay home. In his frustrated condition, this was the last thing he needed to see.

Soon after Moses' victory, Tom Wilkens found himself racing the finals of the 400-meter I.M. These meets move fast. The mighty Tom Dolan was in the race as well. It was widely known Dolan, swimming in his first meet since knee surgery, was still at half-speed and cautious. But Wilkens couldn't stop thinking about him. Dolan's presence pulled Wilkens like a magnet, and for the first 250 meters the Santa Clara swimmer eyeballed his competitor's lane constantly. When Dolan fell back on the breast-stroke leg, Wilkens glanced around him for the first time.

"Uh-oh, that wasn't smart," he thought.

Finland's Jani Sievinen, the world record-holder in the 200-meter I.M., was right next to him. Caught by surprise, Wilkens hammered the first half of his freestyle leg and managed to gain a body-length lead. Then he protected it all the way to the finish as Sievinen's last-lap charge failed. Wilkens won; Sievinen was second. Dolan coasted in four seconds later.

Hanging on the lane line and gasping for breath, Wilkens did not yet know an official had disqualified him for a one-handed breaststroke turn (the rules require a two-hand touch on breaststroke and fly). That mistake was going to cost him thousands in prize money. He waved tiredly to the crowd. Two lanes away, Dolan didn't acknowledge the fans, even though, like Moses, this was his hometown crowd. The King of Swimming was breathing hard, but not nearly as hard as Wilkens. He quickly hopped from the pool and as he walked by Wilkens' lane he casually spit on the deck. Dolan had a full goatee and had worn two suits for the race, the second one for extra drag to intentionally slow him down.

Later that evening, Wilkens raced Moses in the 200-meter breaststroke. It wasn't the first time they had raced, but it had new significance, both because Moses was suddenly the most talked-about swimmer in the sport and because this specific race signaled his coming-out party in the 200-meter breaststroke. He was so new he was still learning how to swim beyond 100 meters. Grote, of course, had planned to be swimming right next to them. When the race began, Moses took off like lightning, astounding Wilkens. At the halfway point, the Santa Clara swimmer was in fourth place and more than a body length behind his new Virginia rival.

"A full body length already?" Wilkens thought while suppressing a shiver of panic. "Man, this guy is for real."

Wilkens began a dramatic charge that was reminiscent of the Santa Clara International five months earlier. He easily swept past two swimmers, and by the last lap was closing on Moses considerably. They came toward the finish with Wilkens clicking into a higher gear as Moses was fast running out of gas. But Wilkens couldn't catch him. Moses buried his head, elongated his body into an exclamation point, and hit the wall a finger ahead of Wilkens. The crowd exploded. How incredible was this? As Moses himself admitted, he was barely capable of completing a full-volume, average collegiate workout. Yet he had just beaten the best. There was no longer any doubt that this was the most naturally talented late-blooming breaststroker since a blond San Diegan named Kurt Grote had emerged on the scene six years earlier. Seconds after he won, Moses made what appeared to be the sign of the cross. Only it wasn't that; it was the "Dirty Bird," a jerking, two-armed movement the NFL Atlanta Falcons employed to signify a total butt-kicking.

Sports Illustrated's Olympic reporter, Brian Cazeneuve, was on hand to write a profile about either Lenny Krayzelburg or Jenny Thompson, the two biggest names in swimming. At the Pan Pacifics, Krayzelburg had set three backstroke world records, while Thompson, the new 100-meter butterfly world record-holder, was simply untouchable in anything she swam. But after watching Moses take out Wilkens, Cazeneuve called his New York editors. Forget the other two, he said; the real story was Moses. He started typing:

> Some golfers might throw up their hands in surrender after a slice or a shanked five-iron, but how many pack up their clubs and become world-class in a fallback sport? Swimmer Ed Moses had done that with only two years of full-time training. So meteoric has his rise through the national ranks been that he has to have answered the commandment of his sign-waving mother, Sissy: PART THE WATER, MOSES . . .

Wilkens wasn't the only Santa Clara swimmer frustrated with a runner-up finish. In the finals of the men's 100-meter butterfly, Dod Wales was pitted against his former college roommate and close friend, 6'7" Sabir Muhammad. The two men knew each other's race plans as well as they knew their own. Muhammad would blast off the blocks, try to establish a lead, and then hang on. Wales would build his first 50 meters and charge at the end. The race started, and Muhammad took his commanding lead. He fully realized Wales liked to hang back, so he threw more speed into the race's front half than he normally would. Wales wasn't the kind of swimmer who changed strategies. Muhammad was dying by the race's end but he beat the Santa Clara swimmer by nearly a second. There was a tremendous lesson in that. Muhammad waved gleefully to the crowd and then gave the angry Wales a playful hug. The lesson was this: While Wales' systematic approach was his greatest weapon, it was also his greatest exposure. Wales had lost to a close friend this time, but any competitor who studied him was going to know exactly how he raced.

"Dod, you know why you lost?" Jochums asked afterward.

"Yes, I already know so don't . . ."

"You *lost* because you went out too slow," Jochums said, lifting his voice to override Wales'. "You can't hold back. You're smarter than me, but there's things I know. I'd rather see you die ten feet from the finish than know you had leftover energy after a race."

And that pretty much set the tone for the meet. If mistakes were going to be made, now was the time to make them. Wales nodded and filed the defeat in his vast mental library. He knew that very soon there'd be no more room for error.

. . .

Early December. The World Cup and several other autumn meets were over and the team was now deep into a difficult training cycle. On this cold morning, all swimmers save one had already departed for the weight room. Standing twenty-five feet back from the pool was Jochums. He positively radiated fury. In the water was Wilkens, who angrily slashed through a long pulling set. From the pool rose hundreds of separate wisps of vertical fog. They were about 12 inches long and rose gently into the air, where they performed slow pirouettes. They swirled and caught the sunlight, and twinkled once and then dissipated into the morning. A person could watch them for hours. In the space between swimmer and coach, wetted down and pasted to a kickboard, was a yellow notepad sheet filled with writing. The kickboard was propped in the gutter next to Wilkens' lane like a tombstone.

Their fighting had only intensified in the past month. Humans are remarkably predictable this way. A worthwhile fight will escalate to a pitch. Then it either is resolved or becomes irreconcilable, which is itself a kind of resolution. Jochums was pushing toward some undefined moment of truth. It was as if he wanted to break the swimmer's spirit and then build it back up. He continued to be adamant that Wilkens needed to be tougher and meaner. He continued to heap buckets more criticism and pressure on Wilkens than on any other swimmer. None of the others could have handled it. Part of it was the coach's own anxieties. Wilkens and the Olympics consumed the coach's waking thoughts and had even infiltrated his dreams.

The swimmer had returned from the FINA World Cup meet absolutely certain Jochums' 1950s barracks approach was destroying his Olympic chances. The training failed to develop speed. No elite swimmer trained this way anymore. So when Jochums had resumed his never-changing workouts, Wilkens had nearly blown his top. Had the coach been blind in Maryland? Did he somehow miss the disqualification in the 400-meter I.M.? How about the loss to Moses in the 200-meter breaststroke? Don't forget another race, the 200-meter I.M., in which Wilkens took third. After that competition, Wilkens had flown directly to Canada for a second World Cup meet, where he was whipped in the 400-meter I.M. by much weaker competition. If that wasn't proof there was a serious leak in the boat, nothing was. Wilkens began rehearsing what he needed to say to Jochums. And Jochums, steeped in his belief in the Greeks' *agon*, the theory that from conflict rose excellence, had been lying in wait. He knew Wilkens was popping with new ideas. The coach was spoiling for the fight that would settle once and for all who was in charge.

"Some buy what I sell, some don't, but it's up to them to decide," Jochums had said days earlier, after Wilkens let it slip that he'd been talking to an independent stroke guru who had recommended several training changes. Jochums was incensed by that. He trusted no one on the other side of Santa Clara's gate, least of all an outsider coach.

"Tom buys my program, but he wants something to push against because he's not yet sure if it's real," Jochums had continued. "When my son, Rick, was three years old, I swatted him for misbehaving. He spun on me so fast I didn't know what to think. This little man wanted to kick the ass of whoever hit him. I liked that. I liked that a lot. Stubbornness reveals your courage and character. I know Tom's going to come after me, and when he does, what's important is how hard I push back."

On this morning, Jochums had called the same main set that he called every week at least once or twice, 3 × 800 freestyle. It was a descend set, which meant each 800-yard swim was to be faster than the previous one. Wilkens did it, and afterward automatically swam the same 400-meter lungbuster he performed four times a day, five or six days a week. When he finished, he began to suggest how his training should be modified. He had rehearsed the speech beforehand with Bitter and it was supposed to come out clear and logical. But the words became mixed up and garbled—and they came laced with an accusatory tone.

Jochums had yelled at him to stop thinking and start swimming. And instead of backing down, for the first time Wilkens had yelled back. He said he knew what his body needed and he was sick of being told otherwise. He'd been successful long before Dick Jochums had entered his life. He'd won four NCAA titles training under someone else, hadn't he? He was sick of this crap, sick of the relentless one-on-one practices long after his teammates had finished. He wanted to know why he couldn't race them in practice and why Jochums held him to a higher standard without delivering the promised results. Jochums exploded and sent him on a major pulling set. Oddly, no matter how angry they became at each other, the swimming set was never compromised. It was as if the integrity of training was something sacred. Wilkens pushed off and Jochums stormed into his office. They were redefining tough love.

Jochums had sat at his desk and drew three vertical columns on a yellow notepad. In the first column, he listed every Olympic swimming event. In the second, he wrote all the corresponding world records that his swimmers had set over the years. Column three was where he put the corresponding No. 1 rankings that his swimmers achieved. In parentheses, he noted all his American records. It had taken fifteen minutes, and when he finished, he had leaned back and reviewed the list with satisfaction. Damn, it felt good to be alive. Who needed coffee when you had numbers like this: twenty-five world records, sixty American records, and about twenty No. 1 rankings? He was about to include his twelve Olympic medals but decided to hold off. Better to save those for another time. The coach had ripped the sheet off the pad, marched to the pool, and dipped it in water. He pasted the wet paper to a red kickboard and leaned the board against Wilkens' gutter. Then he had stepped back, folded his arms, and waited.

In the water, Wilkens was fuming because Jochums never listened to him. At the rate he was going, he would end up like Tim Shaw—strung out by a coach's one-way bullheadedness until there was nothing left. He finished the set and hadn't fully lifted his head from the water when Jochums was already at the pool's edge and screaming in his ear.

"You listen to me, asshole! When you can say you've trained a world record-holder or a number one–ranked swimmer in every event except two then—and only then—can you start telling me what to do! What have you done? You've been number one in the world in the breaststroke one year and in the I.M. the next. You know what? Big deal! You know how many people can say the same thing? Hundreds. You can be one of the greatest ever, you know it and I know it, but it has to start in your heart. All you're doing is playing head games. You and your second-guessing! You know what? There are no quick fixes out there. If you think you can do a better job than me, say so now and we'll shake hands goodbye. I'll give you my goddamn stopwatch and say good riddance. There's plenty of others who may not be as talented, but they want it more. Those are the people I want to coach."

The coach momentarily looked as if he might leap into the water to settle this once and for all. Wilkens, his eyes big with fear, backed away cautiously and finished the workout without uttering another a word. He was disgusted. The words were exceedingly unfair, because Tom Wilkens was nothing if not dedicated. His entire life was swimming. This fight had resolved absolutely nothing except to guarantee that there had to be at least one more blowup. That is how humans work. There has to be a winner and there has to be a loser, and both have to feel respected when it's over. When Wilkens climbed from the pool at the end of practice, he angrily swung his swim bag at the perched kickboard and sent it skittering across the deck. He hadn't bothered reading it. He knew what it said.

. . .

The weeks between Thanksgiving and New Year's are crucial for training because they offer six weeks of uninterrupted focus. If swimming has a boot camp, this is the time for it. Nationwide, yardage and intensity substantially increase. From an early age, swimmers are programmed to believe the Christmas holidays represent the most important training period of the year.

As the Santa Clara Swim Club marched toward the end of the year, everyone was on edge. The jangled nerves had originated with Grote and his inexplicable injury. Then unease had infected Wilkens and Jochums. Soon all dozen or so people living for the Olympic Trials were consumed by anxiety and doubt. Backstroker Blahnik disappeared and Wales turned sullen. One of the country's best female freestylers just up and quit. Every day brought the team twenty-four hours closer to Trials and it was terrifying to consider how much work remained. Pale and droop-shouldered from three weeks of twice-daily, body-emptying workouts, by late December the swimmers complained constantly. They swore viciously at slow times, spoke little during practice, and afterward showered and hurriedly dressed so they didn't have to hang around and socialize. Meanwhile, the financial scandal was an invisible acid eating away at everything. The cold rain and early darkness only made it worse.

And there was another force at work. The moment the new millennium arrived at 12:01 A.M. on January 1, 2000, a line was going to be crossed. Every Olympic Trial swimmer seeing the emblazoned numbers "2000" would be paralyzed by one thought: *Now it's for real.* The Olympic Trials. The Olympics. Sydney. One chance. You spend a decade thinking about the 2000 Olympics and they are nothing more than an elusive possibility, a faint light on the horizon's edge. Now they stand right in front of you. Press out, follow through, head down, stretch to the wall. Touch first or second. A missed taper would be damnation. A third place would be agony unlike any other.

The Santa Clara swimmers had knotted worries that were beginning to seriously bunch their guts. But they were strong and proud, so they shielded weaknesses from each other. But they had to vent somehow, and so between their complaints about bad swimming and sore shoulders they collected around a common problem. That problem was the Olympic Trials' horrendous scheduling.

U.S.A. Swimming had made a very bad decision about the 2000 Olympic Trials. Two years prior, after months of argument, debate, backroom politics, and analyses, the sport's 500-member House of Delegates, a mix of coaches, officials, athletes, and volunteers, had elected to hold the 2000 Olympic Trials a mere thirty days before the start of the Sydney Games. It was a terrible move.

Historically, the U.S. Olympic swim team had performed far better when Trials were held months in advance of the Games. In 1988, just 35 days had separated the qualification meet from the Seoul Olympics, and the United States only won eighteen medals, just eight gold. In 1992, there were 141 days—nearly five months—separating Trials from the Barcelona Games, and U.S. swimmers responded with 27 medals, 11 gold. A similar gap was allowed for the 1996 Atlanta Games, and the team captured 26 medals, 13 gold.

The counterargument came partly courtesy of *Swimming World Magazine*, which analyzed every World Championships, Pan Pacific Championships, and the Olympics (plus their respective qualification meets) between 1968 and 1998 to determine the optimum interval between the trial meets and their subsequent championships. According to the data—which carried significant weight—American swimmers performed their best at championship meets when the qualification meet had been only five weeks earlier.

But one problem with that analysis is that there is a world of difference between other qualification meets and the Olympic Trials.

The Olympic Trials are simply too emotionally and physically draining to put so close to the Olympics. It is like playing in the seventh game of the World Series twice in the same month. Recovery is required. Returning to a level of sustained hard work is necessary. Psychological refocusing is imperative. Thirty days is barely enough time to pack a toothbrush and get a passport. The other countries were obviously tickled pink by the development.

In 1998, U.S.A. Swimming's House of Delegates voted to hold the Trials right before the Olympics. The vote was so contentious that the organization revoted in 1999 but reached the same outcome. Why would the delegates ever jeopardize the United States' Olympic chances by this schedule? It had to do with control. College coaches wield lots of it, and in 1992 and 1996 they hated the way the springtime Olympic Trials disrupted their seasons. The country's best collegiate swimmers had spent the school year thinking about Olympic berths, not NCAA championships. Some of the best had abandoned their college teams altogether to train with a hometown coach. The NCAA championship meets were fiascos, with some athletes training right through them. In addition, when Trials and the Olympics are separated by several months, the newly anointed Olympians earn their berths and then return to their training clubs as celebrity heroes. There is a general concern that they lose their focus.

But there was another issue that influenced this scheduling. The overwhelming majority of people in the House of Delegates would not be directly involved with swimmers who were considered Olympic-team favorites. For these people, their goal was to see their swimmers enjoy fast, season-ending swims. So what difference did it make to put Trials right next to the Olympics? If anything, one of their swimmers could be a late-blooming surprise. Even the Santa Clara coaches felt that way. Of course, those hurt most by the tight scheduling were the country's very top swimmers. They had to enter Trials thinking not only about making the team but also about the Olympics immediately following. Psychologically, that represented a tremendous strain. Where do the best swimmers put their focus, on Trials, the world's most competitive meet, or on the subsequent Games? And that's where it gets sinister. The later Trials were scheduled, the more likely it was that a top athlete thinking too much about the Olympics could be thrown off his or her game. If that happened, a dark horse racing on the taper's extreme edge, a person who'd have nothing left to give in Sydney, would slip into a coveted Olympic spot. It was going to occur; it was only a question of how often. America loves the underdogs, but not when they triumph this way. Even the Santa Clara swimmers who considered themselves to be those underdogs were disgusted with the situation.

But that was the reality. After the Olympic team was selected, the new Olympians had to immediately report to a Pasadena training camp that would last until departure for Sydney. The Olympic coaching staff would have one daring shot to make the 2000 Olympics successful. At the camp, the swimmers would immediately be forced into intense training designed to create a hole of fatigue. From there, they would launch an abbreviated taper that hopefully would engage as the Olympics began. It was inherently a strategy full of risk and downside, and as the New Year arrived it was yet another thing to worry about. All the Santa Clara Swim Club athletes and coaches were in a funk as the holidays hit. What they needed was a serious pick-me-up. And then, just like that, they got it.

CHAPTER ELEVEN

When the new millennium arrived, everything magically seemed to change for the better. Outside the gate, e-commerce transactions over the holidays had beaten all predictions, signaling a mass-market embrace of online shopping and a boon to the Silicon Valley economy. The housing market in the neighborhoods around the swim center was the hottest in the nation. The rain had stopped, too.

But there was a buzz on the pool deck that had nothing to do with money or the triumph of high technology. It came from whispering and pointing, from mothers sitting on deck, and from rambunctious children who had suddenly lowered their voices in respect. It came, too, from gaped-mouthed adult recreational swimmers, especially the men, who for once paused on their way to the locker room to watch Jochums' workouts. Who cared about Grote, Wilkens, or the others? Swimming was once again a spectator sport. Dara Torres had joined the Santa Clara Swim Team.

Professional model, ESPN2 sports commentator, three-time Olympian, Tae-Bo infomercial queen, *Sports Illustrated* swimsuit girl. Thirty-two years old. Seven years gone from the sport. In the midst of one of the most improbable comebacks ever seen in sports. Now a favorite to make the Olympic team in its marquee events, the 50-meter and 100-meter freestyle. She also had a shot at the 100-meter butterfly, and perhaps three Olympic relays. All that and Dara Torres was now wearing a blue Santa Clara bathing cap.

Six months earlier, she had sat in the SCSC bleachers during its international meet and decided to return to the sport. At the time, she weighed

143 lbs. and could bench-press 95 lbs. Now, half a year later, she was 160 lbs. and racking 185 lbs.

Torres gracefully moved back and forth across the pool while a crowd of about twenty-five people stood on deck and watched. Her stroke was as pure and beautiful as a musical note. That day in July when she had slipped into the water for the first time, Stanford and head Olympic women's coach, Richard Quick, had halted her after two minutes and said, "Dara, we don't swim like that anymore." In the weeks that followed, he had re-engineered her 1980s stroke, which planed high on the water's surface and was scull-based, by making her swim lower and emphasizing her core body power. The results spoke for themselves. In her first competition in more than seven years, she had swum lifetime best times at the World Cup Series meet in Maryland and won two silvers and two bronzes. That had been in November. In December, she had competed at the U.S. Open in San Antonio and her times fell again. The 50-meter freestyle race in particular was spectacular. She won it in a best time and it was .3 seconds faster than the former world record she had set fifteen and a half years earlier. The swim had ranked her No. 3 globally for all of 1999.

Touching second in that race was one unhappy Jenny Thompson, the world's best female swimmer and Torres' Stanford training partner. Thompson, the 1999 U.S. Olympic Committee Sportswoman of the Year, had originally been excited to train with Torres. But that was before Torres showed what she could do. One simply does not retire from the sport for nearly a decade, blithely announce a comeback, and after just 150 days of training beat the world's best swimmer. And if one *does* do that, one cannot expect life to resume as normal afterward. The Stanford pool had a gate similar to the Santa Clara Swim Club's, and soon after the Texas meet a tearful Torres had found herself and her bags on the outside of it.

In a much later article titled "Breaking Up Is the Right Thing to Do," *San Jose Mercury News* sports columnist Ann Killion wrote:

For years [Thompson] has been the biggest fish in the Stanford pool.

And then last fall, Torres, thirty-three, showed up. She had been retired for seven years, after winning a gold medal—

along with Thompson—in the 400 freestyle relay at the 1992 Olympics. She wanted to train with Quick (at Stanford). She was inspired and awed by Thompson's times at the Santa Clara meet. Within months, she was keeping up with Thompson in the pool.

And the tension built.

"It was like an Olympic final in every practice," Quick said. "It's not good for anybody. I don't want people to be destroyed by practice."

Both women are older. Both are likely on their final Olympic dreams. Both are incredibly competitive. Both were vying for their coach's attention.

"It was a war," said one insider. "A fiasco."

Torres was now at Santa Clara because Jochums had struck a deal with Quick. The Olympic coach would train Torres in an empty lane several mornings per week. In the afternoon, Torres would swim with the Santa Clara men under Bitter's watchful eye. In the first days of practice, she barely missed breaking the short-course American record in the 100-yard freestyle, from a push, no less. Had she dove, she might have broken the record.

"She is the first superstar we've had in this program," Bitter said reverently as he watched her. "Her stroke is the most perfect I have ever seen. It is an honor to have her here."

Jochums felt the same way. Torres was his kind of woman, a roughhouser and a smart aleck who could take an insult and sling one right back. He needed more like her in his male-dominated program. She worked harder than most of his men, and shame was a coach's friend. But Machiavellian layering was also at work. Any favor the Santa Clara coach could deliver the mercurial Quick, who would influence the selection of the assistant coaches for the 2000 Olympic Games, was smart business.

The first morning at SCSC, Quick came an hour early for her practice and fidgeted with his wristwatch until Torres arrived. He was undoubtedly nervous because on some level there was implicit betrayal going on. Jenny Thompson, his premier swimmer for nearly a decade, had no idea Quick was still coaching Torres. In fact, she wouldn't find out for several months. Quick was in a remarkable bind. As the women's Olympic coach, his primary responsibility was to develop the fastest American team possible. In a sense, it was his duty to provide expertise to both women. But Thompson and her Stanford teammates sure weren't going to see it that way.

In the days that followed, Quick began giving Torres some of the most intense workouts ever seen at Santa Clara. He was a relentless taskmaster who walked alongside her shouting for entire sets. Jochums watched and paced, clearly uncomfortable being relegated to a secondary position in his own pool. For her part, Torres never backed down from the practices' intensity. One morning, she did a long set of all-out 50-meter freestyles on a substantial rest interval of 1:30. Lap after lap, for more than thirty minutes, Quick walked next to her, bent at the waist and yelling for her to ignite at certain moments. It was a brutal set designed for failure, but she averaged a fast 28 seconds from start to finish. When it was over, she hung in the gutter and tried not to get sick while Quick wrote her times in a notebook. Then he thanked Jochums and hurried to his car to get back to his Stanford team. Jochums visibly relaxed when he had his pool to himself again.

· · ·

Dara Torres had huge hands. They were slender and feminine, but they were the size of books. A person seeing them on an armrest would do a double take, and then be compelled to find out to whom they belonged. They could only be the hands of an athlete.

Swimming's love affair with the hazel-eyed Torres began in 1981 when she won her first national title at the tender age of fourteen. She was ebullient, tan, and tomboyishly cute, a child of privilege out of a ten-bath home in Beverly Hills. Hers was a lifestyle of towering palm trees, Rolls-Royces, and power-chic couples with their beautiful marriages and sensational divorces. Her father, a real-estate magnate who was behind the Aladdin Hotel in Las Vegas, had been about fifty years old when she was born the fifth of six children. Her parents' eventual split was something so traumatic that even years later she still couldn't easily talk about it.

Growing up, she had soaked up the attention her speed and beauty had brought her. But she also had exuded a tremendous vulnerability, for Torres had a deep need to be loved. Something about her was strangely reminiscent of Marilyn Monroe. It was her mix of brash strength, hopefulness, and little-girl fragility. Two years after her first national championship title, she broke the world record in the 50-meter freestyle with a time of 25.62. She did it again in 1984 (25.61). She was the fastest woman alive, but this was four years prior to the 50-meter freestyle becoming an official Olympic event in 1988. She qualified for the 1984 and 1988 Olympics as a relay and 100-meter freestyle swimmer (in 1988), and she captured three Olympic relay medals, a gold, silver, and bronze.

During that time, she competed at the University of Florida, where she won the maximum twenty-eight All-American honors and became one of swimming's most visible and gregarious personalities. Publicly she seemed to have everything going for her: fast times, beauty, smarts, friends. But privately she was often in a spiral of confusion and fear. Behind closed bathroom doors, she suffered from bulimia, and for five years it controlled her life. An eating disorder is insidious and all-encompassing. Female swimmers in particular are susceptible because of the sport's focus on the perfect body, the near-naked exposure of a swim-suit, and the fact that hard work often results in bulky muscles in the back and shoulders. The one time Torres summoned the courage to ask for help, the counselor to whom she told her secret treated her dismis-sively. In both the 1984 and 1988 Olympic Trials, she had been a favorite in the 100-meter freestyle and 100-meter butterfly (and the 50-meter free-style in 1988, its first year in the Olympics). But she was notorious for mishandling her nerves and only succeeded in qualifying as an individual once, in the 100-meter freestyle in 1988. And in that event, she entered the 1988 Olympic Games ranked No. 1 in the world and finished sev-enth. Done in by her own self-doubts and fears, she became Exhibit A in choking under pressure.

After her second Olympics in 1988, she had quit swimming and re-turned to Florida to complete her degree. Needing to be active, she won a second athletic scholarship, this time for volleyball. After graduating in 1990, she landed an internship with CNN/NBC in New York City. It was there, several months later, that she was busy cataloging videotapes when she looked up to see a story on an Olympic figure skater making a comeback. *Intriguing,* she thought as the skater glided across the ice.

At that moment, one of her colleagues popped through the door and said, "Guess what?"

Torres wanted to ask the name of the skater. Why was he making another Olympic run after already achieving his dream? What had he missed the first time? Everything that related to the Olympics made her revisit her own career, which in turn filled her with regret and dissatisfaction. Always good, never great when she had to be. A choker. At fourteen, the fastest woman ever without working very hard. At nineteen unable to qualify individually for the only meet that mattered. Now twenty-four, life's answers were no clearer. Was it that same feeling which had driven the skater back to the ice?

"Guess what?" her colleague said again. "Nicole Haislett just broke your American record in the one-hundred-meter freestyle."

Torres lived and died by signs. She believed the universe had a benevolent force that took special interest in people and occasionally intervened to redirect their lives. It was God, but it wasn't God, at least not the God described in the pulpits or shown on stained-glass windows, and she couldn't explain it any better than that. For a woman with both her deep insecurities and her urgent hopefulness, it was somehow essential to believe a force watched over her. Watching the skater make a comeback at the exact instant she heard this news was a sign. Now she needed confirmation. Every sign has one.

A few days later she was at dinner with Chuck Daley, who was then basketball coach of the Detroit Pistons and who was going to coach the 1992 Olympic Dream Team. She and Daley were represented by the same agent and the coach started teasing her about a comeback. *What made him bring that up?* she thought. Halfway through dinner, she realized this was the confirmation she needed, and within two months she was back at the University of Florida practicing with Haislett, an undergraduate there. In 1992, at the ancient age of twenty-five, Torres raced in her third Olympic Trials and finished fourth in the 100-meter freestyle. That earned her a trip to the Barcelona Games on a relay and a gold medal in the 4 × 100-meter freestyle. She was also elected Olympic team captain. But she felt like a total failure because she had missed making the team in an individual event. The medal, along with the others she had won in the two earlier Olympiads, went into a box under her bed.

"I was instantly ashamed of that medal," she said later. "It was a reminder of everything I couldn't do. I'd meet people who would say, 'Oh, you're a swimmer; were you good?' It'd get out that I was in the Olympics, and they'd say, 'Wow, what's your name?' When they wouldn't know it, they'd ask, 'What stroke?' I'd say, 'Freestyle' and hope it'd end there. But if they knew swimming, they'd say, 'What event?' and I'd have to say, 'It was just a relay.' By then I'm talking with my head down because I'm too ashamed to look in their faces."

In public she was an energetic flirt brimming with confidence, beauty, and the shimmering vibrancy of the here and now. Black limos, private airplanes, the finest dining New York City had to offer. After Barcelona, she wanted to be rid of swimming and threw out her suits and goggles—saving only her early-1980s Speedo "bug-eye" goggles for sentimental reasons. She married a sports television producer, but it didn't work out and it was one of those subjects she couldn't talk about. She joined the fabled New York–based Wilhelmina Models and did various modeling gigs that provided sporadic but entertaining work.

Then one day in late 1993, *Sports Illustrated* called looking for the first athlete to appear in its swimsuit issue, and suddenly her swimming, which she'd fully left behind, landed her an opportunity that would change the course of her career. After the famous issue appeared, she became an on-air personality with Fox, TNT, ESPN2, and the Discovery Channel. Her job was to be fun in a spontaneous way, a little breathless and the center of attention in a circle of rowdy men—something she had done all her life. There she was on Saturday morning, flexing her bicep while standing in a pickup's flatbed with a gaggle of shirtless and boozed-up good-old boys, all of whom were clearly in love. There she was swimming with sharks on the Discovery Channel and rapping about a skater's life on a hockey program called *NHL's Cool Shots*. Her laughter, deep and rich as soil, was infectious. People opened up to her.

That was the public Torres, the cosmopolitan diva. Only those who inched their way through the defenses, traps, and barbed wire ever met the private Torres, a fragile woman trying to find her way in the world. This was what she had in common with Marilyn. Torres was at once independent but vulnerable, intuitive yet insecure. Kindness and love came off her like heat, but so did her fears. If you were a man, you wanted to hold and protect her. If you were a woman, you were guarded. There was no question she owned a heart the size of Manhattan. But she worried endlessly about how she was perceived, tried her utmost to please, sometimes made stupid blunders, and often believed she had failed when she hadn't. Because her face was her commerce, there was a strong need to make people realize she was also very smart.

Manhattan was perfect for her, not only because it offered 24-hour stimulus but because she could be a celebrity one minute and anonymous the next. She vastly preferred anonymous, but she was too vibrant to slip into a room unnoticed. All the while, it took six years—from 1992 to 1998—to feel good about that relay in the 1992 Olympics. Isn't that odd? It was such a great accomplishment, yet she couldn't see that. She never talked about swimming, but her story was always a step behind.

In 1998, U.S.A. Swimming's nationals were held in Long Island, and she was cajoled into presenting awards for one event. Ironically, the winner of that one race was Tom Wilkens. The pool made her clothes and hair stink of chlorine and she told friends, "Thank God I'm out of that; how could I have done it for so long?"

Months later, in spring 1999, her boyfriend at the time joked, "You get a gleam in your eye when you talk about swimming. You should make a comeback."

"Yeah, right," she said. Her friend must have seen something, some firmness settling around her mouth, because he continued teasing her.

"Why don't you drop it, okay?" she snapped, surprising them both. "You're driving me nuts with all this."

"All what?" he said.

She didn't know. She hadn't thought about swimming for years, but within days began having a recurring dream in which she stood on the starting block before a swim race. Was this a sign? What for? She loved her New York life. The dream came every night until she became possessed with the idea of swimming again. Clearly, she had unfinished business. And clearly it was able to consume her life in a matter of days. Since defeating her eating disorder—or at least holding it at bay—control over her body had been one of the most important things in her life. As a result, she was an exercise fiend who had stayed at an Olympic level of fitness through a weekly routine of running 20 miles, lifting weights three times a week, spinning on a bike four times a week, and regularly performing Tae-Bo exercises. Her obsession with her diet also had ensured that everything she put in her body was healthy, including supplements such as marine lipids, iron, vitamin C, complex vitamin B, antioxidants, and creatine (perhaps not so healthy). After one week of dreaming, she decided that was enough of a sign. She phoned Stanford's Quick and left a vague message, hoping he'd end the nonsense. Then she couldn't stand to step away from the phone as she waited for him to call back. A comeback after seven years? She was already three years older than the oldest American female who had ever swum in the Olympics; by Sydney, she'd be nearly five years older.

"I know," Quick said when he phoned.

"You know what?" she said. Butterflies slamdanced in her stomach.

"I know you want to make a comeback because it's in your voice," Quick said.

"Am I nuts?"

"Let's talk. I'm enthusiastic about the possibility."

Torres hung up and called her mom.

"Mom, I think I'm coming back," she remembered saying.

"Great, have you made a flight reservation?" asked her mother, who lived in Sun Valley, Idaho.

"To swimming."

. . .

"Mom? I said I want to make a comeback in swimming."

Her mother was supportive, but Torres shuddered at the thought of telling her formidable father, who split time between the Hamptons, Palm Beach, and New York City. They were close, and she frequently hopped a private jet on weekends to visit him in Florida, often traveling with some of the Big Apple's most powerful people. Her father, now in his eighties, could be a severe and practical man, and recently he had been telling her that she needed to take concrete steps in her career. Interviewing harness racers for a cable-access sports station was not what he had in mind. She took him to her favorite Chinese restaurant, a place she had frequented since the early 1990s. It had been years since someone there had mentioned swimming.

Torres was a grown woman terrified of talking to her dad. As they settled in, the waiter approached and out of the blue asked, "You swim still?"

"No," she gulped.

"You should because you're young still," the waiter said. Bingo. Another confirmation.

"Why would she waste her career doing that?" her father asked, slightly peeved.

Torres' stomach sank and swimming was not mentioned again. She always communicated better in letters, so she returned to her apartment and wrote her father a long note trying to explain, trying to find words for something she herself didn't fully understand. Then she packed her things and moved to California. On her first day of Stanford practice, she showed up and simply said to her new coach, "Richard, I'm in your hands."

That had been six months ago. Now in January 2000, she was part of the Santa Clara Olympic effort, currently the only adult woman in this overwhelmingly male world, although a second woman, distance swimmer Julie Varozza, would soon join the group. Torres was racing against the team's best male sprinters, sometimes beating them and then taunting them, "So how's it feel to lose to a girl?" Jochums wanted to know, too, and his language was far more colorful. The days were light.

But the spark Torres brought to the club would only last several weeks. Day by day the sky grew grayer and heavier, and soon enough California's winter rains would close over the pool and bring with them a torrent of Olympic-dream pressures. The most difficult days of the journey were right around the corner.

CHAPTER TWELVE

The rain had returned. It came from the west, hard and sharp-angled. The swimmers turned inward and serious again. The coaches stood silently on the empty expanse of deck and watched puddles grow around their feet. Whatever lightness Torres had brought to the Santa Clara Swim Club in early January was by the month's end washed into the San Francisco Bay with the rest of the rainwater.

This was a bleak, funereal time in everyone's life. The pressure setting like concrete. The brutally difficult workload that seemed to have neither beginning nor end. These were crucial weeks, and they had to be unremitting. The aerobic base being built now might or might not determine the outcome of Trials seven months hence. Already, poolside instruction was moving from major stroke overhauls to refinements and nuances. Every day was another step forward into the longest training cycle of the year. On deck, Jochums was an Ahab figure who let the rain pelt his face. Bitter stood next to him, hunch-shouldered under a colorful golf umbrella. When they spoke, it was in monosyllables and without turning their heads. No one would ever say the Olympic journey was easy.

Wilkens was in another dark zone of exhaustion. But this one was vastly different because concurrently the fear of failure had him by the throat. The fear had started slowly. It began after his mediocre Pan Pacifics performances four months earlier, but now it was all over him, on his skin and in his lungs and behind his eyes. He had become weak-hearted and scared. The unresolved relationship with Jochums only made it worse. When alone, Wilkens was crying. *I'm cracking, I don't believe it,* he thought to himself.

We build our athletes into mythic heroes and when they stand on the blocks or the gridiron or at center court, they exude such unshakable confidence that we are awed. But behind the scenes, they are human like everyone else. Perhaps they are even more so; perhaps they are *über-human*, more human than humanly possible. Maybe they are humane humanists with a human streak a mile wide. It could be so, for they live and die, they suffer, anguish, and triumph, a thousand times every week. Our athletes have become the artists of our time, complete with the requisite passion and internal angst. Their genius is their grace and power, but in expressing themselves they run the gamut of human emotions every day before falling exhausted into bed. Imagine you are an elite athlete chasing one of the purest and most noble dreams in existence. You have a bad day, maybe a bad month. Time is running out. What demons crawl from under the bed to spook you when the light goes off?

For Wilkens, the demons were the predictable kind: *You are not good enough. You are a fool and an imposter.* For Grote, who was still unable to perform a regular workout, the demons were the ticking clock and the feeling that his Olympic dream had become liquid, slipping between his fingers like pool water. His February deadline to quit loomed in front of him.

Wales minded his own business and kept his head down. He alone seemed to be surviving the tension of that winter. It was his ability to separate himself from the group that protected him. Between morning and afternoon practices, he went home and silently worked on the computer, learning how financial markets operated.

The other swimmers were quiet, subdued. By mid-January, no one had seen Blahnik in nearly three weeks. He would have been given the boot, except the coaches knew that was exactly what he hoped would happen. If they ever saw him at the pool again, they'd have a long talk about life and facing fears. But while each swimmer suffered individually, it was their head coach who had it even worse, for he held not just his dream but the collective dreams of all of them. And meanwhile, his demons were more ferocious than anyone would have imagined.

• • •

On deck, Dick Jochums clutched his stopwatch as if it held the truth of the universe. And for a moment, you get to be Dick Jochums. You go into his head to see the world through his eyes. Everything rushes at once. The Olympic Trials gnaw so hard at the gut you can't exercise or sleep. It seems like you and your wife are fighting all the time, and that's your fault. This club you are entrusted to preserve is facing financial ruin and possible criminal investigations. And now your mom is in a Portland nursing home, dying of pneumonia, yet she was the one who had been taking care of your father, who shows signs of early dementia. You care so much about the people in the pool that the ache of love is often overwhelming. It's like a heart attack; you want to squeeze your chest and get aspirin into the bloodstream. These kids are delivering, but not all the way, not yet. And as guardian of their lifelong dreams, what have you missed? Is someone anemic like Shaw was? Is there an overlooked shortcoming or some small judgment error that even now is building into a mammoth disaster? They've been warned. They've been warned as frequently as possible that there will be many tears at Olympic Trials. They've been told that so many hearts will break that the pool deck will seem littered with the shards. Their eyes narrow as they listen and it's obvious that deep down they don't think they'll be the ones devastated. It doesn't matter. The warnings are as much for your own benefit as for the athletes. Wilkens is full of anger and resistance, and Wilkens is the best hope. What about Grote, once the best shot, who now has to use the pool ladder to lift himself from the water? Blahnik? Forget it. Wales and the others? Miracles could happen. But what now? You want it so bad you can feel it pushing the blood through your veins even when you lie down to sleep.

It's a Friday afternoon in January and Wilkens has been home sick for two days with the flu. Still weak, he struggles to complete a set of 5 × 200. Jochums knows the swimmer is hurting, but also feels Wilkens gives up too easily when his body fatigues. Wilkens never gives up. But Jochums wants him to be a warrior at all times. The yelling starts.

To be here, you had to spend years in purgatory paying for accumulated sins and egotisms. They'd all predicted you'd get yours and they had been honest-to-God right. The fact is, the punishment was probably deserved. So you were exiled to the wasteland of selling insurance and construction management, and paid for your trespasses with the worst punishment of all: living a meaningless existence. God always laces His lessons with irony. Anyone can see you are softer now. But you've also heard too many jokes that you've lost the edge and this has become a deep worry. Has an edge been lost, has the sharpness that separates good from great been blunted by the passing years? The anger still flashes, but not like the old days in the salt air of Long Beach or under Arizona's endless sky. Hate and fury are a young man's game.

You can't go back to those days, anyway, because you now carry profound feelings of kinship and empathy for the beaten and downtrodden. You've been there and know what hurt feels like. The swimmers at Santa Clara don't know if they'll make the Olympic team, but they know one absolute truth and that is this: that you'd go to war for them and will watch their backs for the remainder of their days. Is it enough, or will they turn resentful if things don't go their way?

When we die, we choose a moment to replay and relive for eternity. If that were true, would you choose a child's birth, a wedding, the first laugh of a grandchild, the finish of a world-record swim twenty-five years ago, or an Olympic race not yet held? It is incredible how simultaneously easy and complicated life can seem.

"Why are you here wasting my time when you don't give one hundred percent?" Jochums thunders at Wilkens. This is it; this is the fight that decides how their relationship will be from now on. It has come up suddenly. Neither man is fully prepared, but it has started and it must now complete itself.

Wilkens makes an ugly retort out the side of his mouth that only Jochums hears.

"You know, you ought to kiss my ass for all I do for you," Jochums says. The anger is coming up fast.

A frail woman dying slowly in an Oregon hospital room. It is raining, and she is expiring slowly. They removed the I.V. two days earlier, which could be good news or bad. It must be bad, so you get on a plane to say goodbye. Your dad, always the strong one, a man who believed life gave no favors and who had enormous workman's hands, seems to be slowly losing his mind the way a beach erodes. The old man holds her hand all day, and this could make a person weep because it is a moment of complete love in its ember-fading simplicity. Maybe you will have the same when it is your turn, but maybe you will be alone, and that is something to think about. Your father wets her lips with water and you feel too big for the room. There is no place to settle and feel comfortable, and what can be done, anyway? Back in California is something as close to heaven as you will ever find: the brief, elusive grace of a perfect arm-stroke, a glimpse of courage defeating fear, the steady, metronomic sound of hands cutting through water. Oregon rain on windowpanes is always fused with sadness.

Sometimes, when running errands, you forget where you're going because your head is pounding with splits, speeches, and dreams. Once you were being dropped off at home by Bitter and forgot where to turn right. These days someone is always complaining about hearing a repeated story and that, too, is something to think about. Your old man's powerful hands have shrunk to nothing. You don't think your father can outlive your mother by more than a week, and don't know what to do if he does.

"Why you don't you kiss my ass," Wilkens tells Jochums without looking up from the water.

"What did you say? What did you say?" Jochums shouts. He is storming and terrible. Every fiber in his body is coiled and ready to uncork. "Get up here on deck and say that to my face!"

Wilkens is the one who can make the dream come true. The others might get close, but Wilkens is the one who represents the redemption, and nearly every day he transports you back to 1975 in Long Beach. You talk about Shaw because Wilkens is so tough that out of the hundreds of amazing athletes who have swum in your pool, only Shaw can compare.

You're fighting Wilkens because you're scared. Wilkens is scared, too. He doesn't laugh anymore; he doesn't play in the water the way he once did. Blame it on the building pressure, on the Olympic Games, on the torture of having a real shot at greatness. Blame it on the fear that is rising in every swimmer's throat, the jumpiness that seems to grow worse each week. Blame it on love, because the more you love Wilkens, the more you want to fight him.

Wilkens is motionless in the water, not looking at Jochums. If the swimmer looks up, he will see a man much bigger than himself, a man righteous and physical in his anger, someone more willing to cross an uncrossable line. He wouldn't, but maybe he would. This is a truth moment, an instant shimmering in time when two men decide with finality how it is going to be between them. Not just for today, but for all time. Twenty seconds pass. Wilkens refuses to move, refuses to look up, and that is what decides it. Jochums has won. There will be no more fights, not like this.

"You are gutless; that's what you are," Jochums *says, spitting each word. "No guts."*

Through all the years, Shaw has come and gone in your mind like a radio station in the mountains. But ever since you found this new one, the memories have become a fixture. You don't have photos of the wife, family, or grandchildren in the cramped office. But on the wall is the blown-up photo of Shaw that is autographed, "To Dick, Thanks for the: past, present and the rest of my life." On a good day when Wilkens touches the wall, he looks up with such simple, little-boy trust that you have to postpone the next set for a minute to tell another Shaw story that only you, he, and Shaw would understand. Bitter would understand the story, too, Bitter who could be head coach nearly anywhere in the country, but who has chosen to stay at Santa Clara and be the world's most loyal right-hand man. As Wilkens pushes off, Shaw's ghost is swimming alongside him. Shaw became the world's best swimmer and was then crushed under the weight of his coach's dreams, and that's partly what this journey to the 2000 Olympics is about. Wilkens, less talented but equally committed, can't possibly understand that he is the redemption for something that happened when he was a one-year-old. There is probably a future Olympian in the pool, and you know you, the coach, could blow it again. And then what?

No guts? Wilkens has more guts than any swimmer you've ever seen. You pace the deck and never stop thinking.

. . .

During this time, Tom Wilkens' workouts had become so demanding that once again he almost invariably worked out alone. He sometimes thought it was to punish him, but that wasn't it. It was to protect the others from his force. He was now performing 4,000 meters backstroke per day, an inordinate amount. It was his weakest stroke, but to win the 400-meter I.M., to challenge for the title of King of Swimming, he had to erase all weaknesses. Nearly every day, Dod Wales would watch Wilkens crushing through another set and ask what he was doing, as if to draw inspiration. Grote watched Wilkens, too, but he never asked, not now.

Wilkens could barely exit from bed he was so tired. The lactic acid sloshed in his heavy legs every time he climbed the stairs to his apartment. But it was the pressure that bore down. He was a bona fide Olympic contender in an Olympic year. Could things be any clearer? Some people's dreams are so big and improbable that they aren't ready for them to come true. *I didn't know it would be like this,* he thought wearily.

Jochums, the most important person in his life right now, was unbearable. Wilkens had always existed in easy agreement with other people. That was his personality. But daily practice had become a trench war. Wilkens had fought for four months before throwing in the towel and giving up. Jochums had won and Wilkens had fallen into line behind him. But that had not dispelled the pressure. The swimmer felt the tension in phone conversations with friends and family, even at the pool when he saw teammates watching him. He was a consummate amateur athlete, but thanks to his 1999 season he had achieved numerous performance milestones and would earn more than $100,000 from U.S.A. Swimming and Speedo, his primary sponsor. It was an amount of money that overwhelmed his imagination. He wasn't arrogant about this; he was terrified. Welcome to the big leagues.

He was home watching television, too tired to do anything except finger the remote control. A commercial for a Chevy truck appeared. In it, the man buys his vehicle when his daughter is a toddler, and the 30-second story follows them through twenty years of ups and downs as she advances from a clumsy beginner skier to a serious competitor to an Olympian. At one point, the daughter must have fallen in competition, because in the cab of the truck the father tenderly tells her she'll bounce back. As Wilkens watched it, his chin trembled. He began crying and couldn't stop.

The swimmer often lay in bed staring at the American flag he had tacked to his wall. *I have no right to this dream,* he thought. The flag was something he brought to international meets, and it was the single piece of evidence in his bedroom that he was a swimmer. He wondered what would happen if he suddenly decided to stop driving the 1.8 miles from his apartment to the pool. Would it lead to seismic shifts in China? Would anyone even notice? Wilkens sighed. His family wouldn't care as long as he was happy. Coach Bitter, his roommate and closest confidante, would understand. The rest of humanity would never know the difference. Only one person, Jochums, would be affected.

In December and January, Wilkens had come to dread swimming. He was going to hurt for months and set up incredible expectations, and then he'd realize, too late, that he wasn't good enough after all, that his quest had been a cosmic waste of time. He was haunted by thoughts like that. Wilkens was living in a liminal period, the transitional state of uncertainty and doubt that accompanies any major change. The liminal period is one of the only common experiences that exist in nearly all cultures and religions. First, a subject begins—symbolically—as one kind of person. Then he or she goes through a rite of passage to symbolically become somehow different. It could be a Christian baptism or a manhood ritual that means four days in a jungle with a knife. It might even be a term of student teaching to earn a teaching certificate. In every case, before the rite of passage is completed, the participant exists in a disordered and marginalized space of confusion. That was exactly where Wilkens was now. And comparing it to a spiritual journey was not accidental. Not for Wilkens, not for anyone at the Santa Clara Swim Club.

Wilkens called home and sounded so listless that his parents suggested they fly out to see him. He rejected the idea. But from his bed he could view the fifteen family photos that sat on his bureau and he wondered how disappointed they were going to be when he failed. His girlfriend, a Stanford medical school student, had her life mapped out for the next eight years. Recently she'd begun asking about his career plans and long-term goals. Did he have any? In bed, he sighed. How could he explain what he was trying to accomplish? But she was right; he didn't have a career. Nor did he have any plans for one and that began to worry him, because like nearly every other swimmer training for the Olympic dream, his understanding of the future faded into a white nothing on September 23, 2000, the last day of Olympic swimming in Sydney.

Swimming is such a solitary and lonely sport. Wilkens knew just how bad his doldrums were because he felt empty when he drove to Stanford and sat in the chapel's dark pews listening to mass. This was supposed to be his last refuge, yet the prayers sounded stupid in his head. The chapel's gilded ceiling, which had once appeared so inspired and divine, looked like knockoff baroque. Flat as the wafer on his tongue, that was how he felt.

In mid-January, shortly after the final blowup with Jochums, Wilkens arrived at the coach's office. He had decided to put fighting behind them and start fresh. A long time ago, he had sworn up and down that regardless of what happened in life he would never display weakness in front of his coach. It was a pledge on par with his Olympic commitment. As they began to talk, Jochums started droning in his gravelly voice about the usual, about believing in the system and sticking to the basics of the process. Without warning, Wilkens began crying. The tears ran down his cheeks as he choked and tried to stop. Jochums was positively stunned; during the previous weeks he'd been so caught in the storms of his own passion that he had missed the emotional toll it was taking on his favorite swimmer. The coach backed off considerably, but subsequent days passed with no improvement. Wilkens swam apathetically, like a kid in detention. Then one afternoon, he was at home again watching television when the NCAA cross-country championships came on. The swimmer recognized the look of intensity on the slack and pain-filled faces of the gaunt male runners.

"I miss that," he said aloud. "They're not thinking about pain. I am. They're enjoying the hurt. I don't. They must have been scared at some point, but they're not now. I can be that way, too."

Every day for the next two weeks, he leaned against the image of those runners, and little by little he began to feel better. Jochums gave the same sets, but gone was his combative tone. In late January, with no rest whatsoever, the swimmer flew to New Jersey for the 2000 Burgdorff Invitational, a small regional meet near his hometown. It was both a homecoming and a way to escape California. Wilkens was slowly feeling better and he needed to prove something to himself. The world rankings had started fresh on January 1, 2000, and he decided to put his name so far at the top that every competitor would know he had to go through Tom Wilkens to win an Olympic gold.

Sometimes basketball players like Kobe Bryant pop into a local YMCA to play pickup. And sometimes swimmers like Wilkens show up at dinky regional invitationals. In the 400-meter I.M. against kids five to eight years younger, he gave an eight-lap demonstration in power and aggression that ended in 4:19.87. It was far and away the fastest time in the world. In the 200-meter I.M., he swam a 2:02.20, which was nearly good enough to have qualified for the 1996 Olympic Team. Both times put him No. 1 in the world in the medley events. No one swam this fast so early in the season. Ever. Wilkens' liminal period of uncertainty and transition seemed over. He was back, and no one had to know he'd been gone.

. . .

Grote didn't know about Wilkens' troubles because he was consumed with his own. He badly needed another painkiller shot but had waited until after New Year's. Somehow he had half-convinced his brain that he'd awake in the new millennium free of hurt and ready to race. On January 1, he felt like weeping as he limped from bed. How was it possible to hold inside this much frustration? Wilkens. Moses. Norment. Linn. Salyards. Hansen. The names of the top U.S. breaststrokers spun through his head. When Grote closed his eyes he could see them swimming lap after lap and getting stronger each week. Why him? Why this senseless, stupid injury? He took his fourth cortisone shot, and felt the familiar burn of the milky white liquid working into his leg. Within a few days he could swim tentative breaststroke. That was how it had gone with the first three shots. But after a week or so, the pain had always returned.

In late January, Stanford hosted the hottest men's college dual meet of the year, No. 2 Cardinal versus No. 3 Arizona. Grote had made the unusual decision to swim a 200-yard breaststroke time trial in the middle of the meet. This was his test. If he didn't swim an acceptable time, he was quitting the following week on February 1.

It felt strange to stand on a starting block again. The last time had been five months earlier in Australia for the Pan Pacs relay. How fast dreams can unravel. Stanford swimmers called out encouragement from their bench. A number of Santa Clara swimmers in the stands joined them. But they paid little attention because this looked like only another mundane time trial, just a quick dip to gauge speed. No one knew what was at stake, for Grote had not mentioned his possible retirement to anyone. But somehow Dara Torres intuited the swim's importance. Maybe she just recognized what it was to be down and out. As Grote stepped on the block, she hushed everyone in the stands around her.

He was guardedly optimistic about this swim. Earlier in the week, he'd delivered a 1:05 in the 100-meter breast, which was not far from his fastest practice time. Thanks to the cortisone, the knee had not hurt at all.

"You can still get back to where you need to be," Jochums had said. "Look how strong you've become. You can still make it. There's not much time, but there's enough."

Grote had looked at the coach for a long time. He used to distrust this man. Now every cell in his body ached to believe him. To celebrate the good news, he took Amy to dinner at a Mexican restaurant. He was bubbling and gleeful, the way he used to be. Amy, glimpsing the man she had married, was overjoyed. Now she was in the Stanford stands by herself, wringing her hands and smiling in a way that was supposed to look hopeful.

Grote had prepared for the time trial by watching a video of the 1997 U.S. nationals. He almost never relived his old triumphs because it wasn't his style. But that meet had been special. He'd won both breaststroke titles and had never been more beautiful in the water. He had put in the video, sat back on the couch, and stared at the oversized television screen in his living room. He let himself reexperience the moment and the feeling of greatness. When it was over, he had rewound the tape to watch it again.

He began the Stanford time trial and moved with long glides and great control, as if ruminating on each individual armsweep. On deck, the oblivious collegiate swimmers chatted. Grote had no snap to his recovery and didn't resemble a jeweler at all, but he finished the 200 yards in 2:00.79, a respectable time. As usual, Amy read the scoreboard and didn't know whether to be excited or disappointed. Trying to study Grote's face, she said tentatively, "He's not smiling, so he might not be happy."

But she was dead wrong. Grote was happy. The time was no great shakes, but that didn't matter because he had pushed the knee as hard as he could and it hadn't hurt at all. For now, nothing else mattered. There was a glimpse of the old champion as he climbed from the pool and nodded to himself. His Olympic dreams were still alive. The last thing he wanted to do was retire now.

. . .

The same afternoon across the country, the University of Virginia was meeting the University of North Carolina in a conference showdown.

Two of the country's top five breaststrokers swam for North Carolina, but as one of them plaintively explained to a *Daily Tar Heel* reporter, "It's pretty tough going into a race [when] you pretty much know you don't really have a shot."

Virginia's Ed Moses cleaved the waters and sailed to easy victory in both the 100-yard and 200-yard breaststrokes (53.45 seconds and 1:57.53 respectively). Afterward—as the *Daily Tar Heel* would report in righteous anger—Moses turned to the UNC bench and mockingly bowed. *Take that.* Then he failed to shake hands with his vanquished foes, a breach of etiquette in a sport bounded by good sportsmanship. Moses was taking no prisoners.

. . .

By mid-February, the bright spots had begun to appear if someone was willing to look hard enough for them. Wilkens had bounced back from his January blues. Grote's knee was finally on the mend. Several times per week Dara Torres blew past the men and posted practice times that would almost certainly qualify her for an Olympic relay spot—not that she was limiting herself to relays anymore.

But the most positive force in the water was also the least noticeable. Every day, Dod Wales' butterfly looked stronger and faster. Since he swam in a vacuum that precluded rivalries and comparisons, it was sometimes hard to judge his progress. But Jochums had been right; the Pan Pac relay swim had redefined the swimmer's courage and confidence. Even though he had lost at the FINA meet in November, he subsequently experienced great performances at two European meets. He had treated the travel like a business trip and was so methodical he had never experienced jet lag despite a nine-hour time difference. In both competitions he won races and gained crucial technique feedback. Returning to Santa Clara, he had witnessed the on-deck tensions between Jochums and Wilkens. He had recognized Grote's ongoing hardship and knew Blahnik, by his absence, was probably deep in avoidance mode. Eyes hardened and mouth set, through the dark weeks Wales had focused on staying even-keeled. After finishing his workouts, he rarely hung around to socialize. It was the smart thing to do. He was scared, too, but emotion wasn't about to control his life.

"There is no doubt in my mind that I can make the Olympic team," he said firmly. "But that is a result and I'm interested in the process. If you do everything right, when it's all over you're able to look in the mirror and know you couldn't give anything else. That's how it's going right now."

That was the essence of what Jochums preached, right down to the same phrases. Their fighting had abated since the fall, and in the ensuing months Jochums' most vocal critic had begun to sound an awful lot like him.

The coach himself had regained a measure of his footing. About this time, his mom finally passed away in the Portland nursing home. They had removed her I.V. weeks earlier, but she was a fighter and had clung to life longer than anyone expected. When it was finally time to go, it had been an easy and gentle release. Jochums was not there at the end, but that was okay. They had loved each other tremendously and had already said their goodbyes. She died just as Santa Clara was leaving for a meet in Washington State. En route, Jochums detoured to Oregon to pay his respects and grieve with his family. And then, because the meet wouldn't wait, because his swimmers needed him, and because the Olympics were one of the most important dreams a man could ever possess, he and his sadness continued to Washington. While his mother's funeral service was being conducted, he was several hundred miles away at the swim meet, coaching with all his heart.

CHAPTER THIRTEEN

On Saturday March 4, 2000, the sky was low and file-cabinet gray. The swimmers grumpily filed through the gate for their afternoon swim. The week's twelfth and final swim workout was nothing more than a gut-check exercise, a brief, five-minute race simulation that existed solely to measure progress and build heart at the end of a long week. Most swimmers spent more time changing in the locker room than they did in the water.

Today was the final day of the hard training that had started five months earlier in late November. Beginning Monday, Santa Clara Swim Club would ease into a taper for the U.S. nationals three weeks down the road. Jochums originally had planned to work hard straight until Olympic Trials, but the winter had proven so unexpectedly difficult that he switched plans to give the swimmers some rest. He expected to see tremendous speed at nationals, not just to boost their confidence, but to boost his own. If there were any problems, nationals would be one of the last places to see them.

Gut-check Saturday was always a very private and passionate practice. No parents, no visitors. A swimmer would be brought into an empty lane to deliver all-out effort for one short swim. A week earlier, Sergey Mariniuk, Santa Clara's Moldovan Olympian, had been biking by the club when he saw people on deck and came inside. The sun had been out that day and Jochums, in a great mood, magnanimously had invited him to sit down, then wasted no time contrasting Wilkens' work ethic with Mariniuk's nonexistent training. Mariniuk had grinned because the juxtaposition was striking indeed. For Wilkens, life was swimming. Meanwhile, Mariniuk, already assured a place in the 2000 Sydney Olympics, hadn't swum in four days, opting instead to surf in Santa Cruz for exercise. When he did intermittently practice, it was in the mornings when the pool was mostly empty and he performed his esoteric, hour-long workout of straight swimming with no intervals or sets. The coaches would watch and say nothing. His bike ride hadn't even been cross-training; he was taking a casual ride after working all day in his back-yard. His own backyard, one that he paid a mortgage on. Standing next to Jochums while they watched Wilkens chase his American dream, the blond, pale-skinned immigrant had gleamed with his own version of it.

When the Moldovan still lived inside the U.S.S.R. sports machine, he had been allowed to be good at three things: swimming, coaching, and Ping-Pong. Swimming had been the whole of his present; coaching was expected to be his future. Ping-Pong was his one allowed diversion. In his lifetime, he had swum more laps than most entire teams but now, in his twentieth competitive season, Mariniuk was adamant that the sport would not rule his life. In contrast to Wilkens, who lived 24 hours a day for swimming, Mariniuk had a meditative, almost holistic outlook that equally incorporated his job, marriage, lifestyle, and athletics. His various ambitions slid easily against each other, one moving to the fore while another glided to the back.

"You here to do some racin' or you just spyin' on the competition?" Wilkens had called out to Mariniuk. They both had beamed. Wilkens flexed his biceps and asked, "Do they look bigger to you?" Mariniuk assured him they weren't. The younger swimmer was happy and buoy-ant. There was joy in his lane again.

Wilkens told Mariniuk and Jochums to pay close attention because he was about to pop a fast time. And then he did exactly that. He turned in a 200-meter I.M. that made Mariniuk shake his head in amaze-ment and declare no one in the Soviet Union had ever swum that fast in practice.

And that was when the juxtaposition had become even more sharp and pointed. Wilkens and Mariniuk were the only two men in northern California who could possibly give each other a race in the two medleys. In fact, they were two of the top five medley specialists in the United States. Each day they could have been training side by side, feeding off each other's hunger. On a primitive level, both wanted it very badly. They could only imagine how much faster they both could become. But

Mariniuk resisted that urge with all his might. For two decades he had lived like Wilkens—with nothing existing except the black line on a pool's bottom—and he had made the decision not to be like that anymore. There was serenity in this, a kind of peaceful relinquishment. But for any Olympic hopeful, Mariniuk's abbreviated approach must have seemed a rude slap. Why should it be so easy for him?

When Wilkens had finished his swim, Mariniuk abruptly became anxious to leave the complex. Moments later he bid them farewell and rode off.

"Tom, you just made Sergey go home to take a long look in the mirror," the coach had chortled, and it was true. Days later, Mariniuk had sat at his kitchen table and with his index fingers measured a distance of 24 inches.

"I used to work this hard," he had explained, indicating the open space on the table. "And I would go this fast." He moved his right finger in six inches. "Now . . ." He closed his fingers until they were a mere inch apart. "I do this and only go a tiny bit slower. I'm okay with that. Maybe I devote my life to swimming and make the Olympic finals again. Or maybe I do all the things that are important to me and in the Olympics I swim three seconds slower. Neither wins a medal. But when I give up those three seconds, I live a full life."

But what if? What if he were to train with Wilkens? What if the two of them in their matching Santa Clara caps went stroke for stroke each and every day and turned themselves into invincible supermen? Didn't he ever think of that? Didn't it haunt him that he had gone to two Olympics and both times had barely missed a medal? Mariniuk looked strained when he answered.

"I think about it all the time," he said. Then he switched topics.

That was a week ago. Today, Mariniuk was nowhere in sight, even though Jochums had invited him to return. One by one, individuals entered lane one and were tested against the clock. The younger ones went first. Then came Dara Torres. She performed a descending set of 5 × 100-meter freestyle. Her final swim was only two seconds slower than the American record. Once again, if she had dove instead of pushed off the wall, she unofficially might have broken it. This was becoming commonplace for her. Even so, she was disgusted with the effort and felt she had let the coaches down. She punched the water. The public Torres would have smiled. But here she could be herself, and her need for perfection made Grote's perfectionist tendencies look rookie. She warmed down in an irritated funk.

Now Wilkens. He moved into the gut-check lane. Since Monday he had already swum 75,000 meters, including 8,000 meters that morning. When Jochums told him the set was 2 × 800-meter I.M.s, Wilkens moaned and complained he was too tired to swim that much.

He sounded so pathetic that Jochums said, "Jesus, don't cry," and dropped the set to 2 × 600-meter I.M.s.

Wilkens smiled conspiratorially at Bitter, who was also on deck. Earlier in the day, the swimmer had decided he was going to flip an all-out 400-meter I.M. He felt fatigue in his marrow, but thanks to the way Santa Clara emphasized daily speed, he also knew he could summon adrenaline at will. It had been weeks since his last fight with Jochums, and the head coach had resumed bearing down the usual way, talking smack, talking passion, talking guts. Wilkens was now fully embracing it, enjoying the aggressive give-and-take. All day he'd been dreaming of slam-dunking a fast swim on his coach. He was definitely not the same swimmer who had cried over a television commercial six weeks earlier.

Wilkens began the first 600-meter I.M. It was slow, Mariniuk-slow, with long, thought-out glides and perfect hand placement. Watching, Jochums fretted that his swimmer was breaking down. When Wilkens finished, he had 30 seconds to rest.

"Can I do an all-out 400 I.M.?" he asked.

Jochums thought for a half-second and said, "Sure, I'll wheel and deal since we're at the end of the week. The deal is that you have to break four-thirty for it to count."

Wilkens pushed off. His best-ever practice time was 4:31, accomplished just several weeks earlier. At the end of that set, he had vomited into the gutter.

The first 100-meter butterfly was 59.8 seconds, which was a gunshot that got everyone's attention. A dive would have made his time eclipse the split he delivered seven months earlier during the finals of Sydney's 1999 Pan Pacific Championships (58.32 seconds). Wilkens churned through the backstroke with huge shoulder rotation and tremendous hand speed. The hours staring at the sky were paying off; it was obvious in his glowing strength and turnover. The backstroke split was 1:08.2, only 2.2 seconds off his Pan Pac split (1:05.97). The other swimmers stopped what they were doing to cheer as Wilkens started breaststroke. By now Jochums was walking at a fast clip alongside his swimmer. The coach usually strolled no more than halfway down the pool, but today he was traveling from one wall to the other, holding his stopwatch at arm's length like a compass so he could read it and watch Wilkens at the same time.

Wilkens looked smooth, like this didn't hurt a bit. But as he lifted his body to breathe on breaststroke, everyone could see the purple splotches that striped across his back as if he'd been whipped. They indicated severe oxygen debt. Then at the 250-meter mark, Jochums looked at his watch and yelled so loud everyone froze, "Holy mackerel!"

There are days when magic happens. Wilkens' breaststroke split of 1:12.2 was .2 seconds *faster* than the Sydney race. By now the other swimmers knew they were an audience to something they would probably never see again. Wilkens fought during the 100-meter freestyle to keep his kick steady and his stroke long and full. He felt the week's miles burning in his legs. The second lap was pure pain, but his kick rose to a plume and the turnover stayed steady. He glided into the wall with his head up. The split, 1:02.8, was a mere one second off his equivalent Pan Pacs split.

"Jesus Christ!" Jochums exclaimed. "Jesus, Jesus Christ!"

The coach twice shouted "Woo-hoo!" in a baffling, high-pitched falsetto. "Damn yes!" he said, trying to recover his normal voice. He was breathing hard.

Wilkens momentarily looked like he was going to get sick in the gutter again. He didn't smile; he didn't talk. He looked bestial and aggressive, like he had just killed something.

"Get your heart rate."

Wilkens put his index and middle fingers against his carotid artery. It was just under 200 beats per minute.

"That was four-twenty-three-point-zero," Jochums told him. A 4:23.0? They were both serious, full of business. How they responded to this was a measure of their respective manhoods.

One of the other swimmers sang out from across the pool, "Hey, Tom, you going to take your heart rate after you set the world record?"

Wilkens ignored him and Jochums read off the splits. The swimmer's whole being radiated something primitive and intense. Jochums bent toward him.

"You did something special today," Jochums said quietly. With that, he stood up and walked away. He had to find a quiet place to slow his heart.

Bitter approached and said simply, "Good job." Then he, too, walked away. The pool deck was empty.

Even without subtracting an approximate two-second cushion for a dive, this time was 1.5 seconds faster than Wilkens' fourth-place finish at Minnesota nationals the previous August. Even without the dive, it was fast enough for fifth at the 1999 Pan Ams, sixth at the 1999 Pan Pacs, and tenth at the 1996 Olympics. It was the twenty-sixth fastest time in the world in 1999, and based on the early 2000 rankings, it was unofficially the world's No. 2 time after his own January 4:19.87 performance.

Wilkens spit in the water, glanced at the big pace clock, and began his warmdown.

. . .

No one's situation contrasted more sharply with Wilkens' than Tate Blahnik's, and that was not a desired thing. Sitting at his office desk, Jochums thought long and hard about the backstroker. Then he dialed Blahnik's number.

The coaches had already tried a variety of methods to engage Blahnik on his terms. Nothing had worked, so in December they had fallen back on yelling at him football-style. After all, that was what they did best. But they quickly learned how someone fighting depression-like symptoms responds to brute shouting. They had yelled and Blahnik promptly vanished for a week.

Next, they had experimented with a hands-off approach, biting their lips and letting Blahnik—and only Blahnik—slip through days of listless, unmotivated swimming. He would disappear for several days and upon his return they would greet him like a long-lost relative. When he didn't talk or answered only in monosyllables, they had smiled and found something to praise about his stroke. All comments were to be positive; that was the guideline. They knew Stanford's frequent use of surprise monster sets, which toughened most swimmers, had always landed like neutron bombs on Blahnik, so they tried to give him the intended workouts several days in advance. They knew he felt like a commodity, like nothing more than a time and a placing, so they engaged him like a friend by sharing jokes and telling stories. This last part had been easy; Blahnik was not only one of the most genuine people on the team, he was also one of the most likable and possessed a rich sense of irony and humor. He didn't have to counter their jokes, but they had watched the corners of his mouth, hoping to see him smile. This approach had lasted from late January to mid-March. But although Blahnik had begun swimming more regularly, no real inroads were being made.

There were things Dick Jochums did very poorly. Managing money and trusting outsiders were two obvious examples. Working with women was arguably a third. But there were other things at which he was exceptionally gifted. One was building an athlete's confidence and self-worth.

Forget the times, the glory, and the thousand goals either achieved or missed. Forget the miniscule amount of money that could be earned in this ridiculously poor sport, or the number of trophies that could fit on a shelf. When all was said and done, when the pace clocks were put away and the sky had turned yellow and rose, Jochums could look at Santa Clara's stilled waters and know with certainty that he was building champions for life. It was what he and Bitter did best and what mattered most. The thought of it got them out of bed in the morning. Anyone knowing Jochums only casually would find his overboard efforts with Blahnik completely at odds with his image as a belligerent, uncompromising taskmaster. But in fact, this was the real man.

Yet so far, nothing had worked. Blahnik had checked out of the hotel and left his key at the front desk. He said he was only pretending to swim so he could continue receiving the $1,400 monthly living stipend U.S.A. Swimming gave him for being ranked No. 3 in the world. He said he used to hate the sport but now couldn't summon enough interest to invest emotion in it. He had engineered a form of passive nonresistance that Gandhi himself would have appreciated. Blahnik never raised his voice, never acted defiant, and never defended his actions. The U.S. nationals were in several weeks and he wasn't sure whether he'd go. It was fear that paralyzed him—fear of repeating the misery of placing third in the 1996 Olympic Trials, fear of repeating the disappointment of senior year NCAAs, fear of being vaporized by the man he had defeated at both the 1996 Olympic Trials and the 1998 NCAA championships, Lenny Krayzelburg. And now there was another swimmer to think about, a young, teenage star from southern California named Aaron Piersol who was threatening to take over Blahnik's position as the No. 2 American backstroker in the 200-meter distance.

None of this was new or secret. The truth was that he cared so much he had shut down his feelings. A weird and powerful self-preservation system had been engaged. He couldn't be emotionally hurt by something if he didn't care about it.

Jochums was no psychologist, and the Santa Clara pool teemed with more than twenty other swimmers ready to lie across railroad tracks for the chance to swim in the finals of an Olympic Trials. Ranked No. 3 globally going into an Olympic year? Blahnik virtually walked on water. But the coaches couldn't want it for him. Their patience finally eroded, in mid-March they had waited in vain for him to show up so they could offer him the choice of changing attitudes or leaving the program. When after six days he still had not visited the pool, Jochums, who never called his swimmers, picked up the phone.

· · ·

Discoursing with Blahnik was like throwing a ball at a pillow and expecting it to bounce back.

"Oh, he's good all right," thought Jochums as they talked. "He knows how to set me off and how to avoid the issue. He's smarter than I am."

Jochums gripped the phone harder. He understood he was dealing with something larger than swimming. Blahnik could quit and go through life as one kind of person. Or he could overcome this, and six months from now walk away with his head high regardless of the outcome at Olympic Trials. But Jochums had no idea how to initiate the latter scenario. As the coach spoke, he found himself growing unexpectedly emotional. He was moments away from cutting Blahnik loose, and in trying to make the swimmer see the lifelong importance of this journey, Jochums had suddenly realized he was being forced to explain and rationalize the most important things in his own life.

A club newsletter recently had been published, the first in a long time.

These types of newsletters are always charmingly parochial, full of exclamation points and reminders that not-for-profits can only flourish with the help of "volunteers like you." But Jochums had used his column, "From the Deck . . .," to blast and bring "into the light of day" the scurrilous "rumors about various problems or actions" regarding the club's ongoing financial emergency and the possibility of criminal activity. So much for energizing his audience. The writing was that of an angry and defensive man. He had then gone on to describe how the Santa Clara program, beginning with the learn-to-swim group and continuing all the way to the senior elite group, was designed for a single meet that took place every four years, Olympic Trials. Everything else was a stepping-stone to that moment, he had said. This had not gone over particularly well with the age-group parents, especially the ones with the youngest swimmers, who were interested in making the sport fun for their kids.

Now Jochums had the newsletter on his desk. He picked it up and could feel tears actually building behind his eyes. He wasn't going to start blubbering on the phone to a swimmer, but this was an important moment for both him and Blahnik. The two of them came from vastly different worlds. They thought differently, acted differently, owned opposite political views, and wanted separate things. Yet they were twined together on the same life journey, like it or not. The five Olympic rings, the dreaming, the decade of training, the triumphs, the fears. Jochums was scared as hell, too; they all were. The coach gripped the phone even harder and asked Blahnik to listen as he began reading from his column:

> To make this team is going to be sweet, to fail is going to be very painful. Either way, the sun will come up the next day and life will go on. But those who strive, those who leave nothing on the table, those who will take the risk, will all be winners. Life is truly sweeter for those who truly live it. The world belongs, and will always belong, to the people who participate. Those who stand on the outside, who never risk, who never fail, cannot now, or will they ever, understand the beauty of each breath of life. So don't feel sorry for those who fail, feel sorry for the majority that never participate. They'll just never understand, let alone feel, all that life can and should be.

They talked a while longer. Blahnik didn't quit and Jochums didn't ask him to leave. Instead, they agreed to meet at the end of the week.

. . .

It was the three of them, Blahnik, Jochums, and Bitter. There were tears and difficult moments. Bitter would leave the room knowing it was the best coach/swimmer meeting he had ever witnessed. They talked about Blahnik's senior year, when he came to believe he would redefine the backstroke at NCAAs and then felt so betrayed when he was strategically used in other events before his big race. Those particular feelings had been bottled up for nearly a year. *It wasn't your failure,* the coaches told him. *It was the failure of the system.* In the middle of the meeting, Wales was pulled into the meeting. Wales had been captain that year, and he was asked whether the team had realized the personal consequences of putting Blahnik in two unfamiliar events before he could shoot for the 200-yard backstroke record. Wales said everyone on the team knew it would wreck Blahnik's body before the backstroke. But they also knew that even if he didn't set the record, he would still win the event and capture the necessary points.

"How the hell did you, the team captain, let this happen?" Jochums boomed.

Wales would have felt justifiably ambushed. At Stanford you swam for team first, individual second. Yet the coaches weren't indicting Wales; they were just trying to free Blahnik from his profound sense of failure.

After Wales left, Blahnik said he wanted to quit then and there. But they wouldn't let him. *This is a fork in the road of life,* they said. *This is as important a thing as you will ever face.*

They talked for more than an hour. The coaches promised Blahnik that from now through Olympic Trials there would be no pressure and his only requirement was that he care about the consistency of his practice. For the time being, he didn't have to look at the pace clock or participate in fast sets. That would eventually come on its own.

"Tate, I will make one promise to you," Jochums told the swimmer. "If you finish dead last in Trials and you have offered your best shot, you are a champion forever and I will be proud of you until the day I die."

They gave him until Monday to decide whether to stay a swimmer or retire. And when he showed up for practice the next week, looking embarrassed and frightened, they simply nodded and gave him the first set.

. . .

By the end of March, the team was readying itself for the spring nationals and Jochums felt a thousand times better than he had the previous August, before the last nationals. There'd be no repeated mistakes. The coach wrestled swimmers into the pool, squirted others with water bottles, and told World War II stories until they rolled their eyes and asked for the next swim set.

"Can we get going?" Grote called out. He was eager and spirited. His knee was on the mend and some days he felt no pain at all. Lately, he'd been smiling more, quipping between sets, and acting generally happy. It seemed sometime during the previous weeks Grote had taken it upon himself to improve his mood. If nothing else, these last six months had managed to both toughen and soften him. A year earlier, there were people who considered him one of the more self-focused athletes in the sport. No one would ever say that again.

"Kurt, come over to lane two and show me what you have," Jochums said. "Dara, get out of that lane so he can swim."

"First Stanford, now here," said Torres. "Everywhere I go, I get kicked out."

Torres had already completed an easy 2,000 meters, so she paddled to Bitter and asked what to do next. "Take a shower," he said. She lingered in the water, her mirrored goggles glinting up at him. She said, "I feel guilty getting out. There's girls probably doing sets of two thousand meters all-out right now."

"Explain how that is going to help you win the sprint freestyle events, and I'll let you stay in," Bitter said. He stared at her until she shrugged and headed to the locker room. The male swimmers stopped what they were doing to watch her. They loved the afternoons when she was in the water with them. Torres' presence had changed the dynamic of daily practice, made it more complex and dimensional. There was less swearing and more efforts to impress. She seemed to bask in their attentions. And meanwhile, there was no question in anyone's mind that they were all part of something extraordinary. Torres was going to turn the swimming world on its head at nationals.

With Jochums standing over him, Grote began a six-lap set, 6 × 50-meter breaststroke. He looked strong, but after just two laps, he inexplicably stopped. He stopped and he pulled off his goggles and he climbed from the pool and he disappeared into the locker room. It happened so fast that no one noticed except the coaches. A moment earlier, his lane had seemed sun-speckled and bright; now it was vacant and forlorn. His first lap of breaststroke had hurt his knee. The pain had come as a pinching surprise. On the second lap, he suddenly had experienced a shooting pain that began in his knee but radiated into his whole leg. All the hope he had been accumulating had fled, and he needed to escape before his friends could witness his disintegration.

This is supposed to be easy. You work hard; you live right. You train like a demon and perform all the small acts of kindness that on a cosmic level make you a good person. All you want in return is a chance. Armsweep out, armsweep in, curl legs, arm recovery, kick, and glide. Six simple motions, but when one, the kick, is faulty, the whole operation tumbles down. There was so much tragedy and sadness in the world that in the scheme of it all, this setback was not even consequential enough to be a joke. But that didn't make the pain or heartache any easier. If anything, the fact that something so inconsequential caused so much heartache added an element of cruel mockery.

Two weeks earlier Grote had taken his fifth cortisone shot, even though both he and the doctor knew by now that the medicine wasn't helping, that they were just co-conspirators unable to look each other in the eye. Grote knew he couldn't take much more of this. He stayed in the locker room for more than a half hour, exploring the sediments one finds at rock bottom. Occasionally Jochums glanced toward the clubhouse but made no move toward it. No swimmer was going to go to the bathroom until Grote emerged.

When he finally appeared, he was dressed in street clothes and crestfallen. The Olympics were all he ever thought about now. He stood on the pool's edge, and the other swimmers pretended they didn't see him. Not only does bad luck jump from one person to another, but before a big meet it is particularly contagious.

"This is so hard," he said as he watched his teammates sprint effortlessly down the pool. He was mostly thinking out loud. "It's not . . . it's not working. None of it. I'm so excited for the others, the way they're swimming, the chances they've created for themselves, but at the same time—"

Wilkens interrupted him. The younger swimmer, the only one to acknowledge Grote's presence, had ducked and bobbed under several lane lines to reach the side of the pool where the world champion was standing. Wilkens asked for mechanical help on his breaststroke. It had been a long time, many months, since Wilkens had asked Grote for help. Incredibly, the two of them spent hours per day together and had still never once broached the world champion's injury. It was like a shattered glass table in the middle of a family room that neither parents nor children ever explained to each other. This was Wilkens' way of showing respect, of telling Grote that he still mattered and that he would, somehow, recover in time.

Wilkens swam a lap and Grote watched. The frustration of seeing Wilkens travel so fast and effortlessly without much daily breaststroke training would never go away. Theirs was such a complex relationship. Even so, their trust in each other was complete. Grote made a subtle adjustment to Wilkens' hips and they began to practice it together. As they did, the moment became sainted and beautiful. Several other swimmers looked on, curious. There was the clothed veteran, standing on deck and pantomiming a swim stroke he could not perform in the water. There was his protégé, in the pool and doing the actual swimming for him.

After several minutes of this, Wilkens returned to his lane and began a medley set. Grote watched with a mixture of pride and envy. Jochums walked over and they stood together. Wilkens' set was a speed exercise, a series of 100-meter swims that simulated the middle laps of a 200-meter I.M. Swimming the first lap backstroke and the second lap breaststroke, he turned in a 1:02.0. Grote waited until Wilkens pushed off again and said, "My God, that's so fast."

They watched Wilkens tear down the pool. Jochums' mouth was working back and forth, like he was fishing for words. Wilkens turned at the pool's far end.

"Look, there's no one hurting more for you than me," the coach suddenly said. "I know this is ripping through your heart no matter how well you think you're hiding it. I know what this means to you. I saw how bad it hurt when you were swimming earlier, because you turned your foot inward to protect the knee and even then you couldn't stop the pain from coming. Just don't forget what you're capable of. You get your legs together and you are on that Olympic team. On it. Your power hasn't gone away; we just can't access it now. We're going to do this together, every step of the way."

Grote seemed to dissolve. His shoulders slumped and his face grew soft. He was not a person who easily talked about the things that mattered most in his life. He swallowed and looked ready to speak, but Jochums abruptly stepped away because Wilkens was about to finish his swim. If Grote was stung, he didn't show it.

Wilkens' 100-meter swim had mimicked the last two laps of the 200-meter I.M. (the breaststroke and freestyle). His time was 59.7, and it was easily the fastest breast-to-free 100 meters Jochums had ever seen. Grote gasped. Wilkens looked disgusted.

"I made three mistakes on the breaststroke," the swimmer said. "The set was wasted. At this rate I won't ever—"

"That's the best you've ever been, you hear me?" Jochums overrode. "That was beyond great and that's all you need to know."

In so many ways, sweet Tommy Wilkens was truly still a rookie. He had no clue how fast he was moving. Would it ever occur to him to look up the splits for the 200-meter I.M. world record, set six years earlier in Rome by Finland's Jani Sievinen? Because if he did, he would see that his own first 100 meters, the back-to-breaststroke swim, was 1.8 seconds faster than Sievinen's equivalent split, and his own breast-to-free swim was .9 seconds faster than Sievinen's. Comparing a broken practice set in an afternoon workout to a race held during the finals of the 1994 world championships is completely ridiculous, but there it was.

Grote waited for Jochums to return and finish their conversation. But the coach's thoughts had turned now to Wilkens, and he walked right past Grote on his way to the clubhouse. In nature, it takes generations to see Darwinian evolution in action. In sports, it takes only a moment.

But Jochums had been right; Grote still had a viable chance to make the Olympic team. He was the most successful and experienced swimmer at Santa Clara. Weight lifting and pulling had made his upper body so strong he probably possessed double the power Wilkens did. He would be ready to go the second he could swim two laps pain-free. In the coming week, the world champion would return to his doctor and insist on another cortisone injection. They would briefly argue about the rising health risks and the medicine's obvious ineffectiveness. Then with weary resignation the doctor would stick the needle into Grote's knee for the sixth time.

Grote now watched Jochums disappear through the clubhouse door. He knew he would have to scratch the upcoming U.S. nationals meet, which meant his next big race would be Olympic Trials. After one last glance toward the doorway through which Jochums had stepped, Grote sighed, gathered his swim bag, and limped to his car.

CHAPTER FOURTEEN

The carnival atmosphere before a swim meet often makes a better spectacle than the actual races do. In the water, hundreds of athletes are so bunched together that the pool surface turns into a gigantic, writhing organism. The swimmers slip through the water gently. They tweak hydrodynamic problems no one on deck can see. Literally 100,000 or more refinements must occur each lap during a crowded warm-up period. The bright caps and glinting goggles. The arms pulled grotesquely behind the head to stretch them. Fingertips dragged lightly across the water's surface to reinforce high-elbowed swimming. There are flat stomachs everywhere, and they are part of magnificent torsos that are sculpted with muscle. The men have shining earrings and tattoos showing college mascots. Occasionally, a woman walks by with the Olympic rings tattooed near her ankle. Nervous flutter kicks send plumes of whitewater into the air. Massive, loose-jointed shoulders roll. The average swimmer's triceps are so loose they are nearly impossible to stretch because the body's skeleton can't accommodate the necessary range of motion. In locker rooms one can sometimes find empty aerosol cans of a slippery, all-over body oil which supposedly makes swimmers less resistant in the water. Sometimes there are also bits of sandpaper lying around, left by athletes who sand down their palms to improve their feel of the water. They say the world's most intuitive swimmers can sense the water catching in the whorls of their fingertips.

The 2000 U.S. nationals were being held at the Weyerhaeuser/King County Aquatic Center in Federal Way, Washington. Located 30 minutes south of Seattle, the pool was built with logging and lumber money, though wood is nowhere to be seen inside the facility. It is a complex modeled after the Indianapolis Natatorium and is one of the prettiest pools in the United States. Yet it is a complete anomaly in the state of Washington, which has only three 50-meter pools inside its borders.

It was late March 2000 and as the swimmers warmed up, the speakers blared Matchbox 20, Madonna, and the ever-present Dave Matthews Band. Swimmers stroked and breathed, flipturned and fretted. Anxious was the mood of the meet. At Olympic Trials, the mood would be Freaked Out, but here it was Anxious. This was a critical competition, for it represented the last serious dress rehearsal before the Olympic Trials in four months. The athletes needed to boost their confidence and their coaches needed to gauge their training. Many athletes were testing new race strategies. More than a few were deciding which events to focus on at Trials. Hundreds of others were dying to make their Trials' cuts.

Twenty minutes before any meet begins, officials will convert the two wall lanes into one-way sprint corridors. The other lanes will bulge with additional bodies as the two end lanes clear to let it happen. Coaches yell, "Hrrpt!" and their sprinting swimmers turn into rockets, leaving a trail of wake behind them. Five minutes before a meet starts, the officials run a final test on the starting equipment. The shrill *beep-beep-beep* is the unofficial signal that it is time to clear the pool. The standard image in the minutes before a swim meet begins is that of a peeved official standing at the pool's edge and marshalling the last swimmers out of the water. The pool then grows empty and glassy. After such turbulence, the sight of such a large, still body of water is oddly ethereal and calming. On deck, bass blares from dozens of Walkmans, the headphones perched atop colorful bathing caps.

. . .

That first night of competition, Wilkens missed Tom Dolan's stunning and wholly unexpected return to the top of the sport because he had been out eating dinner with his family. Dolan was magnificent, winning the 800-meter freestyle in his fastest time in six years. The King of Swimming had returned and was better than ever.

The knee injury had done something to Dolan. Before he was hurt, he had grown complacent with his status as the world's best swimmer. What had been left to prove? He already owned an Olympic gold medal, two world championship titles, a world record, and the unofficial designation of being the best American male swimmer of the 1990s. All evidence had pointed to a comfortable final year culminating with a second Olympic victory and a great retirement. But the knee had changed all that. Dolan had been reignited and he had the aura of a righteous underdog, a sense that he'd been victimized by some great unfairness. It had fueled his comeback. It was Dolan versus the world again, just as it had been when he had set the 400-meter I.M. record six years earlier.

"If people are going to forget about me, that will be their mistake, not mine," he told reporters after his victory in the 800 freestyle.

After his dinner, Wilkens had returned to the aquatic center to see how Dolan had fared. Wilkens' great moment, the one he thought about day and night, was the chance to race a healthy Dolan in the 400-meter I.M. and it was fast approaching. The Santa Clara swimmer located the posted results for the 800-meter freestyle and scanned for Dolan's name. He started near eighth place, expecting to find the King of Swimming somewhere in the mix. His finger slid upward through the names, and when he reached the top and saw the time, a wave of nervousness hit his stomach.

"Okay, it's you and me," Wilkens said with a shaky smile. "Let's bring it on."

The 400-meter I.M. came two days later. In the prelims, Dolan swam first. He posted a surprisingly fast time, 4:18.67, which was now No. 1 in the world for the year. But he never glanced at the scoreboard. The moment he touched the wall, he pulled himself from the water and sauntered past Wilkens, as if to say, *That was fast as hell, and it cost me nothing.*

If that was Dolan's way of playing a head game, it worked. The part of Wilkens that would always be an impish boy now had to outdo him. Wilkens posted a slightly faster time and retook the No. 1 ranking. He, too, pulled himself from the pool the instant he touched. He had never before climbed so swiftly out of a pool.

"Tit for tat," Wilkens thought.

That night in the finals, the spectators buzzed with the excitement. Energy crackled in the air, fueled by Dolan's improbable comeback, the world's top two times posted in preliminary heats, and this unlikely challenge to the King of Swimming's throne. People knew Wilkens' name, but he was not fully defined for them.

"He owns three of the top five fastest times ever in this event," the announcer cried. "A two-time U.S. Swimmer of the Year, a twelve-time national champion, the 1994 and 1998 World Champion, 1996 Olympic gold medalist and current world record-holder in this event . . . Tom Dolan!"

The crowd exploded. Dolan inspired intimidation and awe. Wilkens was so deep into a cone of concentration that he never heard the announcer introduce him. Then they stepped onto the starting blocks, the electronic starter sounded, and Wilkens found himself already 35 meters into the race.

The plan had been scripted six months earlier by Jochums: Attack during butterfly, where Wilkens had a small advantage. Be aggressive but prudent on backstroke, which was Wilkens' weakest link and Dolan's second strongest after freestyle. Dolan liked to say he attacked on breaststroke, but the backstroke was where he usually ended races. He owned history's eighth-fastest 200-meter backstroke. During the medley he typically administered a *coup de grace* during the stroke's second lap (the third lap of the eight-lap race), when seemingly on command he would move into overdrive and in seconds establish a lead so large no one could challenge him. Wilkens' plan was to stay close until breaststroke, the third leg. The instant it began, he would have to attack and gain the lead. Then he would have to widen it on breaststroke's second lap. Dolan owned the freestyle, which meant Wilkens would only triumph if after breaststroke he was too far ahead for Dolan to catch.

The two of them swam butterfly together and turned almost simultaneously at 100 meters (:57.6) with Wilkens owning a slight but insignificant advantage. They had neutralized each other and now the real race began.

"There he is, perfect," Wilkens thought as they started backstroke and he saw Dolan was inches behind. Nearly three hundred miles. That was how much backstroke Wilkens had swum the previous six months. His arms now churned beautifully through the water; his hips rolled deep, and his hands grabbed still water to hurl his body forward.

"If I can stay even, I can win," Wilkens thought over and over. "If I can stay even, I can win."

Just three laps into the race, no one else in the pool was remotely close. At the third wall, Wilkens turned first (1:30.10) with Dolan a surprising 1.3 seconds behind. As they came off the wall, Dolan made a strong, visible move, just as Jochums predicted he would. In seconds,

Wilkens' comfortable lead vanished. This was chess, and Dolan had just attacked with his queen. The smart, academic thing for Wilkens to do was nurse his small advantage and preserve all his strength for breaststroke. But glancing over, Wilkens saw Dolan suddenly swimming at his shoulder and he made the opposite decision. It was time to go blow-for-blow with the King of Swimming. It was the most reckless strategy possible.

"Let's race," Wilkens thought.

It was as if a switch had been turned off. Dolan had been steadily gaining, he had been raising his ax for the *coup de grace* . . . and then he wasn't. Wilkens surged ahead, pulling so hard he nearly lifted himself out of the water. He turned at the 200 meters with half of a body-length lead. His split, 2:02.23, was nearly .7 seconds below world-record pace. People who knew swimming, who understood how untouchable Dolan's world record was, who knew how unbeatable his backstroke was, were already on their feet and screaming. During his underwater pull, Wilkens could have looked for Dolan. That was what he normally did during races.

But instead, as he rocketed through the quiet he inexplicably had a crystal-clear vision of the NCAA collegiate cross-country runners he'd seen on television three months earlier. *They're enjoying the hurt*, he had thought at the time. *I can be that way, too.* He broke through the surface and began stroking aggressively, knowing he had a momentary advantage and had to press it.

"Sharp technique on the first lap," he told himself. "Be smart; stay in correct stroke."

For nearly every 400-meter I.M. swimmer, the first lap of breaststroke is an eddy in the race, a point to recover from the first four laps as the emphasis switches from the arms (butterfly and backstroke) to the legs (breaststroke), before returning to the arms (freestyle). This is a time to conserve energy and prepare for the final 150 meters. But there was no slowdown for Wilkens. By the roar of the crowd he knew he was moving, but he had no idea that by now all the spectators were on their feet, or that the announcer had grown hoarse from screaming, or that Dolan, mighty Dolan, had fallen back not three feet, but three *body lengths*. Wilkens flew over the water, rising so high above the surface his pectorals were visible. He lunged so far forward his whole body seemed to shoot through the hole in the water his hands made. Breaststroke during the 400-meter I.M. (as opposed to pure breaststroke racing) normally over-emphasizes the kick. But Wilkens was swimming these 100 meters as if they were a race by themselves.

When he turned to begin his final freestyle leg he was so far below the existing world record that the entire frenzied natatorium fell silent for a heartbeat. Then it erupted in a roar. What the fans didn't understand was that Wilkens' race was designed to be faster on the front end, while Dolan's world record from 1994 was delivered on the final freestyle leg. Swimming by himself, Wilkens charged the last 100 meters, staying in stroke, visibly correcting his hands every time they slipped, and never breaking his six-beat sprinter's kick. It was textbook swimming. He turned to look for Dolan. But he couldn't see him. The King of Swimming was too far back.

Wilkens hit the wall in 4:13.84, a best by 3.28 seconds in a sport that celebrates improvements measured in tenths of seconds. He felt aggressive and full of power, animalistic and angry the way he became during his very best practices. There was no smile, no joy. Very seriously and very solemnly he raised his finger to show he was No.1. Dolan touched nearly four seconds later. The established order in the world of swimming had just been upended.

Six years earlier, Wilkens had dreamed about this race and tonight it came true exactly as he had envisioned it that first time. Right now he didn't care. He didn't care that the time would have won every Olympic gold medal in every Olympic 400-meter I.M. ever swum. He didn't care that it was the second-fastest time in the world for the previous half decade, and that it came after only five days of rest. No past, no future. Only the present. That, and the single, burning thought that lit up his whole mind.

"There," he thought as he shook hands with Dolan. "I kicked your ass."

· · ·

To celebrate, Jochums took Bitter out to dinner. Cocktails, wine, meat, laughter. There was a rib-cage expansiveness of men feeling immortal in the wash of a victory. Jochums' development of his swimmer had been perfect. The coaches let themselves dream aloud for hours and revisited every stroke of the race. Later, back in the hotel room they shared, they watched Tom Selleck in a bad Western and still couldn't stop talking. The race. The backstroke leg. The way the stroke had held together on freestyle. The night could have lasted forever. Bitter finally clicked off the light, and in the darkness he listened to his boss spin stories and weave dreams that spanned the past, present, and future. Bitter listened until he finally fell asleep to the sound of Jochums' happy voice.

· · ·

That night he had refused all interviews. But the following evening, Tom Dolan returned to the aquatic center and delivered one of the most masterful races in recent nationals when he upset the defending national champion, Chad Carvin, in the 400-meter freestyle. Dolan swam the first 200 meters against Carvin's lane line, which enabled him to ride the faster man's wake. Then, at the halfway mark, Dolan changed speeds and literally climbed up Carvin's back. Dolan, his body out of alignment, his kick erratic, and his arms chopping through the water, clawed into the lead and won on a heroic last-lap sprint (3:49.59). Now he would talk. He practically pushed his way into the media room, and instead of sitting on an elevated platform like the other winners, he held court in the middle of the room. Six journalists circled. Dolan had a lot on his mind and didn't wait for anyone to ask a question.

"Last night sucked," he began. "I haven't lost the 400 I.M. in a real race in seven years. That was not me swimming. I'm a lot better than that . . . We talked before the race about going for the world record; that's how good I was feeling. I don't know what happened. I shouldn't swim so bad when I've trained so well . . ."

He talked for several minutes, not caring that the journalists had already written and published their 400-meter I.M. stories. The king had been knocked from his throne. Dolan couldn't explain the unexplainable, he said several times. But that didn't mean he wouldn't try. He launched into a mesmerizing monologue, a rapid-fire burst of pent-up frustration. Not once did he glance at the journalists who were gamely trying to scribble in their notepads before they gave up one by one. Was Dolan even pausing to breathe? What was most striking, beside his anger, was his intelligence as he cleanly linked one thought into the next. Above all, he made it abundantly clear that Wilkens, whose name he absolutely refused to say, would never defeat him again. Someone asked how he had dealt with the loss, and Dolan just shrugged. He failed to mention that after the race, he had returned to his coach's hotel room and flew into a rage so frightful the guests staying in the adjacent rooms on either side had called the front desk to report a fight.

But despite those vows to never lose to Wilkens again, the next night the Santa Clara swimmer did win again, this time in a far closer 200-meter I.M. Since his victory, Wilkens had been on top of the world and exhibiting a joyful exuberance. He would think about the Olympic Trials and the Olympic Games later; right now he wanted to savor his moment. The victory was making his head spin and his giddiness couldn't be repressed.

"Tell me my stroke rate, but not my time," Wilkens told Jochums the next night as he warmed up before finals. "But only if the time is slow. If it's fast, I need to know that. But if it's not, put it in perspective for me. So I don't worry. I want to know. But only roughly."

On deck, Jochums stared him down until Wilkens faltered and said, "Or, just do what you want."

"Thank you," said Jochums.

What a difference one race had made. As far as everyone at the meet was concerned, there was a new king of the sport. More than a few were privately pleased to see the unfriendly Dolan deposed. As the 200-meter I.M. finals began, the announcer—the same one who had virtually ignored Wilkens during the first 200 meters of the 400-meter I.M. race—immediately told the fans they were watching the two greatest swimmers in the world. Wilkens controlled the first three laps, but on the final 50 meters Dolan began a tremendous freestyle surge. In the last 25 meters alone, he closed a body-length lead. Wilkens won, 2:00.67 to 2:01.21, but the margin was far closer. Only Dolan's arm rotation—his final stroke was not ideally timed for touching the wall—possibly cost him victory. His freestyle split was nearly two seconds faster than Wilkens'. If you were Wilkens' coach, you would look at that number for a long, long time. Anyone swimming that ferociously on the last lap of a race that he will ultimately lose is not going to disappear. Condensed in that two-second differential was all of Dolan's fire, anger, and power, and it was an awesome thing to behold. That number was going to haunt Jochums from now until Olympic Trials.

After the 200-meter I.M. race, an almost surreal scene developed in an otherwise empty media room. Wilkens sat in one chair chatting to the *New York Times.* Dolan sat in another chair less than eight feet away and talked to two reporters. Neither athlete acknowledged the other. Dolan was asked what he thought about Wilkens. Choosing his words carefully—and still avoiding using Wilkens' name—Dolan said it was great the United States had two 400-meter I.M. swimmers who could take first and second at the Sydney Olympics. It would be, he said, just like the 1996 Atlanta Olympics. He smiled bloodlessly at that. The reference was unambiguous. Dolan had won the Olympics while his U.S. and former collegiate teammate, Eric Namesnik, took second. Moments later, Dolan stood up. "It's hard to feel threatened," he said loudly. "This summer certain people better be prepared to swim much faster if they even want a shot at being close." He turned and walked out of the room.

• • •

Three strokes into the most defining race of her comeback, Dara Torres thought, *This is it.*

It was the same line she used to consecrate every race. It was an offertory prayer that had been first uttered nearly twenty years earlier, a talisman to ward off the evil spirits. Like Grote, she avoided fixing on the other racers, but tonight she couldn't help herself. She glanced at her main competition in this, the national finals of the 100-meter freestyle. The race was seven seconds old and Martina Moravcova, a phenomenal Slovakian swimmer and multiple-time European champion who trained at SMU, was already a foot behind. Torres' archrival, Jenny Thompson, had skipped the meet to compete in a short-course-meter championship in Greece.

I've always known I am better than my best times, Torres had thought often through the years. First, she had been tripped up by adolescent nervousness and anxieties. Then she had developed the eating disorder. She'd been a mess, hadn't she? Racing used to terrify her; now nine months into this comeback it made her feel what? Serenity? Peace? It didn't have an easy name, but it washed through her every time she stared down her lane. Until she found it during this comeback, she hadn't known it was something she had been looking for all her life.

"I feel like I have a bond with the water," she had said shortly before nationals began. "It's a relationship between my hands, my body, and the water. I can actually *feel* how the water is moving around me and I can adjust to it. I never sensed it before. I think I'm made of water."

Torres rented a modest apartment in Menlo Park, an affluent city bordering Palo Alto and Stanford. Sometimes after dark, she drove to the university pool and hopped its high fence. There were actually two pools inside the compound, one a 50-meter lap facility, the other a 25-yard competition pool. The latter was obscured from outside view, and it was there that Torres would peel off a pool cover and get in. One of the fastest women of all time would swim as slow as possible. And in those moments, she felt a rightness that existed at no other time in her life. When this comeback was over, no mattered how it ended she knew she wanted to do something in life that would help people. She didn't know how or what, only that there would be a sign to guide her. There always was. It was a whimsical and girlish thought, one full of hope and second chances. Drifting in Stanford's moonlit pool, with the warm water lapping and holding her body, she would feel the joy and security of being complete. The only other time she felt this same new calmness was in the moments before a race.

Now she powered through the race's first 50 meters so gracefully that technique specialists could have filmed the lap for a documentary on perfect stroke. But coming into the wall, she made a rookie blunder and began her flipturn two feet too soon. A swimmer's turn is a tight somersault that cleanly transfers speed from one lap into the next. It's a critical part of every freestyle race because pushing off the wall is when a swimmer achieves her second-fastest speed, after the dive. When the turn is fouled, it's a devastating error because a swimmer must restart from a nearly stopped point. Torres started her flipturn too early, meaning she dropped her hands to her hips and then had to leave them there while she cursed and waited for her decelerating body to glide into the wall. But even with the error, she turned .2 seconds below the pace for the American record. How could this be? She was nine months into her comeback and it still defied the imagination. No swimmer—male or female—had ever returned like this. Not just in the United States, but anywhere in the world.

The mistake reduced her four-foot lead over Moravcova to inches. Torres wanted to look for her, but in a race as fast as the 100-meter freestyle even the smallest distraction can mean the difference between winning and losing. So she buried her head, held her breath, and clawed forward. They came to the finish together. Every thirty-two-year-old needs a thrill like this. Torres touched, spun around to view the scoreboard, and saw she had won her first national championship in a decade. Remarkable. Nonetheless, she was angry. The time (54.98 seconds) was a lifetime best and the fastest performance in the world for the year. But she had wanted faster. And Jenny Thompson's American record had escaped her.

"Smile, Dara," she chided herself. "Everyone's watching you."

She hopped out of the pool beaming and waving. She made a little bow, and in the time it took to perform that small gesture all of U.S.A. Swimming was smitten. Before this meet would end, Torres would engineer the most remarkable return to competition in U.S. swimming history and would be the center of attention in a meet of 800 swimmers. The fans had fallen head over heels.

Over the next several days, Torres solidified her position as a favorite to make the Olympic team in multiple events. In addition to winning the 100-meter freestyle, she captured the national title in the 50-meter freestyle. She was also runner-up in the 100-meter butterfly and third in the 200-meter freestyle. Eight swims, counting prelims and finals, and seven lifetime best times. In a matter of weeks, she would start appearing in major women's magazines, on television, and in the newspapers. Cameras and reporters would follow her through a day of nonstop training that started before the sun came up and ended late in the evening. Sponsors would start lining up.

But even while this was happening, Torres was incapable of understanding the history she was creating. Perhaps naiveté and lack of appreciation are essential parts of what it takes to be great. It can't be emphasized enough how this sport exists on the singular promise of improving times by mere fractions of a second. That thin string of meaning is what fuels swimmers for their entire careers. For this woman to be gone so long and grow so old, and to then repeatedly register lifetime best times that smashed her previous standards defied explanation. Had it been anyone else, the specter of illegal performance enhancers would have raged across the deck the instant she beat the Slovakian in the 100-meter freestyle.

No one knows how prevalent drug abuse is in swimming, but those in the sport fear it is a rampant problem. Certainly it is hard to find an Olympic endeavor more sullied by systematic doping than swimming. In the late 1970s and 1980s, the East German women arrived at meets with grotesque, overbuilt muscles and numerous physical signs of steroid abuse. They rewrote the record books, won gold medals at every competition, and were never caught. It took nearly twenty years for the German court system to expose their systematic doping practices. In the early 1990s, it was believed some East German sports doctors went to China, and soon afterward Chinese female swimmers began making truly unbelievable leaps in the world rankings (in swimming, women seem to derive more pronounced benefits from anabolic steroids than men). Between 1988 and 1992, the Chinese women had averaged twenty Top 25 times per year. Then, during the subsequent twelve months, they posted ninety-three Top 25 swims, and at the 1994 World Championships, Chinese women the swimming world had barely heard of won almost every event. A month later, seven of their top swimmers tested positive for banned substances at the Asian Games, and soon nearly all of them vanished from the rankings as quickly as they had come.

Cheaters in the sport are so incredibly hard to catch that not only is every fast swim suspect, but every fast swimmer is. Never was that truer than in the case of Ireland's Michelle Smith de Bruin, a swimmer of no distinction who in 1996 captured several gold medals at the Atlanta Olympics. Nearly everyone associated with swimming suspected she was dirty, and indeed less than two years later, during a surprise drug test at her home, she turned in a urine sample spiked with lethal amounts of alcohol. Authorities believed she destroyed evidence. De Bruin insisted on her innocence, but FINA, the sport's governing body, slapped her with a four-year ban. Her subsequent appeal to the Court of Arbitration for Sport in Lausanne, Switzerland, was rejected in mid-1999. (Over the years, a total of seven American swimmers have been caught using illegal drugs and publicly identified; of those, three were caught for marijuana.)

Amazing though it was, no one was publicly raising eyebrows at Torres and her swims, at least not yet. She had totally charmed her audience and U.S.A. Swimming had its Cinderella for an Olympic year. But the issue of performance enhancers was eventually going to rise to the fore, and when it did, Torres was going to become one of the most attacked U.S. swimmers in years. For now though, she was the diva everyone wanted to praise, which was ironic, considering she found flaws in every performance. The missed turn. A slow dive on the 50-meter freestyle. A tightening in the 100-meter butterfly. Uncertainty in the 200-meter freestyle. She thought about her age far too often—a thirty-two-year-old racing girls half her age who were in love with the Backstreet Boys, let *that* rattle around the head for a while. Overall, as far as she was concerned, if she had a chisel, she would have reduced her meet to a pile of rubble and then kicked it. That was Torres' perfectionist way. Too many breaths on the 50-meter freestyle, don't forget that.

The overboard self-criticism was nothing new, so when she wasn't castigating herself Torres was having a delightful time. She was everywhere at once, a spotlit debutante taking over the ballroom floor. She was effervescent, nervous, transcendent, and intentionally vague and unsettled. Old-bear coaches received her soft cheek kisses; veteran officials claimed their share of high fives. She prowled the deck looking for familiar faces and throwing off her energy.

Yet if she wasn't shimmering, she was hiding. And here was where the fascinating dynamic between her public and private worlds intersected. She'd walk the deck sending air kisses to various fans and then return to the Santa Clara team area and wedge herself into a cubbyhole between aluminum bleachers and a 32-gallon trashcan. She cranked the volume on her Walkman and waved people away. It was as if she were ducking her own party. She asked her teammates not to talk to her, and whenever someone inadvertently did, she fled to get a massage.

· · ·

Even before Wilkens' 400-meter I.M. swim, Jochums had been having a jolly good time. He never gave team pep talks or group speeches during meets. At a meet where things are going well, pep talks aren't necessary. It's when things go wrong that they are essential. But Jochums generally didn't make that distinction. In Seattle, where nearly everyone wearing an SCSC cap was smiling, he spent the daily sessions joking with his fifteen or so swimmers and constantly giving them either bear hugs or fake punches to the gut. He had nailed the team's taper nearly perfectly by resting everyone at exactly the right time and gloated over it.

"Did it right this time," he boasted. "No screw-ups on my part. I put them in positions to succeed. Now it's up to them."

It was hard to find an unhappy swimmer on the team. That was, until Tate Blahnik appeared on deck. He had built a cubbyhole near Torres and had burrowed into it. But unlike her, he never seemed to come out. The swimmer certainly earned points for consistency. It's no easy task to stay downtrodden and morose for so long. It seemed inconceivable that he hadn't been booted from the team long ago. The swimmer himself was duly amazed that he was still on the team. He'd counted on being free months earlier.

But even when his unhappiness and ongoing efforts to forsake his talent were lumped together, Blahnik still couldn't stop his heart from caring. It was funny the way that four-chambered muscle defeated his own will. Blahnik had worked so diligently at not giving a damn. Then at nationals, he dove in and swam to seventh place in the 200-meter backstroke even though he'd only been training three days a week.

Blahnik didn't like that result one bit. He didn't like it because he knew he could have come close to winning with a little more training. Perhaps he could have come close if he had just swum hard all four laps instead of not exerting any effort until the final lap, when he looked like a dolphin chasing down sea turtles. But he mostly didn't like the fact that the winner, teenager Aaron Piersol, had scorched a 1:57.03 (more than two seconds faster than Blahnik's best), which made him the new No. 2 American behind Krayzelburg.

Blahnik was so mixed up by his different emotions that for two days, all he could say was "I suck" and then refuse to talk about anything except going home. But once he was willing to engage in a discourse about swimming, the words came flying like a chain off a bike: "I don't care. I'm completely, utterly apathetic. This doesn't matter to me. I can't stand being here. But I don't care. None of this matters. I could care less. I'm sorry, but there's nothing anyone can do to help."

He said that and then the next morning he swam in the prelims of his weaker event, the 100-meter backstroke. He didn't try at all, but once again, his heart defeated his apathy and he made consolation finals. This was getting ridiculous. Even when he was in top shape—which he wasn't close to now—he sometimes struggled to make a second swim in the 100-meter backstroke. Blahnik was a genius at reading people and understanding what was sacred to them. So he stood next to Jochums and without looking at him, blithely announced—the way one farmer might tell another rain is coming—that his only objective for the 100-meter backstroke finals was "to swim without feeling any pain whatsoever." It was a priceless moment. Jochums' fleshy face first twitched involuntarily and then tightened into something ugly and furious. Incensed, he scratched the swimmer from the finals and very nearly threw him in the pool. Enough was enough. If Blahnik didn't care, no one else was going to care for him. The swimmer shrugged, and right there in front of everyone Jochums elected to kick him off the team.

"You decide right now whether you want to stay with this program or quit," Jochums said.

"You don't want me to answer that," Blahnik replied. Teammates stopped what they were doing.

Jochums asked the question again. Blahnik gave the same answer. Jochums asked it a third time. For some crazy, subconscious reason, Blahnik refused to walk away himself. He wanted to be thrown out. Yet Jochums wasn't going to take that step. Finally exasperated by the circular dialogue, Blahnik said, "Okay, fine. I quit."

Jochums stared hard. Blahnik gazed back placidly. A moment passed and then Jochums blinked first. He didn't do that very often, but he did here. He realized Blahnik had beaten him. The coach backed off the ultimatum and told his swimmer to think it over. But maybe it had not been a crazy subconscious urge to be thrown off the team, after all. Maybe what Blahnik needed was to see how far the coach was willing to go for him. If it no longer had anything to do with Olympic Trials, as Jochums had said, then what *did* it have to do with?

The two of them slept on it. The next morning, Jochums, while sipping his morning coffee, arrived at a decision: "He's the most naturally talented one we got, but I can't want it for him. He has to live the dream for himself and he refuses. I won't kick him off the team here in front of his friends, but it's goodbye time when we get home."

But it didn't turn out that way. The day didn't end without Jochums flipping his decision again and offering Blahnik one more chance.

"No mattered how scared you are, swim Trials," he told the swimmer. "Swim them for yourself. If you need me to be the reason you're in the water, that's okay. Say you're swimming because I'm forcing you to. Blame me if things don't work out. I will accept the responsibility. We don't care if you're first or you're last."

The talk came before the meet's last event, the 4 × 100-meter medley relay. Jochums had planned to pull him off, but on an intuitive hunch changed his mind. As Blahnik prepared to race, it was impossible to read his face. He'd let down himself, but would he let down his teammates?

The answer was obvious the moment he jumped into the pool to prepare for the in-water backstroke start. Blahnik jumped in and disappeared beneath the surface. Then he shot into view, half his body rising out of the water as his arms pinwheeled and the surface exploded in a white froth. It was his trademark pre-race move. If it had been an opera, the orchestra would have pushed its musical notes to the rafters in a crescendo of sound, for this was a defining moment. No matter what, Blahnik would not let down his teammates. At 50 meters, he turned third and was just .05 seconds behind Piersol. On the second lap, his lack of training—he hadn't trained a single hard 100 meters in nearly four months, he said—became evident and he visibly tired. But instead of giving up, instead of letting the apathy take over, he fought through the pain and touched third by a hair, giving Santa Clara the perfect positioning. His teammates cheered, not for the swim but for its symbolism and heart. The Blahnik who had entered the water was not the same one who emerged. It was not a momentous change and the effects would be imperceptible at first. But Blahnik was going to complete his career the right way.

"You see, someone may care after all," Jochums told him after the race. Looking at the coach, Blahnik actually smiled.

At the meet's end, Jochums was going to announce that Monday morning's practice was cancelled. He usually did that following a big competition and would then head to the pool and wait to see who showed up anyway. On that Monday, just two of the twenty national swimmers would arrive. One was Blahnik. He showed up the next day, too. And the day after that. In the coming months, Blahnik's consistency would become unwavering, even though he still wouldn't swim hard very often. If Tom Wilkens represented one kind of heroism, Blahnik represented an entirely different sort. Everyone's Olympic journey was leading in different directions, but it was becoming easy to root for all of them.

PART IV

MOMENTS OF TRUTH

May 2000 to the Olympics

THE OLYMPIC CREED

The most important thing in the Olympic
Games is not to win but to take part, just
as the most important thing in life is not
the triumph but the struggle. The
essential thing is not to have conquered
but to have fought well.

CHAPTER FIFTEEN

The weeks of spring blended together and became one sustained block of concentration.

Simple athletic heroism, the kind that never makes newspapers but is real and vibrant, manifested itself daily at Santa Clara. Every day it seemed some lean-muscled and sun-kissed swimmer would punch the air in triumph for a best-ever practice time. By now the coaches knew their athletes better than they knew their own families and the swim center had come to resemble a boxing gym with each athlete managed individually. It was sheer detail work and that made it exhausting. But it was easy, too, easy the way hard work always is. There seemed to be a shimmering radiance stretching around the pool, pointing the way to Olympus. The mission had become joyous again. April came and went. Then May, and finally early June. Every athlete's body clock had become synchronized to August 9, 2000, when at 10 A.M. the first heat of Olympic Trials would begin.

Even so, the pool was quieter now. That was because Torres had vanished. It was the most obvious change after U.S. nationals, although the meet had put into motion major shifts in the lives of several Santa Clara swimmers.

Fast as she had arrived, the diva had returned to Stanford. *Poof.* It was bound to happen, if for no other reason than her Stanford coach could not reasonably expect to continue commuting back and forth to Jochums' pool. But the decision to go back to Stanford had come in part because Torres' chief rival, Jenny Thompson, found out Quick was still working with her. It didn't require much sleuthing; Torres had told her. It's easy enough to imagine Thompson's reaction. Yet once the secret was open, there was no reason for Torres to stay at Santa Clara. Although he shouldn't have, Jochums felt burned by her abrupt departure. In reality, he had gained from the experience. It had been good for him to have a more powerful coach walking on his pool deck. It had even been good—the way bad-tasting medicine is good—to have his workouts reviewed by another coach for one of the first times in nearly thirty years. Proud men don't cater to oversight, but the wise ones hopefully learn from it. Besides, the benefits Torres had brought the club were undeniable. She'd become a celebrity among the younger swimmers, especially the girls. She'd also broken, at least for a while, the perception of Santa Clara as a man's world. And in truth it was Bitter—not Jochums—who had been more directly responsible for her training. The men missed her, both for the bantering and for the daily racing.

None fully understood that by leaving the friendly atmosphere, Torres had walked into a thicket of super-charged emotions, animosities, and white-hot rivalry back at Stanford. Competing women are far more intense than competing men. Men pound their chests, fight, and afterward shake hands because it's over. Women are complicated and sharp, like stilettos, and possess a veiled anger that only dies when they want it to. Torres still couldn't train with the Stanford team, so she waited until the women finished practice before diving into a vacated lane. It was a tense, distracting environment that played on her insecurities and often wounded her. It was surely even worse for Thompson. But what rich irony. Training solo had the unexpected effect of depositing Torres into the best of all possible scenarios. Every day, the head women's Olympic coach either stood at the pool's edge or sat in a collapsible plastic chair and for hours delivered uniquely tailored, one-on-one workouts. Together they continued building her Olympic dream. Both were in awe of what she was accomplishing.

. . .

In early June, Santa Clara's five distance swimmers began a main fast set of 20 × 100-meter freestyle. Almost immediately, it was apparent that Tom Wilkens was struggling. Again.

Jochums swore as he glanced at his watch. It was an afternoon practice and the pool was split lengthwise between sunlight and shadow. It happened every day as the sun dipped behind the broad roof-like covering that protected the bleachers. Jochums' distance group always worked in the darkness while the sprinters played in the sun. It was an allegorical significance particularly appreciated by the sprinters.

The new King of Swimming had felt sick and lethargic for weeks. No snap to his stroke, no bursting power during the hard sets. What had happened? Jochums, frightened of overworking his star and haunted by the old memories, had backed off considerably. Wilkens came into the wall and rested for 10 seconds before his next repeat.

"That was good," Jochums said. "You have good balance on the front of your stroke."

"Bull crap," Wilkens said as he pushed off.

Jochums sighed. "He sees through any false compliment I try to give him. We're dealing with trouble here. It may be his body; it may be his head. I don't know."

Wilkens regularly averaged 1:01 for 100-meter freestyle repeats that were on the 1:10 interval. It was so automatic a person could set a watch to it. Today, he touched the wall in 1:03.

"That's beautiful," said Jochums. "A 1:02 on the next two wins the Olympic gold in the 400-meter I.M. Let's go."

Wilkens fell off the pace and did a 1:05 on each of the last two. When he stopped, he took his heart rate. It was 190 beats per minute, way too high for a set like this. Wilkens could be getting sick. Jochums sent him on a warmdown.

Wilkens was indeed slowed by a low-grade fever, as he discovered when he took his temperature at home. But on a deeper level, he was struggling through an unexpected motivational transformation. The rookie had done it. Tommy Wilkens from Middletown, New Jersey, the college walk-on and average swimmer with extraordinary heart, was now the world's best all-around swimmer. The great American dream had come true for him. It scared him; it thrilled him. Alexis de Tocqueville would have shouted for joy to meet this one. The gold medal in the 400-meter I.M. was all he thought about. But he was finding out again how difficult it is to adjust to part of a dream coming true.

It is so much easier to be an underdog than the man to beat. The expectations are less, the motivation is easier, and the chase is clearer and far more righteous. An underdog stays in the corner, where there's freedom to dare, dream, and plot overthrows. The one on top is on center stage with all eyes upon him and nowhere to go but down. Wilkens had swum his entire career with a burning passion to unseat individuals who were faster. His racing ethos, his code of conduct, his sense of epic adventure—they had all been grounded in his remarkable ability to challenge that which seemed out of reach. That is the true spirit of the American dream. But most of what had made him fast had been turned upside down with his victories over Dolan two months earlier.

The cell phone tucked in the jeans' pocket of the new King of Swimming rang. It always seemed to be ringing now. If the earlier pressure had reduced him to tears of self-doubt, what could it be doing to him now? His agent was signing deals, including one to put his face on the Wheaties box if he hit his targets in the Olympics. That was what his dreams were becoming in the language of commerce and marketability: *targets*. The Olympic-hype machine is a gigantic, swirling vampire. His friends were calling; his parents and sisters were calling. National articles were being written. NBC was developing his storyline and showcasing him on its website. *National Geographic* published a gorgeous, two-page picture of him swimming. The people running U.S.A. Swimming were touting him as the future of the sport. Everyone loved the down-to-earth demeanor and work ethic of swimming's Ripken.

At home, Wilkens' roommate, Bitter, began losing contact with him. Until now, Wilkens had relied on Bitter as a sounding board for his doubts and fears. Bitter would help both Wilkens and Jochums understand and manage each other. A keystone is a wedge-shaped stone in the center of an arch that holds the two parts together, and that was exactly what Bitter was to the head coach and the star swimmer. Now Wilkens was turtling and becoming self-protective. That left both coaches feeling out of touch. About this time, Wilkens' older sister, Lynn, decided she didn't like what she heard in his voice. *My brother needs me,* she told her husband before she hopped a plane and flew from New Jersey to California to spend the weekend with her sibling. But whatever the swimmer was experiencing was imperceptible to most people. What they saw was an athlete on the cusp of glory.

Swimming is about geometrical order. The order is in the breadth and expanse of a waiting pool; it is in the blue plate of water that offers unlimited possibility within a very firm border of four walls. For every swimmer, the pool provides a set of established expectations that is known and honored. Yet suddenly Wilkens had transcended the very place which had made him. Suddenly, the way Santa Clara's creaky gate had always served as the delineation between the pool and the outside world stood in stark relief, as if someone had put a black backdrop behind it and illuminated it with two spotlights. Inside that fence was a world of sweat and hurt. Here lived a gritty kind of honor, one that was largely unacknowledged, one that was very personal and very private.

Now Wilkens had been yanked through the gate and was standing in the chaos of the other side. The pressure of the Olympic Trials would have been hard enough to handle, but now it was coupled with expectations and tangible rewards that had little in common with his old world. After U.S. Nationals, it was suddenly no longer a question whether he would swim three events at Trials, the 200-meter I.M., the 400-meter I.M., and the 200-meter breaststroke. He was going for the trifecta. The 400-meter I.M. was his gold-medal event, and the others were bonuses. This was hubris, both his and his coach's, and the decision was made as much during business conference calls as it was on the pool deck. It was decided even though it had become increasingly apparent that his medal chances in both the 200-meter events were severely diminished, given how alarmingly fast the global competition had become in the first five months of 2000 while Wilkens had voluntarily remained static as he put all his attentions on the 400-meter I.M.

Maybe it was just a coincidence that shortly after becoming the King of Swimming his training hit a plateau. It is a confounding but common enough occurrence in the sport. For no apparent reason, a hard-training swimmer suddenly stops improving, sometimes for weeks. It must be similar to what a mountain climber experiences upon cresting a ridge and encountering a long, naked plain with only the hazy outline of another mountain in the distance. The only thing to do is walk across.

"Enough talking and planning about Trials," Wilkens said one day. "I either want to jump for joy or hide in my room. Let's just start swimming already."

During this time, a person could gauge what demons had pitched tent in Jochums' head by how he talked to Wilkens. The ancient Greek poet Pindar built his many beautiful Olympic odes using stanzas called strophes. Structurally, there is the strophe, which tells one simple truth. Next comes the antistrophe, which can layer on a second, perhaps incompatible, truth.

The final element of this three-part form is an epode, and it reveals a conclusion. By June, Jochums had absorbed into his corpus the dueling messages of strophe and antistrophe, and there were times when his brain seemed to be overloaded by simultaneous opposite thoughts. In the same instant, he could believe equally that his athlete would wear the victor's Olympic laurel and that he would bear the shame of the fallen. Life had been reduced to only two possible outcomes.

"He's coming for you, Tom," Jochums said. They were talking after practice on a warm June day. For every pound of pressure Wilkens felt, Jochums probably felt it four times over. But now the coach had finished with the day's admonishments and encouragements. Now he was just talking. Talking like a tired worker who had clocked out for the week and had pulled up a bar stool for a cold one before heading home.

"Dick, you worry too much," Wilkens said. "Just for today, can't we talk about something else? It's a beautiful day. Let's enjoy it."

"Jesus, he's coming for you," Jochums said again. "I know you think I'm trying to scare you, but that's not it. You think a guy like that packs it in and says, 'Gee, I guess Wilkens is the faster man'? He's still better than you. He knows it and I hope to God you still know it. The only way you win is because you do what it takes to win every day in practice. You got a problem. You're still the underdog even though it seems no one except your coaches will tell you that. But that's not the problem. The problem is that now he believes *he's* the underdog. Before you were just some guy. Now he wants you as bad as you want him."

Wilkens lost his smile and nodded. He actually looked pretty tough as he listened. He knew exactly who Jochums was talking about.

. . .

In the Santa Clara locker room, Grote cinched his tie into a loose Windsor knot. He was getting frighteningly good at it. He finished tucking in his shirt, made certain his wet hair was combed, and walked quickly to his car. He couldn't afford to be late for work.

From the pool, Wales watched him depart and shook his head. This was a thing he could not comprehend. Wales still had another hour of workout to go. Grote disappeared through the gate without looking back, and Wales started the next swim set.

Since Grote's knee's last flare-up, it had improved unambiguously, although the swimmer still felt he was always one kick away from ex-cruciating pain. Meanwhile his mind, which had been so accustomed to juggling various interests and priorities, had been reduced to something akin to a hamster on a wheel. So Grote had tried to find outlets. First was gardening. He had converted his backyard into a mini–vegetable farm. But the miracle of green buds popping through dark soil is only hypnotic for about 10 seconds. Next, he turned to personal investing and tore through books, theories, and the analytics of the stock market. Fi-nally, not knowing how else to distract himself, he had returned part-time to Stanford Medical School. Anyone who wants the brain-numbing effects of feeling stupid, overwhelmed, and exhausted only needs to be-come a med student. Grote's rotation was an introduction to patient care, and it so far had done immeasurable good. If you ever feel the universe has handed you a rotten bowl of fruit, don a white lab coat and spend the day in a children's cancer ward.

Grote still had a viable shot. That was the remarkable thing. Even though he hadn't raced in months, he had a shot and it was as real as any-one's because his talent was so natural and his upper-body strength had become so awesome. By June he looked like a child's action figure, com-plete with muscle cabling across his broad shoulders, arms like cannons, and an abdomen so densely packed with muscle his stomach could clench a pencil vertically. The fearsome package was attached to skimpy, under-used legs. The question was, how soon would his legs be back? And once they had their strength, would he be able to recapture the perfect form that had made him so nearly unbeatable? He would enter the Olympic Trials as the No. 2 fastest American in both events since the 1996 Olympics (Moses was No. 1 in the 100 meters and Wilkens was No. 1 in the 200 meters). But the shorter event was clearly his better chance. Even without great tech-nique, a man with enough strength and determination had the possibility of muscling his way to first or second place in 100 meters.

By the time Wales completed his workout, Grote had almost certainly started his day at Stanford Hospital. He'd be following a doctor on morning rounds, checking charts, and thinking hopefully about his next workout. He could go the whole day without anyone in the hospital asking whether his leg was hurt. That was because the limp had disap-peared weeks earlier. On his own chart, the world champion would have written, *Prognosis improving by the day.*

These days, Wales was lingering in the pool after practice to work on his technique. He had good reason to do so. The swimmer had gone to the U.S. nationals back in March fully expecting to win the 100-meter butterfly and establish himself as an Olympic-team favorite, just as his father had done thirty-two years earlier. But it hadn't happened. In the finals, he had initially bladed through the water with that beautiful and powerful symmetry of his. But he swam the first lap too slow. That was his primary mistake. His secondary mistake had come after the turn, when he looked around and seemed startled to find himself in the middle of the pack instead of in the lead. Thrown off his mental game plan, he had begun to swim reactively. His form, which hinged on proper rhythm, had become visibly unbalanced.

Had those other finalists attacked so early because they knew it would rattle him? One of Wales' teammates liked to say, "The best race of Dod's life will happen on the day nothing unexpected occurs." It was an apt sentiment. As soon as Wales lost his coolness at nationals, he began struggling and faded to fifth. His time, 53.84 seconds, was a half-second slower than his time at the Pan Pacific Championships.

The good news was that he finished as the second American, because three of the faster swimmers were foreigners. He was still No. 2 in the country. Only now, he could number three different individuals who in the past eighteen months had held the No. 1 spot ahead of him. They had names and faces and he was always aware of their progress. But they remained nondescript entities, nothing more than red Xs on a general's battle map indicating the location of enemy encampments. Even so, the law of averages said at least one of those swimmers—maybe more—was going to swim just as fast or faster at the Olympic Trials. That was a thing to think about.

Wales, the essence of deliberate control and contained emotion, was wet-cat pissed after the race. He threw a mini-tantrum that startled and amazed his teammates. Yet it greatly relieved them, because it demonstrated that he, too, was human. Even though he often appeared unflappable, he was not immune to the building pressures they were all experiencing.

In the stands, Wales' pretty mother, J.J., watched in surprise. She had never seen her son express such visceral anger. She watched as he flung his arms in frustration and yelled at Jochums. For the swimmer, a physical breakdown was acceptable, but a mental mistake was not. Fifth place? He should have won. *Good for you,* J.J. Wales thought. *Get mad, son, because it's exactly what you'll need to get through these last months.*

After that meet, Wales had returned to practice with a passionate intensity to correct his blunders. Getting it right was just as important as making the Olympic team and he worked significantly harder than he had been earlier in the year. By June, a Santa Clara swimmer didn't hop into Wales' lane unless he was willing to swim some of the fastest times of his life to keep up.

By now it had become something of an on-deck parlor game to guess who during a particular practice looked the most Olympian. The swimmers mugged for votes, with Wilkens kissing his biceps after a particularly good set and Grote flexing his stomach into a gargantuan knuckle after successfully completing another kick set. Others loudly marketed their every stupendous effort: "Anyone else see that awesome time?" a blond sprinter called out. "Get your autograph now, while it's still free."

Wales was too serious and self-absorbed in his private training to play those games. That was too bad because, methodical as a clock, and now possessing an angry righteousness that coaches love, he regularly tossed down practice times that put him right at the top of the club's Olympic pecking order.

· · ·

Meanwhile, the single Santa Clara swimmer who was already a designated 2000 Olympian was nowhere to be found. A continent away, the Moldovan Sergey Mariniuk took his seat in the airplane. In fifteen hours he would be back in his adopted world of California, and back in his wife's arms. Outside the plane's window, Moldova's beaten-down landscape was thawing after another long winter. Mariniuk exhaled deeply. It was then that the tears began to come, and soon there was no stopping them. He had never wept like this before, never felt this kind of loss. He hid his face, trying to keep his despair private. In the well-lit, crowded airplane cabin that was impossible.

He had been strong for as long as the situation required, for as long as it took a prodigal son and a national Olympic hero, to return to a wasted homeland to bury a father. Several weeks earlier, Mariniuk's dad had been rushed to the hospital with some sort of stomach rupture. Details were vague. In the countries of the former Soviet Union, they always are. Mariniuk had stayed by the phone, and after several days everything seemed fine. His father was recovering nicely. Once released, he would have to restrict his diet and live healthier. Mariniuk had laughed at that; where would a person find fruits and vegetables in that forsaken country?

Then his dad died. Again, details were vague. He father was alive and then he wasn't. While the rest of the swimming world was entering its final weeks of training before the Olympics, Mariniuk had rushed home. When he got there, he never asked what had happened, never visited the hospital or contacted the doctors. That is the fatalistic nature of a Russian. What good would it do? How does one assign blame in a world where everything is already wrong, where the system is broken and hope has long ago fled? Following Russian custom, Mariniuk stayed at the gravesite for three days, toasting the deceased with friends and remembering the good times. A Russian cemetery is a place of activity, bustle, and enterprising commerce. It is also a place where the homeless and the amputated, the drunks and the infected, force themselves on the mourners. They come, one after the other, so desperate for drink that they carry their own filthy mugs, step on the graves, and demand wine and vodka. Mariniuk fled back to California.

It is odd what the mind chooses to remember. For Mariniuk, it was the wind. How it gusted during the outdoor viewing of the open casket. He had tried repeatedly and futilely to smooth his father's hair back in place. It was a gesture of such simple love. In the airplane, Mariniuk cried so hard he thought he would break. And when he returned home, he found his way to the Santa Clara Swim Club, where the crunch of armstrokes could be heard most of the day. Jochums merely nodded when Mariniuk walked slowly through the gate. The swimmers didn't even look up. Mariniuk was so detached from their Olympic movement that no one had noticed his two-week absence. Now, none thought to ask why he looked so sad. The Olympic Games seemed to him both meaningless and essential. He slowly took off his clothes and put on his suit. He tentatively stepped to the pool's edge as if he wasn't sure what to do next. Instinctively, he began swimming.

CHAPTER SIXTEEN

Daily workout was supposed to start at 2 P.M., but on this Wednesday in mid-June two dozen swimmers, many newly arrived college students from faraway places, were still loitering on deck at ten minutes after the hour.

Jochums was not in a good mood. Earlier he had seen a *Swimming World Magazine* article that had highlighted Wilkens and Dolan's medley races at nationals and had painted Dolan's comeback, he thought, in a too favorable light. Jochums had angrily underlined several offending paragraphs about Dolan's toughness, scrawled "Not True" in the margins, and shoved the magazine at Wilkens.

On the far end of Santa Clara's pool was a separate diving well where the Santa Clara Aquamaids, perennially the country's best synchronized swim team, trained. At the 1996 Olympics, about half the U.S. synchro team were Santa Clara athletes, and they had brought home the gold. This year, the pool was a training center for the 2000 Olympic Team, although right now a junior team was practicing with a demanding young assistant coach. Synchro is an incredibly difficult sport and it involves thousands of hours of stop-and-go instruction. This particular coach's creative and brutal negativity was legendary among Jochums' Santa Clara swimmers, especially because a loud-speaker broadcasts her comments throughout the complex. Haunting symphony music floated in the air for approximately two bars and then there was the loud click of a cassette player being shut off. Booming over the loudspeaker, the coach's voice said to a synchro swimmer:

"The thing about you that makes me want to drop off the Golden

Gate Bridge is your arm. It's so far back you look like you should be in the hospital. You're never going to meet a guy."

Down where the swimmers were preparing to begin swimming, Grote laughed while another teammate shivered. It was yet another day to thank God they had an old pushover coach like Jochums. The music played again, but for only two seconds. *Click.*

"Do you have a hearing problem? Because what you're doing is the exact opposite of what I said to do . . . That's absolutely unacceptable. That's a joke, only I'm not laughing . . ."

Wilkens appeared from the locker room. He was still deep in his intense training cycle and looked like he'd been sleeping outside for a month. Halfway to the pool, he felt so tired he lowered himself to the deck's warm concrete and promptly fell asleep. When a friend woke him, he stood up and groggily rubbed his face. He was pale and woozy.

A beat-up and sickly swimmer. An angry coach viciously underlining articles. The distraction of the loudspeaker. The Olympic Trials in a mere fifty days. This was not going to be a happy practice.

Jochums told the dallying swimmers to get in the water, and they instantly knew by his tone that this was not a day to loiter. As a rule, Jochums despised being interrupted during workout. So when a FedEx man delivered a package to him on deck, he was barely civil. Then a stranger wandered through the gate and wanted to know about lap swimming. When Jochums rudely told him to get lost, the man stood there in shock until Jochums repeated himself and pointed sternly to the gate. Finally a club administrator brought him a cordless telephone to take a call. On the phone was an Asian reporter in Hong Kong asking for an interview. Jochums listened for a few seconds, then dismissively handed the phone to Bitter. "Tell her to call back when she can speak English," was all he said.

"Kickboards," Jochums said. Off the swimmers went on a hard kicking set. Two newcomers from Princeton were enthusiastically trying to keep up with the elites. Seeing Jochums' foul mood, none of the regular team dared lose to the East Coast swimmers, and the kick set grew faster and faster. Over the loudspeaker, the music played and stopped, played and stopped. With each loud click of the cassette player shutting off, Jochums grew tenser.

"Why are you so weird? Roll your head! What's the matter with you,

you need to turn the other way! I want, no . . . I want you to bend your leg until it hurts. No! More! Bend it until it breaks; the hospital's nearby. Okay. One-two-three-four, one-two-three-four. Stop! Can't you do the simplest thing right?!"

As the kicking set began, Grote kicked breaststroke. But his face flashed pain and he had to switch to a flutter kick. Jochums saw the change but ignored it. At the set's conclusion, the Princeton swimmers handily beat all the Santa Clara swimmers except one. Wilkens in particular was pathetic-looking. He had grown slower on each repeat until by the set's final 100 meters he was whipped by several sixteen-year-olds and finished dead last. Without being told, the swimmers automatically launched into 200 meters of easy swimming to loosen their shoulders. They knew the drill.

"Surprise, that was very nice. I like that spin a lot . . ."

Jochums divided the team into two groups, one for distance swimmers and the other for everyone else. That's how most swim programs break down their groups during practice. As Wilkens began the main distance set, he looked sluggish. Something was wrong and within minutes, every person in his lane passed him. He didn't try to catch them, and for the first time in months, he looked like another average athlete struggling to get through a workout.

Jochums checked his watch and shouted, "Tom! What is this crap?"

"Why are we always a day late and a dollar short? Why?"

Wilkens was in trouble. He must have felt woozy, because several times he veered dangerously into the path of an oncoming swimmer. Still, he continued, and when the set ended he performed an easy 400-meter swim. But that was it for the swimmer. Jochums laid into him with a string of profanity and told him to go home because he was a quitter.

Wilkens nodded dully, and without protest headed for the locker room. His skin, normally bright red during workout, was drained of color. If this wasn't the image of a sick athlete, nothing was. Ten minutes later, Jochums sat down with Wilkens in the office. What the hell is your problem, the coach wanted to know. Wilkens, too sick to care, managed a shrug. Jochums told him Dolan was going to destroy him. And it was then, on that bright June afternoon, with the dream so real it was being discussed in terms of days, not weeks or months, that Wilkens responded with a sentence no one thought he was capable of uttering.

"I don't care," he told Jochums.

At that moment, the pressure of being No. 1 won. Wilkens was indeed sick, but his malaise was as much mental as it was physical. On the most literal level possible, he was struggling to stay ahead of the entire world. Simultaneously, the Olympic Trials loomed so large before him and his teammates that they seemed to blot out the sun. It had become too much.

This would have to be fixed before Trials. Wilkens needed to be whisked to a remote location where he could focus, but there was no more time. The conversation lasted another thirty minutes, only it was not so much a conversation as it was Jochums venting. Afterward, Wilkens, who truly didn't need that kind of lecture, not that day, went home and fell into bed. Yet, he later drove an hour to San Francisco with his girlfriend to meet his Denver-based agent for a business dinner, because she was in town and he was too polite to cancel. He hated how everyone except Jochums and Bitter was talking as if the Olympics were over.

He grew sicker at dinner and had to leave early. Driving home, he said, "Can we talk about something other than swimming?," so his girlfriend turned in her seat and asked about the future of their relationship. That wasn't what he had in mind. Then his parents called on the cell phone to see how he was doing. It was almost comical. He was being nailed from all sides. "Oh, man," he thought wearily. That evening in his apartment, he spiked a fever and began throwing up. The flu lasted for two days and he lost five pounds off his fat-free frame. Whoever argues that the mind does not control the body lives in a make-believe world. This was Wilkens' time to crack, his forty-eight hours of letting eighteen months' worth of built-up pressure have its way with him. It was another liminal period full of uncertainty and doubt. He didn't answer the phone; he didn't think about swimming. And during the two days in bed, his body actually became his loyal best friend. It took all that pressure, balled it up, and shoved it out of his system. When he finally returned to the pool, he was walking a little straighter.

. . .

Kurt Grote opened the white doors of his backyard shed and pulled out his bike. Until this week, he had not ridden it since hurting his knee ten months earlier. He was full of misgivings and half-regarded the bike as his enemy. But in twenty minutes he was biking in the hills above Silicon Valley.

He felt his knee start to ache. He continued pedaling. "What do I have to lose?" he asked himself.

There is perhaps nothing as sobering in sports as a desperate athlete. Grote didn't deserve this kind of struggle. Find a moral in the downfall of a hard-working athlete and you will have found a bald lie. There is no moral. If there were any lesson to learn, it would be a lesson about hubris, about mankind's vaulting ambition and the recklessness that leads us to believe we are invincible. Unexpectedly, in the past two weeks the knee had grown worse again. The twinge he had felt during his recent kicking set had not disappeared. But he wasn't ready to give up. *Not yet,* the whine of his bike wheels seemed to whisper.

Grote pedaled because he was up against a wall and knew his one remaining chance was to inject strength into his legs. He also knew the fastest way to gain that strength was to engage in the same activity that had caused his tender tendon to fray in the first place.

About this same time, maybe even the same day, on the other side of the country breaststroker Ed Moses was signing the paperwork to officially relinquish his remaining two years of collegiate eligibility and turn professional. The official Moses website was being designed, various business opportunities were being evaluated, and he was locking down a multiyear contract with the sportswear company Adidas that he said would deliver a seven-figure payoff if he achieved each of his performance incentives. That kind of money would put him on the short list of the best compensated American swimmers ever. Adidas was entering the swimwear market for the first time, and had decided to ride its hopes on the backs of the two surest bets in swimming: Australia's teenage sensation Ian Thorpe and the United States' Moses.

In comparison, Grote had gained only one new sponsor in the previous twelve months, a pocket-change arrangement with a struggling Internet sports website. Grote had set up the opportunity himself, which wasn't surprising, because his own agent was busy with her healthy and more marketable clients. In fact, a lot of her recent attention was going to her newest recruit, Moses. The business message to Grote was simple: Out with the old and in with the new.

Not yet. An athlete counted out too early is an athlete fueled by intense passion. Grote climbed steadily up Page Mill Road, leaning forward into a winding road that in places was so steep his front tire ached to rise off the pavement. He pushed the pedals harder, and was amazed not only by how strong his legs felt, but by how good it was to be alone on a sun-dappled road. Here, no one was around to see whether his knee failed him; in fact, no one except his wife knew he was doing this, because they all would have protested. Here, he had the freedom to push himself to the edge of his physical limits and fashion a remarkable comeback.

Eighteen months earlier, Grote had been flinty, hard, and calculating. Now he understood anguish and the covetous feeling of wanting something that he couldn't have. Are there master plans in the universe? On days like this, with the blue domed sky and the towering redwoods around a man, with the feel of muscles squeezing and relaxing in rhythm, a master plan seemed plausible. Maybe for Grote it was as simple as ensuring that whether or not he made the 2000 Olympics, as a future doctor and caretaker he would forever understand the fear and uncertainty gripping the sick and wounded.

Today's ride was 63 miles, which was in addition to the 50 miles he had biked earlier in the week. It was suicide. Or was it? It was the only possible way to have a chance. He could tell his legs were stronger after just the first ride. The bike training had begun the day after returning from a small invitational meet in Irvine, California. Before the 200-meter breaststroke finals there, he had told a competing teammate they both had equal shots at winning. That was fine, except the teammate had never been within eight seconds of Grote's best time. The world champion had narrowly won and afterward resolved to make drastic training changes.

"Is this how I want to end my career?" he had thought on the flight home. "Either I continue fooling myself that I'm going to swim fast at Trials or I get serious and take some risks."

His technique at Irvine had been great. What he lacked was the leg strength to lift his torso high out of the water so it could subsequently surge downward and forward. That was all he had to build. If he could do that, he'd swim again like a champion. The elusive form was there, just beyond reach.

As his bike sailed downhill into the valley, he cautiously applied the brakes. The knee was beginning to throb. He considered taking a shortcut home and resuming tomorrow.

"There are no more tomorrows," he thought grimly. He clicked into a lighter gear and continued pedaling for another 90 minutes. If he couldn't heal the pain in his leg, he was going to push right through it.

CHAPTER SEVENTEEN

In early July, one week before Santa Clara began its final drive to the Olympic Trials, Jochums gathered his team at the far end of the pool, a place they almost never went. Between now and Trials stood just one small competition and the taper. About twenty swimmers circled around the coach, their faces serious and scared. Water dripped off their bodies, formed wet circles on the concrete deck, and slowly fanned out. Many of these athletes had sat in the team meeting room nearly eighteen months earlier when Jochums gave his Olympic dream talk. That seemed a lifetime ago. But their eyes were as hungry now as they had been on that wet spring morning.

Jochums and Bitter had just finished making phone calls to see if they could find the new full-length bodysuits that had just been approved for use at the U.S. Olympic Trials. The best-marketed suit, Speedo's Fastskin, had more than fifty separate panels that were said to mimic shark skin by utilizing tiny, V-shaped ridges to channel water off the body. They were said to reduce a swimmer's time by three percent. The first time Wilkens had tried one had been just days earlier, when he swam his standard set of 20 × 100-meter freestyle. Instead of his usual average of 1:01, he cruised in at 58 seconds.

"That wasn't the suit; that was me," he had quipped to Jochums. The swimmer was looking stronger each day. "I'm feeling great."

"Like hell it wasn't the suit." Jochums had smiled.

No one really knew if a bodysuit provided a tangible benefit, but seeing what it did to Wilkens' times had sent the coaches to the phones to scare some up. They were hard to come by because they were in such high demand. It was a sad day for the sport. Sad because soon everyone was soon going to be wearing bodysuits, and nearly every world record was going to be rewritten. Then swimming would resume as normal, only faster and with a lot less sex appeal. The bodysuit of 2000 offered the sport no intrinsic or lasting value. If anything, it created a new barrier to entry, because a bodysuit can run $350 and needs to be replaced after several meets, while a man's traditional suit is $25 and may last several seasons. Until now, swimming had been the last of the pure sports, in that its equipment hadn't influenced the outcome of a race.

Jochums now looked at his athletes, these people who had become hard and ready, and asked, "Any of you think you're out of shape?"

There was no reply. The swimmers squinted to see him better.

"I'm telling you now the hay is in the barn and stored for winter," the coach said. "For you Stanford folks who need an interpretation, that means we're done with the hard work. Now we sharpen. What you do in the next ten days decides how you do in Olympic Trials. With that said, who feels faster today than last week?"

Several swimmers tentatively raised their hands. Most felt terrible. They'd been breaking their backs for weeks.

"You should hurt and be sore and full of doubt. That's okay because now we're going to drop yards and raise intensity. I realize some of you have doubled your workload this summer. That's now behind you. We have one more tune-up meet and then we have Olympic Trials. The tune-up will be unimportant and you won't be rested. So tell me, because this is what I want to know, how tough are you going to be in this meaningless meet?"

He swept his gaze across his team. Directly behind them, the morning sun reflected off the pool and came at such a sharp angle that the entire surface twinkled and winked. At the same time, the sun was already high enough in the sky that it veined the entire pool bottom with thousands of rippling streaks of light. This was a common enough occurrence. But the effect was substantially more intense and unusual when viewed from this unfamiliar side of the pool. The wind blew gently and that was when it happened. The whole brimming and sloshing body—the chlorine, the water, the sweat, and the tears—suddenly became so infused with yellow light that one was overwhelmed with the certainty that there was gold in the water. And with it came the certainty that the gold in the water had nothing to do with the actual outcome of the Olympic Trials or the

Olympic Games. It had to do with the chase, with the lifetime of dreaming and wanting and the happy pursuit of excellence.

Jochums continued to look at the swimmers who had emerged from this remarkable old pool. There was Wilkens, who had defied every limitation ever imposed on him. Since his physical breakdown and sickness four weeks earlier, both his spirit and his health had been on the mend. Before entering his taper, Wilkens was going to swim a practice 400-meter I.M. in 4:22, which was a full second faster than his stunning practice swim back in March. It suggested great things were in store in Indianapolis. Near him was Wales, nervous about his taper but absolutely certain he would follow in his father's footsteps to the Olympics. Of all the swimmers buying into Jochums' philosophy about building champions through a process, it was Wales, the one who questioned the purpose of nearly every set, who had most fully embraced his philosophy.

Also there was Grote, bowed but not defeated. His thighs were strong from steady biking, and surprisingly his knee was not significantly worse for the activity. Near him was Blahnik, smiling with the knowledge that in either four or eight weeks, depending on how he did, he could hang up his suit. Recently, the company where he'd been working as a computer consultant had offered him a full-time programming job with a starting salary package that represented more money than Jochums earned annually. Blahnik's future stretched before him like the thin orange line of a rising sun. It had made swimming nearly fun again. Those were the four thunderbolts and lightning of the Santa Clara program. But there were fifteen others, each with just as much hope and fear and just as much right to be called a champion.

Jochums was ending his short speech, ". . . make your dream happen, not me or any other coach," he said. "Don't let fear take control of you. Being tough requires taking a step forward when you are in pain. You can question all you want, but don't doubt. Doubt comes from fear. Remember it is all right to be scared, but don't let fear control you. If it controls you, everything you've built will be lost."

. . .

A week later, with the team leaving for Indianapolis in little more than ten days, Kurt Grote finished his kicking set with a final hard 100 meters. He kicked breaststroke, carefully but with power, and without much effort finished in a time of 1:20. It was a time with which Moses, Wilkens, and any other top U.S. breaststroker would be happy. He smiled and tossed his kickboard onto the deck.

"I can do this," Grote said. "My body has never been this powerful."

Every so often during practice, his stroke clicked. He would recapture his world-champion form, swim it for several magical strokes, and then it would vanish. But he knew it was there, elusive. For weeks, he had been meeting with Bitter every day after workout and for an hour of technique work. Before, his race to make the Olympic team had been a race against time as he waited for his tendon to heal. Now, it was still a race against time, but the imperative was to unlock the power his body possessed but he couldn't yet coordinate.

Three days later, he again looked terrible. He was an unbalanced, lurching alien in a pool full of perfect strokers. It was amazing how much his form seesawed from one extreme to another. Breaststroke is so precise. Then at the end of practice, he raced an all-out 100-meter breaststroke. During those two laps, his stroke visibly changed no less than four times as he made hundreds of unseen adjustments to find the right rhythm. Water, 773 times denser than air, is merciless to inefficiency. But even as he struggled, Grote was moving incredibly fast. At 50 meters, he turned in an amazing 29 seconds. He broke the surface after his underwater pull and there it was, his perfect stroke. He was suddenly swimming exactly like he used to, before his knee, before the frustrating months. He dipped, he pulled, and he kicked. He was again the master jeweler bent over his work. It was perfect.

Even from 35 meters away, Dod Wales, leaning on the pool's wall, could see Grote's transformation. "That's exactly it," he whispered. "That's Kurt."

The technique lasted for no more than five strokes; then Grote's hips began to sink and he lost the finesse. But the speed somehow stayed and he touched in 1:03.89.

"Oh my God," a nearby teammate said in surprise.

Grote himself couldn't believe his ears. He had to ask for the time again.

"That's my all-time best," Grote gasped when he heard. "My . . . best ever . . . in . . . a practice."

The only other instance he had swum so fast in practice was immediately before the 1996 Trials, where he had done so well. Suddenly, he was exactly where he needed to be to make the 2000 Olympic team. From across the pool deck, Jochums sang out, "Kurt, I see places where we can gain a second, maybe a second-and-a-half. We're going to surprise the world."

It was improbable; it was incredible. The world had tipped once again. Grote was back. He tried not to smile, tried not to enjoy the moment too much lest the universe see it and strike him down again. Around him, several teammates spontaneously erupted in a cheer. The Olympic Trials began in approximately 300 hours.

. . .

It's impossible to describe the collective intensity of the Olympic moment coming to fruition. It was everywhere at once, in the laughter and shouts, in the hunger of the eyes. Television crews regularly showed up at the pool. The male swimmers went to Safeway and bought extra shaving cream for their legs; they wrote goal times on slips of paper and taped them around their rooms. They inhaled sharply to keep the butterflies from flying out of their mouths. They were nervous and jumpy. They looked at each other with ready eyes and called their parents to arrange meeting points in Indianapolis.

And in the midst of this crucial, delicate time, the other shoe dropped. Santa Clara Swim Club's simmering financial scandal roared back to life and this time it had a target: Assistant Coach John Bitter.

How could Bitter continue to stand on deck and coach? Just 75 feet away, Santa Clara's board of directors was deciding a number of things, including whether to press charges against him. They were sitting in the same meeting room where eighteen months earlier Jochums had outlined his Olympic vision. Through the room's plate-glass windows, the men and women looked stiff-backed and severe. These were people making hard decisions. Jaw set, Jochums strode off the deck to join them, leaving Wilkens to finish his workout alone. That, right there, demonstrated the incredible seriousness of the situation. A person could count on one hand the number of times Jochums had stepped away from Wilkens in mid-workout during the previous two years. As Jochums passed Bitter, neither man acknowledged the other. The Olympic Trials were days away.

Eleven months had passed since the scandal had come to light. No missing money had ever been found. The perpetrator of the crime—if there had been a perpetrator, if there had been a crime—had not been caught. The front-page media coverage and live television reports had come and gone. Jochums was close to securing a low-interest loan from the city of the Santa Clara to pay the nearly $125,000 owed to the government. Though the problem had consumed him for months, he thought he had put the worst behind him. Yet he had failed to resolve many of the unanswered questions. The financial situation was not one that could be pushed into a corner and ignored until it settled, not when the Santa Clara Swim Club's volunteer board of directors still demanded answers. By failing to completely close the issue, Jochums had left open a hole for anyone to prod. He had done this to himself.

The board had begun digging for its own answers and soon enough had arrived at the club's adult Masters program, which was coached by Bitter. Through the years, the club had barely paid attention to this program. For Jochums, the Masters group represented first and foremost a potential threat to the harmony of his age-group team. Second, it was a distraction. Only on the third level did it represent a revenue source. The collection of its dues was not monitored, payments were not recorded, and no up-to-date membership list existed. Bitter coached it twenty hours per week for free because no one else would. Under his watch, the group's revenue had grown from about $20,000 two years earlier to an expected $75,000 in the Olympic year. That represented a significant portion of SCSC's overall annual revenue.

Without Bitter's knowledge, his practices had been watched. Swimmers were counted and revenue contributions were cross-checked. It had been instantly apparent something was wrong, because the revenue totals didn't correlate with the number of athletes in the water. That looked bad. It looked profoundly worse when Bitter subsequently handed over a sack containing about $4,000 petty cash, which represented about a month's worth of dues collection (dues of $4 per workout or $40 per month were paid on an abused honor system that had existed for at least a dozen years). Because the Masters' practice occurred in the evenings after the club shut down for the day, Bitter would finish coaching, secure the building, lock the gate, and go home. He said it made no sense to leave loose money overnight in the office, so at home he'd undress and toss the day's collection into the bag on his dresser. Then for weeks, he inexplicably failed to bring it back to the pool the next morning. He was treating money with the same mindless disregard his boss did. But in light of the year-long financial scandal, this begged the question: Was Bitter suffering from incredibly poor judgment or was he one of the world's most inept and blatant criminals? How many bad business practices can one not-for-profit organization claim at once?

This was abhorrently sloppy and dumb. But it wasn't stealing. That assessment required a leap of faith, but only the smallest one. For one thing, a more loyal coach had never worked at the Santa Clara Swim Club. For another, a thief does not stop a program's entire cash flow and wait for the accountant (in this case, another assistant coach) to ask about it. A coach who spends five years preparing for the Olympic moment does not suddenly—six weeks before Olympic Trials—risk his entire career by taking fistfuls of one- and five-dollar bills. Wilkens knew the money sitting on his roommate's bureau belonged to the Santa Clara Masters. So did Bitter's girlfriend, who was an adult swimmer. Bitter, being inexcusably lazy in this matter, had several times borrowed money from the bag and when Jochums opened it, he found inside dated I.O.U.s for the amounts. And what had he purchased? Equipment and supplies for the club.

There were several legitimate reasons why the annual revenue didn't correlate to the number of people in the water, including heavy winter-time attrition and numerous discounts in place to boost participation. Ironically, the assistant coach had generated significantly more money than previous Masters coaches, and that was one reason the program had appeared on the radar screen.

But Bitter was as good as convicted. He could have cooperated and educated the club's board about the Masters program, which few knew anything about. But furious at being impugned and designated the scapegoat for all the financial problems discovered in the past year, he did a very Jochums-like thing and completely stonewalled. And the more vehemently Jochums defended the man who was likely his best friend, the more needlessly confrontational the situation became.

In the meeting room, the board continued to discuss their options. In the pool, the swimmers preparing for Olympic Trials watched through the windows. Bitter gave his sprinters a brief swimming set to hone their explosiveness. He walked with them as they swam, taking pains to keep his back to the meeting room. But he was distracted.

"What?" Bitter asked Kurt Grote.

"I said, 'How many are we doing?' You were looking right at me."

Had the assistant coach turned around right then, he would have seen the imposing figure of Jochums gesticulating behind the glass to the stiff-backed bodies. Why now of all times? It seemed to Jochums as if his enemies had timed this attack to coincide with Trials. That, too, was part of the problem: Everywhere Jochums turned there were people trying to sort things out, and he was convinced they were the *enemy*. But truthfully, even if there were a crook at Santa Clara, nothing substantial would change if this investigation were postponed until after Olympic Trials. What were fourteen more days? It would have been so easy to take a deep breath. Everyone involved—the coaches, the volunteer board, the city—seemed to genuinely want the club to succeed at the Trials. So why was this being fanned into a roaring fire now? It defied logic.

Strong as he was, Jochums had been cleanly knocked off his game. The apple cart had been tipped and he was trapped beneath it. Just as it was impossible to describe the intensity of the realized Olympic moment, it was impossible to describe how terribly this affected the taper's final days. Bitter held the dreams of the Santa Clara sprint group—nearly ten athletes, including Grote and Wales. Already edgy, Jochums vowed to tear down the club if anything happened to his assistant. He always used anger to force his way, and now he became heated-up with rage when he should have been the calm custodian of these final hours. Wilkens and his expanding pressures were neglected; the other swimmers' fine-tuning became spotty. No one was spared as a grave and troubling thickness settled over the pool.

After that board meeting, the situation became worse. One of the directors, a man as strong-willed and as immovable as Jochums, began showing up for Masters' practices, both morning and evening. The board member was probably the single person in the SCSC community who couldn't be intimidated by the coach. The two of them had ugly, heated exchanges, complete with threats of physical harm. The board member began interviewing Masters swimmers in order to determine their relationship to the club and their level of participation. When that revealed little, he stood on the pool deck and silently observed the Olympic group's closed practices. This was completely unfair. Would Jochums swipe a starting block? It was classic intimidation and it worked brilliantly. Every time Jochums looked up, he saw a patient, steel-eyed presence judging him. Bitter, feeling the heat of being watched, regularly fumbled his instructions to his swimmers. How does one act while under overt surveillance? The pressure of Trials, the swirling accusations, the daily threats—it was a total nightmare and yet no one at SCSC was willing to end it.

The men coaching on deck were no angels, but nor were they bad guys. At the root of all the accusations about missing money lay two coaches' passionate and blind single-mindedness for something that didn't have a dollar sign. They did not deserve this kind of trouble, not now.

Within days, Jochums and Bitter had reached their breaking points. They were the inflamed white line that appears just before bending metal breaks. Anyone familiar with their practices could see how badly they were slipping in their duties.

"Get him out of here," Bitter whispered to Jochums, his voice strained. They were looking at the board member, who sat 50 feet away and watched them carefully.

"I can't," Jochums said tersely. "He has the right to be here."

So this was how the final days of Olympic-dream preparation unfolded. At the pool, Wilkens bore the brunt of the rising tension. He was the one who suffered under Jochums' wrecked nerves. Then at home, he had no relief. He saw Bitter, who was like his big brother, in a pit of despair. Any attack on a friend of Wilkens was an attack on the athlete himself. Bitter had always been the keystone between Jochums and Wilkens. Now, at the exact moment the dream was being actualized, he had been pulled out. The coaches packed their bags with their heads spinning with anxiety and distraction. It was the last thing any of them needed as they boarded the airplane and flew to Indianapolis.

CHAPTER EIGHTEEN

In its eighteen-year history, had the deck of the Indianapolis Natatorium ever been so packed? At the end of an early and meaningless preliminary heat, eight swimmers exited the pool. They walked around the poolside timers and tried to wedge themselves through a narrow passageway that led to the warm-down pool. But they were moving against the flow of traffic and it quickly became impossible to walk forward. More swimmers came up behind, making it impossible to step back. The deck was just too crowded. Still breathing hard, the swimmers who had just finished racing became smashed together in a crush of bodies. The heat winner had swum a personal best time and she was so exuberant that she bounced on the balls of her feet and chanted, "Yes! Yes! Yes!" Directly behind her, another swimmer must have raced dismally, because she sobbed inconsolably with one hand covering her face. The two of them were so jammed together that the sad swimmer's head snapped back each time the happy swimmer bounced. Even after the next heat started, these two athletes remained pinned in the crowd, frozen like the Greek theater masks of joy and sorrow.

Welcome to August 9, 2000, the first morning of 2000 U.S. Olympic Trials.

It was hard to imagine another place anywhere in the world more compressed with intensity. Jochums was tired, hopeful, scared, and serious. A kind of labor-room tension gripped him. This was the moment of truth, the time and place for his five-year tenure at Santa Clara to be judged. In 1996, Santa Clara had managed to put only one swimmer in the finals of the Olympic Trials. What would its twenty-two swimmers do in 2000? Would any capture a first or second place and become part of Olympic history? Jochums had little time to wonder. He had spent his last days in California reading and re-reading SCSC's by-laws to determine whether he could be unilaterally fired in his absence (he couldn't). He was 30 lbs. heavier now than he was when the year started. His eyes were bloodshot. This was decidedly not how anyone had expected to approach the team's most important meet in nearly two decades.

Jochums had been so preoccupied that he had failed to take care of his fake front tooth when it came loose. (He had lost the real one years earlier.) In Indianapolis, it popped out while he was eating at a restaurant. He placed it on the table, began ruminating about the meet, paid his bill, and left without it. What state of preoccupation must a man be in to forget his front tooth? The table was cleared and the tooth was thrown away. The gap in Jochums' mouth was big enough to push a pen through. He kept his lips fastened together for most of the meet.

Every four years, U.S.A. Swimming throws a party called the Olympic Trials. Tickets go on sale a year ahead of time and sell out within hours. The world actually cares about the meet, and television cameras stake out the best positions to watch races. Journalists take up approximately twenty percent of all seating. For a few days, the sport's top athletes grace the front pages of newspapers. Life stories are learned, developed, and bundled into 800-word columns. The public reads the stories and knows exactly for whom to cheer. More than 1,300 swimmers were racing for a total of fifty-two spots, twenty-six for men and twenty-six for women. The meet was so overcrowded because U.S.A. Swimming had lowered its qualification standards to increase participation. No Olympic team ever takes the maximum number of Olympians because there are always several swimmers who qualify in more than one event. The rules are simple: The top two finishers make the Olympic Games, no exceptions. Six spots are open for the 4 × 100-meter and 4 × 200-meter freestyle relays, for four main swimmers and two alternates.

The 2000 Olympic Trials were using a semifinal format, which meant the fastest sixteen advanced from the preliminaries to the semifinals. From there, the top eight made finals. Of the 1,300 participants, perhaps the fastest twenty were grappling with the schizophrenia of having to swim fast enough to make the Olympic team, but also wanting to save their best races for the Games themselves. The eight-day meet had fifteen morning and evening swim sessions (the last day had no morning prelims), and Santa Clara's swimmers only attended if they were competing. That meant nearly all of them missed Kurt Grote race the 100-meter breaststroke preliminaries.

Before his event, he had warmed up slowly, measuring the angles of his armsweeps and adjusting the pitch of his hands. It felt good to be here. Familiar, too. Some of his happiest memories had come in this pool. His legs coiled and uncoiled in a languid kick. Neither he nor anyone else was talking about the knee anymore. Normally, Grote had an established pre-race ritual, but today he broke from it. Today he stopped every two laps to lift his head, look around, and smile. No matter what, the waiting was over.

He was in the final heat of the 100-meter breaststroke prelims. Several lanes away was the first-seeded Ed Moses. Also racing was the event's American record-holder, Jeremy Linn. Linn and Grote had captured the No. 1 and No. 2 Olympic spots at the 1996 Trials and Linn had gone on to win the silver medal. They were the oldest two in the heat and the only ones not wearing the new bodysuits. They stood on either side of Moses as twin pillars of white marble in a world of synthetic black fabric. Was the old guard about to teach the rookie sensation a new trick?

Then they were racing. In four strokes Moses assumed the lead. In lane six, Grote was off the pace, but only by a fraction of a second. As they moved toward the turn, Moses increased his turnover by a hair and he leapt ahead. He wasn't even trying; with the semifinals and finals still ahead, all he wanted to do was flex his power. Moses turned first and a group of swimmers followed. Grote had slipped at 25 meters and was nearly a second behind them. There was a filmy, tranquil feeling to the first lap, as if it were a reminiscence.

"Don't look," Grote thought as he glided in the ethereal quiet of his underwater pull.

But when he broke the surface, Grote was thrust directly into the present. It was impossible not to look, impossible not to see and recognize the unfolding carnage. Moses was in front by ten feet and already taking long glides to conserve his energy. That would have been bad enough. But Grote could see other competitors, too. Nearly all of them.

It was a surreal moment, the closing of the curtain, the extinguishing of a light. It was happening so fast, yet he became aware of every breath, arm movement, and angle. The others pulled farther and farther ahead until Grote was looking at their backs. He began swimming with desperation, and then his knee became part of the race, the pain sharp and cutting, reminding him one last, horrible time of his folly, his hubris, his fallibility. The last vestiges of his breaststroke form collapsed and he was spinning water and jerking his torso upward instead of forward. The harder he kicked, the more his left foot instinctively turned inward to preserve the knee.

When he touched the wall, he couldn't look at the scoreboard. In the stands, his wife, Amy, covered her face and began crying. By the time Grote could face his time, the scoreboard was already scrolling through the event's final preliminary results. He didn't know what to do except watch and wait. The scoreboard blinked through four screens of names before his showed up. He had finished twenty-sixth in 1:04.55, more than a half-second slower than his practice time two weeks earlier. He had needed perfect form to succeed, and today his form had fled him.

The swimmer was overcome with sorrow. Jochums began walking toward him to talk, as always. But midway across the deck, the coach halted, reconsidered, and slowly turned back. Grote warmed down for twenty minutes and then approached a throng of journalists. They were waiting in a media pen, a roped-off area in the farthest corner of the pool. Seven reporters circled, pens and notepads poised. Grote felt numb. They wanted to know how it felt for the captain of Team USA to miss even qualifying for the semifinals. They wanted to know if he was injured. They wanted to know what he thought of Ed Moses. They wanted to know what went wrong. Grote smiled thinly at that last one. *What went wrong?* It would have taken six months to explain. He answered each question patiently and professionally.

"Are you leaving the sport feeling your career was unfinished?" one asked.

That question arrowed cleanly through the swimmer's defenses. Suddenly his chin trembled and his eyes brimmed with tears. He started to speak, couldn't, and he took a small step backward to regain his composure. The media, all men in their forties, shifted awkwardly and waited. It was heart-wrenching to watch. The reporters hated this part of their job, this probing of human sadness and the sense of failure. After a moment, Grote wiped his eyes with the edge of his towel and answered, "My career is not over. I am trying to remember I still have the two-hundred breaststroke."

Soon only one journalist remained. He was from Grote's hometown paper, the *San Diego Union Tribune,* and had followed the swimmer for nearly a decade. He considered Grote one of the great success stories in American sports. In front of this familiar face and the gently prodding questions, Grote began to come unglued. The full realization of what had just happened was beginning to hit him.

Trying to help, trying to staunch the pain of a magnificent career coming to an unfair end, the journalist asked, "But still, you have a better shot in the two hundred, right? That's your event."

Grote swallowed. He blinked several times at the ceiling and then looked at the wall behind the diving tower. On that wall, the name of every modern Olympian is painted in large letters and memorialized forever. Grote's name was there, somewhere under 1996.

Grote looked at the reporter and said haltingly, "No, if I had any chance at all, it was going to be in the one hundred."

And that was when he began to cry.

· · ·

The finals of the 100-meter breaststroke were the following night and Grote stayed in his hotel room. He said he needed to prepare for the 200-meter breaststroke in three days and everyone instinctively understood. They knew he couldn't bear to watch the race.

For every finals, the pool turned into a rock concert, complete with strobe lights, thumping music, and 5,000 people clapping in unison. Entering the natatorium, Ed Moses, his hair dyed gold, saw none of it. He knew without a shadow of a doubt that he would dominate this race. *Touch the wall first,* he thought.

His start was slow, but he immediately recovered and gained the lead. His stroke was so fast, his kick so quick, that no one stood a chance. He never faltered, never showed fatigue, and his lead grew with each stroke until he stretched to the wall in 1:00.44, a new American record and history's second-fastest time. He was just .08 seconds off the world record, which had been set weeks earlier by a Russian. Moses was an Olympian and he was unstoppable.

Taking second was an Auburn freshman named Pat Calhoun, a teenager so obscure U.S.A. Swimming's exhaustive media guide had failed to list him. Except for winning a conference meet earlier in the spring, Calhoun's claim to fame was capturing the 1999 Indiana high school breaststroke title. Someone had to step up to fill the void left by Grote. Calhoun proved to be the man.

Just before Moses had raced, Dara Torres had won her Olympic spot in the 100-meter butterfly. But it hadn't been easy. She was a case study in how pressure can strangle an athlete. The 100-meter butterfly was supposed to be her "fun" event, the one she planned to use as "warmup" for her primary races, the 50-meter and 100-meter freestyles. That was partly true, partly a dig at her main rival, Jenny Thompson, who took the 100-meter butterfly more seriously than life. In the prelims of this race a day earlier, Torres had been loose and giddy. Her primary goal was to quell the nerves that in the past had always paralyzed her at crucial moments. During her swim, she was long and smooth. Her sublime intuition for the water, for its invisible currents, flows, and eddies, was in full force, and she touched in 57.58 seconds, a new American record and the second-fastest time in history. It looked so easy, no one saw it coming.

What a way to swim a prelim race. Torres had been barely out of breath when she finished, which was a good thing, because from that moment on, she had to start talking. It seemed it was midnight and Cinderella was still at the ball. Torres' swim was her second American record in two months, the first having come, fittingly enough, two months earlier at the 33rd Santa Clara International in the 50-meter freestyle. Clearly, Torres possessed a flair for theater, because that 50-meter freestyle record had come exactly one year to the day after she made her comeback decision in Santa Clara's stands. In the race, she had touched in 24.73, then jubilantly lifted her muscled arms skyward and whooped in delight for the first time since her comeback had begun.

Then she did it again in Indianapolis, this time in the 100-meter butterfly. And that was when the long-overdue question was finally asked: Was this implausible comeback legal? In the six months leading to Trials, Torres had become the most reported-on swimmer in the country. Yet the issue of illegal performance-enhancing drugs had never been explored. This was a thirty-three-year-old woman who was now bench-pressing 205 lbs. Her back was the width of a table and her arms were larger than most men's. No woman older than thirty years had ever made the U.S. Olympic team, yet the ancient Torres was favored to do it multiple times. The lack of scrutiny had been so bizarre that finally her coach, Stanford's Quick—a strong anti-doping crusader—had begun wondering aloud to reporters why they hadn't pursued it. And that was how the wheel began to turn. Was she juiced? Were the swims won in a laboratory? After the 100-meter butterfly, the questions came in an avalanche, catching Torres completely off guard. How fickle the media is. For nearly a year, it had overtly, even fawningly, encouraged her to celebrate her long absence from the sport and to play up the role of the forehead-slapping tomboy who can't believe her own success any more than she can acknowledge her beauty. Now the same media wanted an explanation for the mythic rise it had helped create. In the media room, small circles of journalists argued the issue incessantly. By the time Trials would end, Dara Torres' guilt or innocence would be one of the biggest stories in Indianapolis.

Torres was not taking illegal performance-enhancing drugs, at least not to her knowledge. It's critical to note that she passed every drug test she took and that her speed had always been, since age fourteen, otherworldly. She was indisputably one of the fastest, most natural, and most successful swimmers in history. But that said, she was doing everything possible within legal bounds to succeed, and that put her squarely in a gray zone. As the *Washington Post*'s Amy Shipley reported, Torres was on a daily nutritional regime of multivitamins, minerals, amino acids, and protein supplements, including the controversial creatine. The swimmer had always been fastidious about her diet, about taking control of her life through food management, but since late spring, she and other Stanford women swimmers, under the direction of Quick, had been daily consuming more than twenty-five pills, powders, and other forms of natural enhancers at a cost of $500 per month. The only people who should be on a protocol of twenty-five pills per day are those battling HIV. If this were the science of legal sports in the new millennium, then swimming was indeed in for dangerous times. What the elites do today is what the grassroots do tomorrow.

Torres gave a good imitation of a deer in the headlights. There she was, sitting in the pressroom, smiling and swigging a carbohydrate drink while bantering with reporters. Then one asked about steroid abuse. The smile stayed on her face, but now it was false. It was as if someone had dragged something dead and foul into the room. Then came another question, then a third. Torres was so unprepared for the inquisition that her sentences fell apart and she lost her relaxed state of mind for the remainder of the meet. In the butterfly finals, it was a two-woman race against her archrival, Thompson. The media had already proclaimed their rivalry the most dramatic in swimming's recent memory, which of course piled on still more pressure. Instead of the fluid grace she had demonstrated earlier, she tried too hard to push herself through the water with sheer strength. The magical lightness was gone.

"Don't think about Jenny," she told herself 75 meters into the race. "Swim your own race."

Of course if you think of it, you're going to do it. Torres instinctively turned her head to look for Thompson. The move disrupted her next two strokes and she fell behind, although in the big picture it was inconsequential. She touched second in 57.86 (losing by .08 seconds) and felt a bucket of relief pour over her. She was an Olympian.

Her racing wasn't done. Before the meet's end, she would place second in the 100-meter freestyle behind Thompson and convincingly win the 50-meter freestyle. That put her in three individual events. She would also win spots on two relays. After thirteen months of training, Dara Torres, the first American woman swimmer to compete in four Olympics, was going to the 2000 Games in five events, more than any other U.S. swimmer. But nothing comes without a price. Behind the thrill of her success was confusion and hurt over the drug issue. She'd been wounded to the core. As much as anything else, this would have to be remedied in the thirty days before the Olympic Games.

. . .

"Tom vs. Tom." That was how the press happily billed the finals of the 400-meter I.M. The match-up, with its strikingly contrasted two swimmers, had all the rich subtext journalists love. Wilkens was the clean-cut, well-mannered athlete with the work ethic and humble approach. Dolan offered ruthlessness and chilling invincibility. Wilkens worked hard and had emerged as the blue-collar hero. Dolan worked harder but was perceived as a mercenary. Wilkens had been turned into U.S.A.

Swimming's next unofficial goodwill ambassador and was being treated as such. Dolan should have owned that role for much of the 1990s, but he had neither wanted it nor had it ever been offered to him.

Weeks earlier, U.S.A. Swimming had asked Wilkens to be on the cover of its Olympic Trials program. He had agreed but was completely unprepared and embarrassed when he saw the final product. Set against a black background, Wilkens' bright profile and torso dominated the entire cover. His eyes were closed, his face grimaced, and twinkling water from pre-race splashing ran down his body. The image was wholly iconographic. It was a picture of an illuminated savior—a baptismally cleansed one at that—having assumed his anointed place as the new King of Swimming. U.S.A. Swimming had been so eager to develop him into an official poster child that its graphic designers had digitally altered the original photo by turning his yellow Santa Clara cap into a white national-team cap. In the background were chiaroscuro images of several other athletes. But they were so small and recessed that the athletes were barely individualized. The message was that Wilkens had become the essence and personification of American swimming. He was bursting with light and twenty times larger than the others. Here was the hope and future of the sport.

Wilkens was the type of person who holds his ego firmly in check. For this reason, he would always be an amateur athlete posing as a professional. That is, as long as "amateur" describes a person whose pure passion for a sport overrides all other reasons for participating. His parents hadn't raised him to be the center of attention and the most recognizable athlete at the 2000 Olympic Trials. And they certainly hadn't prepared him to fight through throngs of autograph-seekers and parents wanting snapshots. Wilkens tried to accommodate everyone, because that was who he was. If a kid wanted to score Dolan's autograph, he had better be able to motor, because Dolan allowed the public a two-second window of access to him. That was how long it took to emerge from a stairwell and walk across a public hallway to the natatorium's adjacent parking garage.

In the prelims of the 400-meter I.M., the two competitors made their first chess moves. Dolan floated his race to conserve energy and only swam fast enough to make finals. Wilkens elected for an aggressive first strike and swam 4:16.91, his second-fastest time ever. It was quite a statement. Jochums was irritated but also optimistic. If Wilkens could do that in prelims, the sky was the limit in the finals.

They went to their hotels and slept. They slept and then they woke up, thought about the lifetime of work that had gone into this moment, and headed to the pool to race. Now it was the finals and Wilkens, Dolan, and six others stood nervously on the blocks. Wilkens felt a kind of fear and excitement unlike anything he had ever experienced. He couldn't wait for the race to begin.

"Judges and timers, ready . . ." the starter said.

The finalists hit the water simultaneously and Wilkens attacked first. He took the lead as expected. Dolan would wait to make his move on backstroke. Wilkens' race plan was basically the same as it had been for spring nationals, when he upset Dolan. But he was stronger now. Stronger and more confident. He would take the early lead, attempt to neutralize Dolan's offensive move on backstroke, build a lead in breast-stroke, and then try to hold it during the freestyle.

Wilkens looked beautiful on his first lap, strong and in control. But standing on deck, Jochums gripped his watch harder. He knew Wilkens' stroke better than he knew his own face and something was off. He twice checked the swimmer's stroke rate and saw it was unusually high, a sign that Wilkens was spinning too fast through the water. It didn't make sense, especially so early in the race. Jochums swore to himself and waited.

At 100 meters, Wilkens had the lead, but his split (58.00 seconds) was a shade slower than it should have been, especially considering how much higher the stroke rate was. But that wasn't the surprise. The surprise was Dolan, only .18 seconds back. The world record-holder had lost the leg but he had parried one of Wilkens' most important offensive weapons. The leg was a draw, which meant Dolan had effectively won it.

They began the backstroke. This was where Wilkens had ambushed Dolan in the spring, and the defending Olympic champion clearly wasn't going to let it happen again. Through the months of training, Wilkens and Jochums had mentally raced Dolan every day. They had invoked his image, using his face and speed to psyche each other up. All during that time, they did not prepare for the contingency that Dolan might dra-matically change race strategies. Yet he had. For months, the deposed king had trained for this 400-meter I.M. as if it were a 300-meter race with the winner to be declared at the end of breaststroke. It was a huge gamble, for he was willing to exhaust himself to stay close to Wilkens, then trust his heart to carry him to victory in freestyle.

On backstroke, Jochums counted Wilkens' stroke rate and saw once again it was too high. This was inexplicable, and Jochums experienced the familiar feeling of being utterly helpless to help an athlete. In a race, stroke rate is the one thing swimmers can't easily judge for themselves. Wilkens had trained at a specific rate for thousands of hours until it had become second nature. Now it was nowhere in sight. What was going on? If Wilkens thought he could win a stroke-for-stroke slugfest against Dolan, he needed to have his head checked. Yet that was what he appeared to be doing. Just three laps into the race, it was equally possible that Wilkens was either swimming the race of his life or heading for a colossal collapse.

The Santa Clara swimmer still owned the lead at the end of backstroke, but he knew something was off. Now was the time for him to turn this race into a rout. But underwater, he felt his lungs hurting. *Too early for that,* he thought. He wouldn't know about the high stroke rate until Jochums told him, but he felt the first inkling of trouble. And Dolan was much closer than he should have been.

"Now's the time," Wilkens said to himself as he started breaststroke. "This is where you do it."

He swam the pool length and his lead grew. But it was clear Dolan was not going to give away the three body lengths he had lost at nationals. Jochums looked for Wilkens' signature explosion of power, but Wilkens was holding it until the second lap. At the 250-meter turn, Wilkens' lead was six feet when it should have been more. Then the explosion of power came. Only it came not from Wilkens or Dolan, but from a baby-faced teenager from the University of Southern California named Erik Vendt. Vendt, nineteen and one of the smallest finalists in Olympic Trials, was a distance freestyler with a promising 400-meter I.M.; in the spring he had placed second in the event at the NCAA championships. But in truth, he was using this race as a warmup for the 1,500-meter freestyle, which he was expected to win on the meet's last day. It is common enough for swimmers to race an early event to stay sharp. Wilkens and Dolan had been so involved in their own battle they never saw Vendt sneaking up.

Swimming the second lap of breaststroke, Vendt, his head shaved, had broken the cardinal rule of never turning the head to view the competition. When he realized they were only a few feet ahead, he literally did a cartoon double take. He was Elmer Fudd realizing "da wabbit" was within reach. No one, certainly not Vendt, had ever anticipated he'd be this close. The instant he understood where he was, he began swimming like an ecstatic madman.

At 300 meters, Wilkens owned the lead. Dolan and Vendt were a few feet behind, though Vendt had passed Dolan to take second place. Wilkens' breaststroke split was two seconds slower than planned. Now he was in deep trouble, because the men chasing him were two of the world's best freestylers. Wilkens saw how close they were and he began his freestyle leg with a furious six-beat sprinter's kick. This was chess and he was in check. His only hope was to establish a wide lead and hold on.

Between 300 meters and 350 meters he held his advantage. Then he flipturned. A collective groan escaped from the spectators as they saw how slowly he pushed off the wall. He was destroyed with fatigue. They wanted this for him, and they wanted it for themselves, because in Wilkens they saw their own hopes and dreams. Wilkens tore at the water and maintained his lead to 375 meters. That was when Dolan and Vendt pulled even with him. In three strokes, they both pulled ahead.

"No!" Wilkens screamed in his head. "No! No! No!"

It was too late. Dolan and Vendt, now in their freestyle grooves, swam farther ahead. This couldn't be happening. Then with 10 meters to go, Wilkens simply shut down and stopped racing. He had already lost, but in those final five strokes he also gave up. He glided into the wall third, the most horrible place in all of swimming, since only first or second goes to the Olympics. Dolan won with his fastest time in years (4:13.72) to recapture his crown as the King of Swimming. In the biggest upset so far of Olympic Trials, Vendt took second (4:13.89). Wilkens, his head against the pool ledge, had touched in 4:15.69, nearly two seconds slower than his best.

He was shell-shocked. The one race where he could afford no mistakes was the one where everything went wrong from the first lap. All he had to do was swim his best time to make the team (4:13.84), yet he had folded, buckled under pressure. On deck, Vendt was practically doing cartwheels. Dolan was punching the water and screaming with a primal intensity that was shocking. It had been too big a thing, this race, and Wilkens had choked. The Olympic Trials are as beautiful as they are terrible.

For the next hour, he numbly went through the machinations of warming down and preparing for his next race in two days. He grimly met with Jochums, talked to reporters, signed autographs, and worked with a masseuse. His body ached from swimming in such an unfamiliar manner. The evening session ended and 5,000 people cleared out. Wilkens stayed in the pool area. Is it possible to catalog and compare heartache? First Grote, now Wilkens. On the misery scale, who was hurting most? *I lost,* Wilkens thought. *I lost my own race.*

In the cavernous emptiness of the silent natatorium, he didn't know what to do or where to turn. The devastated Jochums had gone off to some dark place, where he cried stinging, bitter tears that no one would ever see. "All this time together and I forgot that underneath the warrior exterior was a boy still learning his way," was all Jochums could say the next day.

After a bad loss, a vacant athletic facility is one of the most mournful places on earth. Wilkens stayed there, unable to face his family. It began to sink in that his dream of an Olympic gold medal had died. He had two more races, two additional chances to become an Olympian, but he realistically couldn't count on winning a medal in either. He couldn't even count on making the team. All his chips had been placed on the sport's decathlon. Eric Vendt? Vendt was an animal, but no one had ever thought he would be anywhere near Dolan and Wilkens. Wilkens couldn't imagine what to do now. He held his head. He choked against the sobs. Nothing made sense. He barely knew where he was.

Wilkens looked up to see his brother-in-law, Brian Retterer, approaching. Retterer was an ex–Stanford teammate who had married Wilkens' older sister Lynn several years earlier. Retterer was one of the best collegiate racers of all time. Ironically, it was Retterer who owned the American record in the 200-yard backstroke that Blahnik had wanted so badly—and missed—at the 1999 NCAA championships. Twice, in 1992 and 1996, Retterer had been an Olympic Trial finalist who failed to make the Olympic team. One of those times, he had touched third.

"Tom, get back in the water," Retterer told his brother-in-law. "Get in, swim, and do whatever you need to do to get through this. You cry; you scream; whatever. You don't come out until you're ready to face forward for the rest of the meet."

Wilkens dumbly nodded and followed Retterer's advice. He began swimming in the empty warm-down pool while three generations of Wilkenses, all of them pale and somber, waited in the upstairs lobby. The lobby overlooked the pool and through the glass wall they watched him move back and forth. The women had wet eyes. The men stared into space and comforted each other by recounting the race over and over until it had hardened into historical, uneditable fact. Wilkens' mother, Laney, listened to them for a while, and when she couldn't take it any longer she went off by herself to pray for her baby.

More than two hours after his race, Wilkens, the last one out of the pool area, appeared before them. He looked smaller and more vulnerable than seemed humanly possible. It was as if the defeat had chopped three inches off his frame and reduced his shoulders by half. His eyes were red-rimmed. He tried to make a weak joke about nobody dying and no one laughed. At that moment, an unseen janitor killed the natatorium's overhead lights. The pool disappeared in darkness.

· · ·

Two days had passed since Wilkens' defeat. Now was the morning of the 200-meter breaststroke preliminaries. The event's world champion, Kurt Grote, began racing and after just 25 meters his knee told him this was the last swim of his career.

He gamely tried to stay with the leaders, and if the race were three laps instead of four, he could have at least finished with dignity. But in the final 50 meters, his body simply broke down. Most of the heat pulled away, first five feet, then ten feet, and finally fifteen. Grote was dead last with 2:23.09, a time he could do during practice any day of the week if his leg were healthy. Afterward, he sat in a plastic chair to watch Moses and Wilkens swim their respective heats. Both advanced to the semifinals, but with very different races. Moses, taking just fourteen strokes per lap, was so powerful that if the guy in charge of Olympic gold had been watching, he would have handed him the medal right then and there. Wilkens, on the other hand, looked jerky and uncomfortable. His stroke was rushed and lacked his usual aggressive power.

After Wilkens swam, the scoreboard ran through the final placings. Hand on his chin in a Rodin pose, Grote abjectly watched the scrolling results. His name finally appeared in thirty-eighth place. He was inconsolably sad. He approached the warm-down pool and watched Wilkens swim back and forth. It seemed like only yesterday that they were ranked No. 1 and No. 2 in the world. Now the world champion's career was over and the protégé's was in deep trouble. Grote had no reason to warm down, so he slowly walked back to the Santa Clara team area.

Wilkens' disturbing prelim race reflected his ongoing struggles out of the water. It is an undeniable fact that the mighty fall faster and harder than anyone else. The 400-meter I.M. loss would take years to become barnacled with the right perspective, insight, and growth. Yet Wilkens had been allowed all of 48 hours to get over the death of his dream. He had no help from Jochums, whose face, disfigured by the missing tooth, was a closed door. The coach was inconsolable and couldn't stop talking about the loss. On deck, people Wilkens didn't know came in a steady, funereal procession to express their condolences. Everywhere he looked, he saw his face on the Trials' program and it made him feel queasy. *Face forward,* Wilkens tried to remind himself. *You still have two events.*

In the 200-meter breaststroke semis, Wilkens swam fast enough to make finals, but things looked bad. He qualified fourth behind Moses and two promising teenagers who were known to swim much faster in finals. Moses, swimming as if on a Sunday stroll, had glided his way to a new Olympic Trials record without seeming to break a sweat.

A person could spend a lifetime in an airless room and emerge for one day to watch a swim meet and be able to identify Wilkens as a swimmer in trouble. It was so obvious that several people within the U.S.A. Swimming hierarchy privately suggested to Jochums that he scratch the swimmer from the finals of the 200-meter breaststroke. They felt a second failure was imminent and that another missed Olympic berth would mentally destroy him. He wasn't going to make the Olympic team in the 200-meter breaststroke, but he still had a shot at the 200-meter I.M., they said. This was a delicate matter and Jochums' predictable response was to immediately tell Wilkens and ask him what he planned to do about it.

In the hours before the 200-meter breaststroke finals, the swimmer napped in his hotel room. When he woke up, he stretched in bed and used the remote control to turn on the television. The screen flickered and suddenly Wilkens found himself in the most surreal moment possible. He was staring at the television screen and the person staring back at him was Tom Wilkens. This was NBC's tape-delayed broadcast of the week's events, and Wilkens had turned it on at the exact instant the camera was panning in on him before the 400-meter I.M. finals.

"God, you look scared," he said to the television. He felt at once all the shame and disappointment scrambling through his body like a million spiders. He wanted to climb out of his own skin. His finger lifted to change the channel, but he stopped it in midair. "No, you have to watch this no matter how bad it hurts. There must be a reason you're meant to see it."

He could see his mistakes clearly on tape—the high stroke rate, the flat breaststroke, the failure to finish a race strong. He could hear how the voice of the announcer, 1984 Olympian Rowdy Gaines, spiked with excitement and surprise as Vendt forced himself into the race. Wilkens had always been an athlete who performed well when he was furious, and this did the trick. Especially seeing the unconscionable give-up at the end, when he fell back so fast that he disappeared off the screen. Cursing and suddenly full of aggression, he rammed his towel and goggles hard into his bag and left for the pool. He knew exactly what he needed to do if he wanted to be an Olympian. He needed to ignore the two teenage stars who were seeded ahead of him and focus on the biggest game of all.

"Take out Moses," he told himself. "Do that, and the rest of the race takes care of itself."

All week, U.S.A. Swimming had been conducting extensive biomechanical research on swimmers that included measuring their stroke rates. Not many athletes realized they could analyze their competition in new and innovative ways simply by checking the data outputs, and Wilkens had been one of the few who took advantage of it. Studying Moses' races, he believed he had discovered a crack in the swimmer's seemingly unbeatable stroke and power. Beginning at about 125 meters, Moses' stroke length began imperceptibly degrading and shortening. It was a classic sprinter's breakdown, but Moses had managed to cloak his fatigue until the final lap. It was nearly impossible for the eye to notice this minor event because by the third lap Moses always owned a well-cushioned lead. So while it seemed as if his vulnerability occurred in the last 25 meters of a race, he was actually decelerating well before then. What would happen if someone were able to push Moses so hard on the third lap that his body entered early distress?

Before the event, Wilkens let all the anger over the 400-meter I.M. loss bubble to the surface. He glowered at the pool while the violent sounds of Rage Against the Machine blasted through his headphones. In lane four, Moses rolled his head slowly on his neck and projected the serene confidence that was his due. His Olympic Trials record in the semis wasn't remotely close to an all-out swim. He knew no one could touch him in this event.

The race started, and in three strokes Moses gained half of a body-length lead. He carried it into the first wall. Turning second was Kyle Salyards, a high school graduate who had deferred college for a year to train for these specific two minutes. Wilkens turned third. In just one lap, he was already more than a half-second behind Moses and his stroke was choppy.

"Hold it steady and together," Wilkens thought as he turned. He saw Moses pulling ahead and wanted to push harder. "Not yet," Wilkens reminded himself. "Swim your own race."

By the second lap, Moses had hypnotized the roaring spectators with strokes that were effortlessly long and fluid. The crowd almost seemed to lean forward with his every stroke, and lean back with him as he broke the surface to breathe. As Moses blazed toward the halfway mark, he seemed to increase his lead with each pull. But as the swimmers turned, the scoreboard revealed a different story. On the second lap, Wilkens, still third by a long way, his swimming uncharacteristically ugly and anxious, had minutely tightened the gap.

"Now or never," Wilkens thought as he turned at the 100 meters. "Do you want the Olympics or not?"

Wilkens attacked before he even broke the surface to begin his third lap. Here was the Wagnerian explosion and thunderous aggression that had been missing in earlier races. Within 20 meters, he drew even with Moses. His back high and scarlet, Wilkens lunged forward on each stroke. His legs whipped underwater, heels smacking together on each kick. This was all or nothing, live or die, for Wilkens was swimming the third lap as if it were the homestretch. He was going to be severely punished on the last lap. The third 50 meters of a 200-meter race is a time when swimmers typically conserve energy for their final sprint. For 15 meters, Wilkens swam even with Moses and Salyards. They must have seen him; they had to have heard the tremulous pitch of the crowd change as it watched the race unroll. Then Wilkens owned the lead. He had it not by a little, but by a lot. Suddenly Moses and Salyards were forced to pick up their paces just to stay competitive.

It was a fearsome display of guts and sheer racing ability. By the time the swimmers reached the third wall, it was clear Moses had been knocked out of his comfort zone. Now the race was a street brawl. No records would be set here. Wilkens turned first, Moses second, and Salyards third. Wilkens' third lap was the fastest in the pool by over .6 seconds. During the four seconds of his underwater pull, he realized how bad he felt and how much he was now going to pay for his early sprint. He had no idea whether his gamble had wounded his opponents, but he knew his own race would come down to heart.

"One lap, one lap," Wilkens urged himself. "Hang on and beat Ed. Beat Ed."

Can people see the future? Do they posses a sublime intuition that lets them read undisclosed truths in the rustle of tree leaves or undulating waves of heated air? More than a year earlier, stretching on the sun-baked concrete of the Santa Clara Swim Club, Wilkens had heard about Ed Moses' first breakthrough swim and had said something completely out of the blue. He had said it mysteriously and wholly without context.

He had said, "I'm confident. I know what needs to be done and I know I'm going to be able to do it."

There were 25 meters in the race and Wilkens still owned the lead. Then the lactic acid began raging through his body like fire in a paper mill. He struggled to keep the stroke long and his hips high for balance. It was no good. He knew he was slipping, knew Moses and Salyards had drawn themselves even again. None of the three had a clue that a fourth swimmer, a late-charger named Brendan Hansen, had caught the group as well. As the four swam toward the finish, they formed a single line, making this the most exciting race yet at the 2000 Olympic Trials. It seemed as if the crowd's roar would blow the top off the natatorium.

"Stay in stroke; stay in stroke," Wilkens whispered to himself. "Please, God, stay in stroke."

Wilkens was mortally wounded, but his derring-do had worked. Even as his stroke disintegrated, in lane four Moses was in even more profound crisis management. His kick was growing weaker on each stroke. The two of them, still barely first and second, would end up swimming the final lap slower than the six other finalists.

Then the unthinkable happened again. With four strokes to go, Wilkens could no longer hold himself together and he appeared to slip to fourth place. Simultaneously, he gauged the distance to the wall and realized with horror that he was going to finish in the middle of a stroke. He'd be compressed like a spring, a disastrous way for a breaststroker to finish. Breaststrokers fully elongate their bodies and stretch to the wall to touch sooner.

You do it like this, Tom. How many times in the previous six years had Kurt Grote shown Tom Wilkens ways to improve his breaststroke? How many tips, backdoor tricks, improvements, and adjustments had the veteran taught the rookie to get him to the wall sooner? With two strokes to go, instinct took over. Wilkens was ten feet from the wall and he performed an awkward, slipping half-stroke to correct his finish. Then he took a final full stroke and shot his exhausted arms over the water instead of through it, because that was quicker, and his body lunged for the wall. It was a finish Grote had taught him.

Not one of the 5,000 spectators knew who finished first through fourth. All heads swiveled to the scoreboard. With his poor eyesight, Wilkens couldn't read it and began to panic. His eyes flashed around the blurry natatorium until they settled on the section where his dozen family members were. What he saw was a crazy, jubilant celebration that threatened to collapse the stadium seating. On that last very stroke, Wilkens had lifted himself from fourth to second. The All-American Everyman was an Olympian.

As Wilkens had discovered in the 400-meter I.M., the Olympic Trials are merciless to race favorites. In lane four, the battered Moses pulled himself from the water, sat in a nearby chair, and buried his head in his hands. He had finished fourth.

The race was much closer than the times indicated. Salyards had won (2:13.21) with Wilkens second (2:13.34), the late-charging Hansen third (2:13.49), and Moses fourth (2:13.53). If Moses had only equaled his semifinal time, he would have won the event. It wasn't pretty, but Wilkens did what he did best: He raced. It put him on the Olympic team.

Tom Wilkens: asthmatic, YMCA swimmer, walk-on. One of the least naturally gifted swimmers in the 2000 Olympic Trials had made the dream come true. It was an amazing comeback against adverse circumstances, and on the next night he returned to the pool to do it again, this time racing for a spot in the 200-meter I.M. He still wasn't swimming his best. All four strokes were off, his body was sore, and his competitors could sense he was vulnerable. Yet a great portion of his confidence had returned, and the race was a fait accompli. There was no 200-meter I.M. equivalent of Eric Vendt to steal the race. The one outside threat was a 200-meter I.M. specialist named Ron Karnaugh, and indeed Karnaugh controlled the first three lengths. But the SCSC group had expected that to happen, and when Karnaugh began to fade on the final lap, the race turned into another duel between Wilkens and Dolan. Wilkens' freestyle, always a weak spot in his medley, was notoriously slow in this shorter race. Dolan convincingly won for his second triumph, but Wilkens finished a strong second (2:00.81 to 2:01.38). Dolan could once again lay claim to being the world's best swimmer. But at that moment, Wilkens had no problem with it. He was an Olympian in a second event. In the coming weeks, Team USA was going to elect him a team captain over Lenny Krayzelburg and Dolan. He'd share the honor with 1996 Olympian Josh Davis of Texas, who at the 1999 Pan Pacific Championships had been captain with Grote. Wilkens would effectively step into the leadership role vacated by his mentor.

The Santa Clara swimmer hung on the lane line, smiling and feeling the pressure slip away. It was a temporary respite, because 72 hours after the meet he would report to the Olympic training camp in Pasadena with his new teammates and begin the preparation for Sydney. But right now, he could die and be happy.

"Now I can say it," he thought. "Tom Wilkens, Olympian. I did it."

. . .

Backstroker Tate Blahnik crouched tensely and waited for the electronic start. When it came, he sprang backward in a beautiful arc, broke the water's surface with his hands, and willed the rest of his long body to follow through the hole his hands had made. Fifteen meters later, he burst to the surface and began racing the finals of the 200-meter backstroke.

Earlier in the week, he had placed a surprising sixth in his weaker event, the 100-meter backstroke. He gave credit to his new and beloved bodysuit, which covered him from wrist to ankle. It made him feel, he said, like a superhero. Perhaps it made him act like one, too, because this was certainly not the same man who had tried so hard for so many months to avoid this meet.

The 200-meter backstroke was his one legitimate shot at Olympic glory. But it was also one of the only races that seemed to have a foregone conclusion. The top finisher would be Lenny Krayzelburg. Second place looked like it was a virtual lock for Aaron Piersol, the teenager from southern California who only several months earlier at nationals had taken over Blahnik's position as the country's No. 2 backstroker. Entering the finals, Blahnik was seeded third behind them. Both Krayzelburg and Piersol were great last-lap swimmers, and Blahnik's only chance for the Olympics lay in gaining an early lead, then fending off Piersol to capture second.

Shortly before the race, Bitter had pulled the swimmer aside and said, "You be the first to put your feet on the wall [at the turns]. Don't look around until the third wall."

If the race were 125 meters, Blahnik, certainly the most reluctant swimmer competing in the 2000 Olympic Trials, would have been an Olympian. With his matchstick arms whirring and his hips rolling, he briefly appeared to be winning the race.

But maybe it was just a trick of the eye, because by the third turn at 150 meters, the scoreboard showed the two favorites were in charge and Blahnik was in third. Coming home in the last 50 meters, Krayzelburg and Piersol began pulling away, and the Santa Clara swimmer underwent a metamorphosis. He had overcome his fears. He had exposed his heart and raced, and it wasn't going to be enough. The eight finalists' arms crashed through the water. If only he had had six months of solid training. If only he had enjoyed his sport. If only. . . . There were so many other potential outcomes that they overwhelmed the imagination. What if Grote's desire had been matched with Blahnik's body?

Blahnik had tried his utmost to stay with Krayzelburg and Piersol, but now they were extending their lead. One thing was certain. Tate Blahnik did not need the psychological burden of another third place. The fatigue in his legs was building and with 25 meters remaining in the race he gave into it. He gave into the fatigue and relinquished the race right then and there. His turnover downshifted and he stretched out his stroke. The full knowledge that he would never have to fight with his sport again must have suffused him with joy, because he seemed to swim ebulliently. But maybe that, too, was a trick of the eye. Perhaps for this athlete, and this athlete alone, it signaled a fitting way to end a career. There would be no Olympics for him, but neither would there be any more pain of losing. As he slowed, two other swimmers swiftly passed him and by the time he reached the wall he was fifth. Later, as he sat on the edge of the warm-down pool for the last time, his face reflected all the unexpected and mixed up feelings he was experiencing. But he couldn't wait for the next morning. It held the promise of being the first day of the rest of his life.

. . .

Wales had avoided the Olympic Trials most of the week by staying in his hotel room and waiting for his 100-meter butterfly on the meet's second-to-last day. To further insulate himself, he was rooming with his non-competing brother, Craig. He did this to escape the emotional up-heavals of joys and sadness that he knew would rip through the team. Wales was making sure every detail was covered, every distraction minimized. It was, of course, a flawed plan. For seven days he waited for his big race mostly by sitting in his anonymous hotel room and feeling the pressure build. Try though he did, he couldn't contain and manage his emotions the way he wanted to. A lifetime of preparing made it impossible to ignore the significance of what was at stake.

But when it finally came time to race, he was ready to join his father as an Olympic butterflyer. Programmatic as always, Wales had analyzed his race so many times he had reduced the margin of error almost to zero. By finals, he knew first place would likely go to a young Maine swimmer named Ian Crocker who had emerged at this meet as an un-expected favorite. But second place was probably the most open Olympic spot in the entire Trials. Anyone could take it, with Wales the designated favorite. Before the race, the Santa Clara coaches voiced the same concern they always did: *Don't swim the first 50 meters too tentatively. Don't save your strength until the end.* It was an especially relevant warning at a meet like Trials, because there are always dark horses willing to risk everything with reckless, hell-may-care races. In the 100-meter events, that usually meant a desperate competitor would swim the first 50 meters at maximum speed and try to hang on. In the 200-meter events, the gamble occurs on the third lap when a person races it like an all-out homestretch sprint. Wilkens had made the Olympic team using that strategy in the 200-meter breaststroke.

"Dod Wales, you don't leave anything behind in the pool tonight," Jochums said.

Wales smiled. It was highly probable he was more in control of his nerves than the coach. "Duh, Dick," he said.

When the race started, the desperate dark-horse competitor immediately revealed himself as a Texas swimmer named Tommy Hannan. Hannan was a backstroke specialist who had already failed to make the team in his primary event, and had spent the last minutes before this race loudly talking in the ready room about partying after finals. Globally, he was ranked No. 70 in the 100-meter butterfly (Wales was No. 12), which gave him license to be as fearless as he wanted. In the first 50 meters, Hannan tore down the pool at a pace no one could match. On the opposite side, Wales swam with measured rhythm and controlled power. It was textbook swimming, but it was what the Santa Clara coaches feared most. For years they had consistently fought against this tentative first lap. But this was Wales' style; it was what had built him into one of the country's best butterflyers. Hannan turned first (24.31) with most of the heat swimming faster than expected to keep up. Wales turned sixth (25.01).

As they came off the wall, Wales seemed to increase his power, particularly in the legs. Simultaneously, Hannan began dying a slow, painful death. Maine's Crocker powered into the lead, but barely. Ultimately, he would win the event. Wales was feeling terrible and at 65 meters said to himself, "This is not the swim that will put me on the Olympic team." It was a funny thought, because anyone could see that he was demonstrably growing faster with each successive stroke. Yet Hannan, even though he was faltering, still owned a great lead. And that was how they swam toward the finish: a meticulous man against a reckless man, both fighting for the same chance at immortality. With each meter, the meticulous man grew stronger while his foe grew weaker. But Hannan's lead was too great. Even though the unknown Texan was on the verge of collapse, even though his arms could no longer extend straight in front of his body, he cleanly beat the surging Wales to the wall (52.81 to 53.41).

Third place at Olympic Trials. It was a horrible, crushing loss. Wales turned to see the scoreboard and his face contorted into a fixture of unimaginable pain. The face could not have belonged to him; it belonged to someone else, someone suffering a terrible and unexpected death. The Santa Clara corps was devastated. After a few moments, Wales climbed from the pool. His face had already returned to normal and he accepted his fate with stoicism and dry eyes. Afterward, since he seemed the one possessing the most control, it was up to him to comfort his distressed family, team, and coaches.

As quickly as possible, he left the pool. Later, the coaches would snap out of their daze and become almost frantic over his safety. *Third place.* The swimmer had so immediately internalized the moment there was no telling what would happen when the nuclear blast went off in his chest. But they didn't need to worry. After dressing, Wales walked outside the complex with his girlfriend and together they sat on the cool lawn. They had been together since high school. She put her arm around his shoulder and he started crying.

When he was ready for whatever was supposed to logically follow, he knew he couldn't go back to California or even stay in Indianapolis. Leaving behind his brother and parents, at 11:30 P.M., he and his girlfriend collected his things from the hotel and drove four hours to his boyhood home of Cincinnati. Sailing directly southeast along the empty and ghostly I-74 highway, the world seemed to end at the edge of his rushing headlights. The beat of tires on pavement became hypnotic. At one point, he said aloud, "All right, what's next?" and began talking about his future. When the car finally rolled down his sleeping street and pulled into his old driveway, there were still several hours until the sun rose. For the first time in years, Wales wouldn't have a plan once the day began. The only thing he knew with certainty was that although he had planned to continue swimming for another year, he would now never race again.

Tiredly, he entered his childhood room and stepped through a time warp. The room had remained unchanged since the day he had departed for Stanford six years earlier. Ironically, during college those four walls had come to represent his only refuge from swimming, because the only time he could visit home was during scheduled training breaks. Now he slowly processed the familiar environment and tried to understand the incredible emotions in his breast. It seemed so jarringly strange to be standing in this room, which he hadn't seen for more than half a year, when his body was smooth shaved and race perfect and the faint odor of rubdown oil still clung to his skin. Just eight hours earlier he had been standing on the blocks for his event. In his swim bag, his racing suit was still wet. Anyone else would have wept.

There was a trophy case in Wales' bedroom that showed the history of his amazing career. He didn't expect to be drawn to it, he didn't even expect to be in the state of Ohio, but there he was, inches from the display and gazing at the various awards with a sense of finality. Maybe later he would pause at his father's framed Olympic medal, but probably not.

"I had a pretty good career, didn't I?" he said aloud. "I'm going to be okay, I think."

Wales would disappear for several months after Trials. He would avoid going to Sydney, even though his father was a V.I.P. there and would present medals during the awards ceremonies. He would avoid friends and not return phone calls. This loss was going to cut miles deeper than Wilkens' defeat, for there was no second chance, no opportunity for redemption. He would never watch the race on videotape. If there would be any consolation, it was that he had swum the race he wanted to. He would have done it differently had he known someone would attack so hard on the first lap, but hindsight is useless. Wales had developed a strategy and had followed it. He had done everything he could. And he had come up several inches short.

Weeks and weeks later, long after the Olympics were over, Jochums would receive a letter from Wales. No other post-graduate Santa Clara swimmer had contacted the coach; none had yet stopped by or even called. Most would come eventually, one by one, in street clothes and feeling oddly out of place on the pool deck now that their dream was over. But early on they needed distance. In his note, Wales wrote that for the remainder of his life he would look back on his years of preparation knowing he had done everything possible to achieve his dream. The letter was perfectly spaced and meticulously free of error, as if several drafts had been written. Wales would say he realized Jochums had always looked out for him, even when they were arguing. He would say every day he looked in the mirror he was proud of himself and his effort. He would close the letter with the word "love."

For weeks afterward, Jochums would keep that note on his desk. He pushed it out of sight under several pieces of mail. But just about every other day, the coach would pull it out and re-read it.

• • •

The 2000 Olympic Trials drew to a close. Tom Wilkens going to Sydney in two out of his three events, but not in his best one. You don't complain when you make an Olympic team, but objectively speaking, it had been a bad for meet for him. Joining him would be Dara Torres, who had a phenomenal meet. Incredibly, the diva was going to the Olympics in the 100-meter butterfly, 100-meter freestyle, 50-meter freestyle, 4 × 100-meter medley relay, and 4 × 100-meter freestyle relay. That was five events, more than any other American swimmer. Also reaching the summit of Olympus were Curl-Burke teammates Tom Dolan in the 200-meter and 400-meter I.M., and Ed Moses in the 100-meter breaststroke and 4 × 100-meter medley relay. Dolan couldn't have asked for a better Trials. Moses had a mixed meet, dominating one event but days later he was upended by Wilkens in his second event.

Kurt Grote and Dod Wales left Indianapolis with very different endings to their careers, but with the same generic misery. For Grote, the 2000 Olympic Trials were a tremendously sad closure to a brilliant career. After his events were over, he wore street clothes to the pool, encouraged friends, and weakly joked about retirement. But he looked so forlorn and bewildered. He never imagined it would end this way. Meanwhile, Wales suffered the searing pain of third place. In contrast was Blahnik, who had finally freed himself from the pain Wales was now experiencing firsthand. He spent the meet's remaining days smiling.

"I guess it's time to go home," Jochums said shortly before the meet ended. As a team, Santa Clara had a triumphant meet, its best Trials since 1972. He and Bitter had done it. There were twenty-six events in Olympic Trials, and Santa Clara's twenty-two swimmers (several of whom were Stanford-trained men wearing Santa Clara's colors) competed in thirteen of them. They had twenty-five semifinals swims, which tied for the most in the country. In eleven of the thirteen events, a Santa Clara swimmer had raced in the finals. In more than fifty percent of them, the club had been mere inches from putting someone in the Olympics. Those inches would haunt the swimmers and coaches for a long time, but overall it was a banner meet, the kind of return that in the business world leads to foaming champagne bottles. That said, there had been no unexpected triumphs or collective sense of victory. Although Jochums had returned the club to its former glory, the spark of accomplishment seemed to be missing.

The coach felt grudgingly good about the overall results, but he had been unable to let go of the 400-meter I.M. Clenched-jawed in embarrassment over the missing tooth, he had sulked at dinner after finals and turned fiendish and petulant during lunch. He flogged himself mercilessly, not for a bad training regime—the old-school approach and his belief in the basics had delivered strong results—but for letting the pressure get to his athlete. In all his strategizing, Jochums had forgotten the simple fact that beneath the hours of training and refining, his cherished athlete, his Ajax, his hope and future, was a young man under unprecedented duress facing the biggest moment of his life.

For decades, Jochums' great ambition had been to coach an Olympic team. Yet toward the meet's end, he requested his name be withdrawn from consideration for an assistant coaching position in Sydney. It was widely known he was one of the favorites to land the coveted job. Even a Tucson paper, which last talked about Dick Jochums when it reported on his problems at the University of Arizona, had stated that he was a likely pick. When he tried to remove his name, the Olympic gatekeepers hesitated. But Jochums insisted until they grudgingly agreed. There is no other name for what Jochums did. In disgrace, the coach had committed hara-kiri for Wilkens' and Wales' third places.

For the entire meet, Jochums, who should go down as one of the best individual motivators in swimming's history, did not hold a formal team meeting. That was not unusual for him, but this was Olympic Trials and that made things different. The Santa Clara swimmers, after leaning against him every day for the previous year, had needed to hear his support and encouragement. They may have embraced the concept of personal responsibility and individualism, but they still needed guidance.

Yet Jochums, his heart aching with love and loss, had descended into a private gloom and left them to fend for themselves. He didn't understand how much these self-reliant, adult swimmers relied on him. In fact, he wouldn't until it was almost too late.

CHAPTER NINETEEN

Santa Clara's Sergey Mariniuk stood gasping on the moonscape deck of Sydney's Olympic pool. The Moldovan was already forgotten. The 18,000 Olympic spectators, the largest crowd to ever watch a swim meet, had already turned their eyes to the next preliminary heat of the 400-meter I.M. Mariniuk's career was over.

Several times he had led. Then his lack of endurance began to show. Midway through the race, he was fifth. He fought against the burn in his lungs, kicked a little harder, and ultimately finished third in the heat. It is difficult to interpret what this man had just accomplished. It's difficult because it was not what we expect when we think about the devotion that goes into the Olympics. Over the previous four years, Mariniuk had trained seriously perhaps six months total, and had just placed twenty-second in the sport's decathlon. His time was a respectable 4:23.57, only five seconds slower than his eighth place at the 1996 Olympics, when he was swimming full-time. Tom Wilkens would have given an awful lot to have been in his place.

Hands on hips, the third-oldest male swimmer in the 2000 Olympics slowly took in the roiling sea of white faces in the stands. Mariniuk looked at the natatorium's cathedral ceiling, its wall-mounted televisions, and 200 photographers. He had been able to finish his career in the fastest pool in the world in front of millions of television viewers. History was being made in Sydney and he was feeling a small part of it. He broke into a grin full of satisfaction but also mixed with sadness.

What makes a person fast in the water? Is it better to train like Tom Wilkens with his years of intensity and hard work, or like Sergey Mariniuk, who in the sunset of his career had sought something mystical in the water? Is it better to have dreamed and lost like Wilkens, or to have lived like Mariniuk and deliver a result he knew could have been better? Somewhere in the irony of their parallel journeys was a message about life. Given enough time, perhaps a person could figure out what it meant.

In the movie version, the camera focuses on Mariniuk because he is one of the elite immortals who made it to Olympus. The camera could just as easily pan to Grote back home in his California backyard. He is lifting a full glass of purple wine and smiling broadly at the surprise retirement party his wife has thrown for him. Half a dozen Santa Clara Trials swimmers are there, sitting in a circle and talking about their futures. The scene could dissolve and recompile to show a silent and meditative Grote standing at midnight in the doorway of his moonlit home office, gazing at the large Olympic flag hanging over his desk. Maybe he even takes out his 1998 World Championship gold medal, just to feel its heft and to remember. The image disintegrates into gray and then reconstructs to another scene, this one showing Wales meticulously avoiding coverage of the Olympics. It isn't easy. He relies on his firm belief in structure and order to hold him upright. He is building a résumé and applying for investment-banking jobs. The awful pain is already dimming, but it will continue to exist for a long, long time. Finally, the camera might show Blahnik, whistling and smiling as he builds sophisticated computer programs.

The great myth of the camera is that a story must ultimately end. The story never ends; it continues unraveling like a limitless double helix that uncoils and weaves through lives even as it splits into different directions. There is a transcendence to the pursuit of greatness. And those who have been on that quest will find the remainder of their days stronger and more meaningful because of it.

There should be transcendence in the Olympics as well, but it seemed Mariniuk had used up his allotment during his first two Olympiads. Until several weeks ago, he had been slated to swim the 200-meter I.M. after the 400-meter I.M. Then Moldova yanked him from the event. That which the kingdom gives, the kingdom can also take away. Mariniuk was replaced with an athlete who swam six seconds slower. The official line was that the new swimmer was an up-and-coming star who needed international experience. It was an interesting argument, considering the athlete was twenty-seven years old and not far from retirement.

The decision was based on a political numbers game: Every nation brings a delegation of state officials and big shots to the Olympic Games, the size of which is determined, in part, by political favors, arm-twisting, and, ostensibly, the number of athletes it has participating. Putting an additional swimmer on the Moldovan team enabled more officials to receive V.I.P. passes. Mariniuk was out of his stronger race, and if from his cozy California home he wanted to complain, they could probably find someone else to swim his remaining event. It made a person yearn for the merciless equity of the U.S. Olympic Trials.

Mariniuk's situation offered a glimpse into how the Olympics work every day on a grassroots level in many countries. Moldova is one of those small, forgotten countries lost in the Olympics' Parade of Athletes during Opening Ceremonies. Its 2000 Olympic team had eight swimmers, which was the total number of individuals who had qualified for the Games' slower "B" standard. None was even going to qualify for semifinals in Sydney. In contrast, Team USA not only had more than 40 swimmers at the Games who could, at least theoretically, win medals, but back home in the United States were several dozen others who would have reached the Olympic finals. After the Olympic Games, most U.S. swimmers were assured celebratory homecomings, complete in many cases with parades, endorsements, and speaking tours. Most swimmers on the Moldovan team wouldn't return home at all. Four athletes and one coach would opt to remain illegally in Australia in what would be the single biggest defection of any country at the 2000 Olympics.

For Opening Ceremonies, Moldovan officials, like officials from many other countries, insisted they—not the athletes—should lead the delegation into the stadium. For the duration of the Games, the same officials spent much of their time sitting in the team common rooms of the Olympic Village in a blue haze of cigarette smoke. There were 48,000 Olympic volunteers helping make the Sydney Olympics the most spectacular global event in history, but somehow Moldova had received only one interpreter for its entire fifty-person entourage. She was forbidden to speak directly with the athletes because her obligation, she was informed, was to meet the officials' needs in a timely manner. Those needs included chauffeured cars, bigger chauffeured cars, charged cell phones, take-out dinners, faxing, and the like. Only a few years earlier, the Olympics had pulsated with East-West tensions. While that is no longer the case, old habits die hard, and the athletes were effectively blocked from outside contact. This type of informal sequestering was actually fairly typical for many countries at the 2000 Olympics. Most foreign athletes would have been amazed by the comparative freedom the members of Team USA enjoyed.

The national head of Moldova's swim federation arrived after a long flight. Looking around, he saw an individual and ordered him to carry his luggage. Startled, the young man had picked up the bags and followed him to his room. The director brusquely dismissed him, never realizing it was his country's own best breaststroker. Over in the United States' massive village, Wilkens didn't carry anyone's bags, not even his own. Porters had been arranged by the American concierge staff. If Wilkens ever had a question—if, for instance, he wanted to double-check the time of his daily massage—all he had to do was pick up the free cell phone he'd been given upon arrival.

Mariniuk dreaded entering the Moldovan apartments. As the only accessible English speaker, he was deluged with questions and requests for favors. But they were nothing compared to the first day, when a Moldovan coach in another sport trapped a teenaged female maid in his room and forced himself on her. He was a terrible assailant and a piss-poor planner; her co-workers were in the next room, and they barged through the door when they heard her scream.

"I was giving her an Olympic pin," the coach had shrugged to Mariniuk.

"You're responsible for making this situation go away immediately," one of the Moldovan officials told the swimmer.

Mariniuk had nodded and, switching to English, promptly told the girl to file charges. He had been incensed. Four years earlier in Atlanta, he had been thrust into a similar assault case by a different coach. This is the Olympics? Both instances were kept quiet, making one wonder exactly how often such things occur. Indeed, before the Games would end, at least one swimmer—an athlete from Uganda—would be arrested on suspicion of rape.

Almost immediately after his race was over, Mariniuk was knocked into bed with a three-day illness. It was as if his body, honed to perform above and beyond its limits for a single eight-lap race, had collapsed from the effort. Afterward, he suddenly found himself enlisted as the de facto expert on immigrating to a new country. If you are fleeing a third-world country,

Australia and New Zealand are difficult places to go because their residency requirements are fairly strict. By the middle of the meet, Mariniuk became so overwhelmed that he abandoned the Village altogether and moved into a nearby house where his wife, who only weeks earlier had surprised him with the news she was pregnant, was staying.

In comparison, the Olympic lives of Wilkens, Dolan, Moses, and Torres looked easy. All they had to do was win medals.

. . .

In the history of swimming, there had never been a swim meet like this. And until the Olympic Games are again hosted in Australia, there will certainly never be another.

From the first heat, the swim-crazed nation of 18 million screeched to a halt. The Olympic Games were one thing; Olympic *swimming* was quite another. In water-bound Australia, swimming is a national obsession, and the people's fanaticism rivals that of Italian soccer fans. For the Olympics, billboards, newspapers, and ATM machines were plastered with swim heroes; a downtown subway station had converted every inch of its advertising space to swimmer-endorsed products. A newcomer descending the station's escalator would be startled to realize the seemingly abstract pattern on the partition between the two moving staircases was really an elongated, fifteen-foot image of an Australian swim hero.

The Olympic Games are about individual athletes and personal excellence. But they are also about national pride, and in the pool the XXVII Olympiad was a grudge match between the United States and their Australian hosts. The Aussies had been lying in wait for the United States ever since the 1999 Pan Pacific Championships, when—thanks in part to Grote and Wales—they had been defeated on the final relay and lost the meet. Now it was a classic David-versus-Goliath setup. The mighty American swim juggernaut swung into Sydney having won 387 Olympic swim medals since 1896, about four times more than second-place Australia. On the first night of competition, Australia scored first when it torched the United States in the men's 4 × 100-meter freestyle relay. It was the first time the United States had ever lost that race in Olympic competition. The Aussie victors stood over the humiliated Americans and taunted them.

Tom Dolan saw it on television. He and the 400-meter I.M.'s new hope, Erik Vendt, were in the Olympic Village shaving down for their medley swims the next morning. Dolan turned to Vendt and demanded they take first and second place to shove it back at Australia. At heart, Dolan was a prizefighter. He needed something to slug against, and the image of a bald Australian swimmer mockingly strumming an air guitar over the United States was enough to motivate anyone. Dolan just happened to take it very personally.

Both he and Vendt advanced to finals, which were the following night. Dolan was seeded second and Vendt was seeded fifth. If you stand on a pool deck long enough, you learn to read swimmers' body language. Dolan, swinging his long arms and fiddling with his goggles, was ready to unleash a vicious race. He never wore a bathing cap, another defiant swing at convention.

The race began. The world record-holder often swam the butterfly segment downplaying his legs to conserve energy. Not tonight. He turned at 100 meters significantly under his own world-record pace from six years earlier. Really, the race was already over. Over the next two laps he uncoiled one of his most incredible backstroke medley legs ever. There was no holding back, no worry that a certain breaststroke specialist might catch him, because the breaststroke specialist was watching the race from the stands. When Dolan hit the halfway mark, Wilkens turned to his U.S. teammates.

"He's going to break the world record," Wilkens said.

Dolan swam his breaststroke strong, as strong as he had at Trials when it had to be his focus. At 300 meters, he was three body lengths ahead of anyone else and more than 1.5 seconds below world-record pace. The one person in the world who might have made it a race cheered until his throat ached. But a cyclone of emotions raced through his blood. Several times, Wilkens had to breathe deeply to get hold of the feelings that were trying to rise up. There was so much for him to prove.

Dolan charged into his freestyle. The other seven finalists were too far back to see. He surged after his 1994 record of 4:12.30. Body twisting, legs too tired to maintain a steady kick, he powered to the wall and touched. Gold medal, new world record in 4:11.76. Tom Dolan, King of Swimming.

He tore his goggles off his head and began screaming with a gorilla rage. His left hand pointed at his team; his right repeatedly slammed the water. There was no joy, just an amazing display of fury and vindication. He didn't hold anything back. "Get up! Get up!" he screamed at the crowd, and at his command 18,000 of them rose.

Here was Tom Dolan in the raw. Team USA had been too intimidated by his ferocity to ever elect him captain, yet at this very minute he was single-handedly shifting the meet's momentum, which had been squarely in Australia's lap, to the United States, where it would remain for the rest of the meet. If Dolan saw his world-record time, he didn't acknowledge it. Meanwhile, in lane two, incredibly, Vendt had moved from eighth place early in the race all the way to second for the silver medal ahead of a Canadian in third. Dolan continued pointing, slashing the water, and screaming at the audience. *There! Look at what I did! Take that, Australia!*

Wilkens watched, cheering and not cheering. It was a moment curled and twisted with confusion, awe, and envy. One of Team USA's youngest members put a hand on Wilkens' shoulder and shook him. *Are you okay?* That seemed to snap the Santa Clara swimmer out of his dream state. Was he a team captain or not? He began rhythmically clapping and leading the team in a cheer for first and second place. He yelled so loud he couldn't hear anything but the sound of his own voice.

"One, two! One, two! One, two!"

Thirty minutes later, the top three finishers stood on the medal dais to receive their awards. They stepped up, one after the other, and when they did they stepped into immortality. Dolan radiated a new, boyish joy. Wilkens watched the two U.S. flags majestically rise alongside the Canadian one and listened to the American national anthem play. He could feel the tears welling under his lids and not all of them were patriotic. The three medal times were 4:11.76, 4:14.23, and 4:15.33. Wilkens' time in the spring, coming off a five-day rest, had been 4:13.84, which meant he would end the year 2000 ranked No. 2 in the world behind Dolan. He swallowed. He knew everyone on the team was watching him, waiting to see if he was strong enough to handle it. So much to prove. He would be racing in two days.

. . .

Forget the commercialism and the bribery scandals, the abuse of performance-enhancing drugs, and the ever-growing professionalism. Underneath all the detritus, all the empty Coke cans, crumpled Visa receipts, positive tests for nandrolene and ephedrine, and the nine-figure basketball-player salaries, the Olympics are still unlike anything else. Breaststroker Ed Moses had thought he understood this, but it turned out he didn't have a clue.

The pressure crashes like a monster tidal wave over everyone, even those who spend every waking moment preparing for it. There is nothing like the Olympic Games. In Moses' case, the pressure was his own fault. He had fanned the expectations with promises of world records and gold medals. Athletes seem to inflict this extra burden on themselves intentionally. Maybe they are bored with the humdrum of winning races. In Sydney, he finally looked like who he was: a twenty-year-old competing in his second major international meet.

An hour before Dolan won the 400-meter I.M., Moses raced in the Olympic finals of the 100-meter breaststroke. The race had offered one of the Games' biggest showdowns, between him and Russia's Roman Sloudnov. The Russian had recently set the world record (1:00.36), and Moses had just missed beating it at Trials (1:00.44). Before the race, both repeatedly promised to break the one-minute barrier. Adding to the excitement was a relative unknown named Domenico Fioravanti of Italy. The unknown Milan native had twice won the 100-meter breaststroke at the European Championships although he was not remotely considered a medal contender. But the willowy Italian had brought to the meet the newest incarnation of breaststroke. It was a long and graceful stroke, and instead of lunging forward like Grote and Wilkens, the Italian held his head high and rigid and looked as if he were leaning back in fright. It was a beautiful display of elegance and it was exactly how a swimmer from Milan, the design capital of the world, should swim.

When the race started, Moses was so quick off the blocks he might have been squatting on a spring. The crowd roared. His churning turnover was nearly twice as fast as the wide-pulling Italian's, and he gained a sizable lead by the 25-meter mark. At 50 meters, he touched first with a commanding lead of 28.60 seconds to Fioravanti's 28.91 seconds. The Russian, a distant third, was already out of the race for gold (29.23).

Moses seemed assured of victory. But something was off. Maybe it was the pressure, maybe the inability to adapt to new demands during the Olympic training camp. His 50-meter split was .36 seconds slower than his Trials swim, a big difference in a 100-meter race. At 70 meters, the fabled quickness that made him so great began to fade. This was expected, but almost simultaneously the Italian clicked into a higher gear. The two drew even and raced for the wall. Moses, growing weaker with each stroke, fought to keep up his high cadence. Fioravanti, artistic and relentless, maintained his long, fluid pace. With five meters to go, Moses sank back. It was over. Fioravanti won in 1:00.46 for Italy's first-ever swimming gold medal. The American touched second in 1:00.73. Moses' time from Trials would have won the gold medal. His epic showdown with the Russian, who finished third (1:00.91), never materialized. Kurt Grote's best time would not have won a medal, but it would have been very close.

Moses was washed in disappointment. Not because of the medal, which awed him, but because he knew he had not swum his best race. He withdrew for a few days to collect his energy. He still had the 4 × 100-meter medley to swim. With that, he would show the world what he could do.

Six days later, it would be time to race the men's 4 × 100-meter medley relay, the final event of swimming's 2000 Olympics. By then, the United States would own the meet and would have delivered one of its best performances ever. There was no question the Olympic coaching staff had assumed the risk of the poor scheduling and had delivered the goods. U.S.A. Swimming would croon that despite the tight scheduling between the Trials and the Olympics, the swimmers turned in more personal best times than ever before. While true, it wasn't mentioned that both the new bodysuits, which could reduce times by three percent, and the world's fastest pool played a role here.

But Team USA was not the invincible squad it once was. The biggest stars of the Olympics were not Americans but the Dutch wonders Inge de Bruijn and Pieter van den Hoogenband, and the Aussie teenager Ian Thorpe. The American men's team in particular had received two serious black eyes in earlier relays. Prior to Sydney, the Americans had won twenty-five of the twenty-six Olympic relays ever contested. But here, the men lost both the 4 × 200-meter freestyle (expected) and the 4 × 100-meter freestyle (one of the most dramatic duels of the meet). Now it was time for the 4 × 100-meter medley, the only remaining relay event the

United States had never lost in Olympic competition. The United States also had held every world record in it since 1971.

Racing in Grote's former place was Moses. He was the relay's linch-pin. Team USA's backstroker, Krayzelburg, would establish the lead. Australia's butterflyer and freestyler would likely neutralize it, and then some. The relay therefore rested on Moses' shoulders, and anyone who cared to watch was going to learn for certain just how good he was.

Krayzelburg gave the Americans the lead, but Australia and Germany were just a whisper behind, far closer than expected. Moses didn't think about his time, his technique, or anything else. He just swam, racing that first lap as if the water were burning his skin. At 50 meters, he turned in 27.29 seconds, a time that defied anything imaginable until that moment. Moses didn't die either. When he finished, his lead was so insurmountable the only way Australia could have won was if its final two swimmers ran along the deck. Two minutes later, the United States secured its victory, smashing the old world record of 3:34.84 with a 3:33.73. Moses' breaststroke split of 59.74 was easily the fastest in history. He didn't just break the mythical one-minute barrier; he redefined the stroke's outer limits. And he had won a gold medal.

• • •

Life was supposed to be drastically simplified the moment a U.S. Olympic swimmer arrived in Pasadena for the pre-Olympic training camp. But for Dara Torres it had only become more complicated.

Rumors that performance-enhancing drugs were responsible for her comeback swirled everywhere, even among her teammates. There were various other whispers as well. Her differences with teammate Jenny Thompson were now public and made for good gossip in the camp. Torres needed people to like her, needed the warmth of acceptance and attention, but she wasn't getting it. Now Cinderella's story could not be told without raised eyebrows and innuendo. Those around her couldn't begin to imagine how deeply the steroid allegations had wounded her. How could she explain that her speed and strength had always been there, they'd simply never been fully accessed? She vehemently, convincingly, denied impropriety. Every drug test came back negative. What more did they want? There was no question her exotic dietary regime had been engineered in a laboratory to enhance athletic performance. But it was done within the rules. Since other members of the Stanford women's team had been on the same protocol, why did it seem members of the media were targeting only her?

Ironically, when she finally arrived in Sydney, the accusations and snipes still flew like spears back and forth across the pool deck. But in Australia there was a bigger target. The Netherlands' Inge de Bruijn, age twenty-six, had set ten world records in a matter of weeks, each more astonishing, more improbable, than the next. Like Torres, de Bruijn was a relatively older swimmer. Like Torres, she had been a world-class performer for years but had never maximized her potential. Like Torres, she also tested negative repeatedly. But the questions about the origins of her sudden speed were unceasing. Amidst the flak, Torres ducked out of the way. The two of them were swimming the same events, the 100-meter butterfly, 100-meter freestyle, and 50-meter freestyle.

In the 100-meter butterfly, Torres easily qualified for the finals. It had been sixteen years since her first Olympic race. The Olympics' oldest swimmer cut a stark image in the new millennium. She wore the same sleek, $350 bodysuit as many others, but she also wore a pair of scratched, vintage Speedo bug-eye goggles resurrected from her 1980s career. The goggles were wildly popular until more attention was paid to hydrodynamics and smaller models emerged. Then there was the way she started a race, which tagged her as a visitor from another era. Every other swimmer in the meet crouched over the front of the blocks before taking their marks. That was how they had been taught. But Torres remained upright and rigid until the last second. That was how *she* had been taught a generation earlier.

From the first stroke of the butterfly finals, it was clear Inge de Bruijn was hunting the world record and everyone else was welcome to tag along and watch from a distance. Torres didn't seem fully ready for this Olympic championship and it took her 35 meters to shift into a rhythm. Once there, she perhaps focused too much on power instead of balance and technique. Even so, for the entire race she was in the medal hunt. Coming into the finish was a flurry of multiple hands stretching for the yellow touchpads. It took her a second to realize she had touched third. A bronze, her first individual medal in four Olympics. Her first reaction was intense letdown. She hadn't won. She had swum a bad race. Torres couldn't hide her disappointment, although she tried to smile because she knew the cameras were on her, talking about the comeback, the impossibility and the enormity of it. The winner, de Bruijn, had broken her own world record with a 56.61 seconds. Second was the Slovakian from SMU, Martina Moravcova (57.97), with Torres third in 58.20. The time bothered Torres. It was more than a half-second slower than the American record she had set at Trials. Jenny Thompson, who many had thought would win the event, touched fifth.

Yet somehow that race freed Torres, because from the instant the bronze medal slipped around her neck, she swam like a different person. An Olympic bronze. Well, now. In the finals of the 100-meter freestyle, de Bruijn again owned the race and set another new world record (53.82) en route to winning. Finishing second was a Swede named Therese Alshammar. But third place was the story. What rich and clever irony the world has. Torres and Thompson—antagonists, combatants, enemies, teammates—touched at exactly the same time (54.47). Everyone in the natatorium knew about their animosities. The stands were filled with hearty Australians who loved comeuppance humor and they burst into delighted laughter.

Only once before had Olympic swimming seen an official tie. That had been in 1984, when two U.S. women tied for gold in the 100-meter freestyle. (Later in the 2000 Games, two American men, Gary Hall, Jr., and Anthony Ervin, would tie for gold in the 50-meter freestyle.) Years ago, international swim races were briefly calculated to .001 seconds, a measurement too small for the naked eye to see, and in 1972 an Olympic gold medal was actually decided by that margin when two men, including an American named Tim McKee, tied for gold in the 400-meter I.M. Officials dismantled the timing system to pick a winner, and ultimately McKee lost by .002 seconds. But one-thousandth of a second is simply too small to determine outcomes. An invisible bulge in the pool wall or a bubble in the timing pad might create a one-millimeter advantage in one lane. That could lead to a victory. Intriguingly, the races are still calculated to .001 seconds, which meant there were swim officials who knew which woman had nipped the other. But they weren't talking.

It seemed like a truck could have been driven through the open space that stretched between Torres and Thompson as they stood on opposite edges of the round medal dais they shared. Torres felt fine now. She'd been ranked only No. 6 in the world in the 100-meter freestyle, but had her second individual medal with a time that equaled her best. Perhaps most important, she had beaten the demons of nerves and fears that used to paralyze her. She was growing more confident and comfortable by the day.

Two days later, she raced the finals of the 50-meter freestyle. She was legitimately exhausted from swimming six out of the eight days—more than any other U.S. swimmer. The 50-meter event, the "splash and dash," was the newest Olympic swim event, having been introduced only in 1988. The three keys are the start, the first several strokes, and the final few meters to the wall. De Bruijn was the top seed in this race, too, and was practically guaranteed her third gold medal. The Dutchwoman had reset this world record four times since May, including the previous day when she obliterated her two-month standard by almost .3 seconds with an incredible 24.13 seconds.

Torres' start and breakout were excellent. De Bruijn's were not. *This is it,* Torres whispered to herself before shutting down all thought processes. The finalists churned down the pool. With 15 meters to go, Torres and de Bruijn were even. Also there was Sweden's Alshammar, runner-up in the 100-meter freestyle. Then de Bruijn hit maximum velocity and moved ahead. Alshammar followed. Torres lost a beat, but righted herself in the final strokes. All three stretched for the wall. They touched in order: de Bruijn (24.32), Alshammar (24.51), and Torres (24.63).

Torres had a third bronze and had bettered her American record. She felt dynamite. But her swimming wasn't done. On the first night of competition, she had won a gold in the world-record-setting 4 × 100-meter freestyle relay. Now less than an hour after taking third in the 50-meter freestyle, she was on the blocks again to anchor the 4 × 100-meter medley relay.

The relay was never a race. Team USA led from start to finish with no threat and shattered a six-year world record that had been held by China's steroid-fueled swimmers. Torres won her fifth Olympic medal in grand style: Her 100-meter freestyle split was the fastest ever recorded (53.37 seconds), beating anything de Bruijn had ever done.

In eight days, Torres captured two relay gold medals and three individual bronzes. She was on two world-record-setting relays and established a new American record in the 50-meter freestyle. Fifteen months after starting her comeback, Dara Torres was not only the most decorated female U.S. Olympic swimmer since 1976 but she was also—along with U.S. track star Marion Jones—the most decorated athlete of the 2000 Olympic Games.

. . .

From the moment he had left Indianapolis after Trials until he arrived in Sydney, Tom Wilkens had worked hard to push the 400-meter I.M. from his mind.

"Get over it," he told himself until it sounded like a broken record. "Life has no guarantees. Look forward. Get *over* it."

Easier said than done. The world around him had changed dramatically. He was no longer considered a candidate for Olympic gold. In fact, it was nearly impossible to find anyone betting he would win any medal. It was his subpar Trials' performance. It was the strength of the international fields. It was everything. A dozen swimmers could capture the 200-meter breaststroke race and in the pell-mell scramble Wilkens was expected to be near the back. In the 200-meter I.M., the story was opposite but looked equally bleak: Few races were so top-heavy with talent. The 200-meter I.M. of course had Dolan. But in addition there was also the race's 1996 Olympic champion; the reigning world record-holder; the current world champion; the runner-up world champion; the event's No. 1–ranked swimmer; and the 1996 Olympic bronze medalist. Wilkens was the winner of 1999 Pan Pacifics, a meet most of these swimmers had not attended, and he had briefly held the No. 1 spot in the event until he turned his focus to the 400-meter I.M. The 200-meter I.M. is a sprinter's event, with each lap an all-out drag race. Except for Dolan, the top racers had trained years for this specific event.

Virtually no swimming analyst believed Wilkens could win a medal. Had any of the observers known he suffered a strained groin the week before the Olympics and was unable to swim breast, they would have patted themselves on the back for the accuracy of their predictions. He had done it during a regular warmup. There was no rhyme or reason for why it happened. It was wrecking his entire pre-meet preparation.

Also wrecking his preparation was the absence of Jochums. During the pre-Olympic camp in Pasadena, while nearly every other coach of an Olympic swimmer showed up to help, Jochums had stayed 500 miles north at Santa Clara, where he bitterly fought with his board of directors. When he wasn't fighting, he was sulking. He visited Pasadena only briefly, and that only was because Bitter and Jochums' wife, Mara, both exploded in anger and forced him to go. The trip was brief and unmeaningful for Wilkens, who was privately grieving over the death of his grandfather. Then, when Jochums joined Team USA in Australia, the coach acted like a zombie—staying in the background and being unduly careful with the Olympic staff not to encroach on their space or question their work. The analogy Wilkens used was that Jochums had dropped him at a bus stop and told him to find his own way home.

The swimmer yearned for the old intensity of the solo Santa Clara workouts with all their passion and heart-searching. He'd even take the fighting. He was in a new, exciting space. Want to understand the meaning of pressure? Make an Olympic team. Wilkens desperately needed Jochums to center and prioritize his world, needed him to sweep out everything that was unimportant. But the coach was a mess. He was still mourning the loss of the 400-meter I.M. at Trials. He was beaten up by his club's internal problems. Perhaps most significant, he mistakenly believed that now was the time Wilkens needed to assume responsibility for his own success. But Wilkens wasn't ready for that. As the Games began, the swimmer wanted to ask for help, but he didn't know how.

. . .

Two days after Dolan's Olympic victory in the 400-meter I.M., Wilkens prepared for the prelims of his 200-meter breaststroke. This was a wide-open race and represented his better medal chance. The groin pain had disappeared, but what Wilkens didn't yet realize was that the injury had bungled his final days of tapering. As would become apparent later, the height of his taper had come and gone before he even raced.

A major flaw in Wilkens' 400-meter I.M. at Olympic Trials was that he swam the prelims too hard. At least that was what everyone had told him until the message was grooved in his head. Now, he wasn't about to make the same mistake twice. This preliminary swim was going to be measured and controlled. His plan was to coast through prelims just fast enough to comfortably qualify for semifinals and go from there. As if to prove he understood the importance of pacing a meet like the Olympics, he didn't wear his regular "shorty" bodysuit, which resembled biker's pants. For important races, he always wore them. Nor did he strategize with his Santa Clara coaches very much.

Assistant Coach John Bitter was in the stands. When he saw Wilkens standing behind the blocks, he could read in his movements that some renegade component of the swimmer's brain was straining to prove the point that he was good enough to be in the Olympics. Wilkens had always hated being labeled an average swimmer with an extraordinary heart. He didn't understand how rare he was.

"No, Tom, you're not good enough to be thinking this way," Bitter groaned. "You have to work for everything you get. Other guys can afford to think beyond the Olympic prelims, but not you."

Wilkens was in lane four and his first lap felt strong. He was far and away the fastest swimmer in this heat. But as he turned, he realized he was in the middle of the pack instead of in the lead. This was a critical moment for him, a chance to make a necessary adjustment, to exert more power and surge to the front. But Wilkens was thinking ahead to the semifinals. He let the opportunity slip by.

"Man, that other guy is out there," was all he thought as he looked at the leader.

He stayed in his race plan, swimming an even pace. Yet his stroke seemed slow and robotic. At the 100-meter turn, he glanced again at the competition. There were several swimmers ahead of him, but he felt comfortable because he was breathing easy. Even so, he increased his speed throughout the third lap. His plan was to use whatever energy was necessary to finish first or second coming home.

In one part of the stands, Bitter leaned forward and waited for the third-lap power burst that never came. In the seating reserved for head coaches, Jochums did the same. On television, Olympic commentator Rowdy Gaines mused aloud that Wilkens shouldn't be swimming like this, because he was the type who needed to tear through every race as if it were the finals. Turning at the 150 meters, Wilkens was fifth.

"This can't be," he thought. "How am I this far back?"

He should have been so far ahead the other competitors needed binoculars to find him. Instead, panic flooded his body. The Olympics are supposed to be about transcendence, not blockheadedness. A professional theorist could pull up a chair and work all day to explain what was happening, but it came down to simple stupidity. Consciously, Wilkens believed he could make the semifinals without swimming all-out. Unconsciously, he was overcompensating for the prelims of his 400-meter I.M. at Trials because he didn't want to make the same mistake twice. The two connected thoughts were a disastrous combination.

Wilkens tore at the water, and his stroke, already shaky because of the groin, became jerking and unsynchronized. He was a flailing rookie again. Suddenly he was burning all reserves, throwing into his swim everything that was supposed to be saved for the semifinals. It was already too late. He touched in 2:16.30. If this were an Elizabethan theatrical performance, he would have been pegged with a hail of tomatoes. 2:16.30? He swam that fast during in-season meets. This swim was on the short list of single-worst performances by an American swimmer in the 2000 Olympics.

As the Australian television announcers told their viewers, "American Tom Wilkens . . . wasn't ever a factor in this race."

The zombie that had been Jochums snapped awake with a torrent of cursing before the race even ended. The coach had seen Wilkens commit so many mindless errors that his brain had overloaded. That swim had been a flaunting insult to all the two of them had built together, all the years, miles, and emotions. Even pace an Olympic race? Ridiculous. Even the world's best athletes race hard off the gun, easing up only when they are assured of reaching the next round. That was not even an option Wilkens should have considered. It was as if a hypnotist had snapped his fingers and suddenly Jochums was back. He was sparking in every direction, furious and hell-bent, as he rapidly walked toward the stairwell leading to the pool. That was where he pulled himself up short and tried to see straight. What good would a righteous explosion on the deck of the Olympic natatorium do anyone? The race was over. *That race is over,* the coach said to himself. He breathed deeply and regained control. It wasn't easy, but he did it. Then he found his swimmer.

"What happened?" Jochums tersely asked.

"I don't know," Wilkens answered glumly.

"Well, swim down and get ready for the next one," Jochums said. "Let's get going."

Wilkens was afraid to ask, but he had to. "Do you think . . . do you think I made semifinals?"

"Tom, you're fifteenth with one heat to go," Jochums told him.

"Maybe only one person will swim faster in the final heat, but I doubt it."

Wilkens waited for a miracle that never came. After the final heat, he was twenty-first, which was one spot better than Mariniuk's placing in the 400-meter I.M. As Wilkens went to the warm-down pool, Jochums completed the transformation to his old self. A six-week fog of self-pity and frustration dissipated. The retreating deference he had shown the U.S. Olympic coaching staff vanished. Jochums was pissed. At this moment, his swimmer's chances of making the finals of the 200-meter I.M. were approximately nil. Medaling? Wilkens had better start praying to his Catholic saints, preferably St. Jude, the patron of lost causes. This was not how Jochums had envisioned the Olympic dream culminating. Wilkens was clearly overwhelmed: by the poor Trials; the recent death of his grandfather; the groin injury which was now surely aggravated; the messed-up taper; his natural inclination to be a good captain by helping everyone around him instead of focusing on himself. It went on and on. The swimmer's confidence lay broken in the gutter. It was clear he was in crisis. Okay, then.

"You listen to me," Jochums growled at Wilkens. "We're going to win a goddamn medal in the 200 I.M. I'm telling you how we're going to swim this race and how we're going to prepare for it. And you're going to do exactly what I say from this moment on."

Wilkens felt immense relief coming through his frustration. His coach was coaching again.

. . .

That evening were the breaststroke semifinals. Wilkens stayed in his room to watch it on television. He became so enraged, so filled with hate, frustration, and self-loathing, that he kicked over chairs, threw objects, and swore vehemently. Usually anger helped his swimming, but not in this instance. The next morning, he looked downright bad in the prelims of the 200-meter I.M. At least he advanced to the semifinals.

In the semis of the 200-meter I.M. later that day, top athletes like Dolan eased up to conserve energy for the finals. Wilkens, who only months earlier was the fastest in the world in this event, no longer had that luxury. His groin was flaring and all four of his strokes felt awkward. By now he knew the taper had been missed because his injury had set it in motion too soon. He had probably peaked two days before his first race. That meant, realistically, he would have trouble swimming near his best times. Swimmers are at the mercy of their tapers and that added to the grimness of the situation. Everyone who cared about him felt a rising lump of fear as he prepared for his semifinals race.

"This is business," he told himself. "You know what you need to do and how to do it. Don't look at cameras or the crowd or anything except the water. Let's do this right."

His butterfly and backstroke were slow but technically sound. But on the breaststroke leg, his money stroke, he swam terribly. The bum leg threw everything out of whack. His angles were off and his weakened legs struggled to hoist his torso high enough to properly lunge forward. The final freestyle leg was full of hurt and struggle. But he didn't panic. The hands didn't slip and he qualified for finals. Yet it was frightening how hard he had worked to get there. He put everything he had into that race. Even so, he only qualified sixth.

"That doesn't matter," he thought. "We all start from zero tomorrow."

He had 24 hours. Life sped up as the hours fled past. He somehow moved his fear and uncertainty out of his consciousness and filled the space with confidence and adrenaline. He was ready to take the offensive, to attack and blast all his troubles out of his way forever. He wanted this race more than anything in life. Wilkens was the underdog again.

Jochums was there, in his face, hovering like a stirred-up mythological force. Bitter slipped into the role of strategist, and convinced Wilkens that his only possible shot at a medal was to accept that for the very first time in his career he could not rely on his breaststroke. He had Wilkens alter it, making the kick much narrower and less powerful. That put the onus for forward movement squarely on the swimmer's arms. The possible negative fallout of such a decision was staggering. Not only would Wilkens willingly neutralize his best weapon, but he would trash his arms before he had even started freestyle. Freestyle is always an arm-based stroke, but never more so than at the end of the 200-meter I.M., because the legs are so wasted. It was a decision that required great courage.

Wilkens tried to read his coaches' faces. They were all thinking the same thing: It is 1,000 times better to die fighting than to live in fear.

In the big picture, these 2000 Sydney Olympics had already proved a marvelous swim meet. When the water would finally grow still, fourteen world records would be set, the most in many, many years at one meet.

Only four of them would be set by the United States, reinforcing the notion that a new kind of international parity, at least on the individual level, was coming to the sport. But the United States still dominated. Wilkens and the other captains would lead Team USA to thirty-three medals, fourteen of them gold. Their closest rival, Australia, would capture just eighteen medals total.

Individually, the meet was a crowning success for the others. Torres was going to go home with two individual bronzes, two relay golds, two relay world records, and the promise of commercial stardom. Tom Dolan's second Olympic gold in the 400-meter I.M. had ended for all time any discussion about who was the most dominant American male swimmer of the era. He was the only American to set an individual world record during the meet, and now he was in the hunt for a second gold in the 200-meter I.M. Ed Moses would depart Australia believing his individual silver would have been gold had he swum a better race. But he would outdo himself by leading the United States to victory and a world record in the medley relay. Sergey Mariniuk didn't win a medal, didn't crack the Top 20, and didn't even get to swim the 200-meter I.M. for which Wilkens was now preparing. But it didn't seem to matter to the Moldovan, who was flush with excitement over his wife's pregnancy. Being there had been its own reward.

In short, Wilkens was surrounded by success. It glowed off the others, and in a small way their triumphs bothered him because his own struggles stood in such sharp relief. But there was no time to dwell on it because the hours had galloped forward, and he suddenly found himself in the ready room, just minutes from his Olympic finals.

In the ready room, he did not think about the past or the future, only the present and the four laps that stretched before him. The room was hushed except for the shushing sound of fabric on fabric as nervous athletes moved about. That, and the faint music coming from Walkmans. The tension was enough to expand and contract the concrete walls. Above and beyond was the low, bestial roar of the crowd. Wilkens could feel its weight, its desires, and its sweating want as it all pressed down on his chest. More than a billion people were said to be watching this race. He was no longer an ordinary person. He had stepped out of that anonymity. This was an ultimate moment of truth, a suspended instant that defines forever who a person is.

Then he was rising from his plastic chair and walked down the dim corridor to the pool. The men around him easily represented the most talented field ever assembled for a 200-meter I.M. The noise swelled, and then he stepped on the deck and into a world of deafening sound and blinding light. His vision briefly spun, tipped, and returned to focus. The still blue pool exploded with reflected light from thousands of camera flashes.

Everything felt right. The nervousness of his earlier races, the collection of setbacks, failures, and emotional upheaval had been vaporized. Wilkens had found the ability to put everything behind him. This was a race like any of thousands of others. He pointed at a camera and winked. He turned to the spectators and looked for his sisters. In the chaos of lights and sounds and thousands of faces, he actually found their handmade poster dancing in the crowd and he waved.

"Let's go," he said under his breath as he turned to his lane. "This is the Olympic Games. Let's hit it."

He stepped on the starting block. He was in lane seven, the spot for the third-slowest qualifier. His body emptied of thought. The soft, friendly voice of the starter told the finalists to take their marks.

And then Wilkens was halfway down the pool, swimming butterfly as hard as he could. Four laps, four sprints. And Wilkens was good for only three of them. With his breaststroke a liability, he needed this lap to be perfect. It wasn't. At 50 meters, he turned sixth.

He was swimming backstroke, his weakest link. He churned his arms furiously, far faster than he had ever moved them before. Halfway down the pool, the beginnings of fatigue began to stir in his chest. But in an Olympic final, you cannot allow yourself to feel pain. As Wilkens finished the length, it was impossible for him to see the competition. He didn't know that on the far side of the pool, in lane one, the defending Olympic champion, Hungary's Attila Czene, was winning the race as outside smoke, just as he did in 1996. Or that Dolan was second and the event's No. 1 swimmer, Italy's Massimiliano Rosolino, was third. But on backstroke Wilkens had improbably passed two people. He was fourth, one spot out of the medals.

"Narrow legs," he thought as breaststroke began. "Use the arms."

Wilkens was swimming beyond his physical limits. He should not have been in the medal hunt, not on this particular day. It is a myth that great athletes outperform themselves under pressure. They access and unleash the potential they already possess. Wilkens was improvising his race, but he was accessing a lifetime of preparation. The best champions become the sum total of their parts. Red Bank YMCA. Stanford. Santa Clara.

What is the Olympic dream when all is said and done? Is it the race or is it the medal? The shortest sentence William Faulkner probably ever wrote is also his truest. "Life is motion," he noted. The transcendence is in the doing and the acting. It is in the chase. Wilkens began swimming his wounded breaststroke and it was ominously flat. For five strokes— about one-third the pool's length—he struggled to rebalance himself with his untried kick. He noticeably fell off his pace, and every fiber in his body fought to switch to his old stroke.

Remember this, because everything you will ever do in life comes down to one message: Never panic. Jochums had said that more than a year earlier. He had said it many times since then, always the same message: *Never panic.* This was his race, too, for without Dick Jochums, Tom Wilkens would have been watching the Olympics on television.

Wilkens resisted changing to his old stroke and suddenly his narrow legs and overworking arms clicked together. And from that moment, the race unfolds in the present, in cinematic slow motion, because that is how it should be remembered, as something that is always happening on another plane, in another dimension.

Wilkens feels the familiar adrenaline and joy of being in a race, any race, rushing through his body. He is flooded with happiness. Winning an Olympic medal no longer matters. He could be in the empty Santa Clara pool racing Tim Shaw's ghost on a rainy morning. He could be in the Red Bank YMCA of his childhood or in the Stanford pool. Joy pushes out everything else. His rhythm perceptibly changes and his swimming becomes nothing short of heroic. He is taking monster strokes, ones that force all his power through the arms instead of the legs. His breaststroke split will be among his slowest in several years, and the arms are already lost for freestyle; that is something he knows and must accept. But when he comes to the final turn, he is, suddenly and implausibly, in contention for a medal. He is third.

Breaststroke as usual has proved the defining moment of this race. The leader, Hungary's Czene, has slipped from first to fourth. The third-place Italian has delivered one of the fastest breaststroke laps ever and assumed the lead. Dolan remains second.

Wilkens turns just .08 seconds ahead of the Hungarian. That is the width of a nickel. The Hungarian is a much better freestyler. Wilkens has no right to be in medal contention, not today. He closes his eyes and thinks, *No slipping. Get . . . to . . . the wall. This will be . . . close.*

His hands cut through the water. They find and grip and hold it as his body rockets forward. There is no slipping whatsoever. The swimmer is in the closest, most important race of his life and he refuses to panic.

Jochums sees that Wilkens is willing his body to stay in proper stroke as it instinctively fights to thrash. That is what Jochums will remember for the rest of his life: the swimmer's refusal to panic. On the other side of the pool, the Hungarian is a demon shark. And what kind of cosmic closure is this? The Hungarian trains at the University of Arizona, where a lifetime earlier Jochums had lost so much.

Tom Wilkens can swim for another twenty years. He can go to three more Olympiads and win in world-record times. But unequivocally this will forever remain the single greatest freestyle lap of his career. He is soaring above his own talent. He is in the sky and brushing as close to heaven as a human can ever get. The pain in his exhausted arms is excruciating, unlike anything he has ever felt. The lungs are overwhelmed; the legs are wasted. Yet this lap is nearly a second faster than it has ever been before. There are others ahead, but he doesn't know how many.

Hand . . . wall, is his last thought. And then he crashes to the finish. The Italian Rosolino has won, barely missing the world record and setting a new Olympic mark (1:58.98). Dolan has captured second in a new American record (1:59.77). And Santa Clara's Tom Wilkens is third (2:00.87). The Olympic bronze medal.

He leaps from the pool, shouting and punching the air. An explosion of relief and joy. If you were to turn on the television right now, you would think Wilkens is the victor, for in the water and then on deck he is throwing one of the week's biggest celebration parties. And that is how it should be, for this is the Olympics. He could swim just three of the four laps properly and his time is only .2 seconds off his best. He has done it. An Olympic medal. Wilkens finds Jochums; they happily greet each other and then the swimmer hurries to his medal ceremony.

The ceremony takes place fifteen minutes later. Wilkens steps onto the medal dais. Jochums watches. The coach sees Wilkens triumphantly raise his arms. He sees him fight back tears as the flags are raised and the first strains of the winner's Italian national anthem begin.

"Tom, you are a racer," Jochums says quietly. It is his highest compliment, for it means Wilkens represents everything of value in his world. For the rest of the evening, there will be a joyous late-night celebration for Wilkens' family, beginning at the pool and later moving to a restaurant. Jochums will have none of it. He has always promised his swimmers that he would step forward to assume the blame when they fail and back into the shadows when they succeed. Now he is blinking back tears of his own, so he finds an exit, pushes it open, and disappears alone into the Australian night.

The ceremony ends and it takes Wilkens forty-five minutes to finish his post-race obligations. He arrives in the private meet-and-greet area reserved for Olympic athletes and their families. The room is crowded and he stands by himself near the back, suddenly awkward and shy. The medal hangs around his neck. On his face is a huge grin. His parents enter the area. They spy him across the room and run to him. All three open their arms. Wilkens falls into their embrace and begins sobbing.

They stand there, the three of them, for a long time. The Olympic medal, intermittently visible through the press of their bodies, glints in the natatorium's phosphorescent light.

AFTERWORD

The news came from Italy just days after the 2000 Olympic Games had ended. A leading Italian newspaper, *Corriere della Sera*, revealed sixty-one Italian Olympic athletes had been allowed to participate in the Olympic Games after testing positive for illegal levels of human growth hormone (hGH). The Italian Olympic Committee (CONI) had suppressed the findings.

Never had such systematic abuse been simultaneously uncovered. Human growth hormone is both a highly illegal and highly effective performance enhancer. But it also occurs naturally in the body, and this was one of the reasons the International Olympic Committee had no approved test for it. Despite that, ascertaining probable abuse is relatively easy. Before Italy's 538 Olympians left for Australia, they were subjected to routine drug testing. Presumably, they figured their hGH levels would not be examined since they were not going to be checked at the Games. But CONI's head of research, Alessandro Donati, had other ideas. Call it a hunch. It was Donati who in the mid-1990s exposed the rampant drug abuse in professional cycling. When sixty-one tests came back positive, the results were suppressed. None of those athletes should have competed in the Games. In Australia, Italy won thirteen gold medals, five of which (thirty-eight percent) were won by athletes with illegal hGH levels. One of those was Massimiliano Rosolino, winner of men's 200-meter I.M.; earlier, he had also won silver in the 400-meter freestyle and bronze in the 200-meter freestyle.

It is impossible to adequately describe the emotions that hit Tom Wilkens when he heard the news. He felt nauseous, enraged, and mugged. When you spend a lifetime pursuing the most remarkable dream possible and then learn you were beaten by a cheater, the whole world suddenly seems spoiled. It must be said that Rosolino vehemently asserts his innocence and perhaps he is a victim, too. The tainted athletes are entitled to keep their medals pending an investigation that will likely stretch on for years, and subsequent legal fights that will perhaps stretch through decades. After all, in 1972 a U.S. teenage swimmer named Rick Demont was stripped of his gold medal after he tested positive for traces of a stimulant that was contained in his prescribed asthma medicine (medicine his team doctors knew he was taking), and that case was still being argued in 2001. Adding to the complications is the fact that the hGH testing was not done at the Games.

Not knowing what to do, Wilkens called Tom Dolan. It's unlikely the two will ever be close, but they have a mutual respect. Dolan hadn't yet heard the news.

"As far as I'm concerned, you won the 200 I.M.," Wilkens told Dolan. "You will always be the gold medal winner in my mind."

"And you will always be the silver medalist to me," said Dolan.

For Wilkens, that was enough. He moved on, returning to his hometown on the New Jersey shore for parades and celebrations. He was the first ever Olympic medalist from the region and instantly became a favorite son. His American dream had come true.

In the United States, an Olympic bronze medal carries no commercial value. Wilkens, of course, didn't get his face on the Wheaties box. He didn't appear on Hollywood game shows with the big-name athletes like Torres and Krayzelburg. He didn't sign any new endorsement deals. And perhaps it is better that way, for he had always been more suited to the grassroots. Everywhere he went, he shared his Olympic story with regular people, people who wouldn't ever be invited to black-tie, post-Olympic events. Most of them had never seen an Olympian before. He spoke to dozens of groups, usually for free. After all, who pays money to hear a bronze medalist? The swimmer particularly loved hitting the elementary schools, where he talked to rapt assemblies and then stayed for hours afterward as he went from class to class to pass around his medal. Six months after the Olympics, it was a safe bet that Wilkens' bronze medal had passed through more hands than most of the U.S. coins in circulation.

During his Olympic honeymoon, there is one small incident worth mentioning. A hometown parade was being held in his honor on the official "Tom Wilkens' Day." The swimmer was in the back of a gleaming yellow convertible, soaking in the cheers. In my mind's eye I see him on that sunny day and I imagine it must represent the height of glory and self-happiness for any twenty-four-year-old. As Wilkens was carried past a church, he noticed a young girl in a wheelchair. She had been at choir practice before her father brought her outside to see their Olympian. Wilkens spotted her and spontaneously leapt from the car. I cherish the image of him leaving his own parade and loping over to her, for it represents to me the essence of who he is. He shook her hand, showed her the medal, and then ran after his motorcade. I imagine that he apologized profusely to the driver for the inconvenience.

After the Olympics, the swimmer was anxious to see what the rest of life had to offer. After all, he had never held a real job. But there was unfinished business. He and Jochums had a long talk about what had gone right and wrong in the months before the 2000 Olympics. The discussion basically boiled down to the way both of them handled, or mishandled, the incredible pressure. Wilkens agreed with the assessment that things could have been done better. They decided to take one more shot at the 400-meter I.M. Realistically, Wilkens couldn't think about Athens in 2004, because it was just too far away and he'd be twenty-eight years old by then. But there were other competitions to consider, beginning with the World Championships in mid-2001. There was still a chance to swim the individual medleys faster than anyone ever had.

In early 2001, Wilkens resumed training at the Santa Clara Swim Club. Soon he could be found there any morning or afternoon. He was easy to spot because once again he was often the only swimmer in the water. The others had retired.

After the Olympic Trials, Kurt Grote resumed his medical career as a third-year student. Within weeks he was working like a dog, sometimes going twenty hours straight in the hospital. The knee eventually mended on its own, as he knew it would. Grote loved the pressures and chaos of the hospital setting. There was no time to think and no time to stop thinking. On his rare days off, he joyfully grabbed a surfboard and headed to Santa Cruz, sometimes surfing near a spot that Sergey Mariniuk had surfed earlier the same morning.

During his surgery rotation, Grote worked at the Kaiser Permanente hospital located across the street from the Santa Clara Swim Club. From the proper hospital window, one could gaze over the treetops and see the swim complex. Grote stopped by the pool to say hello but never brought a suit. That part of his life was over. He was considering a career in emergency medicine, but had also begun talking about pursuing an M.B.A. after he earned his M.D. degree. He had no background in finance or business, but knew he could do it. The mind of a Renaissance man never stops looking for new challenges.

Like Grote, butterflyer Dod Wales had no desire to get into the water again, at least not for a long time. Originally, Wales was the one Santa Clara swimmer who had planned to continue competing beyond 2000. But after his third place, his heart was no longer in it and he retired. After a number of job interviews, he landed a position at a prestigious investment-banking firm with offices in nearby Palo Alto.

After Olympic Trials, backstroker Tate Blahnik happily moved into the working world, but within months the high-flying company he had joined became one of the countless casualties of the dot-com implosion of 2000. It didn't matter much, for Blahnik's skills were in such high demand that he soon found another programming position. Of all the Santa Clara swimmers—about ten—who retired after the Olympic Trials, only one continued regularly swimming. Ironically, it was Blahnik. He wasn't training, but several times per week he was drawn to the pool. In his new freedom, he rediscovered how beautiful the water and the motion of slow armstrokes could be. Those who knew him best were not surprised. Many people wondered if he had any regrets. Indeed, he did. He wished he had not swum that final year. His heart was never in it, he said. During a lunch in early 2001, he smiled more than he had during all of the Olympic year.

Like Wilkens, Moldova's Sergey Mariniuk returned to Santa Clara and resumed living his own American dream. With a baby boy due in mid-2001, he set about renovating his house. Meanwhile, he continued training several times per week with the same slow stroke he had used in preparation for the Olympic Games. In January, he competed in a professional meet in Oklahoma and finished near the top. Why retire when he could still do that? He'd be thirty-six years old for the 2004 Athens Games. There was a twinkle in his eye when he thought about that. His baby boy was born almost a year to the day after his father had died.

For Curl-Burke swimmer Tom Dolan, the Sydney Olympics seemed to signal the end of a brilliant career. Easing into retirement, the undisputed King of Swimming began looking for new challenges. But he knew he could swim still faster, and after half a year away, he returned and began training for the 2004 Games. The best American male swimmer of the 1900s was intent on carrying his excellence into the new century.

Dolan's teammate Ed Moses immediately resumed swimming after the Sydney Olympics and attacked the sport with a new kind of ferocity. Now a professional, within months he had won a new car for his performances at a World Series meet. He was committed to winning both breaststroke events at the 2004 Olympics. In early 2001, he set a new world record in the 100-meter breaststroke and nearly broke the record in the 200-meter event. His 100-meter standard lasted only a short while before his Russian counterpart recaptured it, but that only served to fire up Moses even more.

Then there was Dara Torres. The Sydney Olympics were not a commercial success for NBC, which was part of the reason few U.S. athletes became commercial sensations. But Torres was one of them. Returning to New York City, she instantly capitalized on her new fame. She became a rowdy and sexy reporter for the XFL, the new fledgling professional football league. She turned into an occasional contributor on *Good Morning, America*. She co-hosted *Live! With Regis* with Regis Philbin and was an event hostess during George W. Bush's inauguration. She was even tapped to introduce Secretary of State Colin Powell at a concert. She had too many opportunities coming at her at once and was sometimes on the road for weeks, earning thousands and thousands of dollars nearly every time she told her story. There was little doubt that she was on her way to becoming one of the most successfully marketed U.S. Olympic swimmers ever. The only time she swam was with little kids at clinics.

The story ends, as it should, back at Santa Clara Swim Club. Coaches Dick Jochums and John Bitter returned after the Olympics and resumed their regular duties. The pool was quieter now. The investigation into the financial scandal continued for months and included police interrogations. But eventually both men were exonerated. Bitter had been so stung by the accusations that he quietly began looking for a life out of coaching. Maybe he'd go back to school. But in the interim, he was named the club's co–head coach and given a substantial raise. Meanwhile, Jochums worked toward renegotiating his contract through 2006. The nearly $125,000 that the club had owed the IRS was reduced to $72,000 through a deal, and SCSC was able to pay it off quickly. But in a willful act of defiance, the coaches refused to fully remedy all their loose business practices. They were permanently and stubbornly angry about what they had been put through. Without taking anything away from the deserving athletes who made the Olympics in the 400-meter I.M. and the 100-meter butterfly, Jochums would go to his grave believing the club's decision to press the scandal into a full-blown crisis in the critical final days before Trials had cost Wilkens and Wales Olympic spots in their respective events. Sadly, anyone observing the events would likely concur.

There was a natural letdown in the months immediately after the Olympics. In the pool were developmental swimmers, teenagers who were only beginning to show the first signs of promise. Jochums coached them mechanically and without passion as he waited for Wilkens to return. Bitter found him once sitting on deck reading a spy novel as his athletes moved back and forth. In fact, Jochums' office desk, which in the year before the Olympics had been covered with pages of splits and meet information, soon became cluttered with spy novels and sports biographies.

But by early 2001, the coach was finding his old groove.

"There's the one, right there," Jochums said one morning as he pointed to a swimmer. It was a crisp winter day about five months after the Olympics. You could hardly see this particular swimmer because there was so much steam rising from the pool. "That one there," Jochums repeated. He sounded excited. "There. He has a shot if we do everything right. He can be the next great one."

The coach looked pleased as could be. He stepped close to the pool to yell at the swimmer for some unseen infraction. The kid was just fourteen years old. Jochums was not thinking about the 2004 Athens Games. He was looking at 2008.

ACKNOWLEDGMENTS

I will write many books in my life, but I doubt any will mean as much as this little one does. I could not have told this story without the trust of the individuals who appear in these pages, particularly Dick Jochums, John Bitter, Tom Wilkens, Kurt Grote, Dod Wales, Tate Blahnik, Dara Torres, Sergey Mariniuk, Clayton Jones, Ed Moses, Tom Dolan, and Amy Hunn. I am permanently grateful. I am indebted to dozens of swimmers, coaches, Masters, and parents who helped me understand their world, especially Santa Clara elite swimmers Matthew Pierce, Blake Holden, Justin Ewers, and Julie Varozza. Each of these champions greatly supported this project. Dr. Phil Whitten, the Editor-in-Chief of *Swimming World Magazine* and *Swim,* possesses an unparalleled knowledge of the sport and for two years he patiently shared it with me. In addition to providing innumerable insights, Dr. Whitten served as this book's factual and technical editor. That said, all mistakes are mine and mine alone. Swimmer and professional editor Chapman Greer proved a dear friend for editing early drafts. The incredibly talented Andrea Peiro devoted endless hours to making the book's website a true work of art (www.goldinthewater.com). The husband-wife combo of Dough Sheehy and Kristin Jacobson provided great reader feedback as did Mick Moore, the most poetical swimmer I know. My sister, Tracy Mullen, corrected several key errors late in the game. My parents think every swimmer's parents should be thanked for getting their kids to morning practices year after year. Okay: Thank you, parents. The Stanford men's coaching staff elected not to participate in this book, but I want to acknowledge how much they brought to it. The common denominator bonding the exceptional young men of Santa Clara was their time at Stanford, where

I suspect much of their character was forged. Thank you, too, to Rick Curl and Pete Morgan, the outstanding head coaches of Curl-Burke, who helped me understand their respective swimmers, Dolan and Moses. *Sports Illustrated* Senior Editor Myra Gelband gave me the confidence to write about sports. Without the benefit of the daily stories, data, and statistics from three excellent online sources—U.S.A. Swimming Inc., *Swimming World Magazine,* and Canada's *Swim News*—I would have been lost. Other news sources include the *Washington Post,* the *San Jose Mercury News,* the *New York Times, USA Today,* and the *Detroit Free Press.* JKS said life was so short that a person had to either sail around the world or write a book, and he was, of course, right. This books exists because my agent, Tony Siedl of TDMedia, believed a story would rise from the water, and it is readable because my editor, Pete Wolverton of St. Martin's Press, happens to be the best sports narrative editor in the business. Finally, thank you to the community of the Santa Clara Swim Club. A portion of this books proceeds will be donated toward the team's future Olympic efforts.